Big Data Analytics for Sensor-Network Collected Intelligence

Big Data Analytics for Sensor-Network Collected Intelligence

Edited by

Hui-Huang Hsu
Tamkang University, Taiwan

Chuan-Yu Chang
National Yunlin University of Science and Technology, Taiwan

Ching-Hsien Hsu
Chung Hua University, Taiwan

Series Editor Fatos Xhafa
Universitat Politècnica de Catalunya, Spain

ACADEMIC PRESS
An imprint of Elsevier
elsevier.com

Academic Press is an imprint of Elsevier
125 London Wall, London EC2Y 5AS, United Kingdom
525 B Street, Suite 1800, San Diego, CA 92101-4495, United States
50 Hampshire Street, 5th Floor, Cambridge, MA 02139, United States
The Boulevard, Langford Lane, Kidlington, Oxford OX5 1GB, United Kingdom

Notices
Knowledge and best practice in this field are constantly changing. As new research and experience
broaden our understanding, changes in research methods, professional practices, or medical treatment
may become necessary.

Practitioners and researchers must always rely on their own experience and knowledge in evaluating and
using any information, methods, compounds, or experiments described herein. In using such information or
methods they should be mindful of their own safety and the safety of others, including parties for whom they
have a professional responsibility.

To the fullest extent of the law, neither the Publisher nor the authors, contributors, or editors, assume any
liability for any injury and/or damage to persons or property as a matter of products liability, negligence or
otherwise, or from any use or operation of any methods, products, instructions, or ideas contained in the
material herein.

Library of Congress Cataloging-in-Publication Data
A catalog record for this book is available from the Library of Congress

British Library Cataloguing-in-Publication Data
A catalogue record for this book is available from the British Library

ISBN: 978-0-12-809393-1

For information on all Academic Press publications
visit our website at https://www.elsevier.com/books-and-journals

Working together
to grow libraries in
developing countries

www.elsevier.com • www.bookaid.org

Publisher: Joe Hayton
Acquisition Editor: Sonnini R. Yura
Editorial Project Manager: Ana Claudia A. Garcia
Production Project Manager: Punithavathy Govindaradjane
Cover Designer: Victoria Pearson

Typeset by SPi Global, India

Contents

PART III   BIG DATA ANALYTICS AND SERVICES

List of Contributors

Ahmad Anbar
The George Washington University, Washington, DC, United States

Haytham Assem
IBM, Dublin, Ireland

Christophe Blanchet
CNRS IFB, Orsay, France

Teodora S. Buda
IBM, Dublin, Ireland

Jiannong Cao
The Hong Kong Polytechnic University, Kowloon, Hong Kong

Chuan-Yu Chang
National Yunlin University of Science and Technology, Douliu City, Yunlin County, Taiwan

Jinjun Chen
University of Technology Sydney, Broadway, NSW, Australia

Cen Chen
Hunan University, Changsha, China

Szu-Ta Chen
National Taiwan University Hospital Yun-Lin Branch, Douliu City, Yunlin County, Taiwan

Kang Chen
Southern Illinois University, Carbondale, IL, United States

Zixue Cheng
University of Aizu, Aizuwakamatsu, Japan

Cees de Laat
University of Amsterdam, Amsterdam, The Netherlands

Yuri Demchenko
University of Amsterdam, Amsterdam, The Netherlands

Mingxing Duan
Hunan University, Changsha, China

Tarek El-Ghazawi
The George Washington University, Washington, DC, United States

Weiwei W. Fang
Beijing Key Lab of Transportation Data Analysis and Mining, Beijing Jiaotong University, Beijing, China

Edmond J. Golden III
National Institute of Standards and Technology, Gaithersburg, MD, United States

Chu-Cheng Hsieh
Slice Technologies Inc., San Mateo, CA, United States

Ching-Hsien Hsu
Chung Hua University, Hsinchu, Taiwan

Hui-Huang Hsu
Tamkang University, Tamsui, Taiwan

Qian Huang
Southern Illinois University, Carbondale, IL, United States

Tian-Hsiang Huang
National Sun Yat-sen University, Kaohsiung, Taiwan

Chih-Chieh Hung
Tamkng University, New Taipei City, Taiwan

Pravin Kakar
Institute for Infocomm Research, Agency for Science, Technology and Research (A*STAR), Singapore

Shonali Krishnaswamy
Institute for Infocomm Research, Agency for Science, Technology and Research (A*STAR), Singapore

Chung-Nan Lee
National Sun Yat-sen University, Kaohsiung, Taiwan

Kenli Li
Hunan University, Changsha, China

Keqin Li
Hunan University, Changsha, China; State University of New York, New Paltz, NY, United States

Xiao-Li Li
Institute for Infocomm Research, Agency for Science, Technology and Research (A*STAR), Singapore

Qingyong Y. Li
Beijing Key Lab of Transportation Data Analysis and Mining, Beijing Jiaotong University, Beijing, China

Hai-Ning Liang
Xi'an Jiaotong-Liverpool University, Suzhou, China

Chen Lin
National Yunlin University of Science and Technology, Douliu City, Yunlin County, Taiwan

Xuefeng Liu
The Hong Kong Polytechnic University, Kowloon, Hong Kong

Ming Liu
Beijing Key Lab of Transportation Data Analysis and Mining, Beijing Jiaotong University, Beijing, China

Charles Loomis
SixSq Sàrl, Geneva, Switzerland

Chao Lu
Southern Illinois University, Carbondale, IL, United States

Ka L. Man
Xi'an Jiaotong-Liverpool University, Suzhou, China

Martial Michel
National Institute of Standards and Technology, Gaithersburg, MD, United States

Vijayakumar Nanjappan
Xi'an Jiaotong-Liverpool University, Suzhou, China

Minh N. Nguyen
Institute for Infocomm Research, Agency for Science, Technology and Research (A*STAR), Singapore

Declan O'Sullivan
Trinity College Dublin, Dublin, Ireland

Phyo P. San
Institute for Infocomm Research, Agency for Science, Technology and Research (A*STAR), Singapore

Olivier Serres
The George Washington University, Washington, DC, United States

Kathiravan Srinivasan
National Ilan University, Yilan City, Yilan County, Taiwan

Ming-Chun Tsai
National Sun Yat-sen University, Kaohsiung, Taiwan

Fatih Turkmen
University of Amsterdam, Amsterdam, The Netherlands

Wei Wang
Xi'an Jiaotong-Liverpool University, Suzhou, China

Junbo Wang
University of Aizu, Aizuwakamatsu, Japan

Yilang Wu
University of Aizu, Aizuwakamatsu, Japan

Chen-Ming Wu
National Sun Yat-sen University, Kaohsiung, Taiwan

Lei Xu
IBM, Dublin, Ireland

Chi Yang
University of Technology Sydney, Broadway, NSW, Australia

Jian-Bo Yang
Institute for Infocomm Research, Agency for Science, Technology and Research (A*STAR), Singapore

Zhangdui D. Zhong
Beijing Key Lab of Transportation Data Analysis and Mining, Beijing Jiaotong University, Beijing, China

Preface

There are three sources of information we can collect about the environment and the people in the environment: environmental sensors, wearable sensors, and social networks. Through intelligent analysis of the huge amount of sensory data, we can develop various systems to automatically detect natural and man-made events. Moreover, the systems can also try to understand people's behavior and even intention. Thus better services can be provided to people in an unobtrusive manner.

With the advances in sensor and networking technologies, we are now able to collect sensory data easily. These sensory data can be stored and processed in the cloud. Nevertheless, how to properly utilize such a huge amount of data is another essential issue. We certainly hope that advanced ICT technologies can help us perform intelligent analysis on these data and provide better services to people automatically. Exciting new systems and research results have been developed. This book aims to introduce these ambient intelligence and Internet of Things (IoT) systems, which are based on big data analytics of collected sensory data.

The theme of this book is closely related to two hot topics: the Internet of Things and big data analytics. Systems and technologies introduced in the book can be used as supplementary materials for courses involving these two topics. Researchers, professionals, and practitioners in related fields can also find useful information and technologies for their work. There are four parts of this book: big data architecture and platforms; big data processing and management; big data analytics and services; and big data intelligence and IoT systems. Each part includes three or four chapters. Here we briefly introduce each of the 14 chapters.

Part I: Big Data Architecture and Platforms
1. **Big Data: A Classification of Acquisition and Generation Methods**
   Vijayakumar Nanjappan, Hai-Ning Liang, Wei Wang, Ka L. Man
   This chapter points out that it is very difficult to store, process, and analyze huge amounts of data using conventional computing methodologies and resources. The authors classify the data into digital and analog, environmental and personal. Data types and formats as well as input mechanisms are also highlighted. These will help us understand the active and passive methods of data collection and production.
2. **Cloud Computing Infrastructure for Data Intensive Applications**
   Yuri Demchenko, Fatih Turkmen, Cees de Laat, Ching-Hsien Hsu, Christophe Blanchet, Charles Loomis
   This chapter proposes a cloud-based big data infrastructure (BDI). The general architecture and functional components of BDI are described in detail. BDI is supported by the definition of the big data architecture framework (BDAF). Two case studies in bioinformatics are illustrated in the chapter to provide examples of requirements analysis and implementation.
3. **Open Source Private Cloud Platforms for Big Data**
   Martial Michel, Olivier Serres, Ahmad Anbar, Edmond J. Golden III, Tarek El-Ghazawi
   This chapter tells us that it is beneficial to use private clouds, especially open source clouds, for big data. Security, privacy, and customization are the major concerns. The chapter introduces the most prominent open source clouds in view of big data processing. A case study using an On-Premise Private Cloud is also presented to demonstrate the implementation of such an environment.

Part II: Big Data Processing and Management

4. Efficient Nonlinear Regression-Based Compression of Big Sensing Data on Cloud

Chi Yang, Jinjun Chen

This chapter proposes a compression method for big sensing data based on a nonlinear regression model. It improves the effectiveness and efficiency for processing real-world big sensing data. Regression design, least squares, and triangular transform are discussed in this chapter. It is demonstrated that the model achieves significant storage and time performance gains over other compression models.

5. Big Data Management on Wireless Sensor Networks

Chih-Chieh Hung, Chu-Cheng Hsieh

This chapter gives an overview of data management issues and solutions in wireless sensor networks. There are two possible models: centralized and decentralized. Data management can be centralized for the benefit of computation, or decentralized for energy saving. Three major issues for data management in both models are introduced: storage, query processing, and data collection. Some case studies are also discussed.

6. Extreme Learning Machine and Its Applications in Big Data Processing

Cen Chen, Kenli Li, Mingxing Duan, Keqin Li

This chapter first reviews the extreme learning machine (ELM) theory and its variants. Due to its memory-residency and high space/time complexity, the traditional ELM cannot train big data efficiently. Optimization strategies are necessary to solve this problem. Thus, parallel ELM algorithms based on MapReduce and Spark are described. Finally, practical applications of the ELM for big data are also presented in this chapter.

Part III: Big Data Analytics and Services

7. Spatial Big Data Analytics for Cellular Communication Systems

Junbo Wang, Yilang Wu, Hui-Huang Hsu, Zixue Cheng

This chapter surveys methodologies of spatial big data analytics and possible applications to support the cellular communication (CC) system. The CC system provides the most popular way to connect people. However, it still faces challenges, such as unbalanced crowd communication behavior and video transmission congestion. Spatial big data analytics can help the CC system to provide services with better quality of service (QoS). Challenging issues are highlighted in this chapter.

8. Cognitive Applications and Their Supporting Architecture for Smart Cities

Haytham Assem, Lei Xu, Teodora S. Buda, Declan O'Sullivan

This chapter proposes a cognitive architecture to enable big data applications with sensory data for smart cities. It deals with organization, configuration, security, and optimization. This chapter also reviews related work on location-based social networks and presents a novel approach to detect urban patterns, especially anomalies. This is essential for better understanding of human activities and behaviors.

9. Deep Learning for Human Activity Recognition

Phyo P. San, Pravin Kakar, Xiao-Li Li, Shonali Krishnaswamy, Jian-Bo Yang, Minh N. Nguyen

This chapter presents a systematic feature learning method for the problem of human activity recognition (HAR). It adopts a deep convolutional neural network (CNN) to automate feature learning from raw inputs. It is not necessary to handcraft features in advance. Such a unification of feature learning and classification results in mutual enhancements. This is verified by comparing experimental results with several state-of-the-art techniques.

10. **Neonatal Cry Analysis and Categorization System Via Directed Acyclic Graph Support Vector Machine**

    Szu-Ta Chen, Kathiravan Srinivasan, Chen Lin, Chuan-Yu Chang

    This chapter introduces a neonatal cry analysis and categorization system. From the cry of the newborn, the system can identify different types of feelings such as pain, sleepiness, and hunger. The sequential forward floating selection (SFFS) algorithm is used to choose the discriminative features. The selected features are then used to classify the neonatal cries by the directed acyclic graph support vector machine (DAG-SVM). The system is useful for parents and nursing staff.

Part IV: Big Data Intelligence and IoT Systems

11. **Smart Building Applications and Information System Hardware Co-Design**

    Qian Huang, Chao Lu, Kang Chen

    This chapter emphasizes that a comprehensive understanding of information system hardware is necessary when designing efficient smart building applications. The necessity and importance of application and hardware co-design are discussed in this chapter. A case study is also given to show that application and hardware co-design optimize the smart building design from a system perspective.

12. **Smart Sensor Networks for Building Safety**

    Xuefeng Liu, Jiannong Cao

    This chapter presents the design and implementation of effective and energy-efficient structural health monitoring (SHM) algorithms in resource-limited wireless sensor networks (WSNs). Compared to traditional wired transmission, WSNs are low cost and easy to deploy for building monitoring. Distributed versions of SHM algorithms can help overcome the bandwidth limitation. A WSN-Cloud system architecture is also proposed for future SHM.

13. **The Internet of Things and Its Applications**

    Chung-Nan Lee, Tian-Hsiang Huang, Chen-Ming Wu, Ming-Chun Tsai

    This chapter first compares two lightweight protocols for the Internet of Things (IoT): MQ telemetry transport (MQTT) and the constrained application protocol (CoAP). Both protocols reduce the size of the packet and the over-loading of the bandwidth, thus saving battery power and storage space. The major techniques for big data analytics are then introduced. Finally, intelligent transportation systems and intelligent manufacturing systems are presented as examples.

14. **Smart Railway Based on the Internet of Things**

    Qingyong Y. Li, Zhangdui D. Zhong, Ming Liu, Weiwei W. Fang

    This chapter discusses the framework and technologies for a smart railway based on Internet of Things (IoT) and big data. The architecture of a smart railway, including the perception and action layer, the transfer layer, the data engine layer, and the application layer, is presented first. A case study on intelligent rail inspection is then introduced. This chapter shows that a smart railway is promising in improving traditional railway systems.

ACKNOWLEDGMENTS

This book is a part of the book series "Intelligent Data-Centric Systems." First of all, we would like to thank the series editor, Prof. Fatos Xhafa, for his encouragement and guidance in developing this book. We gratefully acknowledge all the contributing authors of the chapters. This book would not have been possible without their great efforts. We are also indebted to Ms. Ana Claudia Garcia, the editorial project manager, and the whole production team at Elsevier for their continuous help in producing this book. Finally, we thank our families for their love and support.

Hui-Huang Hsu, Chuan-Yu Chang, Ching-Hsien Hsu
September 2016

BIG DATA ARCHITECTURE AND PLATFORMS

BIG DATA: A CLASSIFICATION OF ACQUISITION AND GENERATION METHODS

Vijayakumar Nanjappan, Hai-Ning Liang, Wei Wang, Ka L. Man

Xi'an Jiaotong-Liverpool University, Suzhou, China

ACRONYMS

AUIs	adaptive user interfaces
BAN	body area network
BSN	body sensor network
BSON	binary JavaScript object notation records
BT	business transactions
CLI	command-line interfaces
CPU	central processing unit
CSV	comma-separated values
DA	data analytics
DM	data mining
DS	document store
ECG	electrocardiography
EEG	electroencephalogram
Email	electronic mail
EMG	electromyography
GB	gigabyte
GPS	Global Positioning System
GS	graph store
GUI	graphical user interfaces
HIDs	human interface devices
HTML	hypertext markup language
IoT	Internet of Things
IR	infrared
IUI	intelligent user interfaces
JPEG	joint photographic experts group
JSON	Javascript object notation records
KD	knowledge discovery
KV	key-value stores
LED	light-emitting diode
MB	megabyte
MEMS	Micro-Electro Mechanical Systems
NoSQL	not only structured query language

Big Data Analytics for Sensor-Network Collected Intelligence. http://dx.doi.org/10.1016/B978-0-12-809393-1.00001-5

NUI	natural user interfaces
ORC	optimized row columnar
OS	operating system
PC	personal computer
PNG	portable network graphics
PS	proximity sensor
RC files	Record Columnar files
RFID	radio frequency identification
RPC	Remote Procedure Call
SD	scientific data
SF	sequence file
SI	satellite imagery
SMD	social media data
SoC	System on Chip
VUI	voice user interfaces
WIMP	windows icons menus and pointer device
WSN	wireless sensor network
WWW	World Wide Web
XML	extensible markup language

1 BIG DATA: A CLASSIFICATION

The coinage of the term "big data" alludes to datasets of exceptionally massive sizes with distinct and intricate structures. They can be extremely difficult to analyze and visualize with any personal computing devices and conventional computational methods [1]. In fact, enormous datasets of complex structures have been generated and used for a long time, for example, in satellite imagery (SI), raster data, geographical, biological, and ecological data; data used for scientific research can also be considered as "big data." Nowadays, we see that many different kinds of big data exist in our lives, from social media data (SMD), to organization and enterprise data, to the sensor data on the Internet of Things (e.g., metrological data about our environment and healthcare data).

1.1 CHARACTERISTICS OF BIG DATA

In 2001, Doug Laney characterized big data from three perspectives, *volume*, *velocity*, and *variety* (the 3Vs) [2]. *Volume* refers to the magnitude of data, which usually determines the potential value of the data. *Velocity* refers to speed at which data is generated and processed according the requirements of different applications. *Variety* refers to the nature and different types of data. Later, the research community proposed two additional *V*s: *veracity* and *value*. *Veracity* indicates the trustworthiness and quality of the data. This is particularly important, as big data are usually collected from a variety of sources, some of which may not provide high-quality, reliable data. The term *value* is used to indicate the potential (or hope) that valuable information or insight can be extracted or derived from the big data provided that the data is appropriately processed and analyzed. These characteristics bring new challenges into the data processing and analytics pipeline. As the size of the data is constantly increasing and the velocity of the data generation is higher than the processing speed, scalable storage and efficient data management methods are needed to enable real-time or near real-time data processing by the analytical tools. To ensure the creditability of the analytics, the quality of the data must be taken into consideration, for example, to identify erroneous processes and uncertain, unreliable, or missing data.

2 BIG DATA GENERATION METHODS

In today's digital era, the data unambiguously denote digital data which can be either born-digital or born-analog, but eventually converted into digital form. There have already been large amounts of conventional digital data such as Web documents, social media, and business transaction (BT) data. In recent years, the "Internet of Things" (IoT) has generated vast volumes of data about our physical world captured by sensing devices. Many everyday objects are embedded with a variety of sensors capable of collecting analog data and converting it into digital. Besides conventional data, sensor data are becoming the next big data source.

2.1 DATA SOURCES

2.1.1 Born-digital data

The born-digital data are created and managed using computers or other digital devices. Almost all documents in personal computers are stored in some standardized file formats (e.g., Word or PDF documents). Advances in Internet and World Wide Web (WWW) technologies have enabled computers around the world to be connected so that billions of Web documents can be accessed anywhere. The emergence of Web 2.0 technologies enriched data and media types from text-only to images, videos, and audios, as well as the associated metadata such as temporal and geographical information. We can see now that numerous images and videos are being uploaded to social media websites which are annotated with location information and tagging data related to their contents. Some of the other traditional big data sources include electronic mails, instant messages, medical records, and business transactions.

2.1.2 Sensor data

Recently, billions of physical objects, such as sensors, smartphones, tablets, wearable devices, and radio frequency identifications (RFIDs), embedded with identification, sensing, computing, communication, and actuation capabilities, are increasingly connected to the Internet, resulting in the next technological revolution, known as the "Internet of Things" (IoT). Integration of multiple semiconductor components on a single chip (System on Chip) is the key success of the Internet of Things, which has the potential to revolutionize a large array of intelligent applications and services in many fields.

According to Gartner, the network of connected things will reach nearly 20.8 billion by 2020, with around 5.5 million new devices being connected every day [3]. It is estimated that by the end of 2017, sales of worldwide wearable electronic devices will be increased by 39% [4]. In contrast, there is a 9.6% decline in worldwide PC shipments, which indicates that smart devices are more preferred in the market [5]. It is reported that by 2018, new digital devices that can talk to each other in the household will be common [6]. It is estimated that nearly 3 trillion gigabytes of data are produced in a single day. The high volumes of heterogeneous data streams coming from these varieties of devices bring great challenges to the traditional data management methods.

A widespread example of these portable devices are mobile phones or smart devices, like Apple's watch, have been integrated with varieties of sensors like accelerometer, gyroscope, compass, Global Positioning System (GPS), and more recently sensors that can capture biometric information such as heart rate. Table 1 lists commonly used sensors on smartphones or tablets.

Table 1 Common Sensors Integrated in Smartphones and Tablets

Sensors on Smartphones	Function
Microphone	The real-world sound and vibration are converted to digital audio
Camera	Senses visible light or electromagnetic radiation and converts them to digital image or video
Gyroscope	Provides orientation information
Accelerometer	Measures the linear acceleration
Compass or magnetometer	Works as a traditional compass. Provides orientation in relation to the magnetic field of Earth
Proximity sensor	Finds proximity of the phone from the user
Ambient light sensor	Optimizes the display brightness
GPS	Global Positioning System, tracks the target location or "navigates" the things by map with the help of GPS satellites
Barometer	Measures atmospheric pressure
Fingerprint sensor	Captures the digital image of fingerprint pattern

Sensors built on the Micro-Electro Mechanical Systems (MEMS) are small in size and only have limited processing and computing capabilities. A wireless sensor networks (WSN) can be developed by connecting the spatially distributed sensors using wireless interfaces. There can be different kinds of sensors integrated into a single WSN, such as mechanical, magnetic, thermal, biological, chemical, and optical. A sensor can be either immobile or mobile (including wearable). While immobile sensors are installed on an object at a fixed location [7], mobile sensors are usually installed on a moving object. A wearable sensor is a special kind of mobile sensor and is worn on the human body, which can be used to form a body sensor network (BSN) or body area network (BAN) [8].

The fixed sensors can be installed on earth surfaces like terrain [9], or submerged under the water [10] and under the land [11]. In contrast, mobile sensors can move and interact with surrounding physical environments. Wearable sensors are worn by the users and can convert physical or environmental parameters of wearers such as blood pressure [12,13], heart rate [14,15], bodily motion [16], brain activity [17], and skin temperature [18]. Table 2 summarizes some of the most commonly used sensors in BSNs.

2.2 DATA TYPES

Interactions among physical objects, sensors, and people generate massive amounts of data, which can be either structured or unstructured. Table 3 illustrates some of the examples on the different types of the data.

Table 2 Commonly Used Sensors in Body Area Networks or Body Sensor Networks

Sensor	Function
Blood-pressure sensor	Measures human blood pressure
Camera pill	Measures gastrointestinal tracts
Carbon dioxide sensor	Measures carbon dioxide gas
ECG/EEG/EMG sensor	Measures the electrical and muscular functions of the heart
Humidity sensor	Measures humidity changes
Blood oxygen saturation	Measures blood oxygen saturation
Pressure sensor	Measures pressure value
Respiration sensor	Measures human respiration values
Temperature sensor	Measures human body temperature

Table 3 Data Types and Data Sources

	Structured Data	Unstructured Data
Human-generated	Input data Click-streams	
		Text documents Social media data Mobile data Web page content
Machine-generated	Web logs/server logs	
		Satellite imagery Scientific data Image and video Radar data
Sensor-generated	Fixed sensor data Mobile sensor data	

2.2.1 Structured data

Structured data are usually defined with fixed attributes, type, and format—for example, records in a relational database are generated according to a predefined schema. Compared to unstructured or semi-structured data, processing of structured data is relatively simpler and more straightforward. This type of data can be generated by people, machines, and sensors.

(1) *Human-generated structured data*: the data are created under explicit human involvement using some interaction mechanisms, e.g., data generated through human-machine interface devices like mouse input data and click-streams.
(2) *Machine-generated structured data*: the data are created automatically by a computing device without explicit human interaction, e.g., Web log data.

(3) *Sensor-generated structured data*: the data are generated by the embedded fixed or moveable sensors, e.g., sensor data from smartphones and smart meters.

2.2.2 Unstructured data

Unstructured data are the opposite of structured data, without a predefined data model. Some common examples include text, images, audio, video, and streaming sensor data. Unstructured data are one primary source of big data and are much more challenging to process compared to structure data. *Human-generated unstructured data* include a large number of data types with different nature, such as textual data (Web documents, licensed publications, e-journals, eBooks, organizational records, e-mails, logs), and media data of different types contributed by ordinary users on social media platforms. Examples of *machine-generated unstructured data* include scientific data (e.g., astronomical data, geographic, ecological, biological, chemical, and geospatial data), satellite images of weather, surveillance data, and radar data (e.g., meteorological and oceanographic seismic data).

3 BIG DATA: DATA ACQUISITION METHODS

Human interaction with computers and devices creates vast amounts of data. In the PC era, human interface devices (HIDs), like keyboards and mice, support users in interacting with created digital data. Most of the digital user-generated text data have been created by conventional and widely used major input devices like keyboards and mice (or touchpads in portable computers) with explicit human involvement. Digitized analog data or sensor data are generated using audio and camera devices, known as multimedia data. The introduction of tactile-feedback technology has added an extra dimension to the manner in which people interact with computers. The stylus, a pen-shaped instrument used with tactile-feedback devices and graphics tablets to interact, write on the surface of the screen, making interaction more direct. The stylus and similar haptic-based devices allow users to interact directly with the displayed content with multitouch gestures as an input, in lieu of the physical keyboard and pointing devices. The rise of smart touch-based devices, embedded with sensors, has added diversity to existing interaction methods, enabling richer interactive gesture-based interaction methods.

3.1 INTERFACE METHODS

Communication between the user and a computer system is done through various interface mechanisms, especially using input/output devices. In this section, we review some of the most important ones and their evolution, and describe how they contribute to data generation (see Fig. 1 for a summary).

3.1.1 Command-line interfaces

The command-line interface (CLI) or character user interface (CUI) is one of the first types of interface methods that allows users to send text-based commands to the system. Text commands are converted to appropriate operating system functions. The CLI is the earliest and oldest form of interface, but offers powerful and concise control over programs. As such, the earliest forms of digital text data are created using CLIs. The amounts of data generated are not significant. This is an important feature, as in earlier systems, memory was limited and expensive.

| Command-line interface | Graphical user interface | Multi-touch gestural interface | Natural user interface |

FIG. 1

Evolution of user interfaces, user input methods or data generation.

3.1.2 Graphical user interfaces

The graphical user interface (GUI), popularized by Microsoft Windows, is an interactive visual interface rather than a command or text-only interface. The interactive interface tools are visually represented as windows, icons, menus, and a pointer device, which collectively are known as WIMP. The GUI interface also includes a text interface, called the graphical character-based interface. Presently, GUI is the most common and well-known user interface for computers and some earlier mobile devices like mobile phones and laptops. Gracoli, a hybrid interface, combines the strengths of the GUI and CLI to perform application specific interfaces [19].

3.1.3 Context-sensitive user interfaces

Context-sensitive user interfaces is almost pervasively used within GUIs, and allow users to choose automatically from available multiple options based on the current or previous state of the application process. Context menus in GUIs are the principal example of context-sensitive user interfaces. The primary use of the context-sensitive user interface is to simplify the interface by reducing the number of commands or clicks or keystrokes required to perform a given action. This type of interface plays a crucial role where interface devices have limited number of buttons, like video games controlled by a mouse, joystick, or gamepad. With the emergence of mobile devices, whose main input entry is via a touch-based screen, context-sensitive interfaces have found more uses. A variety of contextual options are provided via distinct taps and gestures on the screen.

3.1.4 Web-based user interfaces

A Web user interface or Web app allows the user to interact with content or software running on a remote server through a Web browser. The content or Web page is downloaded from the Web server and the user can interact with this content in a Web browser, which acts as a client. The distributed nature allows the content to be stored on a remote server, while the ubiquitous nature of the Web browser permits a convenient access to the content. The most common Web applications are Webmail, online shopping, online document sharing, social media, and instant messaging. A vast amount of data exists now, generated by these types of interfaces.

3.1.5 Adaptive user interfaces or intelligent user interfaces

Adaptive user interfaces (AUIs), also referred as intelligent user interface (IUIs), support users' customization of the interface by changing the layout and other elements according to the user or context requirements. AUIs are either user-initiated adaptable or system-initiated self-adaptive. Their aim is to offer efficient, intuitive, and secure way interfaces to users based on their unique preferences, traits, and environmental circumstances.

AUIs are capable of passively recognizing a user's presence, and offer services based on their immediate requirements.

3.1.6 Natural user interfaces
The natural user interface (NUI) is a gesture-based simple and intuitive interface, and allows users to naturally interact with the systems without any physical encumbrances, involving body movements, gestures, and voice.

3.1.7 Voice interfaces
Voice user interfaces (VUI) are based on speech recognition technology and enable users to interact or send commands to computers or smart devices using voice or speech. This is the most natural way of allowing users to interact with computers or smart devices, similar to how one would communicate with other people. The most commonly used voice interaction roles are command- and agent-based interactions. The command-based interaction allows the user to give speech input to the system, most commonly in a simple but specific predefined order. The agent-based interactions recognize natural language as input and provide an appropriate response through text or audio on the system. Apple's Siri and Google's Voice Search are typical examples of voice interfaces.

3.1.8 Gesture-based interfaces
Gesture-based interfaces attempt first to recognize gestures as commands. They distinguish continuous physical moments of the users, organizing the hands, fingers, face, head, and body into a discrete sequence of commands. The successful interpretations of meaningful gestures are recognized by the receiving system, which let users interact with the systems in a more natural way. Sensor evolution also led to the enhancement of novel human gesture-based interaction with smart connected devices in the IoT. The natural, continuous meaningful movements of users, involving their hands, fingers, head, face, and body, can all be part of this process of user-system interaction. This will be an important way of interaction as for instance with the growing emphasis on BSNs where sensors are placed on or attached to the human body to passively capture physiological data and body movements [20].

3.1.9 Multitouch gesture interface
A multitouch interface is a gesture-based interface that supports two or more continuous gestures to interact with touch surfaces. On smart devices, for example, multitouch interfaces allow more direct interaction with applications and are considered to be natural and intuitive gestures. This empowers varieties of actions like taps, swipes, rotations, pinches, and other natural gestures. Touchpads and touchscreens on portable smart devices are powered by multitouch interfaces. The ever increasing dominance of these devices has replaced traditional input devices like keyboards and mice as most data-generating input devices.

3.1.10 Touchless gesture interfaces
Touchless gesture interfaces completely eliminate physical contact with a device directly as by touching or indirectly via a secondary device like a mouse. This is thought to that it make interaction even more natural and intuitive by letting users be free of any physical attachments and involving only their

body movements. Second to voice, human movements without the need for any physical controls are closer to how people interact with one another. Touchless gesture interfaces aim to replicate this type of communication, which is achieved through selections of intelligent sensing devices located around the users. A touchless gestural interface represents an intelligent and a natural user interface method for users to interact with systems using intuitive and unencumbered physical movements and gestures [20].

We next review some input devices and tools that enable the creation of the interfaces we have presented above.

3.2 INTERFACE DEVICES

Input devices enable the user to input data directly into the computer. The best-known HIDs are the text entry device keyboard and pointing devices like the mouse, trackball, light pen, and stylus, and other devices like the joystick and touchscreen.

3.2.1 Keyboard

The keyboard is a typewriter-style device with a series of electronic switches or keys which allow users to send text and alphanumeric data directly into computers. The switches each represent one character. The most common English-language keyboard layout is a typewriter-style QWERTY layout. The standard computer keyboard contains alphabet keys, number keys, punctuation symbol keys, arrow keys, and functional and control keys. The keyboard is the primary peripheral device for data entry. The virtual, touchscreen-based keypad is used in mobile devices to simulate the physical keyboard.

3.2.2 Mice

The mouse allows a user to manipulate objects indirectly using a pointer-like representation by detecting two-dimensional motion in a GUI. The mouse is a hand-controlled device, and typically has one or two buttons. The mouse click is generated by pressing any of the buttons once, holding it, or releasing it immediately. There are different variations of mouse clicks to select objects, move the pointer to the desired location on the display, and input commands into the system. The keyboard and mouse are the most integrated computer peripherals which allow the user to interact with the system. In contrast to the keyboard, the mouse is supported only in GUIs. The trackball is another pointing device very similar to the mouse.

3.2.3 Joystick

The joystick is a control column input device with a lever which controls the movement of a pointer in all directions on the display. Similar to the mouse, joysticks include buttons known as triggers for additional functionality. The joystick is typically used in games and sometimes as a replacement for the mouse in certain situations. Miniature versions of finger-operated joysticks are now adopted in mobile devices.

3.2.4 Stylus

The stylus, a pen-shaped input device, allows the user to input commands to the computer, mobile, and other smart devices via their display. The stylus is used on the touchscreen devices to make selections by tapping, or writing or drawing on the screen, just like using a pen on a notebook. The stylus is more commonly used in portable handheld devices, like laptops and tablets, than on desktop computers.

3.2.5 Touchpad

The touchpad is a pointing device or cursor-controlling device for portable computers. Touchpads function a very similar way to mice and contain a tactile sensor to identify the position and motion of the user's fingers in contact with the pad. Touchpads introduced multitouch gesture-based interface mechanisms. In addition to the taps and swipes features of the touchpad, gesture-based interface allows additional gesture-based application special input methods.

3.2.6 Touchscreens

The touchscreen is a combination of both display and input device. A transparent touch-sensitive panel is embedded on the rigid planar surface that recognizes the touch or press of users' fingers as input. The touchscreen replaced mouse or stylus with users' fingers as an input device, giving the feeling of more directness to users when they manipulate content on the display. Touchscreens have brought in widespread use of multitouch gesture-based input interactions with modern devices.

Besides the above more recognizable input devices, there are a number of emergent ones which are becoming more widely used and support new ways of interactive with computing systems. The integration of these emergent devices is only possible by powerful machines that can capture large amounts of data and process them in real-time. In addition, the development of BANs has made the use of some of these devices feasible. We describe some the emergent input devices next.

3.2.7 Kinect

The Kinect is device that captures body motion of users with them being placed at a certain distance of a display. Its motion sensors translate a user's physical body position and movements into commands. Initially developed for the Xbox game consoles, it is now used for other applications and devices.

3.2.8 Leap motion

Leap is an in-air gestural user interface device. Leap uses two monochromic infrared (IR) cameras and three IR LEDs covers hemispherical area at a distance of 1 m. It is similar to the Kinect but is designed for closer interaction from any display.

3.2.9 Myo

Myo is a muscle-controlled arm worn gestural device. Myo recognizes forearm muscle movements and transmits them wirelessly as valid gestural commands to interact with PCs or other systems.

3.2.10 Wearable devices

Wearable devices or gadgets are electronic devices worn by consumers ubiquitously and continually to capture or track biometric information related to health or fitness. Wearable devices are new manifestations of accessories that people wear, such as Apple's Watch or Samsung's Gear Watch or more dedicated tools like the Fitbit One wireless activity and sleep tracker and monitor. Wearable devices with biometric tracking capabilities represent one of the most important sources of data generation. They will continuously and uninterruptedly record data of different types and from a variety of environments.

As data increase in variety and volume in parallel to the need to support greater velocity in their generation and processing, it is important to have a way to organize them. Organization and management of data will therefore be explored next.

4 BIG DATA: DATA MANAGEMENT
4.1 DATA REPRESENTATION AND ORGANIZATION

Current systems represent data using a binary digital system. The data types are converted into binary digits represented of 1s or 0s called bits. A byte, equivalent to a sequence of 8-bits, is the fundamental unit of storage. Different standards are used to encode data objects by assigning bit patterns together. In order to utilize the storage space efficiently, data are compressed using various compression techniques. One of the major requirements in big data is their low latency in their processing. In contrast with the traditional methods of performing computations on stored data, the data must be processed as it is generated in, or almost near, real-time. Thus low latency is a key requirement in big data analytics (DA).

4.1.1 File formats
The file format is the description of how the collection of data is internally represented on a storage medium in a file. Data processing and query performance are heavily based on the file format. In order to reduce the total number of bytes moved from storage disk to temporary memory, data is often compressed. Data compression methods save time to transfer data, but with a tradeoff that data have to be decompressed. A selection of file formats has significant performance consequences. The compression support reduces the size of data on the disks to maximize input/output and central processing unit (CPU) resources to de-serialize the data. The query performance is mainly based on the amounts of input/output and CPU resources required to transfer and decompress the data. The file formats can be structured and unstructured.

We next describe some important file formats.

Javascript object notation records (JSON)
JSON is an open, lightweight, highly human, and machine-readable standard based on a subset of the Javascript programming language that allows data interchange. JSON is a platform and language independent text format. It uses the conventions from different language families, including C, C++, C#, Java, Javascript, Perl, Python, and others. JSON supports arrays and understands the different type of standard data types, such as strings, numbers, and Boolean values. Computers can easily parse and generate JSON records that can describe complex data structures.

JSON is built on two universal structures: as an object, such as the collection of value pairs, and an array, such as the ordered list of values.

Binary Javascript object notation records (BSON)
BSON is a binary-encoded serialization of JSON-like documents. The value pairs are stored as a single entity called *document*. BSON is also lightweight, traversable, and efficient. The extensions in BSON allow representation of data types in addition to the standard JSON types. BSON supports embedding

documents and arrays with other documents and arrays. In comparison with other binary interchange formats, BSON is more "schema-less."

Comma-separated values (CSV)

Comma-separated values (CSV) is a standard file format for spreadsheet data used to exchange data between distinct applications. The data is represented in a text file; each record is represented as one line, and commas are used to separate data fields in each row. CSV is used to exchange data between Hadoop and external systems.

Sequence file

A sequence file (SF) is a flat, compact binary storage format for serialized key-value pairs. These files provide additional support for two different levels of compression formats like a record and block compressions in addition to the uncompressed format. The file metadata is supported with a "secondary" Text/Text pair key-value list. The files can be easily split and processed in parallel. A SF consists of a header followed by one or more records.

Record columnar files

Record Columnar files (RC files) are intended for efficient and high-performing processing of data. They are flat files and support columnar formats that consist of binary key/value pairs. RC files store columns of a table in a record columnar way by horizontally partitioning the rows into row splits and vertically partitioning them in a columnar way. The metadata of row splits remains stored in keys while data of a row split stored as values. Since being introduced in 2011,[1] RC files have been adopted in major real-world systems for big DA, including in Facebook's Hadoop cluster.[2]

Optimized row columnar files (ORC files)

Optimized row columnar (ORC) files are further optimized and intended to replace RC files. In an ORC file, the collection of the row data is in the columnar format, optimized for compression; these collections of rows are stored in one separate file. This format supports parallel processing of row collections across multiple clusters. The lightweight indexing enables the feature of skipping a complete block that is not required for the requested query. ORC files come with basic statistics on its columns.

Parquet files

The Apache parquet is a columnar file format, and stores binary data in a column-oriented way. The values of each column are organized adjacent to each other, enabling efficient, flexible compression options and encoding schemes. Parquet file format supports all data processing frameworks and data models. A single parquet file size range can reach up to gigabytes, and is optimized to process large volumes of data, typically suited to data warehouse-style operations.

---

[1]He Y, Lee R, Huai Y, Shao Z, Jain N, Zhang X, et al. RCFile: a fast and space-efficient data placement structure in MapReduce-based warehouse systems. In: Proceedings of the IEEE international conference on data engineering (ICDE); 2011.
[2]http://www.slideshare.net/ydn/2-hive-integrationhadoopsummit2010.

Avro files

Avro is a binary data storage format, providing data serialization and data exchange services. Avro supports a rich set of primitive data types. The data efficiently serialize into files or a message. The data and data definition are combined together in a single file or message, making Avro schemas to perform rapid serialization. The data stored in a binary format, making it compact and efficient. The data definition is stored in JSON format, making it easy to read and interpret. The markers in Avro files split large datasets into subsets. Avro files support both primitive data and complex data types. Avro handles data schema changes. The data stored in Avro files can easily be portable between different programming languages.

Avro supports the Remote Procedure Call (RPC) interface in data exchange services to effectively allow different programs to communicate data and information. Avro RPC interfaces and schemas are defined in JSON. Avro heavily relies on its schemas, both data and its schemas are stored in a file.

When describing these different file formats, we have also made some references to data compression. This is an important aspect of the management of big data. We shall discuss some salient aspects of data compression next.

4.1.2 Data compression

In big data, petabytes of data are captured, stored, and analyzed. The high volumes of data generally increase the input/output operations and transferring these large datasets over the network will take considerable time. The real-time DA need efficient management using these disk input/output and network bandwidth resources. Data compression mitigates these problems by not just saving storage space but also increasing the data transfer speed across the network. It is crucial in big data environments to combine data compression and to increase the network transfer to improve the performance of DA activities. Compression of massive datasets certainly increases the utilization of the CPU, as the data must be decompressed to be processed at a later stage.

Hadoop supports multiple compression formats most commonly referred as *codec*—short name for coder and decoder. There exist a set of compiled Java libraries that can be used in Hadoop to perform data compression and decompression. Each codec has one algorithm implementation for compression and decompression. Hadoop supports both splittable and nonsplittable compression algorithms. A splittable algorithm enhances performance as large data blocks are distributed across multiple data nodes and multiple MapReduce tasks decompress data blocks in parallel. Nonsplittable algorithms, on the other hand, combine data blocks together and use one MapReduce task for decompression.

There are a number of Hadoop codecs, which we describe next briefly.

4.1.3 Hadoop codecs

Deflate uses a combination of the Huffman coding, a form of prefix coding and LZ77 compression, which works by finding and replacing redundant data with metadata.

LZ4 is a speed-focused lossless compression algorithm, belongs to a LZ77 based byte-oriented compression scheme. The maximum compression speed is 400 MB/s per core, decompressed speed in multiple GB/s per core, expandable to multicores.

Gzip is a file format, based on the Deflate algorithm, used for file compression and decompression.

Bzip2 is an open format file compression based on the Burrows-Wheeler algorithm, used to compress single files. Bzip2 uses multiple layers of stacked up compression techniques.

Snappy codecs, previously known as Zipply, provide very high speed and reasonable compression. The maximum compression speed is 250 MB/s or more and decompression speed about 500 MB/s or more. Snappy is optimized for 64-bit x86-compatible processors. Snappy assumes little-endian throughout and requires byte-swapping of data in several places for big-endian platform. Snappy is a robust and stable system, and has successfully compressed and decompressed petabytes of data in Google's production environment.

Typical compression ratio for plain text data is 1.5–1.7 ×, for HTML about 2–4 ×, and for image data like JPEGs and PNGs and other compressed formats, about 1.0 ×.

Files, whether compressed or not, need to be organized properly. The organization of files is usually down to databases.

4.2 DATABASES

In contrast to the traditional relational databases, a NoSQL (not only SQL) database is a geographically distributed nonrelational database system. A NoSQL database system runs on multiple cluster nodes, with individual instances of operating systems and built-in storage on each node. This feature support is aimed largely at organizing and analyzing large amounts of heterogeneous data types, regardless of OS. The nodes facsimile data across numerous nodes to ensure that there is no data loss during node failure. The cluster services restore the data from the failed node through a single system image to redistribute the data across the cluster.

4.2.1 Dynamic schema

In contrast to traditional relational databases, which require that database schemas should be defined before data insertion, NoSQL permits data insertion without a predefined database schema. This allows applications to integrate schema iteration rapidly in real-time. The side-code is added by the developers to ensure quality controls by keeping specific fields and data types. This validation method imposes authority on data without compromising the benefits of dynamic schema.

4.2.2 Sharding, replication and auto-caching

Sharding is a method of storing data records across many server instances. This is done through storage area networks to make hardware perform like a single server. The NoSQL framework is natively designed to support automatic distribution of the data across multiple servers including the query load. Both data and query replacements are automatically distributed across multiple servers located in the different geographic regions, and this facilitates rapid, automatic, and transparent replacement of the data or query instances without any disruption. The cloud computing and platform as a service framework makes this feature considerably easier. The most frequently used data are kept in the integrated in-memory database instead of being placed in a separate caching later to maintain the lowest latency and also provide the highest throughput.

4.2.3 NoSQL types

Key-value stores

Key-value (KV) stores, or key-value databases, are the simplest NoSQL databases. KV stores use an associate array data model, known as a *hash* or *dictionary*. In this model, every single record in the database is stored as an attribute name or key, together with its value in a schema-less way. This relationship is known as key-value pair. In each key-value pair, the key is represented by a string and the value is the data for the key. In particular, the key-value stores do not require a query language, but provide a way to store, retrieve, and update data.

Notable key-value databases are Riak, Redis, Memcached, BerkerlyDB, Upscaledb, Amazon DynamoDB, Couchbase, and Project Voldemort.

Table 4 shows the comparison of different NoSQL data-models.

Table 4 NoSQL Data-Model Comparison					
Data-Model	Performance	Scalability	Flexibility	Complexity	Functionality
Key-value store	High	High	High	None	Variable (none)
Column store	High	High	Moderate	Low	Minimal
Document store	High	Variable (high)	High	Low	Variable (low)
Graph store	Variable	Variable	High	High	Graph theory

Document stores

Document stores (DS) record data in a key-value pairs in a structured format which the database can understand. Each document contains data and a unique key is assigned to retrieve the document. It allows the adding of new fields of data by including additional key-value pairs into documents.

The transparent way of storing data remove query limitations by key. This allows content-oriented retrieval of full-page, often semistructured data with a single query and is suited for content-oriented applications. The documents are in XML, JSON, and BSON file formats.

The most notable and popular document databases are MongoDB, CouchDB, Terrastore, OrientDB, RavenDB, and Lotus Notes.

Column-oriented stores

Column databases, as the name suggests, are designed to record data tables as rows of columns of data. The columns of data always group related data as rows and are associated with a unique row key. This inverse feature of relational database systems provides optimized queries over very big datasets and offers very scalable architecture with extremely high performance. The columnar database is highly compressed to save storage space and is also capable of self-indexing. The most popular column-oriented databases are Cassandra, HBase, Hypertable, and Amazon DynamoDB.

Graph stores

These data stores are designed to represent data entities and the undetermined interconnected relationships between these entities as a graph. The entities are similar to nodes with properties. The edges represent relationships with their own properties, including directional significance. The nodes and their relationships are organized as a graph. The relationship is actually persevered and the data are interpreted in different ways based on their relationships in the graph. This supports rapid traversing of joining or relationships. The nodes can have multiple types of relationships with start and end nodes along with their own properties. The properties of the relationships are used to add intelligence to the relationship and also employed to query the graph.

The notable graph databases are Neo4J, Infinite Graph, and OrientDB or FlockDB.

4.3 DATA FUSION AND DATA INTEGRATION

Data are generated from varieties of different sources and each data source carries significant information that is sufficient to analyze and process the data. The data obtained directly from different sources can have some redundant information and can also have heterogeneous representations. Retrieval of meaningful information from heterogeneous datasets has limitations. In order to manage data and retrieve valuable information from data efficiently, it is essential to merge heterogeneous datasets into one homogeneous data representation. Data fusion provides this by combining information from multiple sources to form a unified representation.

Data fusion can be defined as [21]: "A multi-level process dealing with the association, correlation, combination of data and information from single and multiple sources to achieve refined position, identify estimates and complete and timely assessments of situations, threats and their significance." An alternative definition is from Hall and Llinas [22]: "data fusion techniques combine data from multiple sensors and related information from associated databases to achieve improved accuracy and more specific inferences than could be achieved by the use of a single sensor alone."

Data fusion systems are used in a wide range of domains such as sensor networks, text processing, and video and image processing, to name a few. In big data, the high velocity of heterogeneous data types implies the importance of having data fusion. Advance developments in Internet of Things connect networks of sensors. These networks encompass sensor nodes and at least one base station. Every sensor nodes are integrated with sensors, data processing tools, a radio communication system, and a battery. In these networks, raw data may present redundant information and provide sufficient information about its relevance. In multisensor networks, transmitting raw data can cause data collisions and there could be a higher chance of having inaccurate/unreliable information from some abnormal nodes. In order to aggregate valid data to yield effective information, it is essential to process the data. Data fusion facilitates better usage of network bandwidth, a great network lifetime, utilizes the energy resources, and above all offers an efficient and high level of accurate information retrieval. As such, data fusion represents one of the bigger challenges in big data.

5 SUMMARY

The objective of this chapter is to give a broad overview of acquisition and generation methods of big data. In the digital century, the term "big data" has expanded its boundary from scientific data (e.g., satellite imagery data and geographical data) to the sensor data on the Internet of Things (e.g., metrological data and healthcare data). The new boundary adds more characteristics, known as *volume, velocity, variety, veracity*, and *value*—the *Vs* of big data. In the same way, the expansion also brings new challenges into the big data processing and analytics pipeline. In fact, the coinage "big data" unambiguously denotes digital data, either born-digital or converted into digital data from born-analog. The computers or other digital devices are the main sources of born-digital data, whereas born-analog or sensor data are captured by various sensing devices. These data are not only predefined with a data model, known as structured data, but also without any predefined model, branded as unstructured data. Moreover, these massive amounts of data are generated with or without explicit human involvement. The tactile-feedback technology has added an extra dimension to the manner in which human interact with computers or devices. Equally, the rise of smart devices, with embedded sensors, has incorporated more diversity to existing interaction methods.

Different types of big data are created from well-known text-only keyboard to rapidly growing wearable devices and are successfully converted into binary digits, or bits. A selection of file formats, notably JSON, BSON, CSV, and RC files, are used to store the collection of data. The data are compressed to reduce the size on storage disks to maximize input/output and CPU resources.

A geographically distributed nonrelational database system, NoSQL is used to handle unstructured data. NoSQL encompasses the following different types of database technologies: key-value stores, document stores, column-oriented stores, and graph stores. Additionally, NoSQL permits dynamic data insertion without a predefined database scheme compared relational database predefined schema. Data fusion merges heterogeneous datasets into one homogeneous data representation by combining information from multiple sources to form a unified representation.

REFERENCES

[1] Sagiroglu S, Sinanc D. Big data: a review. In: International conference on Collaboration Technologies and Systems (CTS); 2013. p. 42–7.
[2] Laney D. 3D data management: Controlling data volume, velocity and variety. META Group Research Note 6, 2001. p. 70.
[3] Gartner Says 6.4 Billion Connected [Internet]. Available from: http://www.gartner.com/newsroom/id/3165317 [cited 20.04.16].
[4] Gartner Says Worldwide Wearable Devices Sales to Grow 18.4 Percent in 2016 [Internet]. Available from: http://www.gartner.com/newsroom/id/3198018 [cited 20.04.16].
[5] Gartner Says Worldwide PC Shipments Declined 9.6 Percent in First Quarter of 2016 [Internet]. Available from: http://www.gartner.com/newsroom/id/3280626 [cited 20.04.16].
[6] When to Expect Devices and Connected [Internet]. Available from: http://www.gartner.com/newsroom/id/3220117 [cited 20.04.16].
[7] Yick J, Mukherjee B, Ghosal D. Wireless sensor network survey. Comput Netw 2008;52(12):2292–330.
[8] Lai X, Liu Q, Wei X, Wang W, Zhou G, Han G. A survey of body sensor networks. Sensors 2013;13 (5):5406–47.
[9] Akyildiz IF, Su W, Sankarasubramaniam Y, Cayirci E. A survey on sensor networks. IEEE Commun Mag 2002;40(8):102–14.
[10] Akyildiz IF, Pompili D, Melodia T. Challenges for efficient communication in underwater acoustic sensor networks. SIGBED Rev 2004;1(2):3–8.
[11] Li M, Liu Y. Underground structure monitoring with wireless sensor networks. In: Proceedings of the 6th international conference on information processing in sensor networks (IPSN '07) [Internet]. New York: ACM; 2007. p. 69–78. Available from http://doi.acm.org/10.1145/1236360.1236370 [cited 22.04.16].
[12] Espina J, Falck T, Muehlsteff J, Aubert X. Wireless body sensor network for continuous cuff-less blood pressure monitoring. In: 3rd IEEE/EMBS international summer school on medical devices and biosensors; 2006. p. 11–5.
[13] Teng XF, Zhang YT, Poon CCY, Bonato P. Wearable medical systems for p-health. IEEE Rev Biomed Eng 2008;1:62–74.
[14] Paradiso R, Loriga G, Taccini N. A wearable health care system based on knitted integrated sensors. IEEE Trans Inf Technol Biomed 2005;9(3):337–44.

[15] Rienzo MD, Rizzo F, Parati G, Brambilla G, Ferratini M, Castiglioni P. MagIC system: a new textile-based wearable device for biological signal monitoring. Applicability in daily life and clinical setting. In: IEEE engineering in medicine and biology 27th annual conference; 2005. p. 7167–9.

[16] Mattmann C, Clemens F, Tröster G. Sensor for measuring strain in textile. Sensors 2008;8(6):3719–32.

[17] Devot S, Bianchi AM, Naujoka E, Mendez MO, Braurs A, Cerutti S. Sleep monitoring through a textile recording system. In: 29th annual international conference of the IEEE Engineering in Medicine and Biology Society; 2007. p. 2560–3.

[18] Jung S, Ji T, Varadan VK. Point-of-care temperature and respiration monitoring sensors for smart fabric applications. Smart Mater Struct 2006;15(6):1872.

[19] Verma P. Gracoli: a graphical command line user interface. In: CHI'13 extended abstracts on human factors in computing systems (CHI EA'13) [Internet]. New York: ACM; 2013. p. 3143–6. Available from http://doi.acm.org/10.1145/2468356.2479631 [cited 30.03.16].

[20] Garzotto F, Valoriani M. Touchless gestural interaction with small displays: a case study. In: New York: ACM Press; 2013. p. 1–10. Available from http://dl.acm.org/citation.cfm?doid=2499149.2499154 [cited 02.07.15].

[21] White FE. Data Fusion Lexicon, Joint Directors of Laboratories, Technical Panel for C3, Data Fusion Sub-Panel. San Diego, CA: Naval Ocean Systems Center; 1991.

[22] Hall DL, Llinas J. An introduction to multisensor data fusion. Proc IEEE 1997;85(1):6–23.

GLOSSARY

Data analytics It is the science of exploring large amounts of data to discover hidden patterns and correlations, and draw conclusions based on the findings.

Data mining and Knowledge discovery It is an interdisciplinary computational process to analyze data for discovering useful knowledge from data.

Raster data It is a data structure that is represented as a regular grid (rectangular or square) of cells.

Satellite imagery It is the collection images of Earth and other planets collected by satellites.

Scientific research It is the systematic investigation of scientific theories and hypotheses.

CLOUD COMPUTING INFRASTRUCTURE FOR DATA INTENSIVE APPLICATIONS

2

Yuri Demchenko*, Fatih Turkmen*, Cees de Laat*, Ching-Hsien Hsu[†], Christophe Blanchet[‡],
Charles Loomis[§]

University of Amsterdam, Amsterdam, The Netherlands[*] Chung Hua University, Hsinchu, Taiwan[†] CNRS IFB,
Orsay, France[‡] SixSq Sàrl, Geneva, Switzerland[§]

ACRONYMS

API	application programming interface
ASP	application service provider
AWS	Amazon Web Services
BDAF	Big Data Architecture Framework
BDE	Big Data Ecosystem
BDI	Big Data Infrastructure
BDLM	Big Data Lifecycle Management
BDRA	NIST Big Data Reference Architecture
CCRA	NIST Cloud Computing Reference Architecture (NIST SP 500-292)
CEOS	Committee on Earth Observation Satellites
CLI	command line interface
CPR	Capability (framework) provider requirements
CSDI	cloud services delivery infrastructure
CSP	cloud service provider
DACI	dynamic access control infrastructure
DSR	data sources requirements
EC2	Elastic Compute Cloud, IaaS cloud service provided by AWS/Amazon
ECL	Enterprise Control Language by LexisNexis (currently open source)
EDW	enterprise data warehouse
EMR	Elastic MapReduce
ETL	extract-transform-load
FADI	Federated Access and Delivery Infrastructure
GCE	Google Compute Engine cloud
HDFS	Hadoop Distributed File System
HPC	high performance computing
IaaS	Infrastructure as a Service
ICAF	Intercloud Architecture Framework
ICFF	Intercloud Federation Framework, part of ICAF
ICT	information communication technologies
IDE	integrated development environment

IFB	French Institute of Bioinformatics
INCA	Institut National du Cancer (France)
KEL	Knowledge Engineering Language (by LexisNexis)
LMR	lifecycle management requirements
NAPALM	Network Automation and Programmability Abstraction Layer with Multivendor support
NFS	Network File System
NGS	Next Generation Sequencing
NIST	National Institute of Standards and Technology in the United States
NoSQL	Not only SQL (primarily refers to databases for nonstructured and semistructured data)
OASIS	Organization for the Advancement of Structured Information Standards
OCX	GÉANT Open Cloud eXchange
OLAP	online analytical processing
OS	operating system
PaaS	platform as a service
PID	Persistent IDentifier
S3	Simple Storage Service (services of AWS cloud)
SaaS	software as a service
SAML	Security Assertions Markup Language
SDI	Scientific Data e-Infrastructure
SPR	security and privacy requirements
SQL	Structural Query Language (a special purpose language designed for managing data in the relational databases)
TMF	TeleManagement Forum
TOSCA	Topology and Orchestration Specification for Cloud Applications (OASIS standard)
TPR	transformation (applications) provider requirements
URI	Unified Resource Identifier
URL	Unified Resource Locator
VM	virtual machine
VPC	virtual private cloud (a concept proposed by Amazon and a name of AWS cloud service)
XACML	eXtensible Access Control Markup Language
ZTPOM	Zero-Touch Provisioning, Operation and Management

1 INTRODUCTION

Big Data technologies (also called Data Science, Data Intensive, Data Centric, Data Driven, or Data Analytics) are becoming a current focus and a general trend both in science and in industry. The emergence of Big Data technologies indicates the beginning of a new form of continuous technology advancement characterized by overlapping technology waves related to different components of the modern digital economy from production and consumption to collaboration, and general social activity. Modern e-Science, empowered with advances in computing, brings new possibilities for industry to benefit from advanced data processing methods; industry in its own turn offers to the scientific/research community advanced computing, data storage, and communication platforms.

Big Data are currently related to almost all aspects of human activity from simple events recording to research, design, production, and digital services or products delivery, to actionable information presentation to the final consumer. Current technologies such as cloud computing and ubiquitous network connectivity provide a platform for automation of all processes in data collection, storing, processing, and visualization.

The fusion between Big Data and cloud technologies fuels modern data-driven research [1] and provides a basis for modern e-Science that benefits from wide availability of affordable computing and storage resources provided on demand. Modern e-Science infrastructures allow the targeting of new large-scale problems that were not possible to solve before, e.g., genome, climate, and global warming research. e-Science typically produces a huge amount of data that need to be supported by a new type of e-Infrastructure capable to store, distribute, process, preserve, and curate this data. In e-Science, the scientific data are complex multifaceted objects with complex internal relations; they are becoming an infrastructure of their own and need to be supported by corresponding physical or logical infrastructures to store, access, and manage these data. We shall refer to these new infrastructures as Scientific Data e-Infrastructure (SDI) and more generally big data infrastructure (BDI) that will also incorporate specific for industry focus on working with customers, supporting business processes and delivering business value.

Modern research is becoming more and more data intensive and requires using high-performance computing over large volumes of data storage. Cloud computing [2,3] and Big Data technologies [4,5] provide necessary computing and data processing capabilities for data-intensive and data-driven applications in both research and industry.

2 BIG DATA NATURE AND DEFINITION
2.1 BIG DATA IN SCIENCE AND INDUSTRY

Science has traditionally dealt with challenges to handle large volumes of data in complex scientific research experiments, involving wide cooperation among distributed groups of individual scientists and research organizations. Scientific research typically includes collection of data in passive observation or active experiments which aim to verify a scientific hypothesis. The scientific research and discovery methods are typically based on the initial hypothesis and a model which can be refined based on the collected data. The refined model may lead to a new more advanced and precise experiment and/or the previous data re-evaluation. New data-driven science allows discovery of hidden relations based on the processing of large amount of data, which was not possible with previous technologies and scientific platforms. The future SDI/BDI needs to support all data handling operations and processes while also providing access to data and to facilities to support collaboration between researchers. Besides traditional access control and data security issues, security services need to ensure secure and trusted environment for researchers to conduct their research.

In business, private companies will not typically share their data or expertise. When dealing with data, companies always intend to keep control over their information assets. They may use shared third-party facilities, like clouds or specialist instruments, but special measures need to be taken to ensure workspace safety and data protection, including input/output data sanitization.

Big Data in industry are related to controlling complex technological processes and objects or facilities. Modern computer-aided manufacturing produces huge amount of technological data which are in general needed to be stored or retained to allow effective quality control or diagnostics in case of failure or crash. Similarly to e-Science, in many industrial applications/scenarios there is a need for collaboration or interaction of many workers and technologists.

With the digital technologies proliferation into all aspects of business activities and emerging Big Data technologies, the industry is entering a new playground. There is a recognized need to use scientific methods to benefit from the possibility to collect and mine data for desirable information, such as market prediction, customer behavior predictions, social groups activity predictions, etc.

A number of blog and technical press discussions suggest that the Big Data technologies need to adopt scientific discovery methods that include iterative model improvement, data reuse with the improved model, and further collection of improved and extended data. We can quote here a blog article by Mike Gualtieri from Forrester [6]: "Firms increasingly realize that [big data] must use predictive and descriptive analytics to find nonobvious information to discover value in the data. Advanced analytics uses advanced statistical, data mining and machine learning algorithms to dig deeper to find patterns that you can't see using traditional BI (*Business Intelligence*) tools, simple queries, or rules."

2.2 BIG DATA AND SOCIAL NETWORK/DATA

Big Data's rise is tightly connected to the social data revolution, which provided the initial motivation for developing large-scale services, global infrastructure and high performance analytical tools, and currently produces huge amounts of data on its own. Social networks are widely used for collecting personal and marketing information and providing better personalized services starting from custom search advice and recommendation systems to targeted advertisements and precisely targeted campaigns.

2.3 BIG DATA TECHNOLOGY DEFINITION: FROM 6V TO 5 PARTS

Early Big Data definitions were focused primarily on the properties of Big Data that distinguished them from the previous generation of technologies and defined them as 3V, 4V, or 5V of Big Data that included such properties as volume, velocity, variety, veracity, and value. Demchenko et al. [7] proposed to extend the essential properties of Big Data to 6V by adding variability as another important property that needs to be supported by Big Data processing systems during its lifecycle. The proposed 6V definition also distinguishes generic properties such as volume, velocity, and variety, and acquired ones such as value, veracity, and variability that are obtained when data are entered into Big Data systems.

Much research has recognized that Big Data properties only are not sufficient to define Big Data as a new technology. The actionable definition should reflect all of the important features that would provide basis for further technology development. Similar to and extending the Gartner definition [8], Demchenko et al. [7] propose an extended Big Data definition as comprising of the five parts that group the main Big Data features and related components in the following way:

(1) Big Data properties: 6Vs
   - generic properties: volume, variety, velocity
   - acquired properties: value, veracity, variability (or dynamicity)
(2) New data models
   - data lifecycle and variability
   - data linking, findability, provenance, and referral integrity

(3) New analytics
- large-scale and multidimensional datasets analytics
- real-time/streaming analytics, interactive, and machine learning analytics

(4) New infrastructure and tools
- high-performance computing, storage, network
- heterogeneous multiprovider services integration, orchestration, and automated provisioning
- new data-centric (multistakeholder) service models
- new data-centric security models for trusted infrastructure and data processing and storage

(5) Source and target: main and long-tail application domains
- high-velocity/speed data capture from variety of sensors and data sources
- data delivery to different visualization and actionable systems and consumers
- fully digitized input and output, (ubiquitous) sensor networks, full digital control

To reflect all components of the Big Data features, we can summarize them in a form of the improved Gartner definition [8] (structured according to the mentioned above components):

Big Data (Data Intensive) Technologies are targeting to process high-volume, high-velocity, high-variety data (sets/assets) to extract intended data value and ensure high-veracity of original data and obtained information that demand cost-effective, innovative forms of data and information processing (analytics) for enhanced insight, decision making, and processes control; all of those demand (should be supported by) new data models (supporting all data states and stages during the whole data lifecycle) and new infrastructure services and tools that allow also obtaining (and processing data) from a variety of sources (including sensor networks) and delivering data in a variety of forms to different data and information consumers and devices.

3 BIG DATA AND PARADIGM CHANGE
3.1 BIG DATA ECOSYSTEM

Big Data is not just a large storage database or Hadoop (as a platform for scalable Big Data processing) problem, although they constitute the core technologies and components for large-scale data processing and data analytics. It is the whole complex of components to store, process, visualize, and deliver results to target applications. Actually Big Data is "the fuel" of all these processes, source, target, and outcome (or "plankton" to use a biological metaphor).

All of these complex interrelated elements can be defined as the big data ecosystem (BDE) that deals with the evolving data, models, and required infrastructure during the Big Data lifecycle. In the following, we shall provide more details about our vision of the BDE.

3.2 NEW FEATURES OF THE BDI

Big Data technology and Data Science as professional areas and scientific disciplines are becoming new technology drivers and require rethinking a number of current concepts in infrastructure architecture, solutions, and processes to address exponential growth of data volume produced by different research instruments and/or collected from sensors.

The recent advances in the general ICT and cloud computing technologies facilitate the paradigm change in Big Data Science that is characterized by the following features:

- Automation of all Data Science processes including data collection, storing, classification, indexing, and other components of the general data curation and provenance.
- Transformation of all processes, events, and products into digital form by means of multidimensional multifaceted measurements, monitoring and control; digitizing existing artifacts and other content.
- Possibility to reuse the initial and published research data with possible data repurposing for secondary research.
- Global data availability and access over the network for cooperative group of researchers, including wide public access to scientific data.
- Existence of necessary infrastructure components and management tools that allow fast infrastructures and services composition, adaptation, and provisioning on demand for specific research projects and tasks.
- Advanced security and access control technologies that ensure secure operation of the complex research infrastructures and scientific instruments, and allow creating trusted secure environment for cooperating groups and individual researchers.

The future BDI should support the whole data lifecycle and explore the benefits of the data storage/preservation, aggregation, and provenance on a large scale and during long/unlimited periods of time. It is important that this infrastructure ensures data security (integrity, confidentiality, availability, and accountability), and data ownership protection. With current needs to process big data that require powerful computation, there should be a possibility to enforce data/dataset policies that ensure they can be processed only on trusted systems and/or complying with other requirements, in general enabling a data-centric security model. Companies and researchers must trust the BDI to process their data on BDI facilities and be ensured that their stored data are protected from unauthorized access. Privacy issues also arise from the distributed character of BDI that can span multiple countries with different national policies. This makes the access control and accounting infrastructure an important component of BDI.

3.3 MOVING TO DATA-CENTRIC MODELS AND TECHNOLOGIES

Traditional/current IT and communication technologies are operating system (OS)/system based and host/service centric, which means that all communication or processing are bound to host/computer that runs the application software. This is especially related to security services. The administrative and security domains are key concepts around which services and protocols are built. A domain provides a context for establishing security and trust. This creates a number of problems when data are moved from one system to another or between domains, or operated in a distributed manner.

Big Data will require different data centric operational models and protocols, which is especially important in situations when the object or event related data will go through a number of transformations and become even more distributed, between traditional security domains. The same relates to the current federated access control model, which is based on the cross administrative and security domains identities and policy management.

When moving to generically distributed data-centric models, additional research is needed to address the following issues:

- maintaining semantic and referral integrity, i.e., linkage between data at the different stages of their transformation
- data location, search, access
- data integrity and identifiability, referral integrity
- data security and data centric access control
- data ownership, personally identifiable data, privacy, opacity of data operations
- trusted virtualization platform, data centric trust bootstrapping

4 BIG DATA ARCHITECTURE FRAMEWORK AND COMPONENTS
4.1 DEFINING THE BIG DATA ARCHITECTURE FRAMEWORK

Based on the discussion in the previous sections, there is a clear need for a new approach to the definition of the BDE and Big Data Architecture that would address the major challenges related to the Big Data properties and component technologies.

In this section, we shall discuss the Big Data Architecture Framework (BDAF) that intends to support the extended Big Data definition given in Section 3 and support the main components and processes in the BDE. The proposed here BDAF definition is based on the ongoing industry standardization on Big Data at National Institute of Standards and Technology of the United States (NIST) [9] and research in the scientific community. The presented BDAF is compatible with the standardization and industry best practices in Big Data, cloud computing and information systems management, in particular, NIST Big Data Reference Architecture (BDRA) [4], NIST Cloud Computing Reference Architecture (CCRA) [3], and Intercloud Architecture Framework (ICAF) by the University of Amsterdam [10].

The proposed BDAF comprises the following five components that address different BDE and Big Data definition aspects:

(1) Data models, structures, and types
  - data formats, non/relational, file systems, etc.
(2) Big Data management
  - Big Data lifecycle management
  - Big Data models, semantics and transformation
  - storage, provenance, curation, archiving
(3) Big Data analytics and tools
  - Big Data applications and new data analytics systems
  - target use, presentation, visualization
(4) Big data infrastructure
  - storage, compute, high-performance computing, network provisioned on demand
  - BDI provisioning, operational and automation
  - sensor network, target/actionable devices

(5) Big Data security
- data security in-rest, in-move, trusted processing environments
- Big Data systems compliance and dependability
- digital right protections
- privacy and personal information protection

We shall refer to the presented BDAF definition, which is rather technical and infrastructure focused and actually reflects the technology oriented stakeholders. The further BDAF improvement should also consider other stakeholder groups such as data archive providers and libraries, which will play a renewed role in the BDE [11].

4.2 DATA MANAGEMENT AND BIG DATA LIFECYCLE

The first and most important task of data management in Big Data systems is to ensure reliable data storage and access. This functionality is typically supported by data discovery or search services. We have developed web searches of hypertext information quite well. For effective Big Data access, we need to develop new methods for search and discovery in large volumes of interlinked data that may be widely distributed and belong to different administrative domains.

Metadata management is one of the key functionalities in the data management system and the enabler for all other data management functions. Metadata, i.e., data describing data, in essence defines the semantic meaning of data and relation between data components. Metadata reflects data model and data classification. Examples of metadata that can be used for identifying and searching interlinked data include persistent data identifier (PID), filename, URI, record time, author, etc.

The required new approach to data management and processing in Big Data industry is reflected in the big data lifecycle management (BDLM) model shown in Fig. 1 that illustrates the main stages of

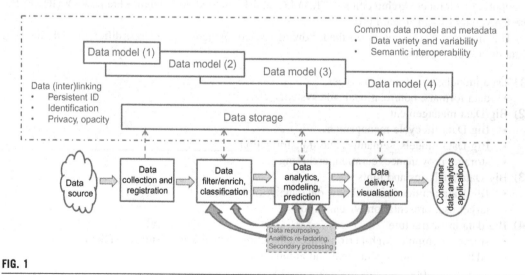

FIG. 1

Big Data Lifecycle in a big data ecosystem.

Big Data Lifecycle and their relations to other components of the BDAF. The following data transformation stages are typically present in Big Data applications:

- data collection and registration
- data filtering and classification
- data analysis, modeling, prediction
- data delivery and visualization

The figure also reflects the iterative character of the typical Big Data processing sequence or workflow. The iterative process allows improving data quality and analytics methods by improving data preparation or selection, or applying improved or different data analytics methods. Data can be also reused for another data analysis purposes, i.e., repurposed.

The data lifecycle model definition is an important research topic in scientific data management where different scientific domain and data character may bring their own specific as described in extensive research by CEOS (Committee on Earth Observation Satellites) [12]. Data preservation and curation community defined their own data lifecycle management model that reflects the scientific research cycle that includes research data handling and scientific results publications [13].

In most cases it is the requirement; in other cases it is business rationality to store and reuse data at different stages. This is needed to be supported by the consistent metadata, data identification, and linkage functionality and infrastructure. When advancing through the data lifecycle stages, data may change their model/structure and consequently metadata; this may also be a consequence of using different systems or platforms at different data processing stages. Linking data during the whole data lifecycle is a significant problem in Big Data lifecycle.

Data curation and provenance are two important services in data management. Data curation applies data cleansing and metadata harmonization as well as formatting for consistent data storage. Data provenance ensures that all stages of the data transformation are documented and sufficient for reproducibility.

4.3 DATA STRUCTURES AND DATA MODELS FOR BIG DATA

Big Data systems and applications will use and/or produce different data types that are defined by their origin or target use. In its own turn, different stages of the data transformation will also use or produce data of different structures, models, and formats.

The following data types can be defined

(a) data described via a formal data model, which are the majority of structured data, data stored in databases, archives, etc.
(b) data described via a formalized grammar (e.g., machine generated textual data or forms)
(c) data described via a standard format (many examples of digital images, audio or video files, also formatted binary data)
(d) arbitrary textual or binary data

Fig. 2 illustrates the Big Data structures, models and their linkage at different processing stages. Data structures and correspondingly data models may be different at different data processing stages; however, it is essential for many applications and data management processes to keep linkage between data at all stages.

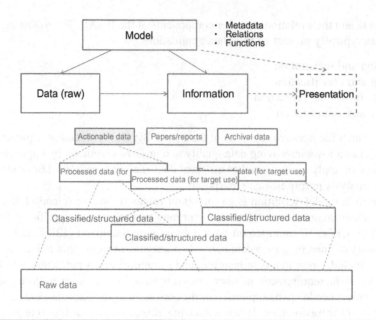

FIG. 2

Big Data structures and their linkage at different processing stages.

A more specific domain of scientific or research data defines the following types of research data [14–16]:

- Raw data collected from observation and from experiment (according to an initial research model).
- Structured data and datasets that went through data filtering and processing (supporting some particular formal model).
- Published data that supports one or another scientific hypothesis, research result or statement.
- Data linked to publications to support the wide research consolidation, integration, and openness.

Once the data are published, it is essential to allow other researchers to be able to validate and reproduce the data that they are interested in, and possibly contribute with new results. Capturing information about the processes involved in transformation from raw data up until the generation of published data becomes an important aspect of scientific data management. Scientific data provenance is widely addressed by the research community and it needs to be taken into consideration by Big Data providers as well.

The generic data types and models include structured data, unstructured data, and semistructured data, and these are well presented in new generation of data-related textbooks and technical publications. In the majority of cases there is a strong relation between data management platforms and tools and the data models or structures they use. On the other hand, data models may significantly define the performance of the data processing systems and applications.

4.4 NIST BIG DATA REFERENCE ARCHITECTURE

The Big Data systems consist of the distribution of data systems across horizontally coupled independent resources to achieve the scalability needed for the efficient processing of extensive datasets.

NIST Big Data Working Group is leading the development of the Big Data Technology Roadmap [9]. A set of documents published in September 2015 as NIST Special Publication NIST SP 1500: NIST Big Data Interoperability Framework [4], it includes seven volumes:

Volume 1: NIST Big Data Definitions.
Volume 2: NIST Big Data Taxonomies.
Volume 3: NIST Big Data Use Case & Requirements.
Volume 4: NIST Big Data Security and Privacy Requirements.
Volume 5: NIST Big Data Architectures White Paper Survey.
Volume 6: NIST Big Data Reference Architecture.
Volume 7: NIST Big Data Technology Roadmap.

The NBDIF defines three main components of the Big Data technology that identify the main challenges in successful adoption of the new technology for research and industry:

- Big Data Paradigm that includes such concepts as domain related data handling ecosystem, data-driven research and production processes or workflows, and required data centric infrastructure and applications design.
- Big Data Science and Data Scientist as a new profession.
- Big Data Architecture (refer to Volume 6 for details).

Fig. 3 presents the NIST Big Data Reference Architecture which is part of the NIST SP 1500 [4] as generalized technology agnostic Big Data system comprised of components or subsystems that reflect the major functional roles in the BDE that are called "Providers." The figure shows two axes that represent the two value chains: information flow or data transformation flow, and platform or infrastructure integration layers.

The following BD-RA Providers and functional groups are defined in BDRA:

- The Data Provider produces and/or supplies data related to specific event or process.
- The Data Consumer is the target of the Big Data transformation and analysis process.
- The Big Data Application Provider includes all services related to data analysis and transformation.
- The Big Data Framework Provider includes all Big Data platform and infrastructure components.
- The System Orchestrator is a separately defined functional role that may include both internal workflow of the Big Data Application Provider and external workflow of the Big Data value added services.

The BDE includes all components that are involved in Big Data production, processing, delivery, and consuming:

- Data Provider
- Big Data Applications Provider
- Big Data Framework Provider
- Data Consumer
- Service Orchestrator

Big Data Lifecycle and Applications Provider activities include

- collection
- preparation

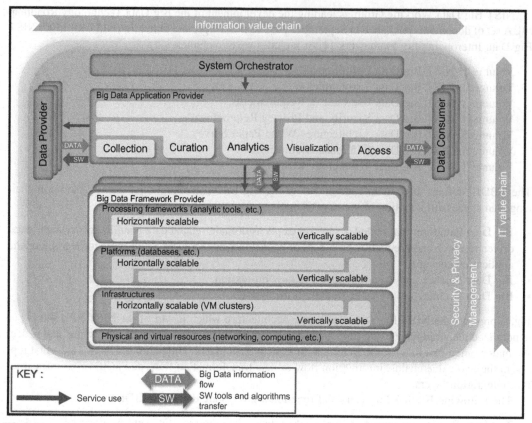

FIG. 3

Big Data Reference Architecture [4].

- analysis and analytics
- visualization
- access

The figure also illustrates the two additional functions Security & Privacy and Management as necessary components of all information systems that are applied to all other functional components and are often defined as separate frameworks of functional planes (e.g., Security Framework or Data Management plane). Data Provider and Data Consumer represent the data source and data target that are defined as separate components of the Big Data definition given in Section 3.

It is important to mention that in NIST BDRA, the Big Data Application Provider is separated from the Big Data Platform Provider. This reflects new features brought to the modern application infrastructure by cloud computing that, by means of virtualization, allow deploying application on-demand on the general purpose cloud-based platforms and underlying infrastructure, and ensure data processing scalability and mobility over distributed multicloud infrastructure.

4.5 GENERAL BIG DATA SYSTEM REQUIREMENTS

This section summarizes requirements to Big Data systems specified in the NIST Big Data Interoperability Framework [4] that are abstracted according to the NIST Big Data Reference Architecture.

The extended data is presented online at the following links:

(a) Index to all use cases: http://bigdatawg.nist.gov/usecases.php.
(b) List of general requirements versus architecture component with record of use cases giving requirements: http://bigdatawg.nist.gov/uc_reqs_gen_ref.php.
(c) List of architecture component and specific requirements plus use case constraining this component: http://bigdatawg.nist.gov/uc_reqs_gen_detail.php.

4.5.1 Data sources requirements (DSR)

DSR-1: Needs to support reliable real-time, asynchronous, streaming, and batch processing to collect data from centralized, distributed, and cloud data sources, sensors, or instruments.
DSR-2: Needs to support slow, "bursty," and high-throughput data transmission between data sources and computing clusters.
DSR-3: Needs to support diversified data content ranging from structured and unstructured text, document, graph, web, geospatial, compressed, timed, spatial, multimedia, simulation, and instrumental data.

4.5.2 Transformation (applications) provider requirements (TPR)

TPR-1: Needs to support diversified compute intensive, analytic processing, and machine learning techniques.
TPR-2: Needs to support batch and real-time analytic processing.
TPR-3: Needs to support processing large diversified data content and modeling.
TPR-4: Needs to support processing data in motion (streaming, fetching new content, tracking, etc.).

4.5.3 Capability (framework) provider requirements (CPR)

CPR-1: Needs to support legacy and advance software packages (software).
CPR-2: Needs to support legacy and advance computing platforms (platform).
CPR-3: Needs to support legacy and advance distributed computing cluster, coprocessors, I/O processing (infrastructure).
CPR-4: Needs to support elastic data transmission (networking).
CPR-5: Needs to support legacy, large, and advance distributed data storage (storage).
CPR-6: Needs to support legacy and advance programming executable, applications, tools, utilities, and libraries (software).

4.5.4 Data consumer requirements (DCR)

DCR-1: Needs to support fast searches ($\sim$0.1 s) from processed data with high relevancy, accuracy, and high recall.
DCR-2: Needs to support diversified output file formats for visualization, rendering, and reporting.
DCR-3: Needs to support visual layout for results presentation.
DCR-4: Needs to support rich user interface for access using browser, visualization tools.

DCR-5: Needs to support high-resolution multidimension layer of data visualization.
DCR-6: Needs to support streaming results to clients.

4.5.5 Security and privacy requirements (SPR)

SPR-1: Needs to protect and preserve security and privacy on sensitive data.
SPR-2: Needs to support multilevel policy-driven, sandbox, access control, authentication on protected data.

4.5.6 Lifecycle management requirements (LMR)

LMR-1: Needs to support data quality curation including preprocessing, data clustering, classification, reduction, format transformation.
LMR-2: Needs to support dynamic updates on data, user profiles, and links.
LMR-3: Needs to support data lifecycle and long-term preservation policy including data provenance.
LMR-4: Needs to support data validation 174.
LMR-5: Needs to support human annotation for data validation.
LMR-6: Needs to support prevention of data loss or corruption.
LMR-7: Needs to support multisites archival.
LMR-8: Needs to support persistent identifier and data traceability.
LMR-9: Needs to support standardize, aggregate, and normalize data from disparate sources.

4.5.7 Other requirements (OR)

OR-1: Needs to support rich user interface from mobile platforms to access processed results.
OR-2: Needs to support performance monitoring on analytic processing from mobile platforms.
OR-3: Needs to support rich visual content search and rendering from mobile platforms.
OR-4: Needs to support mobile device data acquisition.
OR-5: Needs to support security across mobile devices.

5 BIG DATA INFRASTRUCTURE

5.1 BDI COMPONENTS

Big Data applications are typically distributed and use multiple distributed data sources. Data processing and staging also involve using distributed computing and storage resources. Cloud computing presents a right choice as a general purpose Big Data platform. Cloud technologies bring the benefit of building scalable infrastructure services that can be provisioned on-demand and dynamically scaled depending on the required workload and volume of data. The major enabling technology for cloud computing is virtualization of all components of the general computing infrastructure: servers, storage, and network. Virtualization means physical resources pooling, abstraction, composition, and orchestration under the supervision of a hypervisor (a special software for physical resources virtualization) and cloud management software which is the main component of any cloud platform.

Fig. 4 provides a general view on the BDI that includes the infrastructure for general data management, typically cloud based, and Big Data Analytics part that includes data analytics tools and

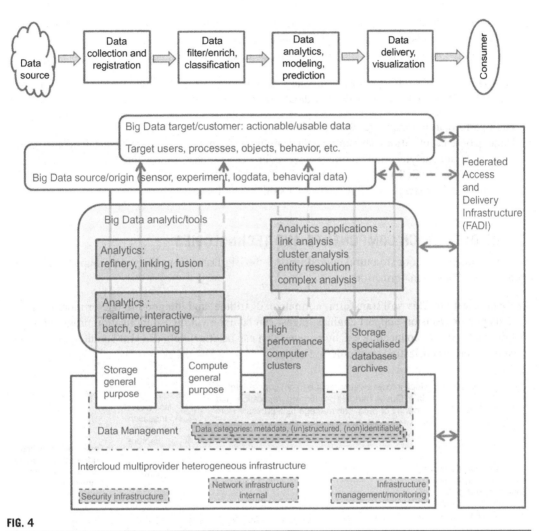

FIG. 4

Big Data analytics infrastructure components and Big Data lifecycle stages.

high-performance computing clusters [5]. The general infrastructure components and services for general data management and user access include

- General purpose data storage and processing infrastructure that is typically cloud based and provisioned on-demand.
- Big Data Management tools: registries, indexing, data search/discovery, metadata, and semantics.
- security infrastructure (access control, policy enforcement, confidentiality, trust, availability, privacy).

- Federated Access and Delivery Infrastructure (FADI) that allows interconnection and interaction of all BDI components; it is typically provisioned on-demand.
- Collaborative environment to support user groups creation and management.

The Big Data analytics infrastructure components are required to support massive data processing required by Big Data applications and other data centric applications:

- High performance computing clusters (HPCCs).
- Hadoop based applications, streaming data analytics and other tools for large-scale data processing.
- Specialist data analytics tools (complex events processing, data mining, etc.).
- Not only SQL (NoSQL) databases for Big Data storage and processing.
- Distributed file systems for large-scale data storage and processing.

5.2 BIG DATA STACK COMPONENTS AND TECHNOLOGIES

Fig. 5 illustrates the major structural components of the Big Data stack. They are grouped around the main stages of data transformation:

(1) Data ingestion: This will transform, normalize, distribute, and integrate to one or more of the Analytic or Decision Support engines; ingest can be done via ingest application programming interface (API) or connecting existing queues that can be effectively used for handles partitioning, replication, prioritization, and ordering of data.

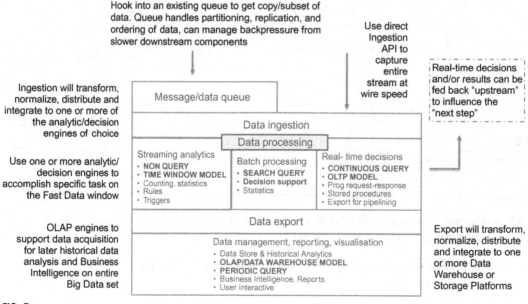

FIG. 5

Big Data stack components and technologies.

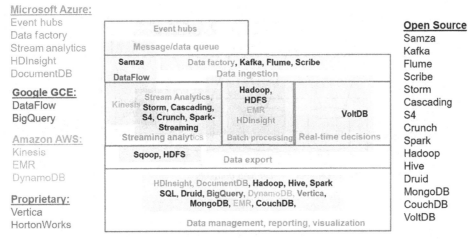

FIG. 6

Big Data analytics platforms and tools corresponding to Big Data stack groups.

(2) Data processing: One or more analytics or decision support engines are used to accomplish specific task related to data processing workflow; using batch data processing, streaming analytics, or real-time decision support.

(3) Data export: This will transform, normalize, distribute, and integrate output data to one or more Data Warehouse or Storage platforms.

(4) Back-end data management, reporting, visualization: This will support data storage and historical analysis; OLAP platforms/engines will support data acquisition and further use for Business Intelligence and historical analysis.

Fig. 6 provides overview of the Big Data analytics platforms and tools corresponding to Big Data stack groups. The majority of software tools are Open Source Software; however, a number of tools and platforms are proprietary and specific for large cloud computing platforms such as Microsoft Azure, Amazon Web Services (AWS), Google Compute Engine cloud (GCE), HortonWorks, and Vertica. A more detailed overview of the most popular Big Data cloud platforms is provided below.

5.3 EXAMPLE OF CLOUD-BASED INFRASTRUCTURE FOR DISTRIBUTED DATA PROCESSING

Fig. 7 shows a general model of data processing stages that are mapped to required compute and storage resources that can be provided by a selected cloud platform.

Fig. 8 illustrates the typical enterprise or scientific collaborative infrastructure that is created on-demand. The infrastructure includes enterprise proprietary, cloud-based computing and storage resources, instruments, control and monitoring system, and visualization systems. Users are represented by user clients and typically reside in real or virtual campuses.

The main goal of the enterprise or scientific infrastructure is to support the enterprise or scientific workflow and operational procedures related to processes monitoring and data processing. Cloud

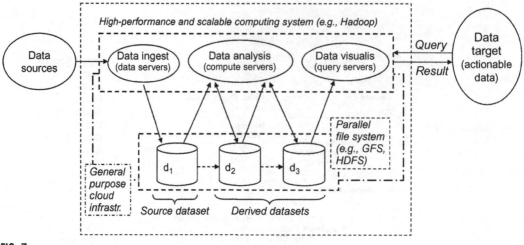

FIG. 7

Data processing stages mapped to compute and storage cloud resources.

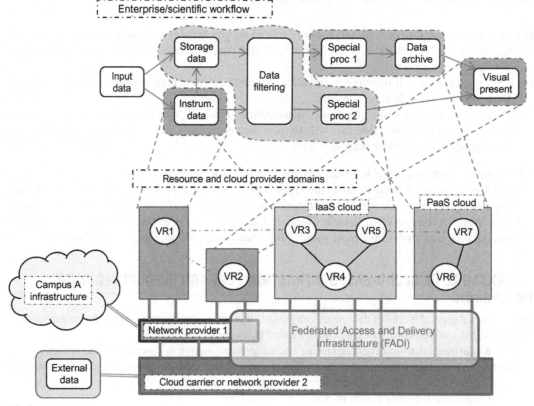

FIG. 8

From enterprise or scientific workflow to cloud-based infrastructure (FADI network connectivity can be provided by a single Network Provider 1 acting as a Cloud Carrier or together with the local connectivity Network Provider 2).

technologies simplify the building of such infrastructure and provide it on-demand. Fig. 8 illustrates how an example enterprise or scientific workflow can be mapped to cloud-based services and later deployed and operated as an instant intercloud infrastructure. Our example contains cloud infrastructure segments infrastructure as a service (IaaS; with virtual cloud resources VR3-VR5) and platform as a service (PaaS; VR6, VR7), separate virtualized noncloud resources or services (where VR1 is an instrument, and VR2 is a visualization facility), enterprise facilities represented by campus A, and additional external source of data B. The network infrastructure plays role of an integrating component for the distributed cloud services delivery infrastructure (CSDI). In Fig. 8, it is represented by FADI to indicate the common approach to use federated access control in multiprovider multidomain environment that in general can use both public Internet and dedicated network infrastructure to ensure required performance and availability. Practical FADI implementation in heterogeneous multicloud intercloud environment may benefit from using such technologies and frameworks as Intercloud Federations Framework (ICFF) [17] and Open Cloud eXchange (OCX) [18] that is practically used by European research community in GEANT-based pan-European network infrastructure [19].

5.4 BENEFITS OF CLOUD PLATFORMS FOR BIG DATA APPLICATIONS

Building a Big Data application on cloud brings the following benefits to whole process of applications development, deployment, operation, and management:

- Cloud deployment on virtual machines (VMs), containers, and bare metal:
  - applications portability and platform independence, on-demand provisioning
  - dynamic resource allocation, load balancing and elasticity for tasks, and processes with variable load
- Availability of rich cloud-based monitoring tools for collecting performance information and applications optimization.
- Network traffic segregation and isolation:
  - Big Data applications benefit from lowest latencies possible for node to node synchronization, dynamic cluster resizing, load balancing, and other scale-out operations
  - clouds construction provides separate networks for data traffic and management traffic
  - traffic segmentation by creating Layer 2 and 3 virtual networks inside user/application assigned virtual private cloud (VPC)
- Cloud tools for large-scale applications deployment and automation:
  - provide basis for agile services development and Zero-touch services provisioning
  - applications deployment in cloud is supported by major integrated development environment (IDE)

6 CASE STUDY: BIOINFORMATICS APPLICATIONS DEPLOYMENT ON CLOUD
6.1 OVERALL DESCRIPTION

Bioinformatics deals with the collection and efficient analysis of biological data, particularly genomic information from DNA sequencers. The capability of modern sequencers to produce terabytes of information coupled with low pricing (less than US$1000 for a human genome) makes parallel use of many sequencers feasible but also causes a "data deluge" that is being experienced by researchers in this field [20,21].

Bioinformatics software is characterized by a high degree of fragmentation: literally hundreds of different software packages are regularly used for scientific analyses with an incompatible variety of dependencies and a broad range of resource requirements. For this reason, the bioinformatics community has strongly embraced cloud computing with its ability to provide customized execution environments and dynamic resource allocation.

The French Institute of Bioinformatics (IFB) [22] provides a good example of a data-driven research organization that has strong demands for modern data intensive technologies and for automation of the applications deployment and management. The IFB consists of 32 regional bioinformatics platforms (PF) grouped into six regional centers spanning the entire country, and a national hub, the "UMS 3601—IFB-core." The IFB has deployed a cloud infrastructure on its own premises at IFB-core, and aims to deploy a federated cloud infrastructure over the regional PFs devoted to the French life science community, research, and industry, with services for the management and analysis of life science data.

The two basic bioinformatics use cases described here have been implemented using the CYCLONE platform for multicloud applications deployment and management that is being developed in the CYCLONE project [23]. The CYCLONE platform is described briefly below. The use cases and proposed implementation address specific challenges in building bioinformatics applications in the cloud. They are transformed into practical technical requirements in a typical cloud federation environment and motivate the necessary cloud infrastructure provisioning and management services and mechanisms.

6.2 UC1—SECURING HUMAN BIOMEDICAL DATA
6.2.1 Description
Continuous decrease of the genome sequencing costs (NGS) allows an increasing number of clinicians to include genome analysis and data into their day-to-day diagnostic practices. Today, most of genomics analyses are realized on the exome, which is the expressed part (5%) of the genome. However, full genome sequencing is being envisaged and will soon be included in daily medical practices.

It is expected that in the near future, some of the genomic data processed on the IFB cloud platform will concern human biomedical data related to patients, and thus will be subject to strict personal data protection regulations. To ensure data security while carrying out the analysis in a federated cloud environment, it is necessary to ensure the security in all involved sites belonging to the federation and ensure their secure/trusted integration (especially if the cloud federation involves both public and private cloud infrastructures).

6.2.2 Workflow
The use case workflow to ensure security of data includes the following steps (see Fig. 9): (1) a biomedical user connects to the cloud through the IFB web authenticated dashboard; uses it to (2) run an instance of the appliance containing the relevant preconfigured analysis pipeline. At step (3) the VM containing genome applications is deployed on the cloud (testbed); then (4) the user signs into the web interface of the VM, (5) uploads the patient's biomedical data, and (6) runs the analysis in a secure environment. Finally, (7) the user gets the results.

The bioinformatics treatment generally relies on a comparison with the current release of the reference human genome hg19 (Human Genome version 19 or GRCh37). The hg19 is a database

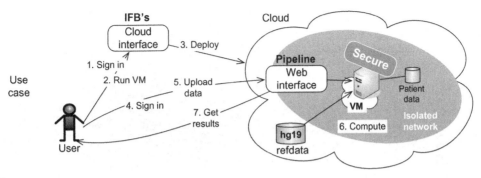

FIG. 9

Functional schema of the use case "Securing human biomedical data." The figure shows the application components and describes the different steps of the workflow.

consisting of many files containing the public genomics data. It can be used remotely (when sufficient connectivity is available) or can be deployed a priori by the cloud providers as a public data set available to all users.

6.3 UC2—CLOUD VIRTUAL PIPELINE FOR MICROBIAL GENOMES ANALYSIS

6.3.1 Description

In post-NGS research, sequencing bacterial genomes is very cheap (a few hundred €). Most of the time, users are no longer intend to analyze a single genome; they want to compare large collections of related genomes (strains). Thus, this brings requirements to increasing need for automating the annotation of bacterial genomes.

The IFB-MIGALE platform (one of the bioinformatics platforms of the IFB) has developed an environment for the annotation of microbial genomes and a tool for the visualization of the synteny (local conservation of the gene order along the genomes) [24]. The platform automatically launches a set of bioinformatics tools (e.g., BLAST, INTERPROScan) to analyze the data and stores the results of the tools in a relational database (PostgreSQL). These tools use several public reference data collections. A web interface allows the user to consult the results and perform manual annotation (manual annotation means adding manually metadata and biological knowledge to the genome sequence). Installing the platform requires advanced skills in system administration and application management. Performing the analysis of collections of genomes requires large computing resources that can be distributed over several computers, generally the computing nodes of a cluster.

The CYCLONE platform supports the cloud services federation and federated identity management widely used by European research and academic community. It allows life science researchers to deploy their own comprehensive annotation platform over one or more cloud infrastructures using federated access control infrastructure and other services federated nationally or internationally among cooperating organizations, such as bioinformatics institutions. Such deployments can be done with the dynamic allocation of network resources for the isolation of the VMs inside a dedicated private cloud, including virtual network and replicated user data.

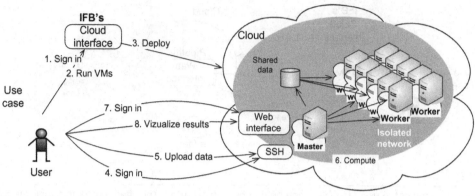

FIG. 10

Functional schema of the use case "Cloud virtual pipeline for microbial genomes analysis." This figure shows the application components and describes the different steps of the workflow.

6.3.2 Workflow

As illustrated in Fig. 10, a bioinformatician (1) connects to the cloud web dashboard, uses it to (2) run and (3) deploy with one click a genomes annotation platform consisting of many VMs, comprising of a master node of the virtual cluster that provides also the visualization web-interface, associated with several computing nodes. Then the user (4) uses secure communication over SSH to connect to the master and (5) uploads the raw microbial genomic data (MB) to the cloud storage. SCP/SFTP protocols are used from a command line tool or a GUI, to ensure AuthN/Z for the data transfer, and to overcome the performance issues of HTTP for large datasets. Still in command line interface, the user (6) runs the computation to annotate the new microbial genomes. The first step consists of many data-intensive jobs performing the comparisons between the new genome and the reference data.

The results are stored in a relational database (provided by a cloud service or a VM deployed within the platform). Then the scientist (7) signs in the annotated data visualization environment provided by the Insyght web-interface to (8) navigate between the abundant homologues, syntenies, and gene functional annotations in bacteria genomes.

6.4 IMPLEMENTATION OF USE CASES AND CYCLONE INFRASTRUCTURE COMPONENTS

The practical deployment of the Bioinformatics use cases is typically done in a progressive manner by the researchers with some assistance from IT and cloud support staff. It begins with a single VM for running an application with security features like in UC1 (Securing human biomedical data). After researchers learn the technology and tools, and their tasks complexity evolves, they start building the complex applications requiring the coordinated deployment of several VMs like in UC2 Cloud virtual pipeline for microbial genomes analysis. Below, these two scenarios are discussed in detail with references to the required CYCLONE platform services and features.

6.4.1 Deployment UC1 Securing human biomedical data

The first bioinformatics use case "Securing human biomedical data" requires a single-VM application supporting enhanced security features such as trusted federated authentication mode. Due to potential data sensitivity, a deployment can be done only on a certified (by the French Health Ministry) cloud infrastructure. The cloud appliance NGS-Unicancer is developed by the bioinformatics platform of the Centre Léon Bérard (Lyon, France, www.synergielyoncancer.fr) in the context of the project NGS-Clinique (INCA—Institut National du Cancer). It provides a simple web interface to launch the biomedical genomic analysis pipeline. The appliance was enhanced by the CYCLONE Federation Provider and is ready for on-demand deployment on the IFB-core cloud infrastructure. The user deploys the appliance NGS-Unicancer through the IFB web interface in "1-click" and uses the CYCLONE federation provider to get access to the VM web interface based on its identity in the federation. The user can then easily upload their data, run the analysis, and get the results. In Fig. 11, the upper part describes the use case workflow, and the middle layer represents the workflow steps that are linked to the related CYCLONE software components and services. The bottom part shows the testbed infrastructure components.

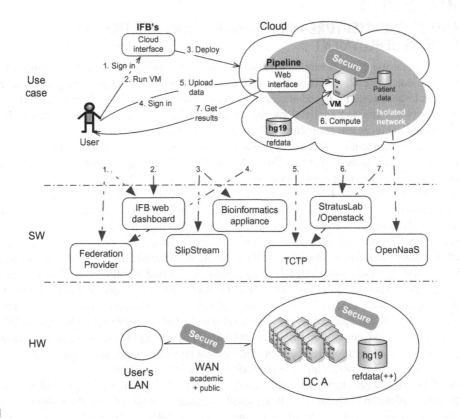

FIG. 11

Functional relations between the use case "Securing human biomedical data" and the CYCLONE components.

6.4.2 Deployment UC2: Cloud virtual pipeline for microbial genomes analysis

The second bioinformatics use case "Cloud virtual pipeline for microbial genomes analysis" is developed by the platform IFB-MIGALE (Jouy-en-Josas, France, http://migale.jouy.inra.fr/). This application requires several components: a user web interface, a relational PostgreSQL database, and a complete computing cluster with a master and several nodes to perform the data-intensive analyses. The infrastructure for running the application in a classical (static) way on bare-metal servers in IFB-MIGALE premises was ported to the cloud and extended with "1-click" deployment features by using the SlipStream cloud deployment automation platform. The VM images were exported from the IFB's private cloud and registered in the Marketplace of the StratusLab community cloud used by the French research community. For further deployments and possible applications migration, the IFB-core produced a deployment recipe based on SlipStream that instantiates the complete application with all the required VMs on the target infrastructure.

7 CYCLONE PLATFORM FOR CLOUD APPLICATIONS DEPLOYMENT AND MANAGEMENT

7.1 GENERAL ARCHITECTURE FOR INTERCLOUD AND MULTICLOUD APPLICATIONS DEPLOYMENT

Multiple, individual use cases for multicloud applications that require cloud and noncloud resources integration into one intercloud infrastructure that executes a single or multiple enterprise or scientific workflows can be abstracted into general scenario (and relevant use cases), as illustrated in Fig. 12. The figure includes two interacting applications, that in general can be multicloud, that contain both application related and management components. The application component interacts with end users while the management component is controlled by an administrator and interacts with the (inter)cloud management software. The figure also shows Cloud Applications Deployment and Management Software and Tools as an important component to support cloud applications deployment and operation during their whole lifecycle. Intercloud infrastructure should also provide two other components or services: federated access control infrastructure and general infrastructure security; and intercloud network infrastructure needs to be provisioned as a part of overall application infrastructure.

Intercloud applications and infrastructure may include resources and services from multiple existing cloud platforms that are provisioned on demand and ideally should allow dynamic scaling and configuration. In the generally distributed heterogeneous multicloud multiprovider environment, the problem of applications integration and management is becoming critical and requires smooth integration with the application workflow and automation of most of development and operation functions, ideally integration with the application specific development and operation (DevOps) tools [25]. Currently, widely used cloud automation tools such as Chef [26], Puppet [11], and Ansible [27] allow only single cloud provider application deployment. They do not solve the problem of multicloud resources/services integration and provisioning of intercloud network infrastructure.

The CYCLONE project attempts to solve this problem by leveraging the original cloud management platform SlipStream [28] and extending its with necessary functionality and components, in particular for intercloud resources deployment and network infrastructure provisioning, enabling federated access control for users and end-to-end security for data transfer, enabling dynamic trust establishment between cloud and application domains.

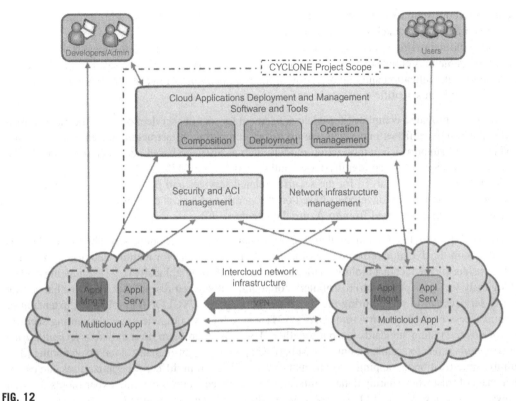

FIG. 12

General architecture for multicloud applications deployment.

Intercloud platforms should deliver open integration environment and preferably standardized APIs, protocols, and data formats, allowing for cross-cloud resources interoperability. Practical Intercloud platform development should target two major stakeholders and user communities: the application service providers (ASPs) as well as their customers to address real-life challenges and problems in a consistent and constructive way.

Effective cloud automation and management platform should allow dynamic cloud resources allocations depending on the workload and application workflow. This task can be solved for the single cloud using its native elasticity and load balancing tools; however, in intercloud environments, such functionality will require involving a real cloud platform load (including resources availability) and application monitoring.

7.2 ENSURING CONSISTENT SECURITY SERVICES IN CLOUD-BASED APPLICATIONS

Since bioinformatics resources may be geographically distributed among different centers, deployment of applications that span multiple clouds requires a consistent security infrastructure in place. For instance, there may be only a limited number of sequencing centers where raw genome data is produced and made available to bioinformatics researchers. Similarly, bioinformatics researchers may have international collaborations such that they need to share their appliances or results with external parties.

Developing a consistent security infrastructure is a challenge in this setting as multiple cloud providers are involved and many stakeholders have a say in security.

Existing cloud providers such as AWS and Microsoft Azure offer tailored services for identity and access management. A cloud developer can make use of these services to build a security infrastructure for managing authentication and authorization in their applications. However, these services are limited or not usable in scientific contexts in various ways:

- They do not provide a complete lifecycle management for security services or allow the management of context in dynamic settings where the necessary computing infrastructure is created on-demand.
- They do not support rich authorization models such as attribute-based access control model. For instance, AWS employs an identity-based authorization model [29].
- Cloud developers are charged for the security-related services and pertinent network traffic. For instance, Azure charges developers based on the number of access control transactions and the quantity of data transferred from/to Azure data centers [30].

In CYCLONE project, two fundamental problems related to security are addressed. The first problem is associated with the dynamic provisioning of a security infrastructure for identity and access management. Considering the fact that bioinformatics research is both geographically (e.g., sequencing center) and logically (e.g., a separate lab) distributed, collaboration between researchers imposes that certain security services are in place during the time of collaboration. CYCLONE employs an extension of dynamic access control infrastructure (DACI) [31] where legacy components implementing security functions over existing standards are put together. The second problem, also called as *dynamic trust bootstrapping*, refers to establishment of trust between partners in on-demand cloud provisioning [32]. With dynamic trust bootstrapping, bioinformatics researchers from different organizations can establish a chain of trust when sharing data, results, and VM instances for reproducing experiments. In what follows, an overview of CYCLONE's solutions to these problems is provided.

7.3 DYNAMIC ACCESS CONTROL INFRASTRUCTURE

DACI presents a virtual infrastructure to provide access control services to an on-demand cloud formation. As depicted in Fig. 13, the following basic security services are provided with DACI:

- *Authentication and identity management service*: provides authentication service, issues, and verifies attribute statements binding to authenticated subjects using the Security Assertions Markup Language (SAML) specification [33].
- *Authorization service*: provides the authorization service compliant with the XACML-SAML profile [34].
- *Token validation service*: issues and validates authorization tokens to improve the decision performance of the authorization service.

These services provide a basic infrastructure for managing access control in dynamic environments. Since CYCLONE use cases involve sensitive data such as sequences of human genome, we extend DACI services with three additional services pertinent to security: encryption service that provides protection of data at rest (or on the move), key management service for storing/exchanging keys, and distributed logging. Moreover, helper tools for assisting the specification and verification of policies are made available [35,36].

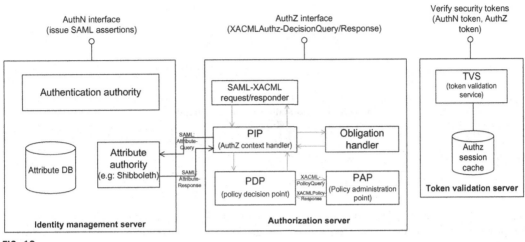

FIG. 13

Security services of DACI.

7.3.1 Dynamic trust bootstrapping

The initialization and deployment of a security infrastructure such as DACI in on-demand cloud provisioning over multiple cloud providers imply that there is a dynamic mechanism to establish trust between involved parties and to populate necessary information for the proper function of the infrastructure. This process, also known as trust bootstrapping, may involve the collection of keys/certificates from all partners, retrieval of list of identity providers (in a federated setting), and so on. Some of this contextual information needs to be provided in a preconfigured manner while other information can be retrieved automatically. For instance, bioinformatics researchers are often affiliated with an organization that is part of a larger network, such as EDUGAIN [37], where the retrieval of certain information with respect to identity of users can be automated.

The implementation of dynamic trust bootstrapping involves additional services such as context management that interplays with DACI components. In CYCLONE, we currently investigate how the bootstrapping process can be integrated to application deployment over a multicloud application management platform such Slipstream [28].

8 CLOUD POWERED BIG DATA APPLICATIONS DEVELOPMENT AND DEPLOYMENT AUTOMATION

8.1 DEMAND FOR AUTOMATED BIG DATA APPLICATIONS PROVISIONING

Modern scientific and industry Big Data applications and infrastructures may include multiple existing cloud platforms. In the generally distributed heterogeneous multicloud multiprovider environment, the problem of applications integration and management in dynamic cloud environment is becoming critical and requires smooth integration with the application workflow and automation of most of development and operation functions, ideally integration with the application specific development and operation (DevOps) tools [25]. Currently widely used cloud automation tools such as Chef [26],

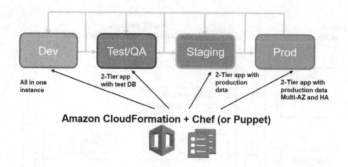

FIG. 14

Cloud-powered services development lifecycle: DevOps—continuous service improvement.

Puppet [11], and Ansible [27] allow single cloud provider application deployment. They do not solve the problem of multicloud resources/services integration and provisioning of intercloud network infrastructure.

DevOps and cloud automation tools are instrumental for enabling the cloud powered applications development model that allows continuous applications improvement as shown in Fig. 14. In the model presented, the developer uses both cloud platform-based deployment automation tools such as Amazon Cloud Formation [38] and external tools such as Chef (of Puppet) to automate application deployment and testing at each stage of the development lifecycle. While CloudFormation provides full functionality for individual cloud resources configuration and provisioning, Chef allows large-scale applications provisioning that involves multiple resources.

Intercloud platforms should deliver open integration environment and preferably standardized APIs, protocols, and data formats, allowing for cross-cloud resources interoperability. Practical Intercloud platform development should target two major stakeholders and user communities: ASPs as well as their customers to address real-life challenges and problems in a consistent and constructive way. The required functionality is provided by the CYCLONE cloud applications deployment platform [23] that is built based on the SlipStream cloud automation and management platform [28].

As an example, bioinformatics deals with the genome sequencing which is computer-intensive and often requires using distributed data sets and computing resources from multiple data centers or cloud providers. Researchers and research institutions are looking for a possibility to automate scientific applications deployment and management as much as it is possible so that they can focus on their main research work/tasks and have complex applications and infrastructure at their fingertips.

The growing demand for automation of applications provisioning acts as a motivator for development of a new concept of applications provisioning, operation and management in clouds defined as Zero Touch Provisioning, Operations and Management (ZTPOM) [39], which allows combined and orchestrated provisioning of cloud researches, distributed applications, and interconnecting them via the dedicated network infrastructure. This trend is also recognized by the TMForum, which has launched its ZOOM (Zero-touch Orchestration, Operations and Management) program in order to develop best practices and standards for a new generation of service provider support systems that will deliver high business agility and rapid new service development [40].

The proposed ZTPOM framework is a necessary and enabling element of the general (Inter-)CSDI that implements the major architectural patterns of the ICAF and ICFF proposed in earlier authors' works [10,17]. The ZTPOM architecture includes such components as the cloud services marketplace and the GEANT OCX [18,41] that serve as customer and cloud provider front-end to access the GEANT network infrastructure [19]. In this way, the OCX solves the "last mile" problem in cloud services delivery, using a community (or corporate) network interconnecting multiple institutions or virtual distributed project oriented research teams. Effective OCX and CSDI operation requires maximum automation of the underlying and interconnected network provisioning and in this way motivates for ZTP-oriented services enabling Big Data application developers to smoothly integrated dedicated network infrastructure services in their multicloud applications.

8.2 CLOUD AUTOMATION TOOLS FOR INTERCLOUD APPLICATION AND NETWORK INFRASTRUCTURE PROVISIONING

Cloud-based applications can be deployed using some cloud automation tools like Chef, Puppet, or Ansible, where, using "recipes" or "cookbooks," an application developer can describe machines configuration in a declarative language, bring them to a desired state, and keep them there through automation. The complete application topology and components interrelationship can be described using a language like OASIS TOSCA (Topology and Orchestration Specification for Cloud Applications) [42], wherein the workflow that invokes different cloud-based services is provided.

However, with the current cloud automation tools, the problem of provisioning intercloud network connectivity remains unsolved, their network configuration capabilities allow only intracloud network configuration for one cloud platform or VPC The Software Defined Networks (SDN) can provide necessary functionality and manageability for network services provisioning in the proposed ZTPOM.

A good example of fusion between cloud-originated technologies and SDN is the recent development of the Network Automation and Programmability Abstraction Layer with Multivendor support (NAPALM) system [43], which implements a common set of functions to interact with different network OSs using a unified API. NAPALM supports several methods to connect to the devices, to manipulate configuration or to retrieve data and uses Ansible [27] to configure network devices as programmable devices. Ansible has benefits over other tools for network deployment and management as it does not require a node agent and runs all process over SSH which simplifies its use for configuring network devices from multiple vendors.

The proposed ZTPOM platform development is based on the SlipStream cloud automation and management platform [28], and intends to solve multicloud applications provisioning and management. The new SlipStream functionality allows intercloud resources deployment and network infrastructure provisioning, enabling federated access control for users and end-to-end security for data transfer, enabling dynamic trust establishment between cloud and application documents.

8.3 SLIPSTREAM: CLOUD APPLICATION MANAGEMENT PLATFORM

SlipStream is an open source cloud application management platform[1] that provides software developers and service operators with the necessary functionality to manage the complete lifecycle of their cloud applications. Through its plugin architecture, SlipStream supports most major cloud service providers (CSPs) and the primary open source cloud distributions. By exposing a uniform interface that

---

[1]Community Edition of SlipStream, is available under the Apache 2.0 license (https://github.com/slipstream).

hides differences between cloud providers, SlipStream facilitates application portability across the supported cloud infrastructures.

To take advantage of cloud portability, developers define "recipes" that transform preexisting "base" VMs into the components that they need for their application. By reusing these base VMs, developers can ensure uniform behavior of their application components across clouds without having to deal with the time-consuming and error-prone transformation of VM images. Developers bundle the defined components into complete cloud applications using SlipStream facilities for passing information between components and for coordinating the configuration of services.

Once a cloud application has been defined, the operator can deploy the application in "one click," providing values for any defined parameters and choosing the cloud infrastructure to use. With SlipStream, operators may choose to deploy the components of an application in multiple clouds, for example, to provide geographic redundancy or to minimize latencies for clients. In order to respond to changes in load, operators may adjust the resources allocated to a running application by scaling the application horizontally (changing the number of VMs) or vertically (changing the resources of a VM).

SlipStream combines its deployment engine with an "App Store" for sharing application definitions with other users and a "Service Catalog" for finding appropriate cloud service offers, providing a complete engineering PaaS supporting DevOps processes. All of the features are available through its web interface or RESTful API.

8.3.1 Functionality used for applications deployment

The bioinformatics use cases described above are implemented using SlipStream's facilities and tools to define applications and its deployment engine through the RESTful API [44].

The definition of an application component actually consists of a series of recipes that are executed at various stages in the lifecycle of the application. The main recipes, in order, are as follows:

- *Preinstall*: Used principally to configure and initialize the OS package management.
- *Install packages*: A list of packages to be installed on the machine. SlipStream supports the package managers for the RedHat and Debian families of OS.
- *Postinstall*: Can be used for any software installation that cannot be handled through the package manager.
- *Deployment*: Used for service configuration and initialization. This script can take advantage of SlipStream's "parameter database" to pass information between components and to synchronize the configuration of the components.
- *Reporting*: Collects files (typically log files) that should be collected at the end of the deployment and made available through SlipStream.

There are also a number of recipes that can be defined to support horizontal and vertical scaling that are not used in the defined here use cases. The applications are defined using SlipStream's web interface; the bioinformatics portal then triggers the deployment of these applications using the SlipStream RESTful API.

8.3.2 Example recipes

The application for the bacterial genomics analysis consisted of a compute cluster based on Sun Grid Engine with a Network File System (NFS) exported from the master node of the cluster to all of the slave nodes. The master node definition was combined into a single "deployment" script that performed the following actions:

1. Initialize the yum package manager.
2. Install bind utilities.
3. Allow SSH access to the master from the slaves.
4. Collect IP addresses for batch system.
5. Configure the batch system admin user.
6. Export NFSs to slaves.
7. Configure the batch system.
8. Indicate that the cluster is ready for use.

The deployment script extensively uses the parameter database that SlipStream maintains for each application to correctly the configure the master and slaves within the cluster. A common pattern is the following:

```
ss-display "Exporting SGE_ROOT_DIR..."
echo -ne "$SGE_ROOT_DIR\t" > $EXPORTS_FILE
for ((i=1; i<=`ss-get
Bacterial_Genomics_Slave:multiplicity`; i++ ));
do
node_host=`ss-get
Bacterial_Genomics_Slave.$i:hostname`
echo -ne $node_host >> $EXPORTS_FILE
echo -ne "(rw,sync,no_root_squash) ">> $EXPORTS_FILE
done
echo "\n" >> $EXPORTS_FILE # last for a newline
exportfs -av
```

9 BIG DATA SERVICE AND PLATFORM PROVIDERS

This section provides a short overview of the major Big Data service and platform providers to give you a starting point in selecting such providers for your company or Big Data related projects. As discussed above, the two main tasks must be addressed when building BDI for a company: general data management and data analytics.

For the first task, you can use existing enterprise IT infrastructure, possibly extending it with or migrating to cloud platform and naturally addressing scalability and on-demand provisioning requirements from the Big Data applications. Making enterprise IT infrastructure cloud based will simplify multiple scenarios of outsourcing general and Big Data services to clouds, in particular in the case of rapid increase of demand, so-called cloudburst scenarios.

Big Data Analytics typically require dedicated infrastructure facilities (dedicated computer clusters) and special applications for data processing and staging. Big Data Analytics platforms are optimized for running massively parallel computational tasks and for processing different types of data, both structured/relational and nonstructured.

Currently most big CSPs provide also special infrastructure or platform components for Big Data and offer Big Data Analytics services. Examples below include AWS, Microsoft Azure, IBM, and LexisNexis HPCC Systems platforms.

Companies specialized on Big Data Analytics are typically offering Hadoop based platforms and Hadoop based data processing services. Example of such providers are Pentaho, Cloudera and SAS, and many others see Ref. [45]. However, some companies may offer other computing and programming for Big Data that are sometimes more effective than Hadoop and MapReduce. An example of such company is LexisNexis and their HPCC Systems platform.

Different types of VM for Hadoop cluster and for high performance computing (HPC) are provided by the major CSPs that are optimized for either computational tasks or working with the storage.

9.1 AMAZON WEB SERVICES AND ELASTIC MAPREDUCE

AWS Cloud offers the following services and resources for Big Data processing [46]:

* Elastic Compute Cloud (EC2) VM instances for HPC optimized for computing (with multiple cores) and with extended storage for large data processing.
* Amazon Elastic MapReduce (EMR) provides the Hadoop framework on Amazon EC2 and offers a wide range of Hadoop-related tools.
* Amazon Kinesis is a managed service for real-time processing of streaming big data (throughput scaling from megabytes to gigabytes of data per second and from hundreds of thousands different sources).
* Amazon DynamoDB highly scalable NoSQL data stores with submillisecond response latency.
* Amazon Redshift fully managed petabyte-scale Data Warehouse in cloud at cost less than $1000 per terabyte per year. It is provided with columnar data storage with the possibility to parallelize queries.
* Amazon RDS scalable relational database.
* Amazon Glacier archival storage to AWS for long-term data storage at a lower cost that standard Amazon Simple Storage Service (S3) object storage.

Amazon also offers a number of public datasets; the most featured are the Common Crawl Corpus of web crawl data composed of over 5 billion web pages, the 1000 Genomes Project, and Google Books Ngrams.

Recognizing the problem of transferring large amount of data to and from cloud, AWS offers two options for fast data upload, download, and access: (1) postal packet service of sending data on drive; and (2) direct connect service that allows the customer enterprise to build a dedicated high speed optical link to one of the Amazon datacenters [47].

9.2 MICROSOFT AZURE ANALYTICS PLATFORM SYSTEM AND HDINSIGHT

Microsoft Azure cloud provides general IaaSs and rich PaaSs. Similar to AWS, Microsoft Azure offers special VM instances that have both computational and memory advanced capabilities. Microsoft Azure provides rich Big Data services [48] specifically targeted for enterprise users, leveraging Microsoft experience in delivering business oriented services for corporate customers.

The Analytics Platform System (APS) [49] combines the Microsoft SQL Server-based Parallel Data Warehouse (PDW) platform with HDInsight and Apache Hadoop-based scalable data analytics platform. APS includes PolyBase data querying technology to simplify integration of the PDW SQL data and data from Hadoop.

Fig. 15 illustrates relations between components of the Microsoft APS that may include components running on Azure cloud and on the premises. Fig. 16 provides a detailed view of all major components of the Microsoft APS.

HDInsight Hadoop based platform [50] has been codeveloped with Hortonworks and offers the same functionality as the original Hortonworks Data Platform (HDP). HDInsight provides comprehensive integration and management functionality for multiworkload data processing on Hadoop platform

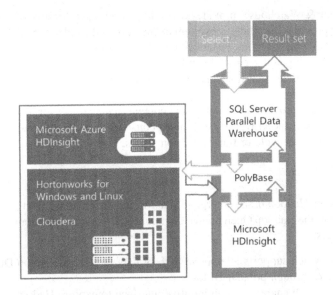

FIG. 15

Microsoft Azure Analytics Platform System ecosystem [49].

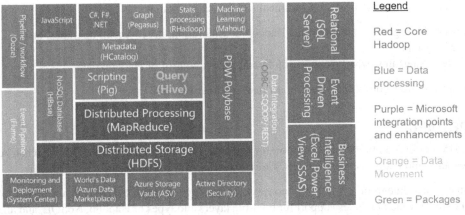

FIG. 16

Components of Microsoft Azure Analytics Platform.

including batch, stream, and in-memory processing methods. Additionally, APS allows integration of HDP with HDInsight on Azure cloud.

9.3 IBM BIG DATA ANALYTICS AND INFORMATION MANAGEMENT

IBM Big Data and information management, known as IBM Watson Foundations [51] includes the following components and capabilities:

- Data Management & Warehouse: provides capabilities optimized for analytics workloads.
- Hadoop System: provides the whole ecosystem to develop, build and use the Apache Hadoop based computing platform with analytics, visualization, and development tools, application accelerators, performance monitoring, and security features.
- Stream Computing: delivers real-time analytic processing on dynamically changing data to support real-time decision making.
- Content Management: provides comprehensive content management service.
- Information Integration and Governance: enables consistent data management and governance across the whole data lifecycle or transformation stages.

9.4 CLOUDERA

Cloudera [52] offers the Hadoop based enterprise analytic and data management platform. Cloudera is an active contributor to the Hadoop Open Source community. Cloudera Open Source platform includes the following products:

- Cloudera Impala, which supports interactive SQL of data in HDFS (Hadoop Distributed File System) and HBase through popular BI tools.
- Cloudera Search, which enables simple intuitive interface to explore Hadoop data.
- Sentry, which provides fine-grained role-based access control.

Cloudera Enterprise is available as a commercial subscription that includes a suite of data management software built for the enterprise and technical support, in particular:

- Cloudera Manager, which simplifies Hadoop configuration, deployment, upgrades, and administration.
- Cloudera Navigator, which supports audit and access control of Hadoop data.

Cloudera also offers consulting, training services, and certification program.

9.5 PENTAHO

Pentaho [53] offers comprehensive platform for data integration and business analytics that can be easily integrated into enterprise applications. Currently offered products include

- Pentaho Data Integration (PDI) (an enterprise-oriented graphical Extract, Transform, and Load (ETL) tool), which includes support for multiple layers and types of Hadoop, NoSQL, and analytic appliance environments.
- Visual MapReduce tool, which significantly simplifies the complex coding normally required for running applications on Hadoop.

- Pentaho Business Analytics suite, which supports the whole data analytics process and includes visualization tools, data mining and predictive algorithms, that is supported with the analytic modeling workbench, BI reporting and dashboard tools.

PDI generates Java-based data integration logic and predictive models for Hadoop. To address a variety of data types used in Big Data applications, Pentaho introduced a data adaptation layer what ensures portability of Pentaho solutions across popular Hadoop platforms from Cloudera, Hortonworks, and MapR.

9.6 LEXISNEXIS HPCC SYSTEMS AS AN INTEGRATED OPEN SOURCE PLATFORM FOR BIG DATA ANALYTICS

LexisNexis offers both comprehensive Data Analytics services and the Open Source HPCC Systems platform that is designed to handle massive, multistructured datasets of Petabytes scale [54,55].

The HPCC Systems has been initially developed as internal application platform and was released to the Open Source community in 2011 to respond to a growing customer base and a need for community contribution.

Figs. 17 and 18 illustrate HPCC Systems data analytics environment components and the HPCC Systems architecture model. It is based on a distributed, shared-nothing architecture and contains two clusters:

- THOR Data Refinery: THOR is a massively parallel Extract, Transform, and Load (ETL) engine, which can be used for performing a variety of tasks such as massive joins, merges, sorts, transformations, clustering, and scaling.

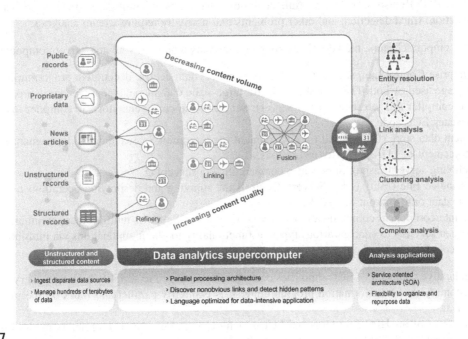

FIG. 17

LexisNexis HPCC Systems data analytics environment.

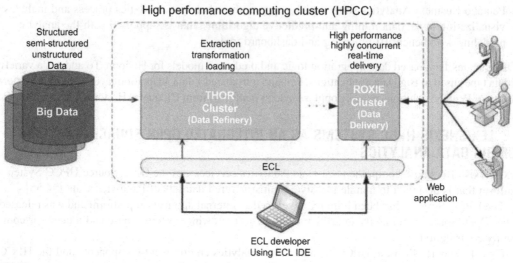

High performance computing cluster (HPCC)

FIG. 18

LexisNexis HPCC Systems architecture.

- ROXIE Data Delivery: ROXIE serves as a massively parallel, high throughput, structured query response engine. It is can perform volumes of structured queries and full text ranked Boolean search. ROXIE also provides real-time analytics capabilities, to address real-time classifications, prediction, fraud detection, and other problems that normally require stream analytics.

Besides compute clusters, the HPCC environment contains other software and server components:

- Enterprise Control Language (ECL): An open source, data-centric declarative programming language used by both THOR and ROXIE for large-scale data management and query processing.
- ECL compiler and job server (ECL Server): Serves as the code generator and compiler that translates ECL code.
- System data store (Dali): Used for environment configuration, message queue maintenance, and enforcement of LDAP security restrictions.
- Archiving server (Sasha): Serves as a companion "housekeeping" server to Dali.
- Distributed File Utility (DFU Server): Controls the spraying and despraying operations used to move data onto and out of THOR.
- The intercomponent communication server (ESP Server): Supports multiprotocol communication between services to enable various types of functionality to client applications via multiple protocols.

The declarative character of ECL simplifies coding; it is developed to simplify both data query design and customary data transformation programming. It is explicitly parallel and relies on the platform parallelism.

The power of the HPCC Systems and ECL is achieved via LexisNexis proprietary record linkage technology SALT (Scalable Automated Linking Technology) that automates data preparation process:

profiling, parsing, cleansing, normalization, and standardization of data. The SALT uses weighted matching and threshold based computation; it also enables internal, external, and remote linking with external or master datasets.

Future development of the HPCC Systems Data Analytics suite includes Knowledge Engineering Language (KEL). KEL is being developed as a domain-specific data processing language that allows using semantic relations between entities to automate generation of ECL code.

10 CONCLUSION

This chapter presented basic definitions and general concepts in the Big Data technologies and discussed their relation to current cloud computing technologies that are considered a technology and a platform of choice for building and deploying Big Data applications. The chapter summarized the research done by the authors and refers to NIST Big Data Interoperability Framework and Big Data Reference Architecture that together provide a conceptual basis for research and development of the cloud-based Big Data applications and infrastructures. The two bioinformatics use cases were used to illustrate effective use of cloud resources and cloud automation tools to deploy and manage bioinformatics applications.

The chapter described the CYCLONE platform that is being developed by the authors in the framework of the CYCLONE project that provides all necessary functionality for multicloud multiprovider applications deployment and management. It uses the SlipStream cloud automation platform for applications deployment and management and includes other necessary components to build and operate complex scientific applications such as federated access control infrastructure, OpenNaaS network infrastructure provisioning, cloud services matchmaking, and optimization.

Currently, after exploring the cloud benefits in reducing capital expenses (capex) by changing them to operational expenses (opex) to rent cloud resources on demand, modern agile companies and businesses are looking for effectives way to reduce increased opex. The solution is seen in cloud deployment and operation automation. For this purpose, the chapter introduced the modern concept of the cloud powered applications development and continuous deployment, also referred to as DevOps (Development and Operation), and provides a short overview of the popular platforms and tools for cloud automation.

The chapter also included short overview of the existing Big Data platforms and services provided by the major CSPs such as AWS, Microsoft Azure, IBM, Cloudera, Pentaho, and LexisNexis. These can provide a basis for fast deployment of customer Big Data applications using benefits of cloud technologies and global cloud infrastructure; however, the necessary use of resources from multiple providers will often require third-party tools for the whole application deployment and management such as CYCLONE or SlipStream platform.

ACKNOWLEDGMENTS

The research leading to these results has received funding from the Horizon2020 projects CYCLONE (funded by the European Commission under grant number 644925), GEANT4 (funded by the European Commission under grant number 691567), and the French programs PIA INBS 2012 (CNRS IFB).

REFERENCES

[1] Grey J. The fourth paradigm: data-intensive scientific discovery. In: Hey T, Tansley S, Tolle K, editors. Seattle, USA: Microsoft Corporation; 2010. ISBN 978-0-9825442-0-4. http://research.microsoft.com/en-us/collaboration/fourthparadigm/.

[2] NIST SP 800-145. A NIST definition of cloud computing, National Institute of Standards and Technology; September 2011, Gaithersburg, MD; 2011. Available from: http://csrc.nist.gov/publications/nistpubs/800-145/SP800-145.pdf.

[3] NIST SP 500-292. Cloud computing reference architecture, v1.0, National Institute of Standards and Technology; September 2011, Gaithersburg, MD; 2011. Available from: http://ws680.nist.gov/publication/get_pdf.cfm?pub_id=909505.

[4] NIST Special Publication NIST SP 1500. NIST Big Data Interoperability Framework (NBDIF), National Institute of Standards and Technology; September 2015, Gaithersburg, MD; 2015. Available from: http://nvlpubs.nist.gov/nistpubs/SpecialPublications/NIST.SP.1500-1.pdf.

[5] Demchenko Y, Membrey P, de Laat C. Defining architecture components of the big data ecosystem. In: Second international symposium on Big Data and Data Analytics in Collaboration (BDDAC 2014). Part of the 2014 international conference on Collaboration Technologies and Systems (CTS 2014), May 19-23, 2014, Minneapolis, MN; 2014.

[6] Gualtieri M. The Forrester wave: big data predictive analytics solutions, Q1 2013. Forrester Research; 2013. January 13. Available from: http://www.forrester.com/pimages/rws/reprints/document/85601/oid/1-LTEQDI.

[7] Demchenko Y, Membrey P, Grosso P, de Laat C. Addressing big data issues in scientific data infrastructure. In: First international symposium on Big Data and Data Analytics in Collaboration (BDDAC 2013). Part of The 2013 international conference on Collaboration Technologies and Systems (CTS 2013), May 20-24, 2013, San Diego, California, USA; 2013.

[8] Gartner. Big data definition. Gartner; 2011. Available from: http://www.gartner.com/it-glossary/big-data/.

[9] NIST Big Data Working Group, http://bigdatawg.nist.gov/; 2015.

[10] Demchenko Y, Makkes M, Strijkers R, Ngo C, de Laat C. Intercloud architecture framework for heterogeneous multi-provider cloud based infrastructure services provisioning. Int J Next-Gener Comput 2013;4(2).

[11] Puppet: cloud automated provisioning and management, https://puppetlabs.com/. Accessed June 2016.

[12] Data Lifecycle Models and Concepts, CEOS Version 1.2, Doc. Ref. CEOS.WGISS.DSIG, 4 April 2012. Available from: http://wgiss.ceos.org/dsig/whitepapers/Data%20Lifecycle%20Models%20and%20Concepts%20v12.docx.

[13] DCC Curation Lifecycle Model. Available from: http://www.dcc.ac.uk/resources/curation-lifecycle-model. Accessed June 2016.

[14] European Union. A study on authentication and authorisation platforms for scientific resources in Europe. Brussels: European Commission; 2012 Final Report. Contributing author. Internal identification SMART-Nr 2011/0056. Available from: http://cordis.europa.eu/fp7/ict/e-infrastructure/docs/aaa-study-final-report.pdf.

[15] Broeder D, Lannom L. Data type registries: a research data alliance working group. D-Lib Mag 2014;20 (Number 1/2). http://www.dlib.org/dlib/january14/broeder/01broeder.html.

[16] Reilly S, et al. Report on integration of data and publications; 2011. October 17. http://www.libereurope.eu/sites/default/files/ODE-ReportOnIntegrationOfDataAndPublication.pdf.

[17] Demchenko Y, Lee C, Ngo C, de Laat C. Federated access control in heterogeneous intercloud environment: basic models and architecture patterns. In: Proceedings of IEEE international conference on cloud engineering (IC2E), March 11, 2014, Boston, MA; 2014.

[18] Demchenko Y, Dumitru C, Filiposka S, Matselyukh T, Regvart D, de Vos M, et al. Open Cloud Exchange (OCX): a pivot for intercloud services federation in multi-provider cloud market environment. In: Proceedings of IEEE 4th international workshop on cloud computing interclouds, multiclouds,

federations, and interoperability (Intercloud 2015), at IEEE international conference on cloud engineering (IC2E), March 12, 2015, Tempe, AZ; 2015.

[19] GEANT Pan-European Network. Available from: http://www.geant.org/Networks/Pan-European_network/Pages/Home.aspx. Accessed June 2016.

[20] Marx V. Biology: the big challenges of big data. Nature 2013;498(7453):255–60.

[21] Stephens ZD, Lee SY, Faghri F, Campbell RH, Zhai C, Efron MJ, et al. Big data: astronomical or genomical? PLoS Biol 2015;13(7). e1002195.

[22] French Institute of Bioinformatics, CNRS IFB UMS3601. Available from: http://www.france-bioinformatique.fr/. Accessed June 2016.

[23] Demchenko Y, et al. CYCLONE: a platform for data intensive scientific applications in heterogeneous multi-cloud/multi-provider environment, In: Proceedings of IEEE IC2E conference, 4–8 April 2016, Berlin; 2016.

[24] Lacroix T, Loux V, Gendrault A, Hoebeke M, Gibrat JF. Insyght: navigating amongst abundant homologues, syntenies and gene functional annotations in bacteria, it's that symbol!. Nucleic Acids Res 2014;42(21). e162.

[25] Davis J, Daniels K. Effective DevOps. O'Reilly; USA, 2015. ISBN 978-1-4919-2630-7.

[26] Chef: cloud automation deployment and DevOps platform, https://www.chef.io/chef/. Accessed June 2016.

[27] Ansible IT automation tool, http://docs.ansible.com/ansible/. Accessed June 2016.

[28] SlipStream cloud automation, http://sixsq.com/products/slipstream/. Accessed June 2016.

[29] Ruoyu W, et al. ACaaS: access control as a service for IaaS cloud. In: Proceedings of international conference on social computing (Socialcom), Washington, DC; 2013. p. 423–8.

[30] Microsoft Developer Network (MDSN), https://msdn.microsoft.com/en-us/library/hh446535.aspx.

[31] Ngo C, Membrey P, Demchenko Y, de Laat C. Policy and context management in dynamically provisioned access control service for virtualised cloud infrastructures. In: The 7th international conference on availability, reliability and security (AReS 2012), 20-24 August 2012, Prague, Czech Republic; 2012, ISBN 978-0-7695-4775-6.

[32] Membrey P, Chan KCC, Ngo C, Demchenko Y, de Laat C. Trusted virtual infrastructure bootstrapping for on demand services. In: The 7th international conference on availability, reliability and security (AReS 2012), 20-24 August 2012, Prague; 2012.

[33] Assertions and protocols for the OASIS security assertion markup language (SAML) V2.0. OASIS Standard, 15 March 2005. Available from: http://docs.oasis-open.org/security/saml/v2.0/saml-core-2.0-os.pdf

[34] SAML 2.0 profile of XACML 2.0, version 2.0. OASIS Standard, 1 February 2005. Available from: http://docs.oasis-open.org/xacml/2.0/access_control-xacml-2.0-saml-profile-spec-os.pdf.

[35] Turkmen F, den Hartog J, Ranise S, Zannone, N. Analysis of XACML policies with SMT, In: Principles of Security and Trust. POST 2015. Lecture Notes in Computer Science, vol 9036. Springer, Berlin, Heidelberg.

[36] Turkmen F, Foley SN, O'Sullivan B, Fitzgerald WM, Hadzic T, Basagiannis S, et al. Explanations and relaxations for policy conflicts in physical access control. ICTAI '13 Proceedings of the 2013 IEEE 25th International Conference on Tools with Artificial Intelligence, IEEE Computer Society, November 4–6, 2013, Washington, DC; 2013.

[37] EDUGAIN, http://services.geant.net/edugain/Pages/Home.aspx.

[38] Amazon CloudFormation, https://aws.amazon.com/cloudformation/.

[39] Demchenko Y, Grosso P, de Laat C, Filiposka S, de Vos M. ZeroTouch Provisioning (ZTP) model and infrastructure components for multi-provider cloud services provisioning, In: Proceedings of IEEE IC2E conference, 4–8 April 2016, Berlin.

[40] Zero Touch Network-as-a-Service: agile, assured and orchestrated with NFV. TMForum, July 2015, https://www.tmforum.org/events/zero-touch-network-as-a-service-naas-agile-assured-and-orchestrated-with-nfv/.

[41] Filiposka S, et al. Distributed cloud services based on programmable agile networks. In: Proceedings of TERENA networking conference (TNC16), 13-16 June 2016, Prague, Czech Republic; 2016.

[42] Topology and Orchestration Specification for Cloud Applications, version 1.0. Candidate OASIS Standard. 25 November 2013, http://docs.oasis-open.org/tosca/TOSCA/v1.0/os/TOSCA-v1.0-os.pdf.

[43] Network automation and programmability abstraction layer with multivendor support (NAPALM), http://napalm.readthedocs.org/en/latest/. Accessed June 2016.

[44] SlipStream API documentation, http://ssapi.sixsq.com/.

[45] Big Data Vendors, http://www.bigdatavendors.com/; 2016.

[46] Amazon Big Data, http://aws.amazon.com/big-data/.

[47] AWS DirectConnect, https://aws.amazon.com/directconnect/; 2016.

[48] Microsoft Azure Big Data, http://www.windowsazure.com/en-us/home/scenarios/big-data/.

[49] Microsoft Analytics Platform System, http://www.microsoft.com/en-us/server-cloud/products/analytics-platform-system/#fbid=ck8LbRWe4MP.

[50] HDInsight Solutions, https://azure.microsoft.com/en-us/solutions/big-data/.

[51] IBM Big Data Analytics, http://www-01.ibm.com/software/data/infosphere/bigdata-analytics.html.

[52] Cloudera: the Hadoop based platform for big data, http://www.cloudera.com/content/cloudera/en/home.html.

[53] Pentaho: business analytics and business intelligence, http://www.pentaho.com/.

[54] HPCC Systems, http://hpccsystems.com/.

[55] Middleton AM. HPCC systems: introduction to HPCC (high performance computer cluster). LexisNexis Risk Solutions; 2011. May 24.

GLOSSARY

Big Data "Big data is high-volume, high-velocity, and high-variety information assets that demand cost-effective, innovative forms of information processing for enhanced insight and decision making" (Gartner definition).

Big Data 3V Big Data generic properties: volume, variety, and velocity.

Big Data 6V Big Data properties: volume, variety, velocity, value, veracity, and variability.

Cloud (end)user A person or organization that uses/consumes cloud-based services. A cloud user can be also a cloud customer.

Cloud computing A model for enabling ubiquitous, convenient, on-demand network access to a shared pool of configurable computing resources (e.g., networks, servers, storage, applications, and services) that can be rapidly provisioned and released with minimal management effort or service provider interaction. This cloud model is composed of five essential characteristics, three service models, and four deployment models (NIST SP 800-145).

Cloud customer A person or organization that maintains a business relationship with and manages service obtained from cloud providers.

Cloud infrastructure as a service (IaaS) The capability provided to the consumer is to provision processing, storage, networks, and other fundamental computing resources where the consumer is able to deploy and run arbitrary software, which can include operating systems and applications. The consumer does not manage or control the underlying cloud infrastructure but has control over operating systems, storage, deployed applications, and possibly limited control of select networking components (e.g., host firewalls).

Cloud platform as a service (PaaS) The capability provided to the consumer is to deploy onto the cloud infrastructure consumer-created or acquired applications created using programming languages, libraries, services, and tools supported by the provider. The consumer does not manage or control the underlying cloud infrastructure including network, servers, operating systems, or storage, but has control over the deployed applications and possibly configuration settings for the application-hosting environment.

Cloud service provider (CSP) A cloud provider is a person, an organization; it is the entity responsible for making a service available to interested parties. A cloud provider acquires and manages the computing infrastructure required for providing the services, runs the cloud software that provides the services, and makes arrangements to deliver cloud services to cloud consumers through network access.

Cloud software as a service (SaaS) The capability provided to the consumer is to use the provider's applications running on a cloud infrastructure. The applications are accessible from various client devices through either a thin client interface, such as a web browser (e.g., web-based email), or a program interface. The consumer does not manage or control the underlying cloud infrastructure including network, servers, operating systems, storage, or even individual application capabilities, with the possible exception of limited user-specific application configuration settings.

Community cloud The cloud infrastructure is provisioned for exclusive use by a specific community of consumers from organizations that have shared concerns (e.g., mission, security requirements, policy, and compliance considerations). It may be owned, managed, and operated by one or more of the organizations in the community, a third party, or some combination of them, and it may exist on or off premises.

CYCLONE EU-funded project that develops multicloud applications deployment and management environment (http://www.cyclone-project.eu).

Data provenance Data provenance documents the inputs, entities, systems, and processes that influence data of interest, in effect providing a historical record of the data and its origins. The generated evidence supports essential data management activities such as data-dependency analysis, error/compromise detection and recovery, and auditing and compliance analysis.

Data Science Also known as Data Intensive, Data Centric, Data Driven, or Data Analytics.

DevOps DevOps (development and operations) is a practice that combines and integrates both software development and software of applications operation while automating the process of software delivery and infrastructure changes.

e-Infrastructure e-Infrastructure refers to new research environment in which all researchers—whether working in the context of their home institutions or in national or multinational scientific initiatives—have shared access to unique or distributed scientific facilities (including data, instruments, computing, and communications), regardless of their type and location in the world. It embraces networks, grids, clouds, data centers, and collaborative environments, and can include supporting operations centers, service registries, Single Sign On, certificate authorities, training and help-desk services.

e-Science Innovative way of conducting scientific research based on using variety of ICT services and powered by e-Infrastructure.

Federated cloud The cloud infrastructure that involves multiple heterogeneous clouds from different providers that use a federation mechanism to share, access and control combined infrastructure and services. A federated cloud typically combines multiple private clouds and may include also private cloud. Federation members remain independent, however, having common policy in resources sharing and access control, including federated identity management. Cloud federation may include provider side federation and customer side federation. Community cloud the most probably will adopt federated cloud model.

GEANT (1) Pan-European Research Network; (2) Acronym for EU funded project to support GEANT network development.

Hadoop An open-source software framework for distributed storage and distributed processing of very large data sets on computer clusters built from commodity hardware.

HPCC Scalable parallel processing computing platform by LexisNexis (alternative to Hadoop).

Hybrid cloud The cloud infrastructure is a composition of two or more distinct cloud infrastructures (private, community, or public) that remain unique entities, but are bound together by standardized or proprietary technology that enables data and application portability (e.g., cloud bursting for load balancing between clouds).

Identity management (IDM) This describes the management of individual principals, their authentication, authorization, and privileges within or across system and enterprise boundaries with the goal of increasing security and productivity while decreasing cost, downtime, and repetitive tasks.

Intercloud The general model for a cloud infrastructure that combines multiple heterogeneous clouds from multiple providers and typically also includes campus/enterprise infrastructure and noncloud resources.

The intercloud model may use the federated cloud model or implement more specific common control and management functions to create a kind of Intercloud virtual private cloud.

Metadata Data that provide information about other data. Two types of metadata exist: structural metadata and descriptive metadata. Structural metadata are data about the containers of data. Descriptive metadata use individual instances of application data or the data content.

Orchestration The automated arrangement, coordination, and management of complex computer systems.

Private cloud The cloud infrastructure is provisioned for exclusive use by a single organization comprising multiple consumers (e.g., business units). It may be owned, managed, and operated by the organization, a third party, or some combination of them, and it may exist on or off premises.

Public cloud The cloud infrastructure is provisioned for open use by the general public. It may be owned, managed, and operated by a business, academic, or government organization, or some combination of them. It exists on the premises of the cloud provider.

Recipe In the context of cloud-based applications deployment, recipe mean a blueprint for deploying application on one of cloud platforms under the control of a cloud automation system such as Chef, Puppet, or SlipStream.

SlipStream Smart cloud automation and management platform.

Topology Topology of a network or service is arrangement of components and interconnection between them.

Virtualization The process of creating a virtual component or resource. Virtualization includes physical resources abstraction (including pooling or segmentation), logical composition, and deployment or physical resources configuration to allocate required/assigned virtual resources.

OPEN SOURCE PRIVATE CLOUD PLATFORMS FOR BIG DATA

3

Martial Michel*, Olivier Serres[†], Ahmad Anbar[†], Edmond J. Golden III*, Tarek El-Ghazawi[†]

National Institute of Standards and Technology, Gaithersburg, MD, United States[*]
The George Washington University, Washington, DC, United States[†]

1 CLOUD COMPUTING AND BIG DATA AS A SERVICE

According to the National Institute of Standards and Technology (NIST)'s definition of cloud computing, "Cloud computing is a model for enabling ubiquitous, convenient, on-demand network access to a shared pool of configurable computing resources (e.g., networks, servers, storage, applications, and services) that can be rapidly provisioned and released with minimal management effort or service provider interaction" [1].

Cloud computing provides a tremendous advantage for Big Data applications as it can be made to scale to meet the computation and storage needs of those problems.

NIST's Cloud Computing Reference Architecture [2] defines multiple service models, such that when we separate the different components of an On-Premise cluster by its roles and responsibilities, we find the following nine components: Application, Data, Runtime, Middleware, Operating System, Virtualization, Server, Storage, and Networking.

There are different kinds of cloud computing options available; Software as a Service (SaaS), Platform as a Service (PaaS), and Infrastructure as a Service (IaaS), each with its advantages and disadvantages. Fig. 1 compares those.

SaaS All of the nine components are controlled by the service provider. SaaS uses web frontends to provide managed applications whose interface is accessed from the provider's servers. As most applications can be run directly from a web browser, they eliminate the need to install and run applications directly on the user's computer, but push the compute and storage resources to the SaaS provider. In general, users are subscribing to a specific software or service; for example, web-based email.

PasS The user controls the choice of Application and Data, but the remaining seven components, from Runtime to Networking are controlled by the service provider. Also known as *Cloud Platform Services*, they provides a platform allowing users to develop, run, and manage applications and reduce the complexity of building and maintaining the infrastructure typically associated with new application development.

IaaS The user is able to control the Application, Data, Runtime, Middleware, and Operating System, and the service provider controls the remaining four components. IaaS relies on services that abstract the user from the details of the infrastructure: they are self-service models for accessing, monitoring, and managing data-center type infrastructures for compute (virtualized or bare metal), storage, networking, and networking services (e.g., firewalls).

Big Data Analytics for Sensor-Network Collected Intelligence. http://dx.doi.org/10.1016/B978-0-12-809393-1.00003-9

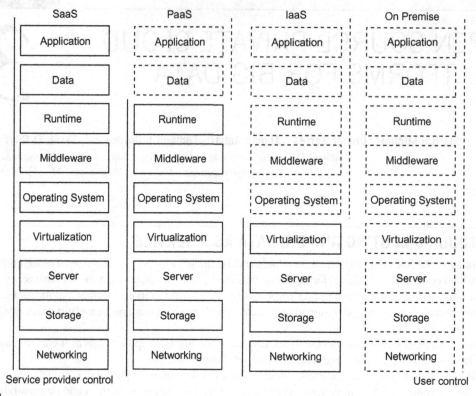

	SaaS	PaaS	IaaS	On Premise
	Application	Application	Application	Application
	Data	Data	Data	Data
	Runtime	Runtime	Runtime	Runtime
	Middleware	Middleware	Middleware	Middleware
	Operating System	Operating System	Operating System	Operating System
	Virtualization	Virtualization	Virtualization	Virtualization
	Server	Server	Server	Server
	Storage	Storage	Storage	Storage
	Networking	Networking	Networking	Networking

Service provider control   User control

FIG. 1

On-Premise, IaaS, PaaS, SaaS.

Although it is not represented on the figure, Big Data as a Service (BDaaS) is an extension designed to work on specific Big Data problems, which consists of extensive datasets, primarily in the characteristics of volume, variety, velocity, and/or variability, that requires a scalable architecture for efficient storage, manipulation, and analysis. As a consequence, it is becoming popular as many businesses identify themselves as facing Big Data challenges and opportunities. Big Data platforms are notoriously complex and building an in-house framework can be really challenging. As such, BDaaS solutions can alleviate such overhead from these businesses. Cloud-based BDaaS offerings currently fall into one of three categories:

[Core BDaaS] offers a Big Data platform, with a limited set of components, often limited to Hadoop and HDFS.
[Performance BDaaS] offers optimized infrastructure to reduce virtualization overheads and enable building hardware servers and networks adequate to core Hadoop requirements.
[Feature BDaaS] focuses on productivity and abstraction, to get users quickly started with Big Data processing and applications. This includes web and programming interfaces as well as database adapters pushing Big Data technologies into the background.

As the research community investigate more models related to Big Data architectures, an Open Science Big Data Analytic Technology Research and Development Model (as can be seen in Fig. 2)

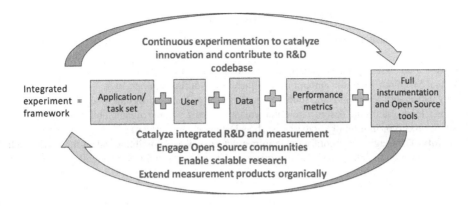

FIG. 2

Open science Big Data analytic technology R&D model.

presents a solution that enables researchers to bring their experiments to the data. In doing so, the complexity of accessing large data sets is reduced as the data is collocated to the compute needs. Using it on an IaaS allows for full separation of running experiments, so that a single infrastructure can support multiple concurrent problems while at the same time be reconfigurable to run controlled experiments. Furthermore, using an On-Premise Private Cloud facilitates the aggregation of benchmarks and compute performance metrics as well as add means to protect that data from exposure or exfiltration. We will discuss their uses in the following section, after presenting some well-known public cloud infrastructures as well as discussing the advantages of the cloud for Big Data.

1.1 PUBLIC CLOUD INFRASTRUCTURE

A cloud is considered *public* when its services are rendered over a network that is open for public use (including clouds that are pay-per-use). Security consideration needs to be considered for services (applications, storage, and other resources) offered to a public audience or over a nontrusted network. Some popular large public cloud solutions are

Amazon Web Services (AWS) [3] Launched in 2006, AWS is a collection of cloud computing services on Amazon.com's on-demand computing platform. Amazon *Elastic Compute Cloud* (EC2), which provides scalable virtual private servers and *Simple Storage Service* (S3), which provides Web Service-based storage, are its most used and known services.

Google Cloud Platform [4] Started in 2008 with its App Engine component, this cloud computing platform is part of a suite of enterprise solutions which provides a set of modular cloud-based services with support for Compute (such as App Engine, Compute Engine, Container Engine), Storage (such as Cloud BigTable, Cloud Storage), Big Data (such as BigQuery, Cloud DataFlow), and Services (such as Cloud EndPoints).

Microsoft Azure [5] Released in 2010 by Microsoft, Azure is a cloud computing platform and infrastructure for building, deploying, and managing applications and services through a global network of Microsoft-managed datacenters that provides both PaaS and IaaS services.

1.2 ADVANTAGES OF THE CLOUD FOR BIG DATA

Big Data workload characteristics make it a natural candidate for processing on the cloud:

Data velocity Cloud elasticity and scalability make it ideal to adapt to data velocity. Its capability to easily add new Virtual Machines when the amount of data increase or during peak periods.

Data variety Different frameworks and tools can be deployed to handle different kind of data.

Data volume Cloud systems are designed to reliably handle a great volume of data, both in term of storage (such as block or object) or in term of databases (such as Database as a Service).

Data variability The usage of a reconfigurable infrastructure makes it possible to adapt the understanding and model processing on the cloud system in response to data whose meaning is changing.

2 ON-PREMISE PRIVATE CLOUDS FOR BIG DATA

Private clouds provide an environment where the hardware, storage, and network are dedicated to a set of users and solve some of security concerns presented by public clouds.

After discussing the security of cloud systems and the advantage of *On-Premise* Private Cloud, we will, in the next section, introduce some selected Open Source Cloud Environments.

2.1 SECURITY OF CLOUD COMPUTING SYSTEMS

Cloud computing brings important conveniences but also come with new security advantages and risks. Cloud computing benefits from better availability. Its deployment can be performed in different zones, and virtual machines running on bad nodes can be automatically migrated. An added benefit is that the virtualization also reduces the collocation of different software on the same servers, reducing security issues. This deployment model often facilitates updates and fixes.

Yet new security risks are also created; a common architecture is susceptible to attacks and may compromise all the services running on the connected cloud. As such, an attacker can target many elements of the cloud platform: the cloud web interface and Application Programming Interfaces (API), the authentication system, the segregation of users and data (virtualization layers, storage systems, networks) [6–8].

Some, but not all, of those new risks are mitigated by private clouds.

2.2 ADVANTAGES OF ON-PREMISE PRIVATE CLOUDS

An On-Premise Private Cloud, where the hardware/access is available on the premises where the users are location (rather than at a remote facility), also has its own specific advantages:

Security It is greatly increased as the access can be limited to private networks. Conformance to specific encryption or storage regulations or constraints is easier to fulfill.

Privacy Often, private and proprietary code, software, or data is developed and tested on large-scale systems. Using such software on an On-Premise Private Cloud, where network components, as well as Network Address Translation (NAT), can be controlled, facilitates a level of proprietary information protection and limits the chances of exfiltration.

Customizability The hardware can be customized to the exact requirements of the application: CPUs, coprocessors, accelerators, and networks can be tailored to the workload. Similarly, the software can be customized through the use of Open Source components.

Accessibility On-Premise Cloud solutions allow for high-bandwidth and low-latency, as well as physical collocation and access to the hardware if needed.

Cost Collocation of multiple clusters in the same cloud architecture help lower costs. At scale, and when the usage of tailored architecture is required, important cost-savings can be obtained when compared to the cost of storage and usage of public clouds for long-running experiments.

3 INTRODUCTION TO SELECTED OPEN SOURCE CLOUD ENVIRONMENTS

Many solutions are available to build On-Premise private clouds. Open source software (OSS) is crowd-sourced and can be freely accessed, used, changed, and shared by anyone. The open factor makes it possible for many developers to collaborate on enhancing and adding features to those software.

In this section, we will detail the architectures and features of the most widely deployed open source solutions, after which, in the next section, we will discuss means of doing heterogeneous computing in the cloud, introducing the use of specialized hardware.

3.1 OPENNEBULA

OpenNebula is an Open Source Software (released under an Apache License, v2.0) providing an IaaS cloud computing solution. It supports private, hybrid, and public clouds with a small focus on private cloud. The core is written in C++ and the rest in Ruby. It provides standard cloud interfaces (Amazon EC2, OGF Open Cloud Computing Interface, and vCloud) [9]. For its hypervisor, it supports Xen, KVM, and VMware. For storage (for VM images), the users can choose to use either a file-system backend (shared directory mounted from SAN/NAS), a vmfs (VMware store, only for the VMware hypervisor), LVM, or Ceph. Similarly for the network, multiple backends are available (such as a simple firewall without network isolation, Virtual LAN tagging, restricted network through ebtables [10], etc.).

A typical base installation of OpenNebula (see Fig. 3) [11] will be composed of a Front End with the management daemon, the scheduler, and the web interface server, a shared storage system and two networks (one for service and storage, one for public traffic). A set of hosts (Hypervisors) will run the virtual machines [12].

OpenNebula has a fairly centralized architecture but is modulable through the use of plugins (see Fig. 4). The native OpenNebula cloud API (XML-RPC) is accessible to the user and can be used for customization [13].

OpenNebula refers to any storage medium as *Datastore*. There are three main classes for OpenNebula datastores (Fig. 5):

System Datastores These are used by OpenNebula to hold images for running virtual machines (VM). An image for a VM is simply a contained copy of that VM, which may include an OS, data files, and applications.

Images Datastores These hold the disk images repository. Disk images are virtual disks that can be attached or detached from running VMs. Disk images can also be cloned or snapshotted.

Files and Kernels Datastore These are special datastores that can be used to store plain files (not disk images).

Storage
Front end
Service/storage network
Public network
Hypervisor
Hypervisor
Hypervisor
Private network

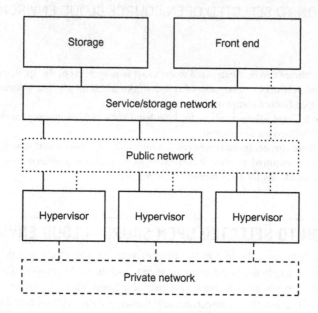

FIG. 3

OpenNebula: high-level reference architecture (Apr. 2015).

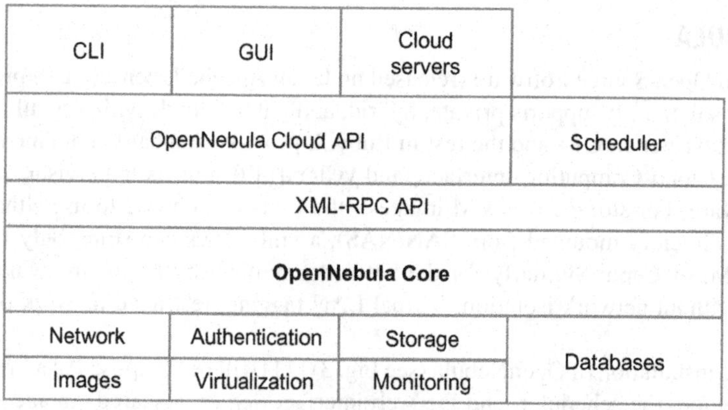

CLI
GUI
Cloud servers
OpenNebula Cloud API
Scheduler
XML-RPC API
OpenNebula Core
Network
Authentication
Storage
Databases
Images
Virtualization
Monitoring

FIG. 4

OpenNebula: anatomy.

Data stores
System
Images
Files
Network
Hosts

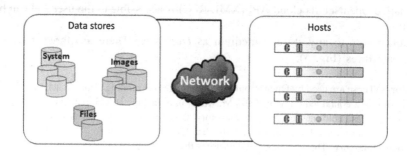

FIG. 5

OpenNebula storage overview.

3.2 EUCALYPTUS

Eucalyptus [14] is an open-source software suite designed to build private/hybrid cloud computing environments [15] compatible with Amazon Web Service's EC2 and S3 [16]. Eucalyptus was initially released in 2008 by Eucalyptus Systems, Inc., and acquired by HP in 2014. It is currently known as HP Helion Eucalyptus.

Eucalyptus provides the different components shown in Fig. 6 and its Logical Model is shown in Fig. 7 [17], such that a basic Eucalyptus installation will contain the following components:

Cloud Controller (CLC) A Java [18] program that provides high-level resource tracking and management. Only one CLC can exist in a Eucalyptus cloud.
User Facing Services (UFS) Implements web service interfaces that handle the AWS-compatible APIs. This component accepts requests from command line clients or graphical/web-based interfaces.

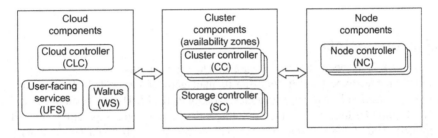

FIG. 6

Eucalyptus components overview.

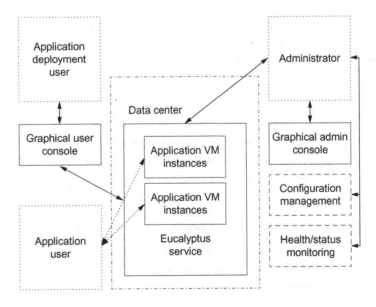

FIG. 7

Eucalyptus: logical model (General Purpose 4.0 Large, 2014).

Cluster Controller (CC) Manages existing Node Controllers and is responsible for deploying and managing Virtual Machine (VM) instances. CC also allows VM instances to run under different types of available networking modes.

Node Controller (NC) Runs on any machine that hosts VMs, and interacts with both OS and hypervisor to maintain the life cycle of the instances running on each of the host nodes.

Eucalyptus has two storage services:

Storage Controller (SC) It has a similar purpose as the Amazon Elastic Block Store (EBS) and can interface with various storage systems (NFS, iSCSI, SAN devices, etc.). EBS exposes storage volumes that can be attached by a VM and mounted or accessed as a raw block device. SC supports SAN, which enables enterprise-grade SAN devices to host EBS storage within a Eucalyptus cloud. Volume snapshots are stored in Walrus.

Walrus (WS) It is the Eucalyptus equivalent to AWS S3 and offers persistent storage to all of the VMs in the Eucalyptus cloud and can be used as a simple HTTP put/get *Storage as a Service* solution.

3.3 APACHE CLOUDSTACK

Apache CloudStack is an open source software for deploying public and private IaaS clouds. It is Java-based, and enables hypervisor hosts using its management server. It is designed to be Hypervisor agnostic, and currently can support XenServer/XCP, KVM, Hyper-V, and/or VMware ESXi with vSphere. It provides user management, multitenancy, and account separation. It interfaces with network, compute and storage resources via a native API or a web-based UI. It manages storage for instances running on the hypervisors and orchestrate network services with built-in high-availability for hosts and VMs. It includes VLANs, security groups, virtual routers, firewalls, and load balancers (Fig. 8).

In 2008, CloudStack was a project of a start-up known as VMOps (later renamed cloud.com), which was purchased by Citrix in 2011. In Apr. 2012, Citrix licensed CloudStack under the Apache Software License v2.0 and submitted CloudStack to the Apache Incubator that it graduated from, in Mar. 2013.

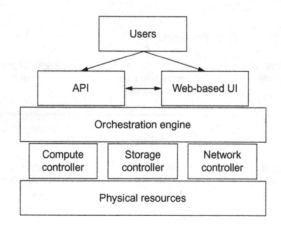

FIG. 8

CloudStack: architecture.

The minimum production installation has one machine running the CloudStack Management Server and another machine being the cloud infrastructure (i.e., one host running hypervisor software) [19]. It can be extended to have multiple management servers with redundancy and load balancing through the use of a common MySQL database.

CloudStack's storage model consists of two types of storage: primary and secondary. There is no ephemeral storage in CloudStack. All volumes on all nodes are persistent:

Primary Storage For virtual disks volumes for all the VMs running on hosts in a CloudStack cluster.
Secondary Storage For Operating System's images, ISO disc images, and disk volume snapshots.

CloudStack also provides plugins that enable the use both OpenStack Swift and Amazon S3.

3.4 OPENSTACK

OpenStack [20] is an Open Source Cloud Computing platform that supports all types of cloud environments. Fig. 9 shows a high-level view of its architecture: the project aims to easily separate and access the Compute, Networking, and Storage components needed to work with a cloud system through simple implementation, massive scalability, and a rich set of features. Fig. 10 presents a simplified view of the conceptual architecture used by OpenStack, where

Nova is the *Computing Engine* that deploys and manages the lifecycle of virtual machines and other instances to handle computing tasks. Its responsibilities include spawning, scheduling, and decommissioning.
Neutron is the *Network Controller* that offers a Software Defined Network (SDN) interface that enables fast and managed network communications. Neutron allows higher levels of cloud scaling and multitenancy using a variety of software-defined networking technologies into the cloud. The networking framework provides services like firewall, load-balancing features, and intrusion detection.

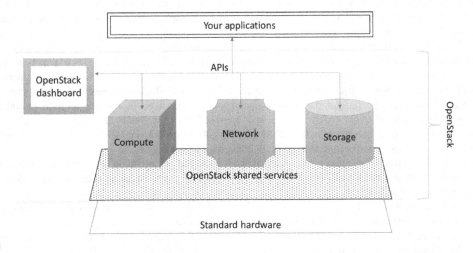

FIG. 9

OpenStack architecture.

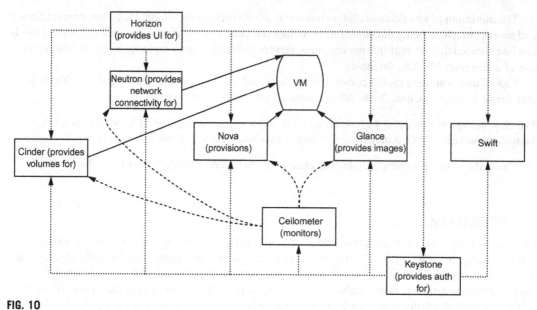

FIG. 10

OpenStack simplified conceptual architecture.

Cinder and Swift are *Storage Systems*. They store objects and files, and are a block storage component for user control when data access speed is essential. *Cinder* is a Block Storage service designed to present storage resources that can be consumed by *Nova* by virtualizing pools of block storage devices. In contrast, *Swift* stores and retrieves arbitrary unstructured data objects via a RESTful API and is highly fault tolerant with a data replication and scale-out architecture. Backends such as Ceph, LVM, Gluster, NFS, ZFS, and Sheepdog can be used for Object, Block, and File storage, but only Ceph and Gluster handle all three types. Both *Cinder* and *Swift* commonly use *Ceph* as a storage backend. *Ceph* is "strongly consistent," which means that read data will be always up to date. This is in contrast to Swift's native backend which is "eventually consistent," meaning that read data have the potential to be stale until consistency has been achieved. This may not matter for certain data types or use cases; the backend selection depends on the use case and the type of data being stored. These backends are based on commodity hardware solutions, making it simple to extend storage components to an additional local cloud as the volume of data increase. They can be deployed between multiples sites where each site's storage can be configured as a single-shared pool or separate pools, allowing for Regions and Zones which can be deployed across geographic regions. OpenStack's *Swift* provides access to streamed data, be it local or remote, via an industry-standard RESTful API. All objects are stored with multiple copies and are replicated in as-unique-as-possible availability within zones and/or regions.

Keystone is the *Identity Service* that provides an authentication and authorization service for other OpenStack services, as well as a catalog of endpoints for all OpenStack services, including user, projects, roles, token management, and authentication.

Glance is the *Image Service*. It uses virtual copies of hard disks images for deployment of new virtual machine instances. Compute makes use of this during instance provisioning.

Ceilometer is the *Telemetry Service*. It keeps a verifiable count of each user's system, monitoring and metering the OpenStack cloud for benchmarking, scalability, and statistical purposes, as well as billing.

Horizon is the *Front End* portal, a web-based self-service to interact with underlying services and provides a quick glance at components and resource usage on the cloud and manage instances.

Heat is the *Orchestration Component* that supports the definition of cloud resource specifications and enables the management of infrastructure for cloud services (not represented on this figure, as it orchestrates the other services). It orchestrates the multiple composite cloud applications by using either a native Heat Orchestration Template format (based on YAML) or an AWS CloudFormation template format.

API enable the extension and interfacing of core components, as well the integration of user's applications within the cloud operating system.

As OpenStack is designed and developed in a modular fashion. In addition to the core services, optional and typically less mature services are often added. Referred to as "Big Tent," these projects expand an OpenStack cloud and include new functionality. The "Big Tent" includes projects such as the following:

Trove is Database as a Service, designed to run entirely on OpenStack to allow users to quickly and easily utilize the features of a relational or nonrelational database without the burden of handling complex administrative tasks.

Sahara provides a simple means to provision a data-intensive application cluster on top of OpenStack and to define Hadoop [21], Spark [22], and Storm [23] clusters by specifying parameters (such as version, cluster topology, nodes hardware details, etc.) and having Sahara deploy the cluster in a few minutes. Sahara also provides the means to scale an already provisioned cluster by adding or removing worker nodes on demand.

Barbican is designed for the secure storage, provisioning, and management of secrets such as passwords, encryption keys, and X.509 Certificates.

Ironic is the OpenStack Bare Metal Provisioning Program designed to facilitate the provision of physical hardware (as opposed to virtual machines). A bare metal deployment might be needed for—but not limited to—computing tasks that require access to hardware devices which cannot be virtualized.

Manilla is designed to establish a shared file system service for OpenStack that provides coordinated access to shared or distributed file systems across OpenStack Compute instances.

Rally is a benchmarking tool that automates and unifies multinode OpenStack deployment, cloud verification, benchmarking, and profiling.

Congress aims to provide an extensible open-source framework for governance and regulatory compliance across any cloud services (e.g., application, network, compute, and storage) within a dynamic infrastructure. It is a cloud service whose sole responsibility is policy enforcement, and uses a policy language to define its rules.

Designate aims to provide a *DNS-as-a-Service* (DNSaaS) component that integrates with *Keystone* for authentication and includes a framework for integration with *Nova* and *Neutron* notifications (allowing auto-generated DNS records), as well as integration support for PowerDNS and Bind9.

Magnum is a container orchestration engine with an asynchronous API that is compatible with *Keystone*, and with multitenancy implementation. It uses *Heat* to orchestrate an OS image which contains *Docker* [24] or *Kubernetes* [25] and runs that image in either virtual machines or bare metal in a cluster configuration.

Murano introduces an application catalog to OpenStack, enabling application developers and cloud administrators to publish various cloud-ready applications in a categorized catalog.

The Community App Catalog is a collection of ready-to-use applications, Murano packages, Heat templates, and Glance images that can be easily deployed into an OpenStack cloud.

Internally, OpenStack services are composed of several processes. All services have at least one API process, which listens for API requests, preprocesses them, and interacts with other parts of the service. For communication between the processes of one service, a message broker is used. Users can access OpenStack via the web-based user interface implemented by the *dashboard* service, via command-line clients, and via issuing API requests through tools like browser plug-ins or curl.

Those features make OpenStack a stack platform capable of great failover and resilience. They also provides OpenStack with a massively scalable architecture [26]. It is without doubt the most mature stack-based cloud control model. It has the backing of large industry players like Dell, HP, and IBM, alongside a long list of contributors.

3.4.1 Using Docker with OpenStack

Docker [24] allows an operator to package an application, including all of its dependencies, into a standardized unit called a *container* based on multiple *Union File Systems* (UnionFS) that creates layers wrapping everything needed to run. Doing so guarantees that a docker *image* will always run the same, regardless of the host operating system. The *Docker Engine* is the core component of the Docker platform that runs Docker containers. Docker core advantages are that it is

[Lightweight] containers on a single machine share the same operating system kernel, enabling faster start time, and more efficient RAM usage. The UnionFS being a layered file system facilitates the sharing of common files, making disk usage, and reuse more efficient.

[Secure] containers isolate applications from one another, and allow containers to communicate using network services.

Containers differ from Virtual Machines. While the latter need to have every component needed by the guest operating system to run, the former shares the kernel with other containers, running isolated processes on the host operating system's userspace. Using a VM that contains the docker engine will achieve complete isolation and security of containers.

One way to use containers with OpenStack is to rely on its *Magnum* service to make container orchestration engines available, using *Heat* to orchestrate an OS image which contains *Docker* (and *Kubernetes*) that is available only to the tenant that started the component, and can deploy it either on VMs or bare metal. One can also manually create and populate a VM, or use a configuration and deployment management tool (such as Ansible, Puppet, or Chef), or import a specialized *Murano* package from the *OpenStack App Catalog*.

Docker also provides its own tool to facilitate the deployment of Docker Engines on systems. *Docker Machine* is a tool which can create Docker hosts (including on OpenStack) and facilitate their linking in order to create distributed Docker infrastructures [27].

3.4.2 Sahara

Sahara's Elastic Data Processing (EDP) facility allows the execution of data-intensive jobs on virtual clusters. This provides a simple means to provision data processing frameworks (such as Hadoop, Spark, and Storm) on OpenStack. Sahara supports data sources in Swift, HDFS, and Manilla [28]. Sahara also allows the addition or removal of worker nodes on demand to existing clusters. In addition to the API interface, it provides a UI interface that is integrated with the *Horizon* dashboard service.

Sahara provides two types of workflow abstractions:

Cluster Provisioning Where a user specifies the version of Hadoop and the cluster configuration, including cluster size, topology, and other configuration parameters. Sahara will then provision VMs, and install and configure the data processing framework. While using this cluster, the user can scale it by adding or removing nodes as desired. Finally the user can terminate the cluster when it is no longer needed.

Analytics as a Service In this scenario, the user can select one of the predefined elastic data processing framework versions. The next step is job configuration, such as choosing job type, and providing the job script and the input and output data location. Finally, the user submits the job and waits for the results. The provisioning of the cluster and job execution will happen transparently to the user. The cluster will be removed automatically after job completion.

3.4.3 Ironic

Ironic allows for the provision of bare metal machines (without virtualization) [29]. This can provide higher performance by removing the virtualization overhead and offer higher security by limiting the usage to a single tenant; it also allows the use of hardware that does not support virtualization pass-through.

Ironic usually uses IPMI and PXE to control and remotely boot a compute node. OpenStack also supports trusted boot which will check components such as the BIOS, on-board ROMs, and the kernel/ramdisk to make sure that the node requested can be trusted through a verification of its trust chain.

Currently, ironic only works with flat networks. This is an important limitation for bare metal instances as this prevents a correct segregation and limits the networking options with virtualized instances. However, work is underway to extend the Neutron ML2 plugin to support VLAN reconfiguration of the top-of-rack switches. The newly provisioned baremetal machines will be configured to use one or multiple VLANs allowing for a correct network segregation.

4 HETEROGENEOUS COMPUTING IN THE CLOUD

In order to process Big Data workloads efficiently in the cloud, accelerators have become more commonplace. For example, GPUs can provide tremendous speedup for many scientific, image processing, or analytic applications. For example, with BigKernel, a high-performance CPU-GPU communication pipelining for Big Data-Style Applications [30], the authors show an average speedup of $3\times$ on their tested kernels (Kmeans, word count, movie preference prediction, sentiment analysis, sequence mapping, merchants affinity). It is possible to request instances that offer access to an accelerator such as a CUDA GPU, a coprocessor, or even an FPGA.

After presenting a couple of specialized modes, in the next section, we will present a case study for an existing On-Premise Private Cloud infrastructure.

4.1 EXCLUSIVE MODE

Accelerators are not always designed with sharing or virtualization in mind. In most cases, accelerators are provided to the user in an exclusive mode, which mean that the resource (e.g., a GPU) will be completely allocated to that specific user. In that mode, a virtual machine can get complete access to the device through the use of a PCI pass-through; this removes the use of emulated drivers to communicate with the device [31], and often provides the best performance [32] and the best security.

4.2 SHARING MODE

In order to improve the utilization of the often very expensive accelerators, it is important to have the ability for multiple tenants to share a device. gVirtuS [33] and vCUDA [34] use a substitute CUDA library in the guest OS which is responsible for issuing RPC calls to a daemon in the host system;

the daemon allows multiple guests to share a CUDA device efficiently. Nvidia Docker [35] is an effort to containerize GPU applications in order to—among other things—facilitate the ease of deployment, isolate individual accelerators, run across heterogeneous environments, and greatly ease the creation of reproducible builds.

The issue of sharing devices is also presents for network adapters. In order to use a high-performance network interface such as Infiniband across multiple VMs, one can take advantage of Single Root I/O Virtualization (SR-IOV). A physical PCIe interface can create different PCIe virtual functions, each of them having their own PCI Express Requester ID (RID) that the IOMMU and Hyper-V can identify. Different virtual PCI functions are assigned to the VMs and through PCI pass-through, the guest VMs device driver can directly communicate with a PCIe virtual function and take full advantages of hardware features like RDMA, IB verbs, etc. [36].

A hybrid approach developed for GPUs does not use the SR-IOV technology, instead it uses a mediated pass-through approach where VMs have a limited pass-through to the device for performance and privileged operations are mediated in software by the hypervisor. The NVidia Grid VGX and Intel XenGT use this approach [37, 38].

5 CASE STUDY: THE EMS, AN ON-PREMISE PRIVATE CLOUD

The evaluation management system (EMS) is a system designed on top of OpenStack for the NIST (part of the United States' Department of Commerce). NIST's Information Technology Laboratory (ITL) has a long history of collaborating on test and evaluation matters with different agencies. ITL's Information Access Division's Multimodal Information Group (MIG) is a prime example with its evaluations in Speaker Recognition [39], Surveillance Event Detection [40], Multimodal Event Detection [41], Keyword spotting [42], Machine translation [43], etc. MIG has developed efficient methods for ingesting the output of analytic systems for performance evaluations. MIG has also developed validation best practices for system submissions through system performance reporting, and recently, an automatic data-driven scoring server with result sequestration capability, which has been adapted for other evaluation challenges.

One of MIG's evolving challenges in running these evaluations involves the movement of data. When a participant (often a private company, a research institute, or an university) needs to provide results for a given evaluation, it first needs to obtain a copy of the evaluation data so that it is possible to run algorithms on that input. Use of this data is controlled by a user agreement, but its distribution—specifically for video analytic processing where data content and its potential privacy concerns need to be addressed—is becoming more and more difficult as sizes can easily reach hundreds of gigabytes, making these datasets difficult to manage. A corollary is that once evaluation data is made public, its reusability is diminished. The monetary cost of generating reference data from a given evaluation data is high. Therefore, the need to keep this reference data protected in order to allow for multiyear use and general reuse is paramount.

In this effort, MIG is developing a framework to bring the algorithm closer to the data and as such is working toward the Open Science Big Data Analytic Technology Research and Development Model introduced in Fig. 2. At the same time, MIG's effort is also looking to prevent data exfiltration as well as protection of a participant's intellectual property.

The EMS integrates hardware and software components for easy deployment and reconfiguration of computational needs and enables integration of compute- and data-intensive problems within a controlled cloud. The EMS enables the collection of metrics on independently running instances as well as aggregation of overall performance metrics on the core problem. This design allows for testing of different compute paradigms as well as hardware accelerations in order to assess how a given evaluation is best studied. This infrastructure supports the integration of distributed as well as parallelized computations, thus providing a flexible hardware architecture for running projects on the system. Performance metrics for individual applications, their data, network, and memory usages are aggregated in order to compute per-application metrics as well as global project metrics. This enables direct comparisons between different algorithmic approaches for a given project and supports studies of hardware accelerations or compute paradigm shifts.

MIG's EMS team is developing an extendable and reconfigurable research approach for running such evaluations, and employing OpenStack to help to solve this problem. This solution currently relies on a given application being run from a container's image, limiting the network access of the application in order to make it impossible for the application to push data out or to retrieve additional content that was not provided from within its original containers. The host itself is a Linux virtual machine that has network mounts to the source data and a storage pool for the application's temporary files and results. This virtual machine shares the source data as a read-only container volume, and the application-specific data store as a read/write volume. The application's container host virtual machine is run behind a firewalled non-NAT-ed (nonroutable) Virtual Private Network.

The EMS has integrated hardware resources within a private cloud testbed (Gigabit and Infiniband networks, Tesla GPUs, Intel Phi Coprocessors, high memory compute nodes, high storage data nodes) using a local OpenStack deployment. Fig. 11 presents the mapping of the current architectural design.

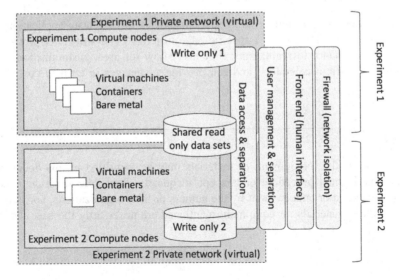

FIG. 11

Evaluation management system (EMS)'s core concept.

The team's framework is built to support in-house technology evaluations and to allow for apples-to-apples benchmarking of a given algorithm against a known set of hardware, with future iterations running on different compute paradigms and hardware facilities, including GPU and Intel Phi High Performance Co-Processors.

Following its Open Science Big Data Analytic Technology Research and Development Model roots and looking at providing some components of a BDaaS solution, the EMS is also the On-Premise infrastructure for a novel Data Science Evaluation (DSE) [44] series run by NIST. The EMS will allow for the DSE to both support systems in a variety of software platforms as well as to support benchmarking of the systems' performances. The EMS's infrastructure will be used to run a custom developed Virtual Machine containing selected Big Data frameworks and aimed at allowing DSE participants to collocate their algorithms with the data hosted by the DSE servers. A wrapper controlling the evaluation procedures and data access will ensure that a participant's algorithm is able to work on provided data sets.

6 CONCLUSION

Cloud computing is essential for Big Data applications; it allows the quick provision and management of resources for computation and storage, at scale. All cloud computing platforms support specific Big Data facilities such as object storage or scalable database.

In this chapter we have seen that a good variety of well-developed and robust open source solutions are available. They offer, on top of the base cloud architecture, many specific components targeting Big Data processing. For example, in OpenStack, one can use Trove to quickly deploy large No-SQL databases, Heat can be used to deploy complex cloud infrastructure composed of different components to create complex analytical pipelines, and Sahara can deploy large Hadoop processing clusters.

Private clouds offer some important additional advantages for Big Data applications (compared to public cloud offerings). They have a specific edge in terms of security and privacy which can greatly simplify conformance to regulations; they also allow for great customization, for example, by the addition of specific accelerators, and can provide advantages in term of cost and improved connectivity.

DISCLAIMER

Certain commercial entities, equipment, or materials may be identified in this document in order to describe an experimental procedure or concept adequately. Such identification is not intended to imply recommendation or endorsement by the authors or their organizations, nor is it intended to imply that the entities, materials, or equipment mentioned are necessarily the best available for the purpose.

REFERENCES

[1] Mell PM, Grance T. The NIST definition of cloud computing. Gaithersburg, MD: National Institute of Standards & Technology; 2011. Technical Report SP 800-145.

[2] Liu F, Tong J, Mao J, Bohn R, Messina J, Badger L, et al. NIST cloud computing reference architecture. Gaithersburg, MD: National Institute of Standards & Technology; 2011. Technical Report SP 500-292.

[3] Amazon web services. https://aws.amazon.com/.

[4] Google cloud platform. https://cloud.google.com/.

[5] Microsoft azure. https://azure.microsoft.com/.

[6] Subashini S, Kavitha V. A survey on security issues in service delivery models of cloud computing. J Netw Comput Appl 2011;34(1):1–11.

[7] Carroll M, Van Der Merwe A, Kotze P. Secure cloud computing: benefits, risks and controls. Information Security South Africa (ISSA). IEEE; 2011. p. 1–9.

[8] Jansen WA. Cloud hooks: security and privacy issues in cloud computing. In: 44th Hawaii international conference on system sciences (HICSS). IEEE; 2011. p. 1–10.

[9] Wen X, Gu G, Li Q, Gao Y, Zhang X. Comparison of open-source cloud management platforms: OpenStack and OpenNebula. In: 9th International Conference on Fuzzy Systems and Knowledge Discovery (FSKD). IEEE; 2012. p. 2457–61.

[10] ebtables firewall tool. http://ebtables.netfilter.org/.

[11] OpenNebula. http://opennebula.org/.

[12] OpenNebula: Open Cloud Reference Architecture. https://support.opennebula.pro/hc/en-us/articles/204210319-Open-Cloud-Reference-Architecture-Rev1-0-20150421.

[13] Toraldo G. OpenNebula 3 cloud computing. Packt Publishing Ltd; 2012.

[14] Eucalyptus. https://www.eucalyptus.com/.

[15] Yadav S. Comparative study on open source software for cloud computing platform: Eucalyptus, OpenStack and OpenNebula. Int J Eng Sci 2013;3(10):51–4.

[16] Nurmi D, Wolski R, Grzegorczyk C, Obertelli G, Soman S, Youseff L, et al. The Eucalyptus open-source cloud-computing system. In: 9th IEEE/ACM international symposium on cluster computing and the grid (CCGRID'09). Washington, DC: IEEE Computer Society; 2009. p. 124–31.

[17] Eucalyptus reference architectures: General Purpose 4.0 large. https://eucalyptus.atlassian.net/wiki/display/EUCA/General+Purpose+4.0+Large.

[18] Java. https://www.oracle.com/java/index.html.

[19] Barkat A, dos Santos A, Ho TTN. OpenStack and CloudStack: open source solutions for building public and private clouds. In: 16th international symposium on symbolic and numeric algorithms for scientific computing (SYNASC); 2014. p. 429–36.

[20] OpenStack. http://www.openstack.org/.

[21] Apache Hadoop. https://hadoop.apache.org/.

[22] Apache Spark. https://spark.apache.org/.

[23] Apache Storm. https://storm.apache.org/.

[24] Docker. https://www.docker.com/.

[25] Google kubernetes containers. http://kubernetes.io/.

[26] Ji C, Li Y, Qiu W, Awada U, Li K. Big data processing in cloud computing environments. In: 12th international symposium on pervasive systems, algorithms and networks (ISPAN). IEEE; 2012. p. 17–23.

[27] Liu D, Zhao L. The research and implementation of cloud computing platform based on Docker. In: 11th international computer conference on wavelet active media technology and information processing (ICC-WAMTIP). IEEE; 2014. p. 475–8.

[28] Corradi A, Foschini L, Pipolo V, Pernafini A. Elastic provisioning of virtual Hadoop clusters in OpenStack-based clouds. In: 2015 IEEE international conference on communication workshop (ICCW); 2015. p. 1914–20.

[29] Rad P, Chronopoulos AT, Lama P, Madduri P, Loader C. Benchmarking Bare Metal cloud servers for HPC applications. In: 2015 IEEE international conference on cloud computing in emerging markets (CCEM); 2015. p. 153–9.

[30] Mokhtari R, Stumm M. BigKernel-high performance CPU-GPU communication pipelining for big data-style applications. In: 28th international IEEE parallel and distributed processing symposium. IEEE; 2014. p. 819–28.

[31] Ravi VT, Becchi M, Agrawal G, Chakradhar S. Supporting GPU sharing in cloud environments with a transparent runtime consolidation framework. In: Proceedings of the 20th international symposium on high performance distributed computing. ACM; 2011. p. 217–28.

[32] Expósito RR, Taboada GL, Ramos S, Touriño J, Doallo R. General-purpose computation on GPUs for high performance cloud computing. Concurr Comput 2013;25(12):1628–42.

[33] Giunta G, Montella R, Agrillo G, Coviello G. A GPGPU transparent virtualization component for high performance computing clouds. In: Euro-Par 2010-parallel processing, 16th international Euro-Par conference, August 31 to September 3, 2010, proceedings, part I. Ischia, Italy: Springer; 2010. p. 379–91.

[34] Shi L, Chen H, Sun J, Li K. vCUDA: GPU-accelerated high-performance computing in virtual machines. IEEE Trans Comput 2012;61(6):804–16.

[35] NVIDIA Docker. https://github.com/NVIDIA/nvidia-docker.

[36] Younge AJ, Fox GC. Advanced virtualization techniques for high performance cloud cyberinfrastructure. In: 14th IEEE/ACM international symposium on cluster, cloud and grid computing (CCGrid). IEEE; 2014. p. 583–6.

[37] Tian K, Dong Y, Cowperthwaite D. A full GPU virtualization solution with mediated pass-through. In: 2014 USENIX annual technical conference (USENIX ATC 14). 2014. p. 121–32.

[38] Maurice C, Neumann C, Heen O, Francillon A. Confidentiality issues on a GPU in a virtualized environment. In: Christin N, Safavi-Naini R, editors. Financial cryptography and data security. Lecture Notes in Computer Science, 437:Springer; 2014. p. 119–35.

[39] NIST Speaker Recognition Evaluation. http://www.nist.gov/itl/iad/mig/sre16.cfm.

[40] NIST TRECVid Surveillance Event Detection Evaluation. http://nist.gov/itl/iad/mig/sed.cfm.

[41] NIST TRECVid Multimedia Event Detection Evaluation. http://nist.gov/itl/iad/mig/med.cfm.

[42] NIST Open Keyword Search Evaluation. https://www.nist.gov/itl/iad/mig/open-keyword-search-evaluation.

[43] NIST Machine Translation Evaluation. http://www.nist.gov/itl/iad/mig/mt.cfm.

[44] NIST Data Science Evaluation Series. http://www.nist.gov/itl/iad/mig/dseval.cfm.

BIG DATA PROCESSING AND MANAGEMENT

EFFICIENT NONLINEAR REGRESSION-BASED COMPRESSION OF BIG SENSING DATA ON CLOUD

Chi Yang, Jinjun Chen

University of Technology Sydney, Broadway, NSW, Australia

ACRONYMS

ANN	artificial neural network
CSMNC	China Strong Motion Network Center
EC	elastic computing
KVM	Kernal virtual machine
LEACH	low energy adaptive clustering hierarchy
PGA	peak ground acceleration
S3	simple storage service
SVR	support vector regression
WSN	wireless sensor network

1 INTRODUCTION

With the fast development of modern science and technology, sensing systems are widely deployed in almost everywhere to benefit everyday life greatly [1,2]. However with the introduction of these sensing systems, new challenges and issues arise. Big data and sensing data are generated with terabyte, petabyte, exabyte, or zettabyte, which offer a direct feeling of big data size [3]. Important challenges come from the big sensing data features including high volume, velocity, variety, veracity, and variability [1,2]. With those five "V" characters, all the data-related manipulations, including storage, filtering, analyzing, and publishing, need to be greatly changed and improved. Due to the great computational power and resources provided by the cloud, it becomes an ideal platform to cope with this challenge of big sensing data. It is well known that the cloud has typical features of flexible stack of massive computing, storage, and software services in a scalable manner to guarantee a low cost, high efficiency, and real-time data services [1,4]. As a result, putting big sensing data processing on the cloud is a popular development trend. Most of current big sensing data processing techniques on the cloud more or less adopt data compression or reduction techniques. However, many problems still exist. For example, how the scalability of the cloud environment can be fully exploited to benefit the big sensing data processing and analysis on the cloud should be further discussed. In addition, in terms of compression technique itself, the special features of big sensing data and the distributed cloud computing model, traditional data compression techniques could not be used directly for big sensing data storage, manipulation, and analysis [4]. Furthermore, the big data compression on cloud has more performance emphases including distributed compression model, good error tolerance, fast real-time compression and decompression. The huge size is one important feature, but not the only one for big data. It can be typically described as the characteristics of five "V"s: volume, velocity, variety, veracity, and variability. Under that theme, big data sets have nearly endless data volume which makes its computation and management exhaust incredible resources. The sources of big data sets are diverse. It means that the format and structure of big data set can change. The data types are far more beyond traditional structured data. The high velocity of big data makes it time sensitive and stream-like. The main challenges of big data processing include capture, recover, storage, search, sharing, analysis, interpretation, and visualization [1,2].

However, previous techniques for compressing big sensing data on the cloud have their own limitation and assumptions for data sets. For example, one data trend-based compression model [5] is suitable for continuous low data rate data sets, while the linear regression model based compression is more powerful to compression high data rate vibrating data sets with a linear relationship. However, in our real-world applications for big sensing data processing, the data generating ratio is getting higher and higher. At the same time, most real-world data sets have more complicated distributions which cannot be accurately described with a data trend or linear regression-based compression model. Based on that specific on-cloud data compression requirement brought by the real-world big sensing data and its inner features, in this chapter, we will propose a scalable nonlinear regression-based approach for efficient compression of big sensing data on the cloud. This research work is motivated by the following real-world data example in Fig. 1.

1.1 MOTIVATION

As shown in Fig. 1A, in a large-scale earthquake event, including the main shock, there were approximately 22,000 aftershocks following the June, 1992 Landers earthquake, California. The high data generating rate earth quake data were sampled in different positions at different time stamps, as shown in Fig. 1A. In each sampling point, there is a data time series as shown in Fig. 1B. It can be observed from in Fig. 1B that even only considering one single time series from the whole deployed earthquake monitoring systems developed in the area described by Fig. 1A, the data changing is pretty bumpy and and it is therefore difficult to use traditional data trends or linear regression model to describe them. For example, the data trend prediction-based compression requires the data generation ratio to be relatively low and the time series does not change violently. However, in the real-world earthquake data example in Fig. 1B, the data trend prediction-based compression will lose most of its opportunity for data compression because the violently changed data will force the prediction model to train the incoming data again and again to guarantee accuracy. When considering the linear regression prediction-based compression approach, a similar problem occurs. This is because under the situation of data set in Fig. 1B, linear regression prediction should frequently calculate the new linear relationship of newly coming data points, which brings lots of computation and time cost. As a result, the compression approach

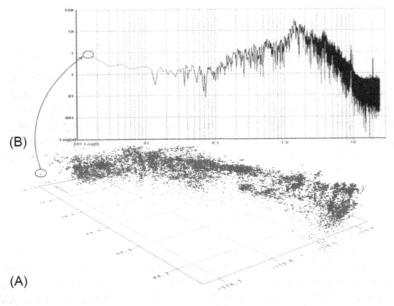

FIG. 1

Motivating example: nonlinear distributed big earthquake sensing data.

may lose its effect. From the above analysis, we find that, if the time series can be better modeled with other relationship which can last a relatively longer period, it will greatly reduce the real data processing required by prediction model training. It means a better data compression performance can be achieved by predicting more. So, in this chapter, we aim to develop a nonlinear prediction model to better approximate the time series in Fig. 1B. In other words, the new prediction model can reduce the frequency for data retraining during the data compression process when encountering big sensing data sets such as earth quake monitoring data sets.

1.2 ORGANIZATION OF THE CHAPTER

The research work in this chapter is organized as follows. In Section 2, we review the related work with the introduction of the related big data compression theory, compression models, data trend prediction, linear regression prediction, and computation approaches for those models. With that, we offer the problem analysis compared to the previous work. In Section 3, a novel big sensing data compression technique based on nonlinear regression model will be proposed to compress high-frequency big sensing data sets such as big sensing data collected by earthquake sensing systems on the cloud. In Section 4, the scalable algorithm for the proposed nonlinear regression based on MapReduce programming model will be offered and analyzed. In Section 5, experiments based on real-world big sensing data are designed on the cloud for testing three performance aspects: compression ratio, time efficiency, and data loss rate. In Section 6, we conclude the work in this chapter.

2 RELATED WORK AND PROBLEM ANALYSIS

In order to process big data sets, different techniques, approaches, and platforms have been designed and developed [6–12]. Whatever the technology is based on, hardware or software, it mainly focuses on three topics: increasing data storage, increasing data processing, and data availability. Data storage has grown significantly with the shift from analog to digital devices in the past 20 years. Similar to storage devices, the computation capability of modern processing devices reaches more than 6.5×1012 million instructions per second. Computation capacity also experienced a sharp increase. Current techniques for big data processing and analysis include classification, parallel computing, distributed computing, cluster analysis, crowd sourcing, regression, spatial analysis, learning, temporal analysis, neural networks, network analysis, optimization, prediction, pattern recognition, data fusion and integration, and visualization.

2.1 RELATED WORK

These current developments offer a solid support for processing of big data in a distributed and paralleled model. Current technologies such as grid and cloud computing all aim to access huge computing power by aggregating multiple resources and offering an integral system view [13]. Among these technologies, cloud computing proves to be a powerful architecture conducted on a large scale, with distributed and paralleled processing for complex computing. Cloud computing [14,15] has offered an approach to abstract and use computing infrastructure. An important aim of cloud computing is to deliver computing as a solution for processing big data, such as large scale, multimedia, and high dimensional data sets. Both big data and cloud computing are the fastest-moving technologies identified in Gartner Inc.'s 2012 Hype Cycle for Emerging Technologies [14,16]. Therefore, cloud computing is a fine answer when talking about big data processing method for different resources.

At present, some work has been done for processing big data with the cloud. For example, Amazon elastic computing cloud (EC2) infrastructure as service is a typical cloud-based distributed system for big data processing. Amazon simple storage service (S3) supports distributed storage. MapReduce [10,11,17] is adopted as a programming model for big data processing over cloud computing. Plenty of recent research has investigated the issues of processing incremental data on cloud. Kienzler et al. [8] designed a "stream-as-you-go" approach to access and process on incremental data for data-intensive cloud applications via a stream-based data management architecture. Bhatotia et al. [18] extended the traditional Hadoop framework [12] to a novel one named Incoop by incorporating several techniques like task partition and a memorization-aware schedule. Olston et al. [9] presented a continuous workflow system called Nova on top of Pig/Hadoop through stateful incremental data processing. Recently, MapReduce has been widely revised from a batch processing framework into a more incremental one to analyze huge-volume incremental data on cloud [11]. MapReduce [19–21] has its disadvantage in terms big data processing over cloud computing. Under the MapReduce programming model for the cloud, a target problem needs to be parallelizable and split into a set of smaller code. Smaller pieces of code are executed in parallel over a cloud computing platform. MapReduce may not be suitable because many iterations are brought for parallel graph processing [22,23]. Firstly, online query support is insufficient. Secondly, graph data cannot be intuitively expressed by MapReduce. Thirdly, each intermediate iteration result of graph data needs to be materialized. The whole graph structure needs to be sent on networks iteration after iteration [23], which incurs huge data movement. That huge amount of intermediate results and data movement may cause time inefficiency, deadlock, errors, and bad performance. Therefore, how to design efficient parallel algorithms for processing big graph data or big streaming graph data becomes an interesting research topic.

Different compression techniques can be widely found in network data processing areas [17,8,18,9,22–27]. Specifically, the work of CAG [24] presented an updated CAG algorithm that forms clusters of nodes with similar values within a given threshold (spatial correlations). The formed clusters remain unchanged as long as the sensor values stay within the given threshold (temporal correlations) over time. With the clustering technique, every time, there is only one sensor data being transmitted, whereas the data aggregation algorithm without clustering requires all nodes to transmit. Low energy adaptive clustering hierarchy ("LEACH") [26] is a TDMA-based MAC protocol which is integrated with clustering and a simple routing protocol in networks systems such as wireless sensor network. LEACH offers an approach to select automatically suitable cluster-heads in terms of energy situation and radio coverage. It solves the technical issues such as topology construction and routing table maintenance. Edara et al. [25] proposed a temporal trend-based time series prediction model which can predict the future data with a small cost in real time. In work [27] proposed by Ail, the spatiotemporal-based clustering and order compression were chosen adaptively for data compression over sensor networks. Except for the above data processing techniques on the cloud, some regression-based techniques are developed for specific data sets with different features. For example, in paper [28], some regression predicting approach is developed to forecast the overdraft of groundwater to provide management strategy support. In Ref. [29], an approach is developed based on spatial-temporal weighted regression techniques for exploring crime events.

2.2 PROBLEM ANALYSIS: REAL-WORLD REQUIREMENTS FOR NONLINEAR REGRESSION

Under the topic of earthquake data processing, regression is a common method adopted for data guessing and predicting. In paper [30], Wenchuan earthquake data set collected by China Strong Motion Network Center (CSMNC) is used. The baseline correction of records was done by CSMNC routinely before the normal processing. There are more than 50 stations with the peak ground acceleration (PGA) larger than 100 gal located within the Longmenshan fault zone. With the collected data, the basic characteristics of the strong ground motions from this earthquake are analyzed with regression models. The attenuation relationships of PGAs from the Wenchuan earthquake are given in this chapter. In addition, shake maps of PGAs are plotted after simulating the PGAs in the near-fault region. The basic characteristics of near-fault ground motion from this event are also summarized. However, the regression model in Ref. [30] is not designed for cloud computing. In paper [31], nonlinear structural identification problems are discussed. Based on the Bouc-Wen model, the paper is generally utilized to simulate a nonlinear structural constitutive characteristic. Specifically, support vector regression (SVR), a promising data processing method, is developed and introduced for versatile-typed structural identification. First, a model selection strategy is utilized to determine the unknown power parameter of the Bouc-Wen model. Meanwhile, optimum SVR parameters are selected automatically, instead of tuning manually. Consequently, the nonlinear structural equation is rewritten in linear form, and is solved by the SVR technique. The paper [32] discussed the problem of predicting PGA with some regression techniques. The probable range of the horizontal component of PGA is predicted as a function of focal depth, earthquake magnitude, and epicentral distance, using an artificial neural network (ANN). Three different ANN architectures (namely Feed Forward, Back Propagation, and Radial Bias Networks) are used to develop the model to decide which model gives a better prediction. In paper [32] an attempt is made to develop a model with the help of ANNs for predicting the probable range for PGA. Thus an attempt is made to replace the traditional methods with faster artificial intelligence techniques. Hence the two different fields, seismology and earthquake engineering, are gelled with the AI techniques for faster and better computational results. Based on the analysis for the above data sets and their related processing techniques, it can be concluded that the earthquake big sensing data has high changing character. In lots of current processing methods, regression can be found. However, these regression techniques have two insufficient aspects or disadvantaged: (1) they poorly support large volume, scalable big data processing with a cloud platform and (2) their focus is on how to predict the future event, but less attention is paid to utilizing the predicting power of regression for data compression. Hence, in the following sections, a novel nonlinear regression-based compression will be developed and introduced.

3 TEMPORAL COMPRESSION MODEL BASED ON NONLINEAR REGRESSION

Based on the previous introduction, we know that the data trend prediction model and linear regression prediction model. Suppose the a data time series $X = \{x_1, x_2, ..., x_i, ..., x_n\}$ represents a data set from a single data source streaming into the cloud for future processing. In each time series, the data distribution is quite discrete where it is difficult to model with data relationship such as data trend. In addition, it may be difficult to find linear relationship or obvious data distribution within a time series.

As shown in Fig. 2, the earthquake monitoring high-frequency data time series can be very bumpy and unpredictable with a traditional data trend model. In addition, if a simple linear regression prediction line is used, most real data is impossible to predict and approximate. In other words, those models lose any effect for compression. Instead of using a simple linear even nonlinear regression line, if the whole time series can be partitioned into continuous sections, in each section, nonlinear regression

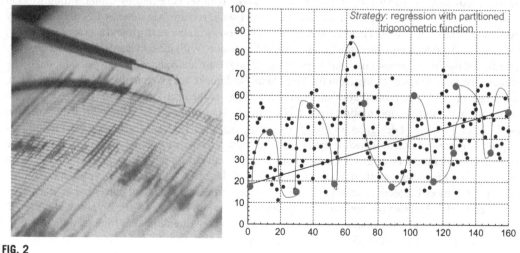

FIG. 2

Nonlinear regression based on partitioned trigonometric function.

should be carried out for calculating data changing and values in both efficient and accurate ways. So, the X will be divided into a group of sections, denoted as $X_{(1,i)}, \ldots X_{(i,j)}, \ldots X_{(k,n)}$, and $X_{(1,i)} \bigcup X_{(i,j)} \bigcup \ldots \bigcup X_{(k,n)}$ is equal to X. With this partitioning, the whole high-frequency data set can be calculated. However, with the above definition, to achieve the compression, three issues should be solved: (1) the nonlinear regression model in each partitioned data section; (2) specific mathematic function and calculation tools adopted in each data section should be offered; and (3) the principle for partitioning each data section of independent nonlinear regression should be proposed. The solutions for these three issues will be offered step by step as follows.

3.1 NONLINEAR REGRESSION PREDICTION MODEL

Due to the complex nature and variety of real-world data, it is very clumsy and inaccurate to use a simple linear relationship to describe the changing and trend of a time series as shown in Fig. 3A. The nonlinear regression modeling should be used to better describe those data as shown by the red curve (dark gray in print versions) in Fig. 3A. Between each two partition blocks, a nonlinear regression function should be calculated for prediction. For example, as shown in Fig. 3B, with the sampled data points from i to $i+l$, some function should be calculated by a nonlinear regression model for inner section prediction. The prediction should be able to approximately simulate the trend of the data points between two red (dark gray in print versions) points as shown in Fig. 3B.

In general, any single variable regression model is to correlate a variable x and a function β, denoted as $Y \approx f(x, \beta)$. It is actually to relate a response Y to a vector of predictor variables $X = (x_1, \ldots, x_k, \ldots, x_n)^T$. Under the theme of nonlinear regression, the function is focused on the fact where the prediction depends on one or more parameters with nonlinear functions. With the limitation of single variable, we can get the nonlinear regression model as the following form.

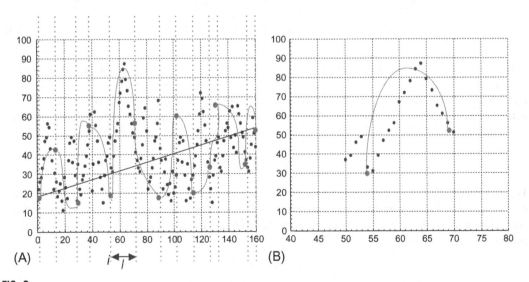

(A)   (B)

FIG. 3

Single independent weighted nonlinear regression.

$$Y_k = f(x_k, \theta) + \varepsilon_k, \quad k = 1, \ldots, n$$

In formula (1), Y_k is a response, f is a function which has known to be with a vector $x_k = (x_{k1}, \ldots, x_{kt})^T$ and its parameter series, denoted as $\theta = (\theta_1, \ldots, \theta_l)^T$. ε_i is used for representing random errors brought by the model. In general, the nonlinear regression models commonly deployed are the exponential decay model, exponential growth model, or logarithmic nonlinear regression model. Firstly, the most often encountered nonlinear regression is exponential decay or growth model, as expressed in Eq. (1). With formula (1), we can further transform and extend it with Fourier transform to benefit our regression process.

$$f(\theta, x) = \theta_1 \exp(-\theta_2 x) \tag{1}$$

The logarithmic regression can be described with Eq. (2) as follows, where c is a certain constant.

$$\frac{\beta f(x, \theta)}{\beta x} = cf(x, \theta) \tag{2}$$

However, the real-world physical processes often need to be model with higher-order differential equations which will result in higher-order exponential function computation models. Specifically, in formula (3), k is the order for the differential equation.

$$f(\theta, x) = \sum_{i=0}^{k-1} \exp(-\theta_{2i+2} x) \times \theta_{2i+1} + \theta_1 \tag{3}$$

Generally speaking, formula (3) is the high-order transformation and extension of formula (1). However, it is short at describing the relational function in terms of regression model application. As a result, formula (4) is used to approximate a large amount of functional shape.

$$f(x, \theta) = \frac{\sum_{i=1}^{k} x^{i-1} \times \theta_i}{1 + \sum_{i=0}^{m-1} x^k \times \theta_{m+k}} \tag{4}$$

Furthermore, the monotonic increasing features in real-world application can be located in variable x, such as time and dosage. Under that theme, nonlinear regression models are also called growth models. Pure exponential models are typical growth models. However, they have short lifetimes due to their mathematic limitations. They are thus often replaced with the following logistic growth curve model in formula (5).

$$f(x, \theta) = \frac{\theta_1}{\theta_2 \exp(-\theta_3 \times x) + 1} \tag{5}$$

The above formula (5), a symmetric growth curve which asymptotes to θ_1 when $x \to \infty$ and to 0 while $x \to -\infty$. In Eq. (5), the parameter θ_2 determines the horizontal position. At the same time, the parameter θ_3 manipulates the steepness. This can be transformed into the Gompertz curve, which generates an asymmetric growth curve as follows (6).

$$f(x, \theta) = \theta_1 \exp[-\theta_2 \exp(-\theta_3 x)] \tag{6}$$

Under the theme of the logistic curve, θ_1 determines the asymptotic upper bound. The parameter θ_2 determines the horizontal position, and the parameter θ_3 controls the steepness. The above set of nonlinear regression models are used for catching data time series curves in our proposed research in terms of data prediction. Finally, the regression process is calculated with nonlinear least square. With the above prediction curves generated by the nonlinear regression, some triangular transform is conducted to improve the prediction accuracy and compression ratio.

To approximate and predict more accurately, unequal weighting methods are developed for processing and predicting time series. Considering the specific requirement of earthquake data sets, three types of weighting approaches are adopted in our work, based on geometric sequence, normal distribution, and Poisson distribution. The system will choose the specific weighting approach for incoming earthquake time series automatically. Due to space limitations, how to achieve the adaptive choice of different weighting methods will not be discussed in detail here. However, the three approaches are adopted including geometric sequence-based weighting, normal distribution-based weighting, and Poisson distribution-based weighting.

4 ALGORITHMS

4.1 ALGORITHM FOR NONLINEAR REGRESSION

Algorithm: Adaptive Nonlinear Regression

input: big sensing data stream $X=\{x_1, x_2, ..., x_n\}$;

prediction error bound e, and user requirement r;

Output: automatically selected non-linear regression model M, and prediction curve $C=\{y_1, y_2, ..., y_n\}$.

(1) 　public void main($X=\{x_1, x_2, ..., x_n\}$, int r, *int e*) throws IOException {

(2) 　　initialize M=null;

(3) 　　initialize(y_1, x_1) 　//$v_1= x_1$ *is used for initializing* y_1;

(4) 　　if(trainingdata(L)==success && f(x,θ)=θ$_1$exp[-θ$_2$exp(-θ$_3$x)] && error.absolute<=e)

(5) 　　　if($r.m$=GeometricSequence)

(6) 　　　　M=m_1;

(7) 　　$$\sum_{k=0}^{\infty} \alpha r^{k} = \lim_{n \to \infty} \frac{\alpha(1-r^{n+1})}{1-r}$$

(8) 　　　if($r.m$=NormalDistribution)

(9) 　　　　M=m_2;

(10) 　　$$w_k = \int_{\frac{3\sigma(k-1)}{m-1}}^{\frac{3\sigma k}{m-1}} \frac{2}{\sigma\sqrt{2\pi}} e^{(-\frac{x^2}{2\sigma^2})}$$

(11) 　　　if($r.m$=PoissonWeighting)

(12) 　　　　M=m_3;

(13) 　　$$\sum \frac{1}{X_0}(X_0 - X_1)$$

(14) 　　Return M;

(15) 　　for (int *round*=1; *round*<=e; *round* ++) {

(16) 　　　*selecting* y_i *to C;*

(17) 　　C(y_i, X){

(18) 　　　for(int i=1;(Distance(y_i, X)<=e)&&length(C)>1;){

(19) 　　　　i--;

(20) 　　　　for(int j=1;j>1;j--){

(21) 　　　　　X=　　;

(22) 　　　　　C(y_i, X);

(23) 　　　　}

(24) 　　　}

(25) 　　}

(26) }

Based on the above compression techniques and scheduling detailed in Section 4, the overall approach for efficient big data processing on the cloud is designed in this section. Specifically, we design related separate algorithms and a roadmap for the proposed spatiotemporal aloud data compressions and afterwards scheduling, which constitute the approach.

Before big sending data compression, adaptive nonlinear regression model will be calculated and calibrated. This data preprocessing normally does not require huge computation resource and power. Therefore, a centralized algorithm is offered first.

In the standard data chunks generation algorithm, there are two important inputs: big sensing data set X and the general application requirement "r" for data processing and error control. The output of this algorithm is an approximate curve data set C, which is a subset of approximate points for the original data set X. As shown in the nonlinear regression algorithm, in line (1), the data exchange time stamp i is counted from 1 to the data exchange application duration, n. Initially, n data items are used for calculating the regression results. In line (2), the variable M is initialized to hold processing modes information. In line (3), y_1 is initialized according to x_1. Line (4) is used for determining the regression conditions. When it is successful, from line (5) to line (13), the different adaptive regression prediction model is activated according to different application requirement brought by the parameter r. Finally, in line (13), the mode information is returned by M in line (14). From line (15), the predicting curve C will be calculated according to a computation approach of least square method. Finally, C is produced.

4.2 NONLINEAR REGRESSION COMPRESSION ALGORITHM BASED ON MAPREDUCE

"Map()" Side Algorithm: Scalable Compression with Non-linear Regression

```
(1)   public static class Mapper extends TableMapper <......,......> {
(2)   public Mapper() {}
(3)   @Override
(4)   public Datatype map(Datatype S={x₁, x₂, ..., xₙ}, Datatype C={y₁, y₂, ..., yₖ}, M)
(5)   throws IOException {
(6)     ImmutableBytesWritable value = null;
(7)     initialize X; // a temporary variable for storing elements from S;
(8)     if(mode.equal(M.m₁))
(9)       Compression.set(S, C.add(GS));
(10)    if(mode.equal(M.m₂))
(11)      Compression.set(S, C.add(ND));
(12)    if(mode.equal(M.m₃))
(13)      Compression.set(S, C.add(PW));
(14)    L=MaxElementSizeof(C); int start=0;
(15)    for( ; S'!=∅; start=start+L){
(16)      X=S'.getlement(start, L);
(17)      for(int j=L; j>0; j-- ){
(18)        S'(C.get(yⱼ), X);
(19)        tag(C.Error<Threshold);
(20)      }
(21)    }
(22)    return S'; // a tagged data set S' for final compression;
(23)    for (int i = 0; i < C.length; i++) {
(24)    try {
(25)      context.write(compressionID,value);
(26)    } catch (InterruptedException e') {
(27)      throw new IOException(e');
(28)    }
(29)  }
(30) }
```

In order to set up the relationship of the reported data and compressed data, the compression algorithm compares the data items from the set S to the calculated data curve C. The scalable compression algorithm based on MapReduce programming model is offered as follows. The algorithm is divided into two components: Mapper side compression algorithm and Reducer side compression algorithm. Firstly, we introduce our Mapper side algorithm. The Mapper side algorithm takes the S and C as its input. The output of the Mapper side algorithm is a data set S which its data element tagged. All the tagged elements are able to be compressed and decompressed based on C. Specifically, the Mapper function is the extension of TableMapper as shown in lines (1) and (2). In line (4), the map() function is initialized and defined. It has S and C as its inputs. Line (5) is the IO exception. From lines (6) and (7), some variables are initialized. From line (8) to line (12), the compression data model is selected and configured. The algorithm from line (8) to line (13) selects the processing model and carries out the main operation for compression. The algorithm from line (14) to line (21), the recursive similarity comparison function, is called again to tag any data element in S to find any $x_i \in S$ which could be compressed. After line (22), the compressed data set S' is returned. The IO exceptions and errors are processed and captured for debugging.

After the processing of map() function of our proposed algorithm, the tagged big data set S should be significantly compressed. The "Reduce()" side scalable compression algorithm extends the TableReducer<> of MapReduce programming model as shown in the algorithm lines (1)–(3). In the algorithmic line (4), the reduce() function is activated. The reduce() function takes tagged big data set, S as its input in line (4). Line (5) is for IO exception. From lines (6) and (7), variable initialization and compression model selection are conducted. From line (8) to line (10), any tagged data element in S is compressed by the compress() function of any element in C. After each function call of compress(), the storage should be updated by a function of update(). The compression path should be indexed for future decompression by a function of index() as show in line (11). In line (14), the combine() function is called for combination. Finally, the consistency of the compressed data is also checked from line (16) to (23).

"Reduce()" Side Algorithm: Scalable Compression with Non-linear Regression

```
(1)    public static class Mapper extends TableReducer <......,......> {
(2)    public Reducer(){}
(3)    @Override
(4)    public void reduce(Datatype S)
(5)    throws IOException {
(6)       ImmutableBytesWritable value = null;
(7)       Compression.set(S, S', C);
(8)       for(int i=0 ; S.getelement.tag()!=∅; i++){
(9)          if(S.getlement(i).tag()!=∅){
(10)            S.getlement(i).compress();
(11)            S.update(storage); S.index(decompression path);
(12)         }
(13)      }
(14)      S'.combine(); S'.consistencycheck();
(15)      return S';
(16)      for (int i = 0; i < S'.length; i++) {
(17)      try {
(18)         context.write(elementID,value);
(19)      } catch (InterruptedException e') {
(20)         throw new IOException(e');
(21)      }
(22)   }
(23) }
```

5 EXPERIMENTS

To verify the effectiveness of the proposed compression based on nonlinear regression model, real-world big earthquake sensing data experiments are designed based on U-Cloud (cloud computing environment at the University of Technology, Sydney) [19–21]. The big sensing data set from earthquake surveillance and monitoring systems is used. Compared to previous big data processing techniques without nonlinear regression models, the evaluation is designed to demonstrate the following gains: (1) the new approach significantly outperforms previous one in terms of cloud resource cost and time cost for data processing and (2) the new approach will not introduce unacceptable data quality loss to most real-world applications for analyzing earth quake data sets.

5.1 EXPERIMENT ENVIRONMENT AND PROCESS

The U-Cloud system is set up as shown in Fig. 4. On top of hardware and a Linux operating system, Kernal virtual machine (KVM) virtualization software is installed for the virtualization of infrastructure and providing unified computing and storage resources. To create virtualized data centers, we install an OpenStack Cloud environment, which is responsible for virtual machine management, resource scheduling, task distribution, and user interaction. Furthermore, Hadoop is installed to facilitate MapReduce computing paradigm and big data processing. In our experiment, there are 100 data collecting nodes are used from earthquake data sources [30] in the real world. The nodes are organized as a hierarchical structure with cluster-head and leaf node. Some data ratio has high frequency. It is a typical heterogeneous big sensing data set. Earthquake shaking and damage are the result of three basic types of elastic waves. In total, there are around 5,000,000 MB data sampled by the whole network. However, due to the heterogeneous features of big earthquake sensing data, some normalization process is taken to filter the original data set.

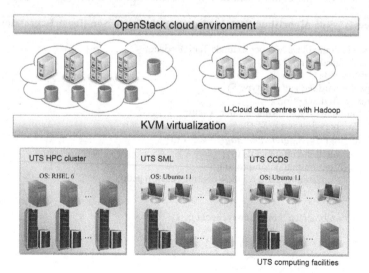

FIG. 4

U-Cloud platform.

5.2 **EXPERIMENT FOR THE COMPRESSION WITH NONLINEAR REGRESSION**

In Fig. 5B, we implemented the compression with linear regression prediction and fed it with the same big earthquake sensing data set. With a total 5,000,000 MB data volume, this compression technique achieves similar compression effect in terms of data size, 100,000 MB. In other words, this experiment results show that the linear regression-based big sensing data compression cannot achieve significant performance gains when encountering earthquake sensing data sets. In Fig. 5C, the proposed nonlinear regression-based compression is implemented and tested. Specifically, around 2,300,000 MB of data from the total 5,000,000 MB testing data are compressed. In other words, 46% of compression ratio can be achieved. It significantly reduced the original data size on the cloud. It will undoubtedly lead to time cost and computation source saving when analyzing the reduced data sets over the cloud platform.

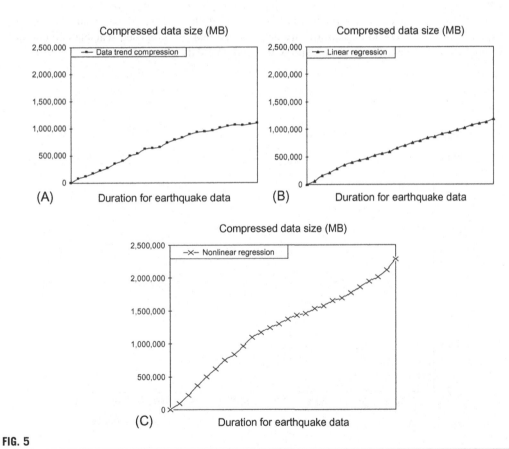

FIG. 5

Compressed data size with different predicting models.

5.3 EXPERIMENT FOR DATA LOSS AND ACCURACY

In Section 5.1, we demonstrated the effectiveness of our nonlinear regression-based compression. However, because the data reduction process of our techniques is not lossless, the accuracy problem is critical to be discussed to guarantee the higher layer data service quality offered to other applications on cloud. In this section the experiment will be conducted to show the accuracy loss and data quality after deploying our data compression over Cloud platform. We aim to prove that under most of applications, our algorithm can achieve efficient big data processing on cloud with acceptable accuracy.

The inaccuracy and error in our proposed compression with nonlinear regression mainly come from regression prediction computation model and compression error bound based processing. The testing results are demonstrated in Fig. 6. Specifically, we use as the parameter L from 10 to 50 data items used for regression to conduct accuracy test. As shown in Fig. 6, with the increase of compression ratio from 0% to 90%, the data accuracy decreases dramatically. In Fig. 6 the larger the L is, better the data accuracy that can be achieved. The reason is that a larger L means more standard data chunks, hence a more refined similarity comparison to guarantee better data accuracy. It can also be observed in Fig. 6 that with larger L, more accurate results can be achieved. It means that the more data units are involved in regression, the more accurate the prediction model is. With the real-world earthquake big sensing data experiments on the U-Cloud platform, we demonstrate that our proposed scalable compression significantly improves data compression ratio with affordable data accuracy loss.

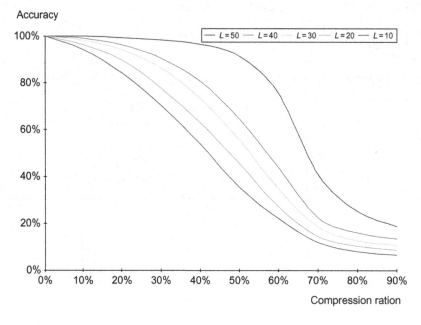

FIG. 6

Fidelity loss with increasing error bounds.

6 CONCLUSIONS AND FUTURE WORK

The cloud promises an ideal platform with massive computation power and storage capacity for processing big data that is of high variety, volume, veracity, and velocity. To reduce the quantity and the processing time of big data sets encountered by the current typical cloud big data processing techniques, in this chapter, by exploring temporal data correlation with a novel nonlinear regression prediction model, scalable data compression was achieved. Specifically, the real-world data sets were compressed according to nonlinear regression-based prediction. During the regression process, some triangular transform and least squares computation were adopted. The output for this novel nonlinear regression model is to generate a prediction curve for compressing big sensing data sets, such as high frequency earthquake data set. The evaluation was conducted over our U-Cloud platform to demonstrate that the proposed compression model could significantly reduce the data size compared to the previous big data processing techniques on the cloud. With the real-world earthquake big sensing data set experiment, the evaluation results also demonstrated that the data processing quality and fidelity loss of our proposed approach met most of the application requirements.

REFERENCES

[1] Tsuchiya S, Sakamoto Y, Tsuchimoto Y, Lee V. Big data processing in cloud environments. FUJITSU Sci Technol J 2012;48(2):159–68.

[2] Ji C, Li Y, Qiu W, Awada U, Li K. Big data processing in cloud environments. In: 2012 international symposium on pervasive systems. Algorithms and Networks; 2012. p. 17–23.

[3] Weiss RR, Zgorski L. Big data: science in the petabyte era. Nature 2008;455(7209):1.

[4] Balancing opportunity and risk in big data, a survey of enterprise priorities and strategies for harnessing big data, http://www.informatica.com/Images/1943_big-data-survey_wp_en_US.pdf [accessed 01.03.13].

[5] Yang C, Zhang X, Liu C, Pei J, Ramamohanarao K, Chen J. A spatiotemporal compression based approach for efficient big data processing on cloud. J Comput Syst Sci 2014;80:563–1583.

[6] Sakr S, Liu A, Batista D, Alomari M. A survey of large scale data management approaches in cloud environments. IEEE Commun Surv Tut 2011;13(3):311–36.

[7] Li B, Mazur E, Diao Y, McGregor A, Shenoy P. A platform for scalable one-pass analytics using MapReduce. In: Proceedings of the ACM SIGMOD international conference on management of data (SIGMOD'11); 2011. p. 985–96.

[8] Kienzler R, Bruggmann R, Ranganathan A, Tatbul N. Stream as you go: the case for incremental data access and processing in the cloud. In: IEEE ICDE international workshop on data management in the cloud (DMC'12); 2012.

[9] Olston C, Chiou G, Chitnis L, Liu F, Han Y, Larsson M, et al. Nova: continuous Pig/Hadoop workflows. In: Proceedings of the ACM SIGMOD international conference on management of data (SIGMOD'11); 2011. p. 1081–90.

[10] Dean J, Ghemawat S. MapReduce: simplified data processing on large clusters. Commun ACM 2008;51 (1):107–13.

[11] Lee KH, Lee YJ, Choi H, Chung YD, Moon B. Parallel data processing with MapReduce: a survey. ACM SIGMOD Rec 2012;40(4):11–20.

[12] Hadoop. http://hadoop.apache.org [accessed 01.03.13].

[13] Wang L, Zhan J, Shi W, Liang Y. In cloud, can scientific communities benefit from the economies of scale? IEEE Trans Parallel Distrib Syst 2012;23(2):296–303.

[14] Armbrust M, Fox A, Griffith R, Joseph AD, Katz R, Konwinski A, et al. A view of cloud computing. Commun ACM 2010;53(4):50–8.

[15] Buyya R, Yeo CS, Venugopal S, Broberg J, Brandic I. Cloud computing and emerging it platforms: vision, hype, and reality for delivering computing as the 5th utility. Futur Gener Comput Syst 2009;25(6):599–616.

[16] Wang L, Von Laszewski G, Younge A, He X, Kunze M, Tao J, et al. Cloud computing: a perspective study. N Gener Comput 2010;28(2):137–46.

[17] Shim K. MapReduce algorithms for big data analysis. In: Proceedings of the VLDB endowment, vol. 5(12); 2012. p. 2016–7.

[18] Bhatotia P, Wieder A, Rodrigues R, Acar UA, Pasquin R. Incoop: MapReduce for incremental computations. In: Proceedings of the 2nd ACM symposium on cloud computing (SoCC'11); 2011. p. 1–14.

[19] Zhang X, Liu C, Nepal S, Chen J. An efficient quasi-identifier index based approach for privacy preservation over incremental data sets on cloud. J Comput Syst Sci (JCSS) 2013;79(5):542–55.

[20] Zhang X, Liu C, Nepal S, Pandey S, Chen J. A privacy leakage upper-bound constraint based approach for cost-effective privacy preserving of intermediate datasets in cloud. IEEE Trans Parallel Distrib Syst 2013;24 (6):1192–202.

[21] Zhang X, Yang C, Liu C, Chen J. A scalable two-phase top-down specialization approach for data anonymization using MapReduce on cloud. IEEE Trans Parallel Distrib Syst 2014;25(2):363–73.

[22] Big data beyond MapReduce: google's big data papers, http://architects.dzone.com/articles/big-data-beyond-mapreduce [accessed 01.03.14].

[23] Managing and mining billion-node garphs, http://kdd2012.sigkdd.org/sites/images/summerschool/Haixun-Wang.pdf [accessed 05.03.14].

[24] Yoon SH, Shahabi C. An experimental study of the effectiveness of clustered aggregation (CAG) leveraging spatial and temporal correlations in wireless sensor networks. ACM Trans Sensor Netw 2005;1–36.

[25] Edara P, Limaye A, Ramamritham K. Asynchronous in-network prediction: efficient aggregation in sensor networks. ACM Trans Sensor Netw 2008;4(4). [article 25].

[26] Handy MJ, Haase M, Timmermann D. An low energy adaptive clustering hierarchy with deterministic cluster-head selection. In: Proceedings of the 4th international workshop on mobile and wireless communications network (MWCN); 2002. p. 368–72.

[27] Ail A, Khelil A, Szczytowski P, Suri N. An adaptive and composite spatio-temporal data compression approach for wireless sensor networks. In: Proceedings of ACM MSWiM'11; 2011. p. 67–76.

[28] Shang RK, Shiu YS, Ma KC. Using geographically weighted regression to explore the spatially varying relationship between land subsidence and groundwater level variations: a case study in the Choshuichi Alluvial Fan, Taiwan. In: 2011 IEEE international conference on spatial data mining and geographical knowledge Services (ICSDM); 2011. p. 21–5.

[29] Yu PH, Lay JG. Exploring non-stationarity of mechanism of crime events with spatial-temporal weighted regression. In: 2011 IEEE international conference on spatial data mining and geographical knowledge services (ICSDM); 2011. p. 106–11.

[30] Yu H, Jiang W, Yang Y, Xie Q, Huang L, Tan P, et al. Data processing and analysis of strong motion records from the Ms.80 Wenchuan, China Earthquake. In: Proceeding of the 15th WCEE; 2012.

[31] Zhang J, Tadanobu S, Susumu L. Non-linear system identification of the versatile-typed structures by a novel signal processing technique. J Earthquake Eng Struct Dyn 2007;36:909–25.

[32] Thomas S, Pillai GN, Pal K, Zuhair M. Prediction of peak ground acceleration (PGA) using artificial neural networks. In: Proceeding of international conference on advances in computer science (AETACS); 2013. p. 270–6.

BIG DATA MANAGEMENT ON WIRELESS SENSOR NETWORKS

5

Chih-Chieh Hung*, Chu-Cheng Hsieh†

Tamkng University, New Taipei City, Taiwan* Slice Technologies Inc., San Mateo, CA, United States†

ACRONYMS

GFS   Google file systems
HDFS   Hadoop distributed file system
RDD   resilient distributed dataset
SQL   structured query language
WSN   wireless sensor network

1 INTRODUCTION

Recent development of various areas of information and communication technologies has contributed to an explosive growth in the volume of data. These data can be analyzed for insights that lead to better decisions and strategic business moves. Amazon Inc. shows us an example that uses data insights to improve business intelligence. The company gained a patent for what it calls anticipatory shipping, a method to start delivering packages even before customers click "buy." This method takes previous orders, product searches, wish lists, shopping-cart contents, returns, and even how long an Internet user's cursor hovers over an item. Analyzing such large-scale, rapid-generated, and various types of data helps Amazon Inc. shorten the delivery time from their hubs to customers, thereby earning great customer satisfactory.

The data sets used in the above example are so-called big data. This term refers to data sets that so large or complex that traditional data processing applications are inadequate. Big data usually has three V characteristics: volume (the quantity of generated and stored data may not be easily handled by conventional databases), velocity (the speed at which the data is generated and processed to meet the demands and challenges that lie in the path of growth and development), and variety (data generated are from multiple sources and in multiple formats). These characteristics of big data bring not only huge opportunities but also huge challenges, including analysis, capture, data curation, search, sharing, storage, transfer, visualization, querying, updating, and so forth.

Thanks to advanced development of big data techniques, these techniques include file systems for big data [e.g., Hadoop distributed file system (HDFS)], noSQL databases (e.g., HBase), data processing models for big data (e.g., MapReduce), streaming techniques for big data (e.g., Storm), query engines (e.g., Impala), big data architecture (e.g., lambda architecture), and so forth. More details will be given in Section 3. Powered by these techniques, including tools and architectures, it is possible for people to collect, store, and analyze big data from diverse sources efficiently. Therefore, people are willing to develop/deploy novel methodologies/devices for collecting data. A wireless sensor network (WSN) is one of the important sources, which can collect data in several kinds of environments easily.

A WSN is composed of small, low-cost, and self-organized sensor nodes. Fig. 1 gives an illustrative example of a WSN. Sensor nodes are able to sense the readings from the environment they deployed, and to communicate with each other within their communication rages in an ad-hoc manner. The readings collected by sensor nodes will relay to "sinks" which can send data outside sensor networks and receive commands from clients and applications. Once the sensor nodes are deployed, sensor nodes could send the sensing readings from the environments to sinks periodically. These characteristics make WSNs a promising solution to collect data in variety of fields, even in areas that people cannot reach easily—for example, in forest areas, battlefields, and volcano areas.

The major challenging issue on the data management in WSNs is energy preservation. Energy preservation means that every computation should reduce energy consumption as much as possible. The energy of sensor nodes is easily exhausted since the sensor nodes are powered by batteries. Once the energy of sensor nodes is exhausted, the whole network is likely to be partitioned into disjoint sub-networks so that some readings cannot be sent to any sink. Decentralization is one of the promising ways to achieve energy preservation, which refers to distributing computation tasks into sensor nodes

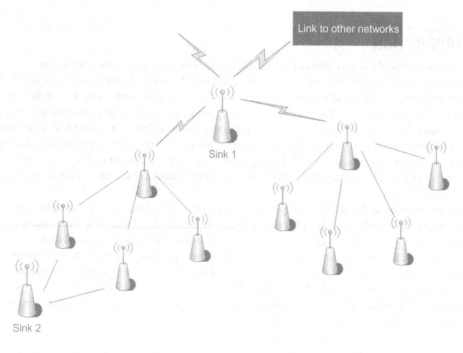

FIG. 1

An illustrative example of wireless sensor networks.

rather than executing them in a centralized way. In a large-scale sensor network, sensor nodes usually relay messages for the others so that the batteries of sensor nodes are easily drained. Communicating with nearby sensor nodes could save more energy of sensor nodes. Therefore, many existing works used this concept to develop their data management approaches.

Decentralization is helpful for energy saving. However, compared to the global approaches, only local information could be obtained in each sensor node in decentralized approaches. Therefore, the design of decentralized algorithms would be more sophisticated, the performance of decentralized algorithms would be limited, and the computation of decentralized algorithms would not be so complicated. Thus, designing data management systems on WSNs in a decentralized way is energy efficient but the complexity of the data management system will be increased significantly. With such constraints and the power of big data technologies, centralization returns and becomes an option when designing the data management system of WSNs. Using big data systems as data management systems for WSNs is reasonable as the readings in WSNs could be viewed as big data since they satisfy the three characteristics: volume (a large amount of sensor nodes may be deployed and keep reporting readings to sinks), velocity (readings are reported in high speed), and variety (heterogeneous sensor nodes may exist in a sensor network). Obviously, there is a trade-off between centralization and decentralization approaches. This chapter will give an overview of both approaches to provide some guidelines to readers when they build a data management system of WSNs.

The rest of this chapter is organized as follows. Section 2 gives an overview of data management on WSNs, including sensors as a database, query processing mechanisms, and data collection approaches. Section 3 introduces state-of-the-art big data tools and frameworks, and concepts. Section 4 demonstrates some successful examples that build high-performance data management systems for WSNs. Section 5 proposes some future directions for whomever may be involved in the relevant research fields of this chapter, i.e., exploiting big data techniques on WSNs. Section 6 concludes the chapter.

2 DATA MANAGEMENT ON WSNs

The purpose of data management in sensor networks is to separate the logical view (name, access, operation) from the physical view of the data. Users and applications need not be concerned about the details of sensor networks, but about the logical structures of queries. From a data management point of view, the data management system of a sensor network can be seen as a distributed database system, but it is different from traditional ones. The data management system of a sensor network organizes and manages perceptible information from the inspected area and answers queries from users or applications. This chapter discusses the methods and techniques of data management in sensor networks, including the difference between data management systems in sensor networks and in traditional distributed database systems, the architecture of a data management system in a sensor network, the data model and the query language, the storing and indexing techniques of sensor data, the operating algorithms, the query processing techniques, and two examples of data management systems in sensor networks: TinyDB and Cougar.

This section introduces three essential components of a data management system: storage, query processing, and data collection. Section 2.1 introduces how the readings are stored among sensor nodes. Section 2.2 gives an overview about query processing mechanisms in WSNs. Section 2.3 describes how data collection could be achieved.

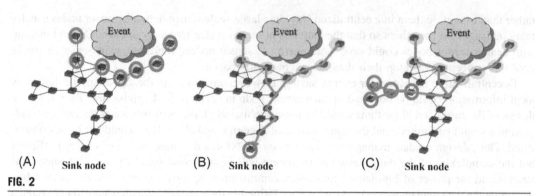

FIG. 2

Data storage approaches. (A) Local storage, (B) external storage, and (C) data-centric storage.

2.1 STORAGE

The first step for data management on WSNs is storage. A naïve approach to store the readings from sensor nodes is to send all the data readings to sinks once a sensor node gets the readings. It is practical in small-scale sensor networks. However, in large-scale WSNs, the large amount of data are generated and relayed by sensor nodes so that the network lifetime will be reduced. The centralized approaches are not practical. To manage such a large amount of data in an energy-efficient way, the decentralized sensor database approaches are usually used for WSNs as one of the most energy-efficient forms of data storage.

The sensor database model views the whole network as a database where each sensor node is the basic unit for storage. The sensor database may be used to store sensor data (the obtained data need to be stored in some way before processing it), to hold the runtime information (e.g., routing tables), and to maintain a history of performance statistics (for performance tuning or debugging).

The widely storage approaches could be categorized into three classes: local storage, external storage, and data-centric storage. Fig. 2 shows three different storage approaches where the cloud-like shape denotes the event, the arrows are the way sensor nodes relaying data, and the circles are the place storing data. *Local storage* refers to the sensor node which measures the physical phenomenon that stores the data. Then, some protocol should be defined in order to allow potential consumers of those data to find and access the nodes where they are stored. The main drawback is the limited memory space of sensor nodes and the local view of storing data. *External storage* refers to the sensor nodes that send back all the readings to sinks, and manage all the data there. The major drawback is mainly from the concern of energy preservation. Data-centric storage mixes the two approaches above together, which defines an event-driven function to decide the sensor nodes where the readings should be sent [1]. That is, relevant data are categorized and named according to their meanings and all data with the same general name will be stored at the same sensor node. Then, when users query the data with a particular name, it can be sent directly to the sensor node that stores those named data.

2.2 QUERY PROCESSING

Query processing in WSNs could be done collaboratively by the server-side and sensor-side. In the server-side, the operation system for sensor networks is executed in the base station, which is responsible for parsing queries, injecting queries into the network, and collecting results as they stream out of the network. Users could submit their queries at the base station. In the sensor-side, the operation system is executed on the sensor nodes, which is responsible for receiving queries, processing queries, communicating, sensing, and sampling.

To provide a user-friendly interface to execute queries, the operation systems for sensor networks usually supports structured query language (SQL)-like query languages. Such languages could describe how users would like data from sensor nodes to be collected, transformed, and aggregated. Note that the query languages usually differ from most significantly from traditional SQL in that its queries are continuous and periodic. The following example gives a declarative query to obtain the sum of light readings from a set of sensors (S1, S2, S3, S4, and S5) every 2 s (i.e., the sampling period is 2 s).

> **SELECT** SUM(light)
> **FROM** S1, S2, S3, S4, S5
> **EPOCH DURATION** PERIOD 2 s

Upon receiving these queries, the sink injects them into the WSN. Routing trees are the most common method of propagating queries and collecting query results from sensor networks, and many routing protocols in various sensor operating systems adopt this approach: the DHV protocol in TinyOS [2], ContikiRPL protocol in Contiki [3], and LiteOS [4]. A routing tree can be viewed as a query tree where the nodes are sensor nodes that participate in the query processing and the edges between nodes represent the routing paths determined by existing routing protocols. Building energy-efficient routing trees with respect to queries, i.e., building routing trees that can minimize the total number of messages of relaying data from sensor nodes to sinks, is an important issue since data transmission are the most costly operation in WSNs.

One of the most popular solutions is to aggregate many messages into one message on their way to sinks. This solution works for some widely used queries, such as MAX, MIN, or SUM,[1] since they can be evaluated inside sensor networks. Fig. 3 shows an illustrative example that the MAX value is going

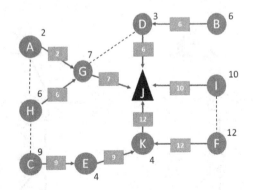

FIG. 3

Executing an aggregation operation MAX.

---

[1]Readers should be aware of that this technique cannot be used in all cases. For some complicated operations, it takes more sophisticated skills to make it work.

to be extracted from this network. The rectangle node denotes the sink in the network. Sensor nodes are in the circle and the number associated with the circle is the reading of this sensor node. The sensor node and the value that a sensor node passes to are represented by the arrowed line and the number associated with the line, respectively. For example, the reading of A is 2 so that A passes 2 to G. G receives the results 2 and 6 from A and H, respectively, and gets its reading 7. In this case, only 7 has to be passed to the next sensor node since the maximum of 2, 6, and 7 is 7. Therefore, G passes 7 to the next node J. This shows the example of using aggregation techniques on MAX operations. Aggregating MAX operations could reduce the total number of messages needed to 10, instead of 17 without aggregation.

In-network aggregate query processing, in which sensor nodes use aggregate operators to reduce the number of messages, thereby conserves energy [5,6]. Similar to the routing tree, a multicast tree is proposed to minimize the transmission cost from a given source to a set of receivers [7–9]. Generally, the solution of finding multicast trees is based on finding Steiner trees, shortest path tree, and so on. Most studies of multicast trees concentrate on how to construct a multicast tree with the minimum communication cost or minimum data-overhead. The authors in Ref. [10] proposed an approach to share the intermediate results among multiple query trees. When multiple aggregate queries are submitted to WSNs, it is possible to generate the intermediate results of these queries. Sharing these intermediate results of queries can further reduce the number of messages involved for these queries. Fig. 4 gives an illustrative example. There are two query trees where Q1 and Q2 are represented as a solid and dashed line, respectively. The grey nodes are data source. Here, the aggregate operation SUM is executed. The number associated with a sensor is the intermediate result at that sensor. Fig. 4A does not share the intermediate results so that the total number of messages for Q1 and Q2 are 5 and 4, respectively, thereby the total number of messages is 9. Fig. 4B shows an example that the intermediate result of S4 can be shared. Therefore, sensor node S7 of Q2 could directly obtain the intermediate result of S4 without accessing readings at S2 and S3. The total number of messages in Fig. 4B can be derived as 7. Compared to the number of messages incurred in Fig. 4A (i.e., 9),

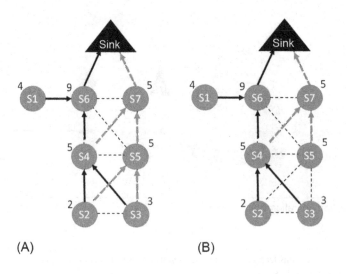

(A)   (B)

FIG. 4

Aggregation technique: sharing routing trees. (A) Without sharing. (B) With sharing.

the reduced number of messages is 2 (i.e., $9-7=2$). Given a set of query trees, it is possible to investigate further how to share intermediate results among queries. In the example in Fig. 4B, Q1 is a backbone and Q2 is a non-backbone. This figure shows that the backbone is performed as usual and non-backbones must adjust their query trees to access the intermediate results of backbones. Clearly, sharing intermediate results among query trees reduces the number of messages involved in multiple queries.

2.3 DATA COLLECTION

Data collection is a fundamental work in WSNs, which could be viewed as a special query to ask sensors to send the information sensed in monitored areas to the sink. The naïve approach for data collection is asking all the sensor nodes reporting the readings to the sink in a given period. Once the number of sensor nodes are huge, this approach may make sensor nodes drain out their batteries easily. To develop energy-saving strategies, some errors from readings collected are usually allowed, since the sensor nodes themselves may have some errors in their measurements. In general, approximate data collection could be roughly realized by probability-based approaches and clustering-based approaches by exploiting the spatiotemporal locality nature of sensor readings.

Probability-based approaches are used to realize approximate data collection with building probabilistic models of sensing readings collected from WSNs [11,12]. The authors in Ref. [12] explored a model-driven architecture, and a centralized probabilistic model was used to estimate the readings of the sensor nodes. Furthermore, the authors in Ref. [11] employed spatial correlation for approximate data collection, where a replicated dynamic probabilistic model is built to predict sensor readings. If the readings are predicted accurately, sensor nodes will not send their readings to the sink, thereby reducing the communication cost. In these works, probabilistic models need to be built and carefully maintained. It is not easy to build appropriate probability models that capture sensed readings fully, because the reading distribution may vary.

Clustering-based approaches are to find some representative nodes which represent a group of sensors so that only representative nodes need to report their readings to the sink. The authors in Ref. [13] derived an extension of a declarative query, termed a snapshot query, for WSNs. Snapshot queries can be answered via a data-driven approach using a linear regression model to predict readings of 1-hop neighbors. The authors in Ref. [14] formulated data gathering into a connected correlation-dominating set problem to select representative nodes. These representative nodes should form a connected subgraph in order to relay sensed data. Thus, the number of selected nodes should be sufficiently large to form a connected correlation-dominating set. The authors in Ref. [15] proposed a centralized algorithm, named EEDC, which partitions sensor nodes based on spatial correlation into disjointed cliques such that sensor nodes in the same clique have similar readings. Furthermore, a round-robin schedule is employed to share the workload of the data collection in each clique. The authors in Ref. [16] proposed a more sophisticated approach to reduce the number of representative nodes based on the fact that one sensor node may represent sensor nodes at a farther distance, rather than only one-hop. Moreover, extending network lifetime should also take remaining energy of sensor nodes into account. According to the concept above, the authors in Ref. [16] modeled selecting representative nodes into a set-cover problem, developed both centralized and distributed algorithms, and proposed the corresponding maintenance mechanisms to dynamically select new representative nodes.

3 BIG DATA TOOLS

In 1969, Edgar F. Codd proposed the famous *relational model* to provide a declarative method for specifying data and queries. Since then, IBM started to build *System R*—a prototype of managing data and allowed users to send a query to retrieve desired information using a standardized query language "SQL." The database management system (DBMS) became a standard of data storage and processing until the 2000s.

Along with the introduction of personal computers and the invention of the Internet, the volume of data are growing so rapidly such that traditional solutions like DBMS are incompetent to satisfy business needs. The term "big data" was then introduced and corresponding ecosystems of big data are developed, contending as well as collaborating with each other to become the new standard.

Most big data systems can be viewed as workflows: an application is represented by a directed graph that chains one job after another. Each job consumes an input data set and output data set. Most of the time, both input and output data sets are immutable. For example, in the Hadoop distributed system, as we shall discuss in Section 3.2.1, jobs are chained by directory names and data are stored to disk.

Despite the fact that expensive I/O operations are expected in such design, the workflow notion is very popular because it has many advantages. (1) Many clients can consume one dataset without affecting each other. (2) Jobs are loosely coupled so that they can be developed in different language and are set to different schedules/priorities. (3) Failure recovery is straightforward—each transition output acts as checking points. (4) Finally, the flow of data processing are easily traceable.

This section will discuss some popular technologies that were developed for the age of big data. We shall start with the data storage, followed by batch data processing, streaming data processing, and end with a discussion on popular architecture design.

3.1 FILE SYSTEM

The foundation of every big data architecture is to find an efficient and reliable way to store a large volume of data for later processing. The two main strategies of dealing with large data are partitioning and replicating: partitioning means cutting sizable data into pieces so they can be stored in different machines; replication means duplicating the data so that a system can achieve fault recovery and augment the throughput. We shall also discuss the idea of caching, which speeds up the data processing through reducing the expensive I/O operations and data transferring across networks.

Apache Hadoop, an open source big data framework, was initiated in 2006, aiming to be a framework for the analysis and transformation for very large data sets. Hadoop consists of seven components where the most obvious ones are a processing component based on the MapReduce paradigm (see Section 3.2.1), and a distributed file system to store data.

Its corresponding storage system, Hadoop distributed file system (HDFS) became a separate project in 2009. HDFS contain two types of nodes: NameNode and DataNode. NameNode record attributes for files and directories like permissions, modification, namespace, and disk quotas, and content are split into large blocks, say 128 MB, into DataNode. Naturally, a client talks to the NameNode to look up its corresponding DataNode locations. Similar to Google file systems (GFS), to achieve fault tolerance, each block has its replica stored in other DataNodes.

Although HDFS and GFS share a lot of commonalities, one of the key difference between GFS and HDFS is the notion of a lease. In HDFS, when a client is permitted to write to the file, no other client can do so. The writing client needs to renew a lease periodically by notifying the NameNode. This design (a lease) allows Hadoop to schedule tasks easily.

The second generation of Hadoop was introduced in late 2012. One of its new key features was YARN (Yet Another Resource Negotiator), a cluster management technology. The fundamental idea is to separate resource management and job scheduling/monitoring. With the help of YARN, Hadoop can easily maintain a multi-tenant environment, with better security controls and better availability.

3.2 BATCH PROCESSING

3.2.1 MapReduce in Hadoop

MapReduce is a programming model for processing and generating large data sets [17]. It contains two main processes: (1) map$(k, v) -> <k', v'>$ and (2) reduce$(k', <v'>*) -> <k', v'>$. The map takes input as key/value pair and produces another intermediate key/value pair. On the other hand, MapReduce is used to aggregate/summarize data—for example, to count the number of words appearing in a document. The map operation breaks content into words:

```
map(String key, String value):
  // key: document identifier
  // value: full text in the document
  for each word w in value:
      Emit Intermediate(w, "1");
```

A reduce operation adds up counts for each word w:

```
reduce(String key, Iterator values):
  // key: a word
  // values: a list of counts
  int result = 0;
  for each v in values:
      result += ParseInt(v);
      Emit(AsString(result));
```

A hidden step in between map and reduce is a shuffle step—redistributing/grouping $<k', v'>*$ by every word w such that the reduce operation above then sums up the total and emits.

MapReduce programs are not guaranteed to be fast or a panacea for every problem. Authors in Ref. [18] concluded that relational databases still have advantages for several scenarios. However, with the release of Apache Hadoop project, one of the most popular frameworks to support the MapReduce paradigm, MapReduce has been extensively adapted to deal with the big data challenge.

3.2.2 RDD in Spark

Probably one of the most promising breakthroughs on data processing would be the project Apache Spark. It was initiated by Matei Zaharia at UC Berkeley's AMPLab in 2009, and later became an open source project in 2010.

One of the main shortcomings of MapReduce is that its data flow overlooks reusability. For most data-centric tasks, to complete a task one must perform many linear data flow: reading data from disk, shredding data into pieces, distributing them among network to conduct a map function to process data, summarizing result in the reduce step, and eventually storing results on a disk. Reading from and then writing to disk are expensive operations that should be avoided when possible, they are even more costly if we have to distribute data into machines across a network.

A new data structure, resilient distributed dataset (RDD), was introduced to greatly "speed up" the process through encouraging data caching and operations grouping. An RDD is a read-only distributed data collection that can be rebuilt if needed. According to research in Ref. [19], Spark can perform 10 times faster than the classical map-reduce system because of the usage of RDDs.

Under the hood, operations are categorized into two types: transformations and actions. Transformations refer to operations that can be further optimized by grouping together. Operations like *map*, *filter*, *sample*, *union*, *intersection*, *groupBy*, etc. fall into this category. For example, assuming a long list of integers are provided, our goal is to divide each number by two, and next to report its square. Two operations are in essence mergeable. A similar concept can be extended to merge operations that require no global knowledge—operations that can be completed in one machine without the need of re-shredding and re-distributing. On the other hand, some operations, such as finding the top N integers, require a global sorting and thus later operations cannot proceed unless the current operation has been summarized. Operations like *reduce*, *collect*, *count*, *first*, *take*, etc. fall into this category.

In Feb. 2014, Spark became a top-level Apache project. In 2015, Spark project has more than 1000 contributors and is now one of the most active open-source projects. Many libraries have been developed on top of Spark, including:

- Spark SQL: allow SQL queries be written against data;
- Spark Streaming: allow user to write streaming jobs the same way you write batch jobs;
- MLlib: implementation of many machine learning algorithms, such as classification and clustering; and
- GraphX: implementation of many graph algorithms, including PageRank, SVD++, etc.

3.3 STREAMING DATA PROCESSING

The classic big data technology, such as Hadoop MapReduce, achieves high throughput of data processing at a cost of having high latency. When data are batch processed, making data available for (near) real-time analysis becomes a challenge. Recalling the steps of MapReduce, shuffling will only start when all map tasks have completed. The wait for shuffling, the scheduling, and the data transferring across nodes all commit to the high latency.

Certain attempts allow the system to reduce its latency. In this section, we are discussing the advances toward real-time analysis, a.k.a. streaming processing. Several real-time/streaming processing systems for big data have been proposed in recent years [20]. The most famous projects include Storm (Twitter), Spark-streaming (Databricks), and Samza (LinkedIn).

3.3.1 Continuous operator model

One of the pioneers of streaming processing is the project Storm. Its initial release was on Sep. 17, 2011, and it became a top-level Apache open-source project in 2014. Storm, MapReduce Online [21], and many streaming databases are often considered to be based on a *continuous operator model* [22]. In the continuous operator model, long-lived, stateful operators process each record and continuously update their internal states, and then send new records out.

Naturally, some operators might malfunction, and to achieve scalability, two common strategies are often used: (1) to have *replication*—two copies of each node are used for processing the same records, and (2) to use upstream backup—rebuild the failed node's state by sending data to the corresponding operator again. The former approach costs two times the hardware, and requires some synchronization protocols like Flux to coordinate; the latter one requires the system to wait when rebuilding the failed node's state through re-running [23].

3.3.2 Discretized stream model

Another stream processing model, *discretized streams* (D-Streams), was introduced in Spark-streaming. The term "D-Streams" comes from the notion of having a never-ending sequence of RDDs. According to the report from Ref. [24], Spark-streaming is at least two times faster than Storm at their study.

Simply put, D-Streams treats streaming as a series of deterministic batch operations, for example, *map*, *reduce*, and *groupBy*, of fixed duration like 1 s or 100 ms. Computations are considered as a set of short, stateless, deterministic tasks, and intermediate states are stored as RDDs (see Section 4.1.3). Since the input data has been chopped into finer granularity, with the help of RDDs, which try to keep data in memory, a sub-second end-to-end latency is attainable.

D-Stream models are stateless and thus recovery can be achieved by *parallel recovery*—when a node fails, other nodes in the same cluster can work in parallel to recompute the missing RDD in that no state information is stored in the failing node. The system may also periodically create state RDDs, say, by replicating every 10th RDD, as checkpoints to speed up the recovery; however, since the lost partitions can be recomputed in any other nodes in parallel, its recovery is often fast. On the contrary, an upstream backup is slow because it depends on a single idle machine to perform the recovery.

4 PUT IT TOGETHER: BIG DATA MANAGEMENT ARCHITECTURE

Until now we have focused on the functions, libraries, and tools that are used for storing and processing data on both WSNs and big data systems. This section will focus on architecture: how to combine pieces into a solution that satisfy user needs.

To achieve the aforementioned properties, *lambda architecture* was proposed in 2013 [25]. One of the authors in Ref. [25], Mr. Marz, is the creator of the Apache Storm project, and during his time working on Twitter, he developed a concept to build Big Data system as a series of layers, consisting of a batch layer, a serving layer, and a speed layer, as shown in Fig. 5.

4.1 BATCH LAYER

Imagine that a user needs to send a query to be answered by the system. One may consider the operation as an equation:

```
query = function (all data)
```

When the size of data are big, to speed up the process, an obvious way is to have some precomputed intermediate stages (views). That is,

```
batch view = function_1 (all data)
query = function_2 (batch view)
```

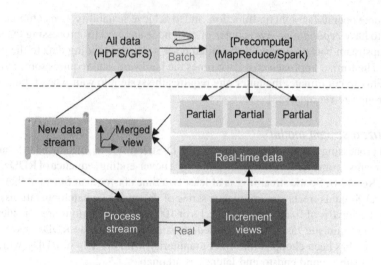

· **FIG. 5**

Lambda architecture.

The batch layer regularly precompute raw data and store output into an immutable, constantly master data set. Batch computations are often simple and straightforward, i.e., acting as a single-thread program, and parallelism comes naturally by consuming only partial input data once at a time—scaling to however many nodes you have available. Eventually, the batch layer produced batch views and these views are then used by the serving layer. In practice, both Hadoop MapReduce and Apache Spark are ideal frameworks to serve as the batch layer.

4.2 SERVING LAYER

The goal of serving layer is to have a framework/application that answers user queries-based views. Since it is usually take a few hours for raw data to be computed, serving queries based on batch views generated from batch layer will be out of data by a few hours. The latency issue can be addressed later by incorporating real-time views generated from speed layer. Cloudera Impala, Elephant DB, and Apache HBase are popular choices for batch-layer output.

4.3 SPEED LAYER

The speed layer aims to reduce the latency by allow arbitrary functions to be computed on the fly based on the incremental data. Instead of accessing the raw data, speed layer updates the real-time views immediately when it receives new data. In practice, stream-processing technologies are often used in this layer, such as Apache Storm, SQLstream, and Apache Spark-streaming.

Every time a batch layer operation is complete, we should discard corresponding pieces in real-time view because they are no longer needed. We can summarize the lambda architecture into the following three formula:

```
batch view = function_1 (all data)
real-time view = function_2(real-time view, new data)
// incremental update
query = function_3 (real-time view, batch view)
```

Note that speed layer require random writes, and thus it is often more vulnerable and complicated, in terms of implementation and operation. If anything goes wrong, one may simply discard the real-time view and in a few hours, the batch layer will help to recover the system into normal state. In practice, not every algorithm can be computed incrementally, and an approximation algorithm is then introduced to get a close answer. For example, HyperLogLog set can be used to compute unique counts [26].

5 BIG DATA MANAGEMENT ON WSNs
5.1 IN-NETWORK AGGREGATION TECHNIQUES AND DATA INTEGRATION COMPONENTS

In-network aggregation is an important concept in both big data management and WSNs. In WSNs, as discussed in Section 2.2, many in-network aggregation approaches are well developed. The main goal is to save more energy for WSNs. The similar functionality exists in the big data systems: data integration components, such as Flume and Kafka, Flume and Kafka are designed to manage data flow, to avoid data explosion, and to unify the data representation. Data integration components usually play a key role in constructing a large-scale system since the incoming data may vary from sources and they may feed in the different destinations. Such systems usually provide data-driven decision and user-defined functions to manipulate data. Therefore, by combining two concepts, it is possible to integrate in-network aggregation techniques in WSNs and data integration components in big data systems.

Authors in Ref. [27] classified the data integration into three categories: complementary, redundant, and cooperative data integration. Fig. 6 shows illustrative examples of these three categories, which

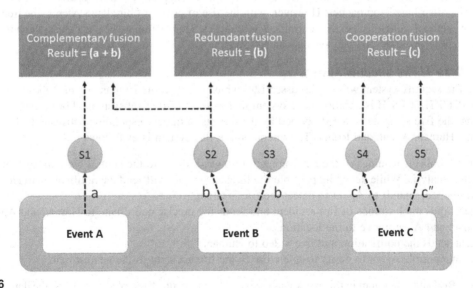

FIG. 6

Three categories of data integration.

are borrowed from Ref. [27]. Complementary data integration is performed when source nodes obtain different pieces of data that need to be fused in order to complete the scene. In the redundant fusion approach, if two source nodes share the same piece of data, the data is first ranked and fused into a high-quality single piece of data. This approach therefore offers trustiness and reliability of sensed data. Cooperative data integration is used when independent sources are fused their data to produce a new piece of data. Cooperative data integration is suitable for the body sensor networks. The killer applications for body sensor networks are human-centric applications like health and sports monitoring. To choose where the data integration modules should be put, one should consider the complexity of the computation needed and the scale of a sensor network. For example, regarding cooperative data integration, the computational power of sensor nodes cannot afford complicated operations but the meaning of readings from different sensor nodes should be checked mutually to make sure the event described by these readings. Moreover, the body sensor networks are usually on a small scale. Therefore, this data integration would be better to put in the big data system (i.e., data integration should be done in a centralized manner).

To conclude, as main sources of big data, exploiting in-network aggregation could prolong the lifetime and contribute to reduction of data volume of the big data, thus accelerating of the values discovery process from this big data. However, the decision where the data integration component is put should be taken the scale of wireless networks and the computational complexity of operations into account.

5.2 EXPLOITING BIG DATA SYSTEMS AS DATA CENTERS

A very popular way to combining WSNs and big data systems is to deploy WSNs as data sources for big data systems and to construct the components of big data systems as a center of data storage and analytics. Interestingly, in early 2000, almost all the centralized approaches were evolved into the corresponding distributed approaches. However, with the rise of power of big data systems, the trend of data management comes back to the centralized approaches. This section gives two cases, which follow this concept to integrate big data systems and WSNs.

5.2.1 Case 1: Fire security system

Here, a fire security system will be discussed [28] which is called the Human Agent Robot Machine Sensor (CFS^2H). CFS^2H is a multi-agent system that consists of five subsystems. For ease of understanding, the five subsystems are described by the objects in the corresponding subsystems: Sensor, BigData, Human, Agent, and Robot. The interaction of this system is as follows:

1. Sensors collects readings of the environment, to send readings to the central big data system for further analysis. While detecting possible fire threats, Sensors will send the notification to Human, and send commands to Agent to detect the fire location.
2. Agent finds the locations of fire accident and sends the precise coordinate to Human and Agent.
3. Human and Agent move to the location.
4. Agent sends the notification and live video to Human.
5. Human controls Agent to direct people close to the fire accident to the nearest exit.

Here, the BigData subsystem in this work was designed to be a centralized place where all the data from all other subsystems could be processed. While every subsystem has to communicate with two or three other subsystems, BigData subsystem has to communicate with all of them. Its main role is to be a central data analyzing and processing station. It should be able to receive and send data to any subsystem. In case of any danger, BigData subsystem has to send warnings and commands to proper subsystems to acknowledge them about it. More specifically, WSN and BigData subsystems establish communication with other subsystems and exchange information without any obstacles. The BigData subsystem stored all the incoming data; received readings from Sensor, query from Human, location and temperature from Agent, location and current state from Agent, and sent current state to Human, and threshold (used to detect fire accidents) to Sensor.

5.2.2 *Case 2: Environment monitoring system*

An air quality monitoring system is discussed here [29]. Authors in Ref. [29] built an environment monitoring system which consists of WSNs to collect the readings of air pollutant, like SO_2, CO, NO_2, and so on, and a big data pipeline to import, process, and store data from sensor nodes.

The whole system is shown in Fig. 7, which is borrowed from Ref. [29]. This system consists of three parts:

1. Data Acquisition Module (DAM): This module includes the sensing-related devices, such as sensor nodes and sinks.
2. Message Oriented Middleware (MOM): This module is responsible for the communication between DAM and DPM. This component transmits the information obtained from the base stations to the processing and storage system, providing independence of operation for both modules. A MOM is a

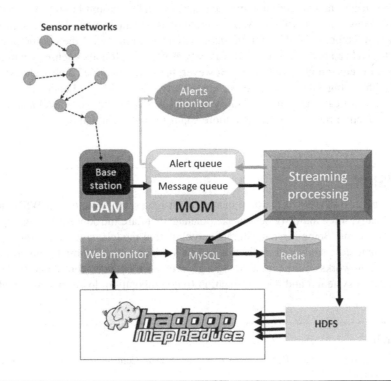

FIG. 7

The architecture of the environment monitoring system.

distributed component that provides asynchronous messaging between applications as well as reliable information delivery mechanisms, guaranteeing the independence of their architectures. This module could be built by message queue systems, such as RabbitMQ or Kafka.

3. Data Processing Module (DPM): This module operates in both streaming processing system and batch processing manners. Stream processing for detecting and sending real-time alarms if necessary, and for computing some statistics, and MapReduce for further data analysis. As mentioned in Section 4, this work also uses Lambda architecture.

Batch processing is executed every 24 h. The data on HDFS are computed by MapReduce to obtain some statistics and some widely used query results, such as mean temperature of each base station per day, min/MAX/avg levels about pollutants, and so on. For stream processing, Storm is used to execute several operations in real-time where each operation could be represented as a spout or a bolt and the relationship among them could be represented as a Storm topology. For example, statistics were computed in three levels of aggregation: sensor, Gateway, and Base station, which are done by SensorStadisticsBolt, GatewayStatisticsBolt, and BaseStatisticsBolt, respectively. Interested readers could refer to Ref. [29] for more detail. In addition to the components for batch processing and stream processing, an in-memory database Redis is used as a cache to store the information of sensor nodes, including identifier, locations, type of sensors, and so on.

To conclude, this work not only consider the big data system as a centralized storage and processing center, but also consider how to combine message queues, and to exploit lambda architecture in their implementation. However, the role of WSNs remains at a data source. These cases told us that a promising way to combine WSNs and big data systems is to move all the computation to the big data system side and keep operations of WSNs as easy as possible. It makes sense because of the computational power of sensor nodes are limited. However, the well-developed approaches in WSNs have not integrated with the big data systems so far. From Section 5.1, one could understand that it may be possible to put some of easy tasks in big data systems in WSNs by the well-developed algorithms. A future research direction may be to design a more sophisticated architecture to do so.

6 CONCLUSION

This chapter gives an overview of the data management issues and solutions in WSNs and big data systems. Specifically, three major issues for data management are introduced: storage, query processing, and data collection. Some big data storage, computation models, and the architecture are introduced. Finally, some case studies of exploiting big data systems for data management on WSNs are discussed. The future works could aim at taking a good balance between centralization (get computation back to big data systems) and decentralization (put computation down to sensor nodes).

REFERENCES

[1] Shenker S, Ratnasamy S, Karp B, Govindan R, Estrin D. Data-Centric storage in sensornets. SIGCOMM Comput Commun Rev 2003;33:137–42.

[2] Dang T, Bulusu N, Chi Feng W, Park S. DHV: A code consistency maintenance protocol for multi-hop wireless sensor networks. In: Proceedings of European conference on wireless sensor networks (EWSN); 2009. p. 327–42.

[3] Tsiftes N, Eriksson J, Dunkels A. Low-power wireless IPv6 routing with ContikiRPL. In: Proceedings of international conference on information processing in sensor networks (IPSN); 2010. p. 406–7.

[4] Cao Q, Abdelzaher TF, Stankovic JA, He T. The LiteOS operating system: Towards Unix-like abstractions for wireless sensor networks. In: Proceedings of international conference on information processing in sensor networks (IPSN); 2008. p. 233–44.

[5] Madden S, Franklin MJ, Hellerstein JM, Hong W. TAG: A tiny aggregation service for ad-hoc sensor networks. In: Proceedings of symposium on operating systems design and implementation; 2002.

[6] Madden S, Franklin MJ, Hellerstein JM, Hong W. TinyDB: An acquisitional query processing system for sensor networks. ACM Trans Database Syst 2005;30(1):122–73.

[7] Mala C, Selvakumar S. Construction of an optimal multicast tree for group communication in a cellular network using genetic algorithm. Comput Commun 2006;29(16):3306–12.

[8] Ruiz PM, Gómez-Skarmeta AF. Approximating optimal multicast trees in wireless multihop networks. In: Proceedings of IEEE symposium on computers and communications (ISCC); 2005. p. 686–91.

[9] Sheu P-R, Chen S-T. A fast and efficient heuristic algorithm for the delay- and delay variation-bounded multicast tree problem. Comput Commun 2002;25(8):825–33.

[10] Hung C-C, Peng W-C. Optimizing in-network aggregate queries in wireless sensor networks for energy saving. Data Knowl Eng 2011;70(7):617–41.

[11] Chu D, Deshpande A, Hellerstein JM, Hong W. Approximate data collection in sensor networks using probabilistic models, In: In Proc. of ICDE; 2006. p. 48–59.

[12] Deshpande A, Guestrin C, Madden S, Hellerstein JM, Hong W. Model-driven data acquisition in sensor networks. In: In Proc. of VLDB; 2004. p. 588–99.

[13] Kotidis Y. Snapshot queries: Towards data-centric sensor networks. In: In Proc. of ICDE; 2005. p. 131–42.

[14] Gupta H, Navda V, Das SR, Chowdhary V. Efficient gathering of correlated data in sensor networks. In: In Proc. of MobiHoc; 2005. p. 402–13.

[15] Liu C, Wu K, Pei J. An energy-efficient data collection framework for wireless sensor networks by exploiting spatiotemporal correlation. IEEE Trans Parallel Distrib Syst 2007;18(7):1010–23.

[16] Hung C-C, Peng W-C, Lee W-C. Energy-aware set-covering approaches for approximate data collection in wireless sensor networks. IEEE Trans Knowl Data Eng 2012;24(11):1993–2007.

[17] Dean J, Ghemawat S. MapReduce: A flexible data processing tool. Commun ACM 2010;53(1):72–7.

[18] Pavlo A, et al. A comparison of approaches to large-scale data analysis. In: Proceedings of the 2009 ACM SIGMOD international conference on management of data. Rhode Island, USA: ACM; 2009.

[19] Zaharia M, et al. Spark: Cluster computing with working sets. HotCloud 2010;10:10.

[20] Liu X, Iftikhar N, Xie X. Survey of real-time processing systems for big data, In: Proceedings of the 18th international database engineering & applications symposium. ACM; 2014.

[21] Condie T, et al. MapReduce online. NSDI 2010;10(4):313–28.

[22] Toshniwal A, et al. Storm@ twitter. In: Proceedings of the 2014 ACM SIGMOD international conference on management of data. Utah, USA: ACM; 2014.

[23] Shah MA, Hellerstein JM, Brewer E. Highly available, fault-tolerant, parallel dataflows. In: Proceedings of the 2004 ACM SIGMOD international conference on management of data. Paris, France: ACM; 2004.

[24] Zaharia M, et al. Discretized streams: Fault-tolerant streaming computation at scale. In: Proceedings of the twenty-fourth ACM symposium on operating systems principles. Pennsylvania, USA: ACM; 2013.

[25] Marz N, Warren J. Big Data: Principles and best practices of scalable realtime data systems. New York, USA: Manning Publications Co; 2015.

[26] Flajolet P, et al. Hyperloglog: The analysis of a near-optimal cardinality estimation algorithm. In: DMTCS proceedings 1; 2008.

[27] Fouad MM, Oweis NE, Gaber T, Ahmed M, Snasel V. Data mining and fusion techniques for WSNs as a source of the big data. In: Proceedings of international conference on communication management and information technology; 2015.

[28] Khaday B, et al. Wireless sensor network and big data in cooperative fire security system using HARMS. In: Proceedings of international conference on automation, robotics, and applications; 2016.

[29] Garcia Rios L, Alberto Incera Diguez J. Big data infrastructure for analyzing data generated by wireless sensor networks. In: Proc. IEEE Big Data Congress; 2014.

GLOSSARY

Big data Data sets that so large or complex that traditional data processing applications are inadequate.

Data collection A special query which asks all the sensor nodes return their readings.

In-network aggregation The process that many messages are merged into one message is executed inside a wireless sensor network.

Lambda architecture A big data architecture consisting of a batch layer, serving layer, and speed layer.

MapReduce A programming model which consists of two main processes: (1) map(k, v) -><k', v'> and (2) reduce(k', <v'>*) -><k', v'>.

Query processing The approach how query plans are made, queries are distributed, and the query results are collected.

Sensor node A device that can sense the readings from the environment they deployed, and to communicate with each other within their communication rages in an ad-hoc manner.

Storage management The approach that decides where the data are stored.

Streaming data processing Processing data in near real-time.

Three-V Volume, velocity, and variety.

Wireless sensor network A network which is composed of small, low-cost, and self-organized sensor nodes.

EXTREME LEARNING MACHINE AND ITS APPLICATIONS IN BIG DATA PROCESSING

6

Cen Chen*, Kenli Li*, Mingxing Duan*, Keqin Li*,†

Hunan University, Changsha, China* State University of New York, New Paltz, NY, United States†

ACRONYMS

ANNs	Artificial neural networks
BP	Backpropagation
CNNs	Convolutional neural networks
DAG	Directed acyclic graph
ELM	Extreme learning machine
FOS-ELM	Forgetting mechanism to OS-ELM
GEP	Generalized eigenvalue problem
H-PMC	Parallel hidden layer output matrix calculation
HDFS	Hadoop distributed file system
LSH	Locality-sensitive hashing
MLP	Multilayer perceptron
OS-ELM	Online sequential ELM
PELM	Parallel ELM for regression based on MapReduce
POS-ELM	Parallel online sequential ELM based on MapReduce
RBF	Radial basis function
RDD	Resilient distributed data set
SAE	Stacked autoencoder
SDA	Stacked autodecoder
SLFNs	Single-hidden layer feedforward neural networks
SS-ELM	Semisupervised extreme learning machine
SVD	Singular value decomposition
SVMs	Support vector machines
Û-PMD	Parallel Û-matrix decomposition
US-ELM	Unsupervised ELM
V-PMD	Parallel V matrix decomposition
W-ELM	Weighted ELM

1 INTRODUCTION

1.1 BACKGROUND

The ELM was first proposed to train Single-hidden Layer Feedforward Neural networks (SLFNs) [1–3], which is an important category of artificial neural networks (ANNs). Later, it was extended to "generalized" SLFNs, which need not be neuron alike [4]. Compared to traditional training algorithms for SLFNs, the hidden layer of ELM needs not to be iteratively tuned. Theoretical studies have shown that even with randomly generated hidden nodes, the ELM maintains the universal approximation capability of SLFNs. Furthermore, with little human intervention and fast training speeds, the ELM shows excellent performance on applications of big data. Recently, lots of improved ELM algorithms have been proposed, such as a basic ELM [2], a random hidden layer feature mapping-based ELM [3], incremental ELM [4, 5], semisupervised learning and unsupervised learning [6], and so on. These algorithms mentioned earlier have been widely applied in many fields such as predicting protein structure, image processing, cancer diagnosis, big data security, and so on.

With the development of information technology, we are surrounded by huge amounts of data. Because of the memory needed for input data sets and the hight time complexity and space complexity of the ELM, traditional ELM algorithms cannot process huge amounts of data effectively. How to achieve valuable needed information from large-scale data has become an important issue [7–9]. Therefore, it is challenging and necessary to process large-scale data sets by the ELM. Fortunately, MapReduce and Spark have recently become the most popular and important platform for big data. Many parallel ELM algorithms based on MapReduce or Spark have been proposed for processing big data, which contributed to the practicability of the ELM in the era of big data.

1.2 ARTIFICIAL NEURAL NETWORKS

Recently, with the rapid development of ANNs, many improved neural networks have been proved, such as the Feedforward Neural Network, Restricted Boltzmann Machine, Convolutional Neural Network (CNN), and so on. These improved networks have been successfully used to solve the practical problems, such as pattern recognition, intelligent robot, automatic control, predictive estimate, biology, and so on.

The ELM is one of the improved ANN algorithms, which shows excellent performance in lots of applications. This section reviews development of ANNs, and describes the theories and the advantages of the ELM compared to other traditional algorithms for training ANNs.

1.2.1 What are artificial neural networks?

ANNs have been motivated by studying the ways human brain works. Many scientists and researchers have found that human brain works in an entirely different way from the conventional digital computer. A neural network is designed to model the way in which brain performs a particular task. ANNs are usually implemented by software on a digital computer. According to Haykin [10], the definition of ANNs is as follows:

A neural network is a massively parallel distributed processor made up of simple processing units that has a natural propensity for storing experiential knowledge and making it available for use. It resembles the brain in two respects:
1. Knowledge is acquired by the network from its environment through a learning process.
2. Interneuron connection strengths, known as synaptic weights, are used to store the acquired knowledge.

The learning algorithms of ANNs are usually used to perform the learning process, the function of which is to get the appropriate synaptic weights of the network to attain a desired objective.

1.2.2 Architecture of a neuron

Neurons are information-processing units which are fundamental elements of ANNs. Fig. 1 shows the basic architecture of a neuron k, which forms the basis for a large family of ANNs. Generally speaking, the model of a neuron contains three basic elements:

1. A set of synapses, each of which is characterized by a synaptic weight of its own, where $x_1, x_2, ..., x_m$ are the input signals. Specifically, a signal x_j at the input of synapse j connected to neuron k is multiplied by the weight w_{kj}: $w_{kj}x_j$.
2. An adder junction for summing the multiplication of input signals and synaptic weights, which constitutes a linear combiner.
3. An activation function for limiting the amplitude range of the output of a neuron. The effect of activation function are to limit the amplitude range of the output signal to some finite value.

In mathematical terms, the neuron k depicted in Fig. 1 can be described by the following equations:

$$u_k = \sum_{j=1}^{m} w_{kj}x_j \tag{1}$$

$$y_k = \varphi(u_k + b_k) \tag{2}$$

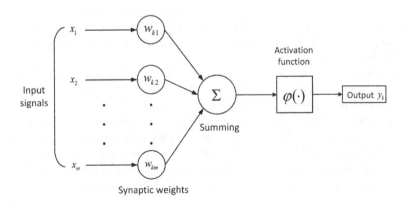

FIG. 1

A basic architecture of a neuron.

where $x_1, x_2, \ldots, x_m$ are the input signals; $w_{k1}, w_{k2}, \ldots, w_{km}$ are the synaptic weights of the neuron k; $\varphi()$ is the activation function; u_k (not shown in Fig. 1) is the linear combiner output for the input signals; b_k is the bias; and y_k is the output signal of the neuron.

1.2.3 Architectures of ANNs

ANNs are constituted by neurons in specific manners, which is linked with the learning algorithms used to train the ANNs. In general, there are three fundamentally different classes of network architectures: Single-layer Feedforward Networks; Multilayer Feedforward Networks; and Recurrent Networks. We can see the details from Haykin [10]. Single-layer Feedforward Networks may be one of the most popular ANNs.

1.3 ERA OF BIG DATA

As we know, with the rapid development of Internet and Internet of Things technologies, recent years have witnessed a surge of data at a fast speed. Due to the development of big data technologies, many decision methods based on traditional experience and intuition have been replaced by data analysis, data mining, and so on [11]. Furthermore, big data plays an important role in predicting and analyzing the problems in many fields such as public health, economics, etc., because the analysis and decision for these fields will depend on huge amounts of data. McKinsey argues that if the healthcare industry in the United States can effectively utilize the data and analyze deeply and efficiently, the cost will be reduced significantly, which will create wealth of about 300 billion dollars for society [12].

In general, industry divides big data into 4V: volume, variety, value, and velocity.

1. *Volume (huge amounts of data)*: From the aspect of data amount, data have reached the PB level (even to ZB level) from the TB level. How to store the huge amounts of data with low cost and manage them effectively are issues that have caused great concern for the information technology industry, while how to analyze massive data quickly and accurately, and get valuable information and knowledge from massive data with data mining or machine learning methods, is becoming an increasingly important and challenging issue in this era of big data.

2. *Variety (multiple data types and sources)*: Various types of data are exploding on the Internet (i.e., text, voice, video, image). As we know, structured data are much easier to be store and analyze with traditional database tools, while other sources (mail, video, microblog, etc.) involve semistructured or unstructured data, reaching 90%, which are difficult to store in a two-dimension relational database.

3. *Value (low-density data value)*: Even in this era of big data, most of the explosive data are not valuable. For example, video files may be more than 1 GB, while only one or two frames are significant. In addition, there are huge amounts of noise data in the Internet, that is, the same report may be republished by diverse webpages, which causes problems for data analysis.

4. *Velocity (fast processing velocity)*: Another feature of big data is its fast growth velocity. For example, the daily trading volume of American stock is up to 7 billion; the monthly visitors of YouTube have reached 800 million and upload almost an hour's worth of videos every second; and more than 100 million micro-blogs are published on Sina WEIBO everyday.

In conclusion, the features of big data are summarized as four dimensional: huge amounts of data, wide-ranging data types, sparse density of data values, and data increasing at a fast rate. Though the era of big data brings many opportunities and conveniences for many fields, all of them will challenge us with many aspects such as data capture, storage, management, and analysis, especially for data mining, and machine learning.

1.4 ORGANIZATION

The contents of this chapter are as follows: Section 2 reviews the traditional extreme learning machine (ELM) and some variants. Section 3 illustrates the shortcomings of the traditional ELM algorithm and the improvements of the ELM for big data. Section 4 shows some representative applications of the ELM such as bioinformatics, image processing, disease prediction, and so on.

2 EXTREME LEARNING MACHINE

2.1 TRADITIONAL APPROACHES TO TRAIN ANNs

As discussed in Section 1, Feedforward Networks may be one of the most popular type of ANNs architectures. A Feedforward Network consists of three basic layers: one input layer, one or multihidden layers, and one output layer. The stimulation from external environments is received by the input layer, while the output of the neural network is sent by the output layer. There are three main approaches usually used in training Feedforward Networks [13]:

1. The backpropagation (BP) method is proposed by Rumelhart et al. [14] based on gradient-descent for Multilayer Feedforward Networks. Additive type of hidden nodes are most often used in such networks. For additive hidden nodes with the activation function $g(x): R \to R$ (e.g., sigmoid: $g(x) = 1/(1 + \exp(-x))$), the output function of the ith node in the lth hidden layer is given by $g(a_i^l, b_i^l, x^l) = g(a_i^l \times x^l + b_i^l), b_i^l \in R$, where a_i^l is the weight vector connecting the $(l-1)$th layer to the ith node of the lth layer and b_i^l is the bias of the ith node of the lth layer. $a_i^l \times x^l$ denotes the inner product of vectors a_i^l and x^l: gradient-descent-based learning algorithms usually run much slower than expected.

2. Support vector machines (SVMs) are proposed by Cortes and Vapnik [15] based on standard optimization methods for a specific type of SLFNs. Rosenblatt investigated perceptrons (Multilayer Feedforward Neural Networks) half a century ago, and suggested a learning mechanism that only adjusted the weights of the connections from the last hidden layer to the output layer [16]. The rest weights fixed the input data are actually transformed into a feature space Z of the last hidden layer as Fig. 2. In this feature space a linear decision function is constructed:

   $f(x) = sign\left(\sum_{i=1}^{l} \beta_i z_i(x)\right)$, where β_i is the output weight between the output node and the ith neuron in the last hidden layer of a perceptron, and z_i is the output of the ith neuron in the last hidden layer of the perceptron. In order to find an alternative solution of z_i, Cortes and Vapnik [15] proposed the SVM, which maps the data from the input space to some high dimensional feature space Z through some nonlinear mapping chosen a priori. Optimization methods are used to find the separating hyperplane, which maximizes the separating margins of two different classes in the feature space.

3. Radial basis function (RBF) network learning is proposed by Lowe [17] based on least-square. For RBF hidden node with activation function $g(x): R \to R$ (e.g., Gaussian: $g(x) = \exp(-x^2)$), $G(a_i, b_i, x)$ is given by $G(a_i, b_i, x) = g(b_i \| x - a_i \|), b_i \in R^+$, where a_i and a_i are the center and impact factor of the ith RBF hidden node. R^+ indicates the set of all positive real values. The RBF network is a

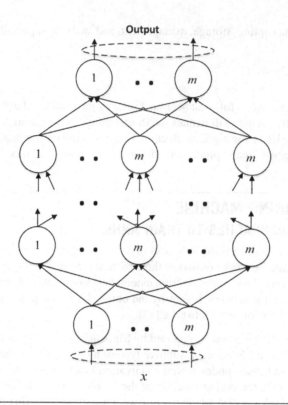

FIG. 2

Multilayer feedforward networks.

special case of SLFNs with RBF nodes in its hidden layer (Fig. 3). Each RBF node has its own centroid and impact factor, and its output is given by a radially symmetric function of the distance between the input and the center. In Lowe's RBF network implementation [17], the centers a_i of RBF hidden nodes can be randomly selected from the training data or from the region of training data instead of tuning, and all the impact factors b_i of RBF hidden nodes are usually set with the same value of Lowe [17]. After RBF hidden nodes parameters (a_i, b_i) fixed, the output weight vector b_i linking the ith RBF hidden node to the output layer becomes the only unknown parameter which can be resolved by the least-square method.

The ELM was originally proposed for the SLFNs [1–3]. In recent years, thanks to the efforts of different scholars and researchers, the ELM algorithm has been continuously developed and extended to the "generalized" SLFNs [4, 5]. Unlike traditional learning algorithms, the original aim of the ELM is to get better generalization performance by reaching both the smallest training error and the smallest norm of output weights. According to the neural network theory of Bartlett [18], for feedforward neural networks, the smaller the norm of weights is, the better generalization performance the networks tend to have. Furthermore, the hidden layer of SLFNs need not be tuned. The parameters of the hidden layer are usually generated randomly. Since in the ELM the hidden layer need not be tuned and the hidden layer parameters can be fixed, the output weights can then be resolved using the lease-square method [13].

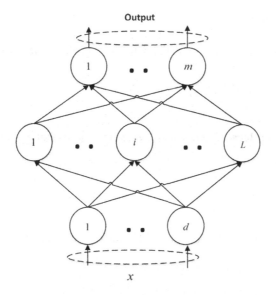

FIG. 3

Single-hidden layer feedforward networks.

2.2 THEORIES OF THE EXTREME LEARNING MACHINE

This section reviews the theories related to the ELM, including the interpolation theory and universal approximation capability of the ELM. The output function of SLFNs with l hidden nodes can be represented by:

$$f_l(x) = \sum_{i=1}^{l} \beta_i g_i(x) = \sum_{i=1}^{l} \beta_i G(a_i, b_i, x), \quad x \in R^d, \ \beta_i \in R^m \tag{3}$$

where β_i denotes the output weight of the ith hidden node; $G(a_i, b_i, x)$ denotes the output function of the ith hidden node; m is the dimension of the output label. For additive nodes with activation function g, g_i is defined as:

$$g_i = G(a_i, b_i, x) = g(a_i \times x + b_i), \quad a_i \in R^d, \ b_i \in R^m \tag{4}$$

The nonlinear mapping functions in ELM can be any nonlinear piecewise continuous functions, while the most popular functions used in ELM is Sigmoid function (Eq. 5) and Gaussian function (Eq. 6).

$$G(a, b, x) = \frac{1}{1 + \exp(-(a \times x + b))} \tag{5}$$

$$G(a, b, x) = \exp(-b \| x - a \|) \tag{6}$$

2.2.1 Interpolation theory

The interpolation capability is investigated by Huang [3–5]. For N arbitrary distinct samples $(x_i, t_i) \in R^d \times R^m$, SLFNs with l hidden nodes are mathematically modeled as follows:

$$\sum_{i=1}^{l} \beta_i G(a_i, b_i, x_j) = o_j, \quad j = 1, \ldots, N \tag{7}$$

That SLFNs can approximate these N samples with zero error means that $\sum_{j=1}^{l} \| o_j - t_j \| = 0$, there exist (a_i, b_i) and β_i such that:

$$\sum_{i=1}^{l} \beta_i G(a_i, b_i, x_j) = t_j, \quad j = 1, \ldots, N \tag{8}$$

where t_j means the actual label corresponding to the input x_j. The above N equations can be written compactly as:

$$H\beta = T \tag{9}$$

$$H = \begin{bmatrix} h(x_1) \\ \vdots \\ h(x_N) \end{bmatrix} = \begin{bmatrix} G(a_1, b_1, x_1) & \cdots & G(a_l, b_l, x_1) \\ \vdots & \vdots & \vdots \\ G(a_1, b_1, x_N) & \cdots & G(a_l, b_l, x_N) \end{bmatrix}_{N \times l}$$

$$\beta = \begin{bmatrix} \beta_1^T \\ \vdots \\ \beta_l^T \end{bmatrix}_{l \times m} \quad T = \begin{bmatrix} t_1^T \\ \vdots \\ t_h^T \end{bmatrix}_{N \times m} \tag{10}$$

where H is called the hidden layer output matrix of the SLFNs [19, 20]; the ith column of H is the ith hidden node output with respect to inputs $x_1, x_2, \ldots, x_N$; $h(x) = G(a_1, b_1, x_1) \cdots G(a_l, b_l, x_l)$ is called the hidden node feature mapping; the ith row of H is the hidden layer feature mapping with respect to the ith input x_i.

Theorem 1 (Huang et al. [2]). *Given any small positive value $\varepsilon > 0$, activation function $g(x)$: $R \to R$ which is infinitely differentiable in any interval, and N arbitrary distinct samples $(x_i, t_i) \in R^d \times R^m$, there exists $l \leq N$ such that for any $\{a_i, b_i\}_{i=1}^{l}$ randomly generated from any intervals of in $R^d \times R^m$, according to any continuous probability distribution, with probability one, $\| H_{N \times l} \beta_{l \times m} - T_{N \times m} \| < \varepsilon$.*

It has been proved by Theorem 1 that for any given data samples, there exists an ELM network that gives sufficient small training error with probability one, when the number of hidden neurons is no larger than the number of distinct training samples [21]. Actually, if the number of hidden neurons is equal to the number of distinct training samples, then with probability one, the training error decreases to zero. Therefore, from the interpolation view, the ELM can fit perfectly to any training set if the number of hidden neurons is large enough. It has also been proved by Huang et al. [2] that from the interpolation capability point of view, if the activation function g is infinitely differentiable in any interval the hidden layer parameters can be randomly generated.

2.2.2 Universal approximation capability

During the past decades, many researchers have studied the universal approximation capability of SLFNs deeply [22, 23]. It is usually assumed that the activation function of the hidden neurons is continuous and differentiable, and the parameters of hidden neurons need to be adjusted during training. However, in the ELM learning paradigm, the hidden layer parameters are randomly generated instead of being trained. However, Huang [4, 5] proved that even with a randomly generated hidden layer, the ELM is still a universal learner.

Theorem 2. *[Huang [3, 4]] Given any nonconstant piecewise continuous function $G: R^d \to R$, if span $\{G(a, b, x): (a, b) \in R^d \times R\}$ is dense in l^2, for any continuous target function f and any function sequence $\{G(a_i, b_i, x)\}_{i=1}^l$ randomly generated according to any continuous sampling distribution, $\lim_{l \to \infty} \|f - f_l\| = 0$ holds with probability one if the output weights β_i are determined by ordinary least square to minimize $\|f(x) - \sum_{i=1}^l \beta_i G(a_i, b_i, x)\|$.*

From Theorem 2, we see that most commonly used activation functions satisfy the conditions that guarantee the universal approximation capability of the ELM. Note that Theorem 2 does not require the activation functions to be continuous or differentiable, thus the threshold function and many other activation function can be used in the ELM. Following the property that the ELM can approximate any continuous target function, it is not difficult to show that ELM can learn arbitrary decision hyperplane for classification tasks, as stated by the following theorem.

Theorem 3 (Huang et al. [24]). *Given any feature mapping $h(x)$, if $h(x)$ is dense in $C(R^d)$ or in $C(\Omega)$, where $C(\Omega)$ is a compact set of R^d, then a generalized SLFNs with such a random hidden layer mapping $h(x)$ can separate arbitrary disjoint regions of any shapes in R^d or Ω.*

Basically, Theorem 3 proves that ELM can approximate any complex decision boundary for classification if the number of hidden nodes is large enough.

2.3 CLASSICAL ELM

2.3.1 Basic ELM

As discussed earlier, the ELM was proposed for "generalized" SLFNs [1] where the hidden layer need not be neuron alike. The output function of ELM for generalized SLFNs is shown in Eq. (11).

$$f_l(x) = \sum_{i=1}^l \beta_i h_i(x) = h(x)\beta \tag{11}$$

Basically, there are two main stages for ELM training process: (1) random feature mapping and (2) linear parameters solving.

1. In the first stage, the hidden layer is randomly initialized to map the input data into a feature space (called the ELM feature space) by some nonlinear mapping functions. Unlike other existing machine learning algorithms such as SVM, which utilizes kernel functions for feature mapping, or deep neural networks which uses Auto-Encoders/Auto-Decoder or Restricted Boltzmann machines (RBM) for feature mapping, ELM uses this random feature mapping. The random generation of the hidden node parameters (a, b) make the ELM more efficient than the traditional BP algorithm.

2. In the second stage, the weights connecting the hidden layer and the output layer, denoted by β, are solved by minimizing the approximation error in the squared error sense:

$$\min \| H\beta - T \|^2 \tag{12}$$

The smallest norm least-squares solution of the above linear system is

$$\beta^* = H^\dagger T \tag{13}$$

where $\|\cdot\|$ denotes the Frobenius norm, $H^\dagger$ is the Moore-Penrose generalized inverse of matrix H.

Thus, the ELM can be summarized in Algorithm 1.

Different methods such as orthogonal projection method, orthogonalization method, iterative method, and singular value decomposition (SVD) can be used to calculate the Moore-Penrose generalized inverse of a matrix.

ALGORITHM 1 ELM OVERVIEW

Require: The training data sets: $\{(x_i, t_i) | x_i \in R^d, t_i \in R^m, i = 1, ..., N\}$;
       Hidden node output function: $G(a_i, b_i, x)$, and the number of hidden nodes: l;
Ensure: The output weight vector: β;
1: Randomly generate hidden node parameters (a_i, b_i), $i = 1, ..., l$;
2: Calculate the hidden layer output matrix H;
3: Calculate the output weight matrix $\beta = H^\dagger$;
4: **return** β.

2.3.2 Essences of the ELM

From the learning point of view, the original aim of ELM [1, 2, 25] is to satisfy several salient targets simultaneously compared with other traditional learning algorithms [14, 26, 27]:

1. *Generalization performance*: The basic goal of the ELM is to reach better generalization performance through getting both the smallest training error and the norm of output weights, that is to minimize

$$\| \beta \|_p^{\sigma_1} + C \| H\beta - T \|_q^{\sigma_2} \tag{14}$$

where $\sigma_1 > 0, \sigma_2 > 0, p, q = 0, \frac{1}{2}, 1, 2, ...$ The first term in the objective function is a regularization term which controls the complexity of the learned model.

2. *Universal approximation capability*: The hidden layer feature mapping need to satisfy the universal approximation capability [13].

3. *Learning without "iteratively tuning" hidden nodes*: ELM theories believe that the hidden layer of the ELM need not be iteratively tuned and the parameters of the hidden layer can be generated randomly.

2.4 ELM FOR CLASSIFICATION AND REGRESSION

This section reviews various improvements and extensions of the classical ELM for classification and regression problems.

2.4.1 Improving stability and compactness of the ELM

How to obtain the output weights is a key step in the ELM. Essentially, this step is equal to solving a (regularized) least squares problem or ridge regression, where an $N \times N$ or $L \times L$ matrix should be inverted [21]. A proper ridge magnitude is usually set to ensure positive definiteness of the matrix to be inverted. However, this method will sacrifice the training accuracy of the ELM. Wang et al. [28] proved that for certain activation functions, such as the RBF function, there always exist input weights such that the mapping matrix H is of full column rank or of full row rank. Then, an efficient input weights selection algorithm is proposed to replace the random feature mapping in the ELM, which improves the stability of the ELM.

As the theories of the ELM mentioned earlier, the parameters of hidden nodes are randomly generated, therefore many hidden neurons are required to achieve matched performance. Because of the large network size of the ELM, its training phase requires a long time. One method is to grow, prune, or replace hidden neurons dynamically during the training process. Huang and Chen [4, 5] proposed an incremental ELM (I-ELM) algorithm, whose main idea is to select new and appropriate hidden nodes from a candidate pool. Therefore, the obtained network can be more compact by getting rid of inappropriate hidden nodes. Later, Feng et al. [29] proposed an efficient incremental ELM called error minimized ELM (EM-ELM) which can add hidden neurons one by one, or group by group. Moreover, a fast incremental ELM called bidirectional ELM (B-ELM) was proposed to reduce the network size of ELM [30]. In pruning ELM (P-ELM) [31], an initial network is built using a traditional ELM; then those hidden neurons with less contribution to the training performance are removed.

2.4.2 ELM for imbalanced data

In some cases, the number of training samples in some classes are much larger than that of other classes. There are also cases where each data point is associated with a unique cost or an importance coefficient. That is to say, in some cases, the data samples are imbalanced. Zong et al. [32] proposed the weighted ELM (W-ELM) to deal with the imbalanced data problem. The W-ELM reweights the training data by adding different penalty coefficients to the training errors corresponding to different inputs. This feature is different from the classical ELM, which treats all training data points equally.

$$\min \left(\frac{1}{2} \|\beta\|^2 + \frac{1}{2} \sum_{i=1}^{N} C_i \|e_i\|^2 \right), \quad \beta \in R^{l \times m} \tag{15}$$

$$\text{s.t.} \quad h(x_i)\beta = t_i^T - e_i^T, \quad i = 1, \dots, N$$

where C_i is the penalty coefficient corresponding to the ith training point.

$$\min \left(\frac{1}{2} \|\beta\|^2 + \frac{1}{2} (T - H\beta)^T C (T - H\beta) \right), \quad \beta \in R^{l \times m} \tag{16}$$

where C is a diagonal matrix whose diagonal elements are $C_1, \dots, C_N$. By setting the gradient to zero, we obtain the closed form solution to β:

$$\beta = \begin{cases} (H^T C H + I)^{-1} H^T C T, & l \leq N \\ H^T (C H H^T + I)^{-1} C T, & l \geq N \end{cases} \tag{17}$$

2.4.3 ELM for semisupervised learning

Semisupervised learning, a learning method that combines supervised learning and unsupervised learning, is a major problem in model identification and machine learning. Semisupervised learning has tremendous practical value. In many tasks, there is a paucity of labeled data. The labels may be difficult to obtain because they require human annotators, special devices, or expensive and slow experiments especially for big data. Furthermore, semisupervised learning is attractive because it can potentially utilize both labeled and unlabeled data to achieve better performance than supervised learning. Semisupervised learning assumes that both labeled and unlabeled data conform to uniform probability distribution. Viewed from this perspective, unlabeled data provide useful information for data learning.

Although the ELM algorithm can be applied in many areas, it is primarily used in the field of supervised learning, such as regression analysis and classification, which greatly restricts the utility of the ELM algorithm. In order to solve the problem, the semisupervised ELM integrates manifold regularization into ELM to extend ELM to the area of semisupervised learning [6].

Suppose that there are labeled data samples $(x_i, t_i)_{i=1}^{l}, x \in R^d, t_i \in R^m$ and unlabeled samples $(x_i)_{i=1}^{u}, x \in R^d$. The SS-ELM algorithm can be described as:

$$\beta = \begin{cases} (I_h + H^T CH + \lambda H^T LH)^{-1} H^T C \tilde{T}, & l \leq N \\ H^T (I_{l+u} + CHH^T + \lambda LHH^T)^{-1} C \tilde{T}, & l \geq N \end{cases} \tag{18}$$

where l represents the number of hidden nodes; N is the number of data samples; H refers to the output matrix of nodes at the hidden layer; L is Laplace matrix whose calculation method is $L = D - S$; S refers to the adjacent matrix of the input data; and S_{ij} refers to the similarity between the input node i and j, which can be expressed using the Gaussian function:

$$S_{ij} = \exp\left(-\frac{\|x_i - x_j\|^2}{2\sigma^2}\right) \tag{19}$$

D is a diagonal matrix whose element is $D_{ii} = \sum_{j=1}^{l+u} S_{i,j}$. We can normalize L in accordance with the formula $D^{-(1/2)} L D^{-(1/2)}$. The calculation of Laplace matrix is given in the following formula:

$$L = I - D^{-(1/2)} S D^{-(1/2)} \tag{20}$$

The process of the SS-ELM algorithm based on Gao Huang's paper [6] is in Algorithm 2.

ALGORITHM 2 SS-ELM ALGORITHM

Require: Labeled data set: $(x_i, t_i)_{i=1}^{v}, x \in R^d, t_i \in R^m$;
  Unlabeled data set: $(x_i)_{i=1}^{u}, x \in R^d$;
  Hidden node output function: $G(a_i, b_i, x)$, and the number of hidden nodes: l;
Ensure: The output weight vector: β;
  1: Construct the graph Laplacian L from both labeled data set and unlabeled data set;
  2: Initiate the hidden node parameters with random input weights and biases (w_i, b_i);
  3: Calculate the output matrix of the hidden node H;
  4: Choose the tradeoff parameter C and λ;
  5: Compute the output weights β using Eq. (18);
  6: **return** β.

$\tilde{T}$ is a matrix of $(v + u) \times m$. The preceding one line of the matrix is the label of labeled data samples. The following u line of data is 0. λ is a tradeoff parameter. Suppose that the sample x_i belongs to t_j, and that the category t_j has $(N_t)_j$ sample data, then the data samples will be granted with one penalty coefficient $C_i = C_0/N_{t_j}$. C_0 is one parameter defined by users.

In order to solve the problem of data bias, Huang introduced penalty coefficient $C_i = C_0/N_{t_j}$ [6]. The method was similar to the weighted ELM (W-ELM) algorithm [32]. In this way, the category with a large number of data samples will not be overfitted, while the category with a smaller number of data samples will not be ignored [6].

2.4.4 Other variants of the ELM

Due to its flexibility, many variants of the ELM have been developed for special applications. We summarize some important variants of the ELM as follows:

1. Fuzzy ELM [33–35]
2. Bayesian ELM [36, 37]
3. Complex ELM [38, 39]
4. Sparse ELM [37, 40]

2.5 ELM FOR UNSUPERVISED LEARNING

2.5.1 ELM for embedding and clustering

The ELM was primarily proposed for supervised learning tasks, such as regression and classification, while relatively few works involve unsupervised learning problems. Recently, Huang et al. [6] proposed an unsupervised ELM (US-ELM) for unsupervised learning such as clustering or embedding, thus greatly expanding the applicability of the ELM. The US-ELM is based on the manifold regularization framework, and its formulation is given by

$$\min_{\beta \in R^{l \times m}} \left(\| \beta \|^2 + \lambda Tr(\beta^T H^T L H \beta) \right)$$

$$s.t. \quad \beta^T H^T H \beta = I_m$$

(21)

where $L \in R^{N \times N}$ is the graph Laplacian built from the unlabeled data; $H \in R^{N \times l}$ is the hidden layer output matrix; and $\beta \in R^{l \times m}$ is the output weight matrix. The US-ELM maps the input data into a m-dimensional space in which the data is well clustered. Therefore, the US-ELM can be used for non-linear dimension reduction or embedding. If the learning task is clustering, then the k-means algorithm is applied to cluster the embedded data in the new space.

It is shown in Huang et al. [6] that the equations above solve the following generalized eigenvalue problem (GEP):

$$(I_l + \lambda H^T L H)v = \Upsilon H^T H v$$

(22)

In the US-ELM, we first solve the above GEP to find the first $m + 1$ generalized eigenvectors corresponding to the $m + 1$ smallest eigenvalues. As in the algorithm of Laplacian eigenmaps, the first eigenvector is discarded while the second through the $m + 1$ eigenvectors is used to compute the output weights of the US-ELM:

$$\beta = [v_2^*, v_3^*, \dots, v_{m+1}^*]$$

(23)

where $v_i^* = v_i / \| Hv_i \|, i = 2, ..., m+1$.

If the number of labeled data is fewer than the number of hidden neurons, Eq. (22) is underdetermined. In this case, the following alternative formulation is used:

$$(I_l + \lambda LHH^T)u = \Upsilon HH^T u \tag{24}$$

and the output weights are computed by:

$$\beta = H^T [u_2^*, u_3^*, ..., u_{m+1}^*] \tag{25}$$

where $u_i^* = u_i / \| Hu_i \|, i = 2, ..., m+1$.

The US-ELM algorithm is summarized in Algorithm 3.

ALGORITHM 3 US-ELM ALGORITHM

Require: Unlabeled data set: $(x_i)_{i=1}^u, x \in R^d$;

Hidden node output function: $G(a_i, b_i, x)$, and the number of hidden nodes: l;

Ensure: For embedding task: the embedding in a m-dimensional space: $E \in R^{N \times m}$;

For clustering task: the label vector of cluster index: $t \in N^{N \times 1}$;

1: Construct the graph Laplacian matrix l from unlabeled data set X;

2: Initiate an ELM network of l hidden neurons with random input weights, and calculate the output matrix of the hidden neurons $H \in R^{N \times l}$;

3: **if** $l \leq N$ **then**

4:     Find the generalized eigenvectors of Eq. (22) corresponding to the second through the $m + 1$ smallest eigenvalues. Compute output weights from Eq. (23);

5: **else**

6:     Find the generalized eigenvectors Eq. (24) corresponding to the second through the $m + 1$ smallest eigenvalues. Compute output weights from Eq. (25);

7: **end if**

8: Calculate the embedding matrix: $E = H\beta$;

9: (For clustering only): Treat E as the new data matrix, and cluster them into K clusters using the k-means algorithm. Let t be cluster assignment vector;

10: **return** E (for embedding task) or t (for clustering task).

2.5.2 ELM for representational learning

Representational learning (e.g., stacked autoencoder [SAE] and stacked autodecoder [SDA]) is effective in learning useful features for achieving high generalization performance. Apart from being used to train SLFNs, the ELM theory has also been applied to build an autoencoder for multilayer perceptron (MLP).

Recently, Kasun et al. [41] proposed an ELM-based autoencoder for learning representations, which performs layer-wise representational learning using autoencoders learned by ELM, resulting in a multilayer feedforward network. According to the experimental results on the MNIST OCR data sets, this approach is several orders of magnitude faster than deep belief networks and deep Boltzmann machines, and the achieved accuracy is highly competitive with that of deep learning algorithms.

3 IMPROVED EXTREME LEARNING MACHINE WITH BIG DATA

3.1 SHORTCOMINGS OF THE EXTREME LEARNING MACHINE FOR PROCESSING BIG DATA

In this era of data explosion, data are produced quickly and extensively, such as kinds of sensors, business transactions, emails, news, images, videos, and tweets. Analyzing these large-scale data sets has become a challenging problem in data analysis. It is necessary for developing an ELM algorithm for training large-scale data sets in this era of big data.

However, the ELM has many shortcomings for training big data. We list just a few shortcomings as follows:

1. *Memory-residency*: The ELM algorithm and its variants are memory resident. That is to say, all the data must be loaded into computer memory in advance. If the amount of data far exceeds one machine's memory, the ELM cannot effectively carry out the calculation. So it is a challenge to process large-scale data sets, and it drives the increasing research of parallel algorithm and distributed processing for the ELM.
2. *Time-consumption*: The processes of calculating the hidden node output matrix, Moore-Penrose generalized inverse of a matrix, Laplace matrix, and matrix multiplications consume a lot of time, when training large-scale data sets.
3. *Difficulty of solving the Laplace matrix for the SS-ELM and US-ELM*: The original SS-ELM and US-ELM algorithm needs to store the data in memory before processing them and then calculates the adjacent similarity matrix of data sets, which takes $O(N^2)$ time and space. Therefore, the original SS-ELM and US-ELM cannot handle large and web-scale data sets, which are usually faced in the era of big data.
4. *Velocity*: In this era of big data, not only the existing data is very large, but also data is expanded with fast growth velocity. The traditional ELM just focused on the existing data. Therefore, it is necessary to develop online ELM algorithms to train the data received sequentially.

3.2 OPTIMIZATION STRATEGIES FOR THE TRADITIONAL EXTREME LEARNING MACHINE

As discussed earlier, there are many shortcomings for the traditional ELM to train large-scale data sets. Optimization strategies have been employed for the traditional ELM:

1. *Efficiency improvement*: Firstly, an orthogonal projection method for calculating Moore-Penrose generalized inverse of a matrix was set out by Huang et al. [24]. Secondly, to extend ELM for online sequential data, Liang et al. [42] proposed the online sequential ELM (OS-ELM), which can learn the data one by one or chunk by chunk with fixed or varying chunk sizes. Thirdly, some methods for improving the efficiency of training large-scale data sets have been proposed, such as a sparse ELM [40]. We also proposed an approximate SS-ELM algorithm, and then paralleled it based on MapReduce.
2. *Parallel algorithms*: Parallel algorithms for the traditional ELM and its variants have been implemented based on MapReduce, such as parallel ELM for regression based on MapReduce (PELM) [43], ELM*: distributed extreme learning [44], parallel OS-ELM based on MapReduce (POS-ELM) [45], etc. Moreover, a distributed ELM algorithm based on Spark is proposed in this chapter.

3.3 EFFICIENCY IMPROVEMENT FOR BIG DATA

3.3.1 Orthogonal projection for ELM

The orthogonal projection method can be efficiently used to calculate the Moore-Penrose generalized inverse of a matrix in ELM [24]: $H^\dagger = (H^T H)^{-1} H^T$ if $H^T H$ is nonsingular or $H^\dagger = H^T (H H^T)^{-1}$ if it is singular. According to the ridge regression theory, it was suggested that a positive value $1/\lambda$ is added to the diagonal of $(H^T H)$ or $(H H^T)$ in the calculation of the output weights β. The resultant solution is more stable and tends to have better generalization performance. That is, in order to improve the stability of the ELM, we can have

$$\beta = H^T \left(\frac{1}{\lambda} + H H^T \right)^{-1} T \tag{26}$$

The corresponding output function of ELM is

$$f(x) = h(x)\beta = h(x)H^T \left(\frac{1}{\lambda} + H H^T \right)^{-1} T \tag{27}$$

Alternatively, we can have

$$\beta = \left(\frac{1}{\lambda} + H H^T \right)^{-1} H^T T \tag{28}$$

$$f(x) = h(x)\beta = h(x) \left(\frac{1}{\lambda} + H H^T \right)^{-1} H^T T \tag{29}$$

Huang et al. [24] show that the solutions (Eqs. 26, 28) are actually consistent to minimize $\|H\beta - T\|^2 + \lambda\|\beta\|^2$, which is the essential target of the ELM, as mentioned before. Thus, the ELM algorithm can be rewritten as follows:

ALGORITHM 4 ELM ALGORITHM FOR LARGE-SCALE DATA OVERVIEW

Require: The training data set: $\{(x_i, t_i)|x_i \in R^d, t_i \in R^m, i = 1, ..., N\}$;
    Hidden node output function: $G(a_i, b_i, x)$, and the number of hidden node number: l;
Ensure: The output weight vector: β;
 1: Randomly generate hidden node parameters (a_i, b_i), $i = 1, ..., l$;
 2: Calculate the hidden layer output matrix H;
 3: Calculate the output weight matrix:

$$\beta = H^T \left(\frac{1}{\lambda} + H H^T \right)^{-1} T \tag{30}$$

or

$$\beta = \left(\frac{1}{\lambda} + H^T H \right)^{-1} H^T T \tag{31}$$

 4: **return** β.

3.3.2 ELM for online sequential data

As mentioned earlier, velocity is the most important feature of big data. The training data sets are always received sequentially with fast growth velocity. However, the traditional ELM assumes that all the training data sets are ready before the training process. Liang et al. [42] proposed the OS-ELM, which can learn the data one by one or chunk by chunk with fixed or varying chunk sizes. OS-ELM has extended the traditional ELM for training online sequential data. OS-ELM is summarized in Algorithm 5.

ALGORITHM 5 OS-ELM ALGORITHM

Require: The training data set: $\{(x_i, t_i) | x_i \in R^d, t_i \in R^m, i = 1, ..., N\}$;

  Hidden node output function: $G(a_i, b_i, x)$, and the number of hidden nodes: l;

Ensure: The output weight vector: β;

  Initialization phase:

  1: Let $k = 0$. Calculate the hidden layer output matrix H_0 using initial training data, and estimate the initial output weight $_0$ as in classical ELM. Let $P_0 = (H_0{}^T H_0)^{-1}$;

  Online sequential learning phase:

  2: Calculate the output weight matrix;

  3: When the $(k + 1)$th chunk of new data $X_k + 1$, $T_k + 1$ arrived, update the hidden layer output matrix as $H_{k+1} = [H_k^T + \Delta H_{k+1}^T]^T$, where ΔH_{k+1}^T is the hidden layer output matrix corresponds to the newly arrived data;

  4: Update the output weights as $\beta_{k+1} = \beta_k + P_{k+1} H_{k+1}^T (T_{k+1} - H_{k+1}\beta_k)$, where $P_{k+1} = P_k - P_k H_{k+1}^T (I + H_{k+1} P H_{k+1}^T)^{-1} H_{k+1} P_k$;

  5: Set $k = k + 1$;

  6: **return** β.

Zhao et al. [46] proposed the forgetting mechanism to the OS-ELM (FOS-ELM) to reflect the timeliness of training data in short-term predictions. The FOS-ELM algorithm is suitable for practical applications which have the feature of timeliness and producing data in a sequent manner. Rong et al. [47] proposed an OS-Fuzzy-ELM for the TSK fuzzy model with any bounded nonconstant piecewise continuous membership functions.

3.3.3 Sparse ELM for classification

A sparse ELM [40] is proposed as an alternative solution for classification, reducing storage space and training time. The traditional ELM obtains the result by matrix inversion, whose computational complexity is between quadratic and cubic with respect to training size. It still requires plenty of training time for large-scale problems, even though it is much faster than many other traditional methods. In the paper by Bai et al. [40], an efficient training algorithm is specifically developed for a sparse ELM. The quadratic programming problem involved in a sparse ELM is divided into a series of smallest possible subproblems, each of which are solved analytically. Compared with SVM, a sparse ELM obtains a better generalization performance with much faster training speed. Compared with a traditional ELM, a sparse ELM achieves similar generalization performance for binary classification applications, and when dealing with large-scale binary classification problems, a sparse ELM realizes even faster training speed than a traditional ELM.

3.4 PARALLEL EXTREME LEARNING MACHINE BASED ON MAPREDUCE

3.4.1 MapReduce and Hadoop

MapReduce is a programming model, which is usually used for the parallel computation of large-scale data sets [48] mainly due to its salient features that include scalability, fault-tolerance, ease of programming, and flexibility. The MapReduce programming model is very helpful for programmers who are not familiar with the distributed programming. The MapReduce framework contains two main phases: the map phase (also called mapper) takes key/value pairs as input, possibly performs some computation on this input, and produces intermediate results in the form of key/value pairs; and the reduce phase (also called reducer) processes these results. The intermediate results produced by the map phase are performed with shuffled operations. Then the data are sent to the reduce phase. In more detail, the data are processed through the following five steps [48, 49] as illustrated in Fig. 4. It should be noted that, for a particular job, only a Map function is strictly needed, although for most jobs a Reduce function is also used.

1. *Input reader*: This reads data from files or databases and converts them into key/value pairs. The data sets are usually divided into splits, for example, the size of a split in Hadoop distributed file system (HDFS) is 64 MB by default, but it can be configured.
2. *Map function*: A map task takes a key/value pair from the input reader, performs some computation on it, and then produces the result in the form of key/value pair as well. The results from map tasks are initially output to main memory buffer, and when almost full spill over to the disk.
3. *Shuffle function*: This function will perform partial reduction so that pairs with the same key will be processed as one group by a reduce task.

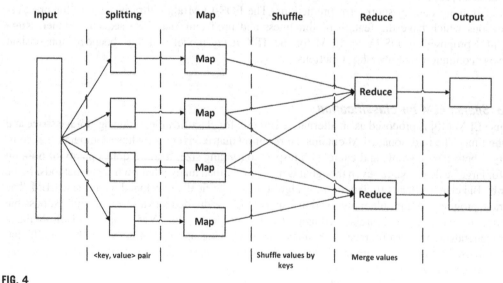

FIG. 4

MapReduce model.

4. *Reduce function*: The user-defined reduce function is invoked once for each distinct key and is applied on the set of associated values for that key; that is, the pairs with same key will be processed as one group.

5. *Output writer*: This is responsible for writing the output to stable storages (e.g., HDFS or databases).

The procedure of data transformation of (key, value) pairs is shown as follows:

$$\text{Map}: \ (key_1, value_1) \rightarrow list(key_2, value_2)$$

$$\text{Reduce}: \ (key_2, list(value_2)) \rightarrow list(key_3, value_3)$$

Hadoop [50] is an open-source implementation of MapReduce. Hadoop consists of two main parts: Hadoop distributed file system (HDFS) and MapReduce for distributed processing. Hadoop consists of a number of different daemons/servers: NameNode, DataNode, and Secondary NameNode for managing HDFS, and JobTracker and TaskTracker for performing MapReduce.

3.4.2 PELM

He et al. [43] designed and implemented an efficient parallel ELM based on the MapReduce framework named PELM; this can cover the shortcomings of the traditional ELM, whose learning ability is weak to process huge data sets. The PELM is based on the orthogonal projection to solve the Moore-Penrose generalized inverse of a matrix [24]. The overview algorithm is shown in Algorithm 4. By analyzing the mechanism of Algorithm 4, it becomes obvious that H is an $N \times l$ dimension matrix, so HH^T is an $N \times N$ dimension matrix. However, in massive data mining, N is always a very large number, so HH^T must be too large a matrix for memory, which makes it impossible to execute the ELM algorithm in the way of memory-residence. In most cases, the number of hidden nodes is much less than the number of training samples, $l \ll N$. According to the matrix theory, in the SVD method, a small matrix $H^T H$ could be calculated instead of the large matrix HH^T. We can therefore get ELM results by $\beta = \left(\frac{1}{\lambda} + H^T H\right)^{-1} H^T T$. Hence, the bottleneck operations $H^T H$ and $H^T T$ need to be parallelized using MapReduce. The remaining operations are performed sequentially.

PELM uses two MapReduce jobs to obtain the final ELM results.

1. The first MapReduce course computes the hidden node output matrix H, which is the independent variables matrix of N samples. The MapReduce computation of hidden layer mapping is just mapping samples to space represented by hidden nodes.

2. The second MapReduce course computes the matrix multiplication $H^T H$ and $H^T T$ in parallel. In the map function, the elements of the hidden node output vector are firstly parsed, and then they multiply each other together to form the intermediate results. In the reduce function, the intermediate results are merged, sorted, and summed to achieve the matrix multiplication $H^T H$ and $H^T T$.

In PELM, after the first MapReduce job obtains the output matrix H, H is written into HDFS. The second MapReduce job should read the output matrix H from HDFS, and then computes the final ELM results. Therefore, there are numerous intermediate results (i.e., $N \times l$ dimension matrix H) transformed during the two MapReduce jobs, which increases the processing time of the ELM based on the MapReduce framework.

3.4.3 ELM*

Xin et al. [44] proposed a distributed ELM based on the MapReduce framework, named ELM*. Unlike PELM, there is just one MapReduce phase in ELM*. Thus, the efficiency is largely improved. By adequately analyzing the property of the traditional ELM, Xin et al. found out that the most expensive computation part of the Moore-Penrose generalized inverse matrix operator in the output weight vector calculation is the matrix multiplication operator. Then the operations are divided into two groups: those to be parallelized by MapReduce and those to be run in a single machine. The calculation of the Moore-Penrose generalized inverse matrix is paralleled on the MapReduce framework. The corresponding output weight vector is then calculated with centralized computing. The experiment results show that the ELM* can learn massive training data more efficiently than the PELM.

When the amount of training data goes beyond some limitations, Algorithm 4 still has two inevitable problems that cannot be solved efficiently with a single computer. One is to compute the hidden layer output matrix H, and another is to compute $H^T H$ and $H^T T$ which are involved in calculating the output weight vector β. The PELM uses one MapReduce job to compute H, then uses a new MapReduce job to compute $H^T H$ and $H^T T$. However, all the calculations are computed within one MapReduce job in the ELM*. Let $U = H^T H$, $V = H^T T$, then

$$\beta = \left(\frac{1}{\lambda} + U\right)^{-1} V \tag{32}$$

On the basis of the formulas of matrix multiplication, we can further get

$$u_{ij} = \sum_{k=1}^{N} h_{ik}^T h_{kj} = \sum_{k=1}^{N} h_{ki} h_{kj} = \sum_{k=1}^{N} g(w_i x_k + b_i) g(w_j x_k + b_j) \tag{33}$$

$$v_{ij} = \sum_{k=1}^{N} h_{ik}^T t_{kj} = \sum_{k=1}^{N} h_{ki}^T t_{kj} = \sum_{k=1}^{N} g(w_i x_k + b_i) t_{kj} \tag{34}$$

According to Eq. (33), we know that the item u_{ij} in U can be expressed by the summation of h_{ki} multiplied by h_{kj}. Here, h_{ki} is the ith element in the kth row of matrix H, and h_{kj} is the jth element in the same row. Apparently, both h_{ki} and h_{kj} are from row h_k of the same training data record x_k, which has nothing to do with the other data in the training sets. Similarly, according to Eq. (34), we know that item v_{ij} in V can be expressed by the summation of h_{ki} multiplied by t_{kj}. Here, t_{kj} is the jth element in the kth row of matrix T. Apparently, both h_{ki} and t_{kj} are from the corresponding rows h_k and t_k, respectively, of the same training data record x_k, which has nothing to do with the other training data as well.

Since U is an $l \times l$ matrix, the computation cost of calculating $(\frac{1}{\lambda} + U)^{-1}$ is very small. At the same time, as V is an $l \times M$ matrix, the computation cost of multiplying V is also very small. Thus, the most expensive computational part in the output weight vector β calculation process is to solve matrixes U and V. However, the processes of calculating U and V are both decomposable. The calculation can be paralleled by MapReduce. Moreover, the other operations can therefore be realized in a single machine.

Therefore, the overview of ELM* is in Algorithm 6.

We can get the details of Map and Reduce function from Xin et al. [44]. In the paper, Xin also proposed an improved *ELM** to improve the efficiency by using the MapClose function provided by the Hadoop framework. The local summation of matrices U and V is first computed in the MapClose function, therefore the computation and communication cost decrease during the shuffle course.

ALGORITHM 6 ELM* OVERVIEW

Require: The training data set: $\{(x_i, t_i) | x_i \in R^d, t_i \in R^m, i = 1, ..., N\}$;
   Hidden node output function: $G(a_i, b_i, x)$, and the number of hidden nodes: l;
Ensure: The output weight vector: β;
   1: Randomly generate hidden node parameters $(a_i, b_i), i = 1, ..., l$;
   2: Calculate the matrix U, V in parallel based on MapReduce with only one MapReduce job;
   3: Calculate the output weight matrix $\beta = (\frac{1}{\lambda} + U)^{-1}V$ in a single machine;
   4: **return** β.

3.4.4 PASS-ELM

According to Section 2.4.3, the proposal of SS-ELM (semisupervised ELM) extends the ELM algorithm to the area of semisupervision learning, which is an important issue for machine learning on big data. However, the original SS-ELM algorithm needs to store the data in its memory before processing them and then calculates the adjacent similarity matrix of data sets, which takes $O(N^2)$ time and space. Therefore, the original SS-ELM cannot handle large and web-scale data sets which are usually faced in the era of big data. To solve the problem, we propose a parallel approximate SS-ELM (PASS-ELM) algorithm based on locality-sensitive hashing (LSH) [51, 52] based on the MapReduce model, without significantly impacting the accuracy of the results. Firstly, an approximate algorithm for calculating the adjacent similarity matrix is proposed to reduce the complexity and occupied memory from $O(N^2)$ to $O(krN) + r\sum_{j=0}^{T-1} O(N_j^2)$, where $0 \le j \le T_i - 1$, $\sum_{j=0}^{T-1} N_j = N$ and N_j is usually small. Secondly, a parallel algorithm is proposed and carefully designed based on the MapReduce model to utilize the flexibility of cloud computing platforms.

In circumstances involving handling a large amount of data, the number of unlabeled and labeled data is far larger than the number of hidden nodes. Therefore, the calculation of output weights should follow the following Eq. (35) according to Eq. (18):

$$(I_h + H^T CH + \lambda H^T LH)^{-1} H^T C \tilde{T} \tag{35}$$

We use U to represent the matrix $H^T CH$ and V to represent the matrix $H^T LH$, and W to represent the matrix $H^T C \tilde{T}$. Therefore, the above formula can be transformed into the following solution:

$$\beta = (I_h + U + \lambda V)^{-1} W \tag{35}$$

In the formula, $(I_h + U + \lambda V)$ is a matrix with l line and l columns. In general, l is quite small (which represents the number of hidden nodes), so the expenditure of calculating the inverse matrix is not high. At the same time, $H^T C \tilde{T}$ is a matrix with h lines and m columns. As a result, the calculation of multiplication of $(I_l + U + \lambda V)^{-1}$ and W does not consume much time, either. H is a matrix with n lines and l columns. H^T is a matrix with l lines and n columns. C is a diagonal matrix with n lines and n columns. L is a matrix with n lines and n columns. $\tilde{T}$ is a matrix with n lines and m columns. Under the situation where the number of samples is quite large, U, V, and W, the calculation of the matrices takes a long time. In addition, the occupied memory is huge. According to the above analysis, the highest cost in the calculation of the SS-ELM algorithm lies in that of the three matrices of U, V, and W.

The major idea of our proposal includes an approximate algorithm, selective parallelization, and efficiency improvement.

Firstly, an approximate algorithm for computing the adjacent similarity matrix for large-scale data sets based on LSH scheme is proposed to reduce the computational complexity, especially for high dimensions. The proposed approximate algorithm can be widely applied, because the calculation of adjacent similarity matrix is necessary for many other machine learning algorithms such as spectral clustering, graph-based semisupervised learning, and so on.

From Section 2.4.3, we can find that the calculation of the Laplace matrix is the key and a time-consuming operation in the SS-ELM. The first step in calculating the Laplace matrix is to calculate the adjacent similarity matrix. The simplest solution for the computation of the adjacent similarity matrix is a nested loop over both relations, which, however, has the disadvantage of quadratic complexities for computation and I/O. However, for example, point p in Fig. 5 has only a small subset of database objects in its ε-neighborhood but a nested loop would calculate the distances to all points. Furthermore, since the cost of computing the adjacent similarity matrix is $O(N^2)$ in both time and space, it becomes computationally infeasible to handle large and web-scale data sets, such as Amazon's customer statistics data sets (3 million records) and Wikipedia Talk network data sets (2 million instances).

LSH [51, 52] is well performed for the Approximate Nearest Neighbor search. In LSH, k AND constructions and r OR constructions are usually used to construct a hash family. The process of constructing hash tables is illustrated in Fig. 6. In this section, we propose an approximate algorithm for calculating the approximate Laplace matrix to improve the performance. There are four steps in the proposed algorithm. Firstly, the algorithm calculates the hash value for all data points by LSH family for l_p norm. Secondly, points whose hash values collide with each other grouped together. Thirdly, similarity values are computed for points in each group to form portions of the similarity matrix. Fourthly, we compute the Laplace matrix on each group as shown in Eq. (20).

A different hash table is constructed by a different hash function group with k hash functions. The points with the same hash value which is calculated by the function group are grouped into the same bucket. The time complexity of calculating the r hash tables is $O(krN)$. Then, for each bucket,

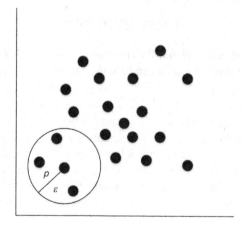

FIG. 5

ε-Neighborhood.

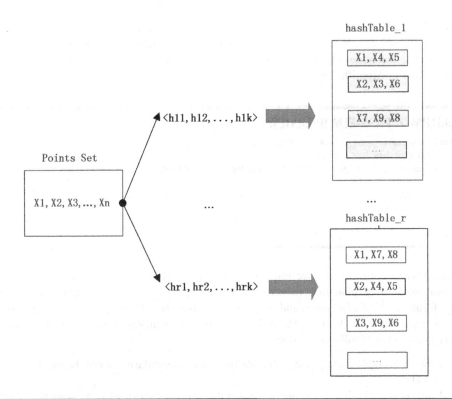

FIG. 6

Implementation by MapReduce.

we compute the similarity by Eq. (19) for the points that belong to one bucket only. Assuming the ith hash table has T_i buckets, each of which has N_j points, where $0 \leq j \leq T_i - 1$ and $\sum_{j=0}^{T-1} N_j = N$, the overall complexity of this step is $r \sum_{j=0}^{T-1} O(N_j^2)$. We notice that if two points are not in any same bucket, the similarity between these two points are zero. The overall complexity of these two step is $O(krN) + r \sum_{j=0}^{T-1} O(N_j^2)$. Although there are some duplicate calculations in the second step, the complexity is much smaller than the complexity $O(N^2)$. After the calculation of adjacent similarity matrix, we can calculate the Laplace matrix by Eq. (20).

The calculation of the approximate adjacent matrix can be easily implemented by MapReduce. In the Map phase, we calculates hash value for all points with r hash groups. In the Shuffle phase, we group the points which have the same hash value calculated by the same hash group together. In the Reduce phase, we calculate the similarity for the points that belong to one bucket through all the buckets.

Secondly, a selective parallelization method is adopted. Analyzing SS-ELM algorithm deeply, the operations can be divided into two groups: those to be parallelized by MapReduce and those to be run in a single machine. This is because some operations run more quickly on a single machine rather than on multiple machines in parallel, as the overhead incurred by using MapReduce exceeds gains made by parallelizing the task. From the analysis above, we can find that the computation cost of the three matrixes of U, V, and W is very high. Therefore, all these calculations can be parallelized by MapReduce so as to improve the efficiency. Once U, V, and W are calculated, one machine is adopted to calculate the final hidden node output matrix. Therefore, PSS-ELM algorithm with a large amount of data can be expressed in Algorithm 7.

ALGORITHM 7 PASS-ELM OVERVIEW

Require: Labeled data: $(x_i, t_i)_{i=1}^{l}, x \in R^d, t_i \in R^m$;
        Unlabeled data: $(x_i)_{i=1}^{u}, x \in R^d$;
        Hidden node output function: $G(a_i, b_i, x)$, and the number of hidden node number: l
Ensure: The output weight vector: β;
  1: Initiate the hidden-node parameters with random input weights and biases (w_i, b_i);
  2: Calculate $U = H^T CH, V = H^T LH, W = H^T C\tilde{T}$ with MapReduce;
  3: Calculate the output weight matrix $\beta = (I_h + U + \lambda V)^{-1}W$;
  4: **return** β.

Thirdly, several optimizations are implemented to improve the efficiency, such as cache-based optimization, skewness exploitation, reduction of MapReduce processes, local-summation for improving the performance of shuffle phase, and so on. Suppose that the data are trained by us have subscript indexes, the input of the whole algorithm is the file in (index, pointValue) form. Our proposed PASS-ELM only needs three MapReduce phases.

1. During the first MapReduce phase, calculate the adjacent similarity matrix based on the scheme described above.
2. During the second MapReduce phase, calculate the diagonal matrix D in an accumulated manner based on the output at the first stage and group the data into buckets based on what described above about matrices multiplication for the calculation of U, V, and W. The matrix C is also calculated during this process. Furthermore, duplicate data need to be removed in this process.
3. During the third MapReduce phase, Laplace matrix is calculated, and then U, V, and W matrices are calculated at the same time in the end.

3.5 PARALLEL EXTREME LEARNING MACHINE BASED ON APACHE SPARK

3.5.1 Advantage of Apache Spark

Although the PELM and ELM* above have improved the learning rate and efficiency of the ELM, the intermediate results generated during the map stages are written onto disks, while during the reduce stages, they are read from disks into HDFS. These processes seriously increase the communication cost and I/O overheads, and degrade the learning speed and efficiency of the system. The several copies for each task within MapReduce is another shortcoming which increases the additional overheads of the system. In addition, if one node cannot work, the tasks in this node will be assigned to other nodes, and reprocessed again, leading to more costs during the process.

Relative to MapReduce, Apache Spark is designed to process data-intensive applications with distributed memory-based architecture, and provides the similar scalability, and fault tolerance characteristics to MapReduce [53]. The most important part in Spark is an abstraction called the resilient distributed data set (RDD), which is regarded as a handle for a collection of individual data partitions.

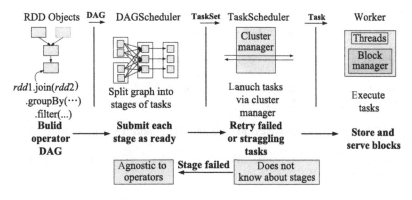

FIG. 7

System scheduling in Spark.

All operations are based on RDDs, and RDDs can be cached in memory across nodes, which can be reused in multiple MapReduce-like parallel operations. So when we calculate the Moore-Penrose generalized inverse matrix, the multiple occurrences of variables and intermediate variables can be cached in memory instead of disks, which reduces the communication costs and I/O overheads. Each RDD contains lists of dependencies on other RDDs, and we call that a lineage, which means that the lost partitions can be rebuilt based on the lineage. That process provides good fault tolerance and if a partition is lost, the RDD can rebuild the lost partition quickly. Based on the dependencies among the RDDs, the DAGSheduler in Spark forms a directed acyclic graph (DAG) of stages for each job, which significantly reduces costs during the computations, and it is an important reason why Spark processes big data faster. Fig. 7 shows the scheduling in Apache Spark.

3.5.2 Parallel ELM on Spark

As we mentioned earlier, the most expensive calculation part is the Moore-Penrose generalized inverse matrix, which is decomposable, so that we can compute this matrix in parallel [54, 55]. In this section, we propose a novel improved parallel ELM based on Spark which is called the SELM algorithm. The algorithm includes three subalgorithms: a parallel hidden layer output matrix calculation (**H**-PMC) algorithm, a parallel $\hat{U}$ matrix decomposition ($\hat{U}$-PMD) algorithm, and a parallel **V** matrix decomposition (**V**-PMD) algorithm. These algorithms adequately exploit the strengths of Spark framework to speed up the process of calculating the Moore-Penrose generalized inverse matrix (M-PGIM). There is no doubt that this accelerates the process of ELM classifying big data. While our SELM maintains a competitive accuracy on the test data, it achieves a significant speedup compared to the baseline ELM algorithm implemented on a single machine. What is more, our SELM algorithm outperforms other parallel ELM algorithms based on MapReduce by exhibiting significant performance improvement in terms of learning rate and efficiency, as well as maintaining the training and testing accuracy.

First, the **H**-PMC algorithm is used to calculate the hidden layer output matrix and it works as follows:

1. Parse the training samples and hidden node data set.
2. Partition the training samples into l partitions according to the rows of the samples.

3. Partition the hidden nodes data set into l partitions according to the columns.
4. Calculate the hidden layer output matrix in parallel.

Then Û-PMD algorithm is developed to compute $(\mathbf{I}/\lambda + \mathbf{H}^T\mathbf{H})$ and it can be depicted as follows:

1. Cache the diagonal matrix $\mathbf{I}/\lambda$ as Broadcast variables and initialization.
2. Calculate the diagonal matrix $\mathbf{I}/\lambda + \mathbf{H}^T\mathbf{H}$.

Finally, the **V**-PMD algorithm is proposed to calculate $(H^T t)$ and it works as follows:

1. Partition training samples result matrix into m partitions according to the columns.
2. Calculate the matrix $H^T t$.

We have mentioned that the most expensive computation part of ELM is the computation of the matrix, and the above parts have calculated M-PGIM, matrix $\mathbf{H}^\dagger$. At that time, all parameters for the SELM algorithm are confirmed, then we implement the SELM algorithm to classify the testing data sets. Fig. 8 shows the SELM for big data classification on Spark.

From Fig. 8, we can find that our SELM algorithm mainly includes two phases as follows. In the first phase (computing output weight matrix using **H**-PMC algorithm, Û-PMD algorithm, and **V**-PMD algorithm), the **H**-PMC algorithm is used to calculate the hidden layer output matrix while the Û-PMD algorithm and **V**-PMD algorithm compute the matrix M-PGIM. The steps of the three mentioned algorithms are similar, and the general process is as follows:

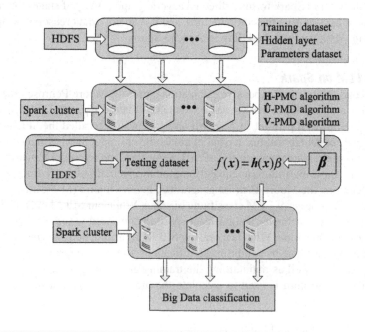

FIG. 8

SELM for big data classification on Spark.

1. Parse the data sets, then divide them into corresponding size of partition in order to reduce the communication costs and I/O overheads.
2. Calculate the corresponding output matrix in parallel.

In the second phase (classifying testing data sets using the SELM algorithm), the SELM algorithm uses the parameters generated by the **H**-PMC algorithm, Û-PMD algorithm, and **V**-PMD algorithm to classify the testing data sets.

1. Compute the hidden layer output matrix of the testing data set **H** in parallel according to Algorithm 1.
2. Parse the data sets, and divide them into corresponding size of partition.
3. Classify the testing data set and, based on the results, analyze the performance of our proposed SELM.

3.5.3 Performance of the SELM under different dimensionality

In our experiments, we have tested the performance of the SELM under different dimensionality. The data sets are S_1, S_2, S_3, S_4, S_5, S_6, S_7, S_8, and S_9. Table 1 gives a detailed description of all data sets.

Dimensionality is an important characteristic of big data. We use several experiments to investigate the influence of dimensionality on the performance of our SELM. At this time, the data sets we used in our experiments are S_1, S_2, S_3, S_4, and S_5, and the hidden layer nodes are 50 while the number of servers is 10. In Fig. 7, our SELM algorithm compares with the PELM algorithm, ELM* algorithm, and ELM*-Improved algorithm.

From Fig. 9, we can find that with the increase of dimensionality called m, the training time and testing time are both increasing. When we increase the dimensionality, we have to spend more time calculating the hidden layer output matrix **H**. We know that it should spend most of the time computing M-PGIM, which contains computing $N \times l$ matrix and $l \times l$ matrix, and increasing the dimensionality of data set does not have a huge influence on the size of M-PGIM. Therefore, the runtime of calculating the matrix **H** increases with the increase of dimensionality while the whole runtime keeps growing slightly.

It can be seen from Fig. 9 that the performance of our SELM is better than the ELM*, ELM*-Improved, and PELM. The PELM has two MapReduce phases, and in the first phase, with the increase of dimensionality, it has spent more cost to compute matrix **H**. At the same time, two MapReduce

Table 1 Detailed Information of Data Sets

Name	File Size	Dimensionality	Sample Size	Training Sample Size	Testing Sample Size
S_1	1.2G	8	10M	6M (0.72G)	4M (0.48M)
S_2	2.26G	15	10M	6M (1.356G)	4M (0.904G)
S_3	3.18G	20	10M	6M (1.908G)	4M (1.272G)
S_4	4.24G	28	10M	6M (2.544G)	4M (1.696G)
S_5	5.08G	35	10M	6M (3.048G)	4M (2.032G)
S_6	1.84G	8	15M	10M (1.24G)	5M (0.60G)
S_7	2.46G	8	20M	13M (1.64G)	7M (0.82G)
S_8	3.88G	8	32M	21M (2.59G)	11M (1.29G)
S_9	4.65G	8	38M	25M (3.1G)	13M (1.55G)

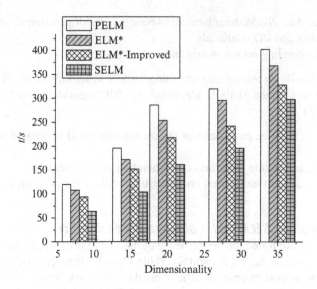

FIG. 9

Runtime under different dimensionality.

phases mean more overhead including computation, communication, and I/O cost, which cause PELM
to take the most time to realize the ELM. Relative to the PELM algorithm, the ELM* algorithm and
ELM*-Improved algorithm use one MapReduce phase to finish classification, which reduce lots of
costs. On the other hand, the ELM*-Improved algorithm leverages the local summation of corresponding elements in the matrix, so that it reduces the transmitting time and has better performance than the
ELM*. Compared with the discussional parallel ELM algorithms earlier, our SELM partitions the data
sets reasonably, which makes sure that most calculations are processed locally. During the computation
process, lots of intermediate results can be cached in distributed memory instead of storing them in
disks or HDFS, which reduces transformation cost significantly, and accelerates the whole computation
process. At the same time, Spark takes less time to recompute the lost data because of *lineage*, while
MapReduce has to redistribute the lost nodes tasks and recompute them, which heavily increases the
overhead. Therefore, our SELM algorithm enhances the learning speed of the ELM.

4 APPLICATIONS

4.1 ELM IN PREDICTING PROTEIN STRUCTURE

Because of the close association between the protein structure and its function, predicting the three-
dimensional structures from protein sequences in molecular design and biological medicine design
are very important [56]. Unfortunately, it is so difficult to predict the three-dimensional protein structures from protein sequences accurately that researchers usually take an intermediate step to predict the
protein secondary structure first, as a three-dimensional protein structure results partially from its
secondary structure. At present, the numbers of known protein sequences have far surpassed the numbers of known protein secondary structures which have been obtained through chemical and biological
methods [57]. There is thus an urgent need to predict protein secondary structure.

Nelson et al. [58] classify protein secondary structure into three consolidates classes including helix (H), strand (E), and coli (C) classes, and among the three classes, the helix and strand classes are the major repetitive secondary structures. The existing predicting methods use the local residue information on a single sequence while the three-state overall per-residue accuracy is only 57% [59–62].

In order to solve this challenging issue, Wang et al. [63] used the ELM to train protein secondary structure framework. First, a new encoding schema statistic vector based on the statistic information of amino acid residues was proposed. After that, in order to improve prediction accuracy further, they used the ELM train for several times and then chose the optimal training frameworks as the final predicting frameworks. In addition, they proposed an effective probability-based combination method, which can also improve the prediction results. Finally, they used helix postprocessing, which was based on biological features to obtain the final secondary structure prediction results. The experimental results showed that the method achieved equally good prediction accuracy as other popular methods at very fast learning speed did.

4.2 ELM IN IMAGE PROCESSING

Nowadays, with the rapid development of digital image processing technologies and an urgent demand for practical applications, image classification and recognition technologies have been developing rapidly. In image processing, image classification technologies are an important applications of pattern [64] and their goal is to develop automatic image processing systems that can help us to process image classification and recognition tasks while providing us with lots of useful information obtained from images. Because of the strong nonlinear approximation capability of these technologies, feedforward neural networks have proved to be the efficient way, attracting more and more attention and obtaining various applications in image classification [65–67]. It is well known that images are so easily corrupted by noise that they are not easily classified by feedforward neural networks. Therefore, using fuzzy rule systems and/or their fuzzy neural systems to classify the noisy images has attracted more and more researchers [68–70]. However, most of fuzzy systems use positive fuzzy rules to classify images, which ignores the valuable negative classification information [71–73].

In order to avoid the shortcoming of discovering negative classification information, Nguyen et al. [74] combined positive and negative fuzzy rules to classify images effectively. However, during the training stage, the learning speed is very slow and the method easily falls in local minima of the cost function of the network [75].

As the newest technology in training the SLFNs, the ELM only updates the output weights while the input weights and biases of the hidden layer are randomly generated [6], which are distinctive advantages over all other learning algorithms of feedforward neural networks. Jun et al. [76] used the ELM to train the positive and negative fuzzy rule system for image classification. Liu and Wang [77] used the ELM to analyze images. There is an increasing trend that more and more researchers will use the ELM to process images.

4.3 ELM IN CANCER DIAGNOSIS

Directing multicategory classifications are an important problems in the cancer diagnosis area, on which just a small number of works have been done. Lots of researches show that direct multiclass classification is much more difficult than binary classification, and the accuracy of classification may drop dramatically as the number of classes increase [78].

The methods of ANNs provide an attractive approach for direct multicategory classification problems [79–81]. Neural network methods not only use one network to map the input data into different classes directly, but also accommodate nonlinear features of the gene expression data easily [81]. However, the accuracy of traditional neural networks is often low [82] and they usually adopt gradient-based learning methods, which easily cause local minima and long training times [79, 80].

In order to avoid these problems, Zhang et al. [83] provided that the ELM is used for directing multicategory classification problems in cancer diagnosis. ELM can avoid local minima and improve the learning rate. They used three benchmarks to evaluate the multicategory classification performance of the ELM. The experimental results show that relative to traditional ANNs, the ELM can produce more accurate classification while reducing training time.

4.4 ELM IN BIG DATA SECURITY AND PRIVACY

We live in an era of big data, from which we can mine new useful knowledge for economic growth and technical innovation. Big data has attracted more and more attention and lots of works have been done on its high volume, value, velocity, and variety ("4V"). There is no doubt that "4V" is challenging while the security and privacy of big data are developing into a hot topic, as we know that if the security and privacy of big data cannot be solved satisfactorily, the concept of big data cannot be widely accepted [84].

Although lots of security and privacy techniques have already been designed, some problems of techniques have to be faced, such as local minima, lower learning speed, long time spending on training stage, etc. As an SLFN, the ELM can avoid the problems mentioned earlier. At present, we are using the ELM to process security and privacy of big data, and we can look forward to good performance by the ELM.

5 CONCLUSION

The ELM was first proposed to train SLFNs, which is an important category of ANNs. The ELM only updates the output weights; the input weights and biases of the hidden layer are randomly generated. Because of the fast and efficient learning speed, fast convergence, good generalization ability, and ease of implementation, the ELM and its variants are widely used in batch learning, sequential learning, and incremental learning. With the development of information technologies, big data has become a hot and challenging issue. This chapter shows distributed ELM algorithms based on MapReduce and Spark in detail, and implements them to process several applications of big data.

REFERENCES

[1] Huang GB, Zhu QY, Siew CK. Extreme learning machine: a new learning scheme of feedforward neural networks. In: Proceedings of IEEE international joint conference on neural networks, vol. 2. IEEE; 2004. p. 985–90.
[2] Huang GB, Zhu QY, Siew CK. Extreme learning machine: theory and applications. Neurocomputing 2006;70 (1):489–501.

[3] Huang GB, Chen L, Siew CK. Universal approximation using incremental constructive feedforward networks with random hidden nodes. IEEE Trans Neural Netw 2006;17(4):879–92.

[4] Huang GB, Chen L. Convex incremental extreme learning machine. Neurocomputing 2007;70(16):3056–62.

[5] Huang GB, Chen L. Enhanced random search based incremental extreme learning machine. Neurocomputing 2008;71(16):3460–8.

[6] Huang G, Song S, Gupta JN, Wu C. Semi-supervised and unsupervised extreme learning machines. IEEE Trans Cybern 2014;44(12):2405–17.

[7] Ranjan R, Wang L, Zomaya AY, Georgakopoulos D, Sun XH, Wang G. Recent advances in autonomic provisioning of big data applications on clouds. IEEE Trans Cloud Comput 2015;3(2):101–4.

[8] Kambatla K, Kollias G, Kumar V, Grama A. Trends in big data analytics. J Parallel Distrib Comput 2014;74 (7):2561–73.

[9] Assunção MD, Calheiros RN, Bianchi S, Netto MA, Buyya R. Big data computing and clouds: trends and future directions. J Parallel Distrib Comput 2015;79:3–15.

[10] Haykin S. Neural networks and learning machines. Upper Saddle River, NJ, USA: Pearson; 2009. p. 32–52.

[11] Zhang J, Chen Y, Li T. Opportunities of innovation under challenges of big data. In: 2013 10th international conference on fuzzy systems and knowledge discovery (FSKD), IEEE; 2013. p. 669–73.

[12] Manyika J, Chui M, Brown B, et al. Big data: the next frontier for innovation, competition, and productivity. Analytics; 2011.

[13] Huang GB, Wang DH, Lan Y. Extreme learning machines: a survey. Int J Mach Learn Cybern 2011;2 (2):107–22.

[14] Rumelhart DE, Hinton GE, Williams RJ. Learning representations by back-propagating errors. Cognit Model 1988;5:3.

[15] Cortes C, Vapnik V. Support-vector networks. Mach Learn 1995;20(3):273–97.

[16] Rosenblatt F. Principles of neurodynamics. Perceptrons and the theory of brain mechanisms. Technical Report. DTIC Document; 1961.

[17] Lowe D. Adaptive radial basis function nonlinearities, and the problem of generalisation. In: First IEE international conference on artificial neural networks. IET; 1989. p. 171–5 (Conf. Publ. No. 313).

[18] Bartlett PL. The sample complexity of pattern classification with neural networks: the size of the weights is more important than the size of the network. IEEE Trans Inf Theory 1998;44(2):525–36.

[19] Huang GB, Babri H, et al. Upper bounds on the number of hidden neurons in feedforward networks with arbitrary bounded nonlinear activation functions. IEEE Trans Neural Netw 1998;9(1):224–9.

[20] Huang GB. Learning capability and storage capacity of two-hidden-layer feedforward networks. IEEE Trans Neural Netw 2003;14(2):274–81.

[21] Huang G, Huang GB, Song S, You K. Trends in extreme learning machines: a review. Neural Netw 2015;61:32–48.

[22] Poggio T, Girosi F. Networks for approximation and learning. Proc IEEE 1990;78(9):1481–97.

[23] White H. Artificial neural networks: approximation and learning theory. International Conference on Intelligent Systems Design & Applications. Blackwell Publishers, Inc. 1992.

[24] Huang GB, Zhou H, Ding X, Zhang R. Extreme learning machine for regression and multiclass classification. IEEE Trans Syst Man Cybern Part B Cybern 2012;42(2):513–29.

[25] Huang GB, Ding X, Zhou H. Optimization method based extreme learning machine for classification. Neurocomputing 2010;74(1):155–63.

[26] Block H. The perceptron: a model for brain functioning. I. Rev Mod Phys 1962;34(1):123.

[27] Block H, Knight Jr B, Rosenblatt F. Analysis of a four-layer series-coupled perceptron. II. Rev Mod Phys 1962;34(1):135.

[28] Wang Y, Cao F, Yuan Y. A study on effectiveness of extreme learning machine. Neurocomputing 2011;74 (16):2483–90.

[29] Feng G, Huang GB, Lin Q, Gay R. Error minimized extreme learning machine with growth of hidden nodes and incremental learning. IEEE Trans Neural Netw 2009;20(8):1352–7.

[30] Yang Y, Wang Y, Yuan X. Bidirectional extreme learning machine for regression problem and its learning effectiveness. IEEE Trans Neural Netw Learn Syst 2012;23(9):1498–505.

[31] Miche Y, Sorjamaa A, Bas P, Simula O, Jutten C, Lendasse A. OP-ELM: optimally pruned extreme learning machine. IEEE Trans Neural Netw 2010;21(1):158–62.

[32] Zong W, Huang GB, Chen Y. Weighted extreme learning machine for imbalance learning. Neurocomputing 2013;101:229–42.

[33] Qu Y, Shang C, Wu W, Shen Q. Evolutionary fuzzy extreme learning machine for mammographic risk analysis. Int J Fuzzy Syst 2011;13(4):282–91.

[34] Daliri MR. A hybrid automatic system for the diagnosis of lung cancer based on genetic algorithm and fuzzy extreme learning machines. J Med Syst 2012;36(2):1001–5.

[35] Zhang W, Ji H. Fuzzy extreme learning machine for classification. Electron Lett 2013;49(7):448–50.

[36] Soria-Olivas E, Gómez-Sanchis J, Martín JD, Vila-Francés J, Martínez M, Magdalena JR, et al. Belm: Bayesian extreme learning machine. IEEE Trans Neural Netw 2011;22(3):505–9.

[37] Luo J, Vong CM, Wong PK. Sparse Bayesian extreme learning machine for multi-classification. IEEE Trans Neural Netw Learn Syst 2014;25(4):836–43.

[38] Huang GB, Li MB, Chen L, Siew CK. Incremental extreme learning machine with fully complex hidden nodes. Neurocomputing 2008;71(4):576–83.

[39] Savitha R, Suresh S, Sundararajan N. Fast learning circular complex-valued extreme learning machine (CC-ELM) for real-valued classification problems. Inform Sci 2012;187:277–90.

[40] Bai Z, Huang GB, Wang D, Wang H, Westover MB. Sparse extreme learning machine for classification. IEEE Trans Cybern 2014;44(10):1858–70.

[41] Kasun LLC, Zhou H, Huang GB, Vong CM. Representational learning with ELMs for big data. IEEE Intell Syst 2013;28(6):31–4.

[42] Liang NY, Huang GB, Saratchandran P, Sundararajan N. A fast and accurate online sequential learning algorithm for feedforward networks. IEEE Trans Neural Netw 2006;17(6):1411–23.

[43] He Q, Shang T, Zhuang F, Shi Z. Parallel extreme learning machine for regression based on MapReduce. Neurocomputing 2013;102:52–8.

[44] Xin J, Wang Z, Chen C, Ding L, Wang G, Zhao Y. ELM*: distributed extreme learning machine with MapReduce. World Wide Web 2014;17(5):1189–204.

[45] Wang B, Huang S, Qiu J, Liu Y, Wang G. Parallel online sequential extreme learning machine based on mapreduce. Neurocomputing 2015;149:224–32.

[46] Zhao J, Wang Z, Park DS. Online sequential extreme learning machine with forgetting mechanism. Neurocomputing 2012;87:79–89.

[47] Rong HJ, Huang GB, Sundararajan N, Saratchandran P. Online sequential fuzzy extreme learning machine for function approximation and classification problems. IEEE Trans Syst Man Cybern Part B Cybern 2009;39(4):1067–72.

[48] Dean J, Ghemawat S. MapReduce: simplified data processing on large clusters. Commun ACM 2008;51(1):107–13.

[49] Doulkeridis C, Nørvåg K. A survey of large-scale analytical query processing in MapReduce. VLDB J 2014;23(3):355–80.

[50] White T. Hadoop-the definitive guide: storage and analysis at Internet scale; 2012 (revised and updated).

[51] Datar M, Immorlica N, Indyk P, Mirrokni VS. Locality-sensitive hashing scheme based on p-stable distributions. In: Proceedings of the twentieth annual symposium on computational geometry. ACM; 2004. p. 253–62.

[52] Indyk P, Motwani R. Approximate nearest neighbors: towards removing the curse of dimensionality. In: Proceedings of the thirtieth annual ACM symposium on theory of computing. ACM; 1998. p. 604–13.

[53] Zaharia M, Chowdhury M, Franklin MJ, Shenker S, Stoica I. Spark: cluster computing with working sets. In: Proceedings of the 2nd USENIX conference on hot topics in cloud computing; 2010. p. 10.

[54] Li K, Yang W, Li K. Performance analysis and optimization for SpMV on GPU using probabilistic modeling. IEEE Trans Parallel Distrib Syst 2015;26(1):196–205. http://dx.doi.org/10.1109/TPDS.2014.2308221.

[55] Yang W, Li K, Mo Z, Li K. Performance optimization using partitioned SpMV on GPUs and multicore CPUs. IEEE Trans Comput 2015;64:2623–36.

[56] Mount DW, Mount DW. Bioinformatics: sequence and genome analysis, vol. 2. New York: Cold Spring Harbor Laboratory Press; 2001.

[57] Lin Z. Bioinformatics basics: applications in biological science and medicine. In: Buehler LK, Rashidi HH, editors. Briefings in Bioinformatics 2008;9(3):256–7.

[58] Nelson DL, Lehninger AL, Cox MM. Lehninger principles of biochemistry. MacMillan; 2008.

[59] Emanuelsson O, Nielsen H, Brunak S, von Heijne G. Predicting subcellular localization of proteins based on their N-terminal amino acid sequence. J Mol Biol 2000;300(4):1005–16.

[60] Garnier J, Osguthorpe D, Robson B. Analysis of the accuracy and implications of simple methods for predicting the secondary structure of globular proteins. J Mol Biol 1978;120(1):97–120.

[61] Rost B. Rising accuracy of protein secondary structure prediction. In: Protein structure determination, analysis, and modeling for drug discovery. New York, NY: Dekker; 2003. p. 207–49.

[62] Zvelebil MJ, Barton GJ, Taylor WR, Sternberg MJ. Prediction of protein secondary structure and active sites using the alignment of homologous sequences. J Mol Biol 1987;195(4):957–61.

[63] Wang G, Zhao Y, Wang D. A protein secondary structure prediction framework based on the extreme learning machine. Neurocomputing 2008;72(1):262–8.

[64] Tang Y, Yan P, Yuan Y, Li X. Single-image super-resolution via local learning. Int J Mach Learn Cybern 2011;2(1):15–23.

[65] Kang S, Park S. A fusion neural network classifier for image classification. Pattern Recogn Lett 2009;30 (9):789–93.

[66] Tzeng YC, Chen KS. A fuzzy neural network to SAR image classification. IEEE Trans Geosci Remote Sens 1998;36(1):301–7.

[67] Zhou W. Verification of the nonparametric characteristics of backpropagation neural networks for image classification. IEEE Trans Geosci Remote Sens 1999;37(2):771–9.

[68] Nakashima T, Schaefer G, Yokota Y, Ishibuchi H. A weighted fuzzy classifier and its application to image processing tasks. Fuzzy Sets Syst 2007;158(3):284–94.

[69] de Moraes RM, Banon GJF, Sandri S. Fuzzy expert systems architecture for image classification using mathematical morphology operators. Inform Sci 2002;142(1):7–21.

[70] Liu D, Wang Z. A united classification system of X-ray image based on fuzzy rule and neural networks. In: 3rd international conference on intelligent system and knowledge engineering, ISKE 2008, vol. 1. IEEE; 2008. p. 717–22.

[71] Mandal DP, Murthy C, Pal SK. Formulation of a multivalued recognition system. IEEE Trans Syst Man Cybern 1992;22(4):607–20.

[72] Pal SK, Mandal DP. Linguistic recognition system based on approximate reasoning. Inform Sci 1992;61 (1):135–61.

[73] Ishibuchi H, Yamamoto T. Rule weight specification in fuzzy rule-based classification systems. IEEE Trans Fuzzy Syst 2005;13(4):428–35.

[74] Nguyen TM, Wu QJ. A combination of positive and negative fuzzy rules for image classification problem. In: Seventh international conference on machine learning and applications. ICMLA'08. IEEE; 2008. p. 741–6.

[75] Tong DL, Mintram R. Genetic algorithm-neural network (GANN): a study of neural network activation functions and depth of genetic algorithm search applied to feature selection. Int J Mach Learn Cybern 2010;1(1–4):75–87.

[76] Jun W, Shitong W, Chung FL. Positive and negative fuzzy rule system, extreme learning machine and image classification. Int J Mach Learn Cybern 2011;2(4):261–71.

[77] Liu N, Wang H. Evolutionary extreme learning machine and its application to image analysis. J Signal Process Syst 2013;73(1):73–81.

[78] Li T, Zhang C, Ogihara M. A comparative study of feature selection and multiclass classification methods for tissue classification based on gene expression. Bioinformatics 2004;20(15):2429–37.

[79] Statnikov A, Aliferis CF, Tsamardinos I, Hardin D, Levy S. A comprehensive evaluation of multicategory classification methods for microarray gene expression cancer diagnosis. Bioinformatics 2005;21(5):631–43.

[80] Linder R, Dew D, Sudhoff H, Theegarten D, Remberger K, Pöppl SJ, et al. The subsequent artificial neural network (SANN) approach might bring more classificatory power to ANN-based DNA microarray analyses. Bioinformatics 2004;20(18):3544–52.

[81] Khan J, Wei JS, Ringner M, Saal LH, Ladanyi M, Westermann F, et al. Classification and diagnostic prediction of cancers using gene expression profiling and artificial neural networks. Nat Med 2001;7(6):673–9.

[82] Lee JW, Lee JB, Park M, Song SH. An extensive comparison of recent classification tools applied to microarray data. Comput Stat Data Anal 2005;48(4):869–85.

[83] Zhang R, Huang GB, Sundararajan N, Saratchandran P. Multicategory classification using an extreme learning machine for microarray gene expression cancer diagnosis. IEEE/ACM Trans Comput Biol Bioinform (TCBB) 2007;4(3):485–95.

[84] Lu R, Zhu H, Liu X, Liu J, Shao J. Toward efficient and privacy-preserving computing in big data era. IEEE Netw 2014;28(4):46–50.

GLOSSARY

Supervised learning The machine learning task of inferring a function from labeled training data.

Semisupervised learning A class of supervised learning tasks and techniques that also make use of unlabeled data for training C typically a small amount of labeled data with a large amount of unlabeled data.

Unsupervised learning The machine learning task of inferring a function to describe hidden structure from unlabeled data.

Single-layer feedforward networks A class of networks consisting of only a single layer of computational units, usually interconnected in a feed-forward way.

Multilayer feedforward networks A class of networks consisting of multiple layers of computational units, usually interconnected in a feed-forward way.

Recurrent neural networks A class of artificial neural network where connections between units form a directed cycle.

Scalability Capability of a system to handle a growing amount of work, or its potential to be enlarged in order to accommodate that growth.

Framework Abstraction in which software providing generic functionality can be selectively changed by additional user-written code, thus providing application-specific software.

Internet of Things The network of physical objects or things embedded with electronics, software, sensors, and network connectivity, which enables these objects to collect and exchange data.

PART

BIG DATA ANALYTICS AND SERVICES

SPATIAL BIG DATA ANALYTICS FOR CELLULAR COMMUNICATION SYSTEMS

7

Junbo Wang*, Yilang Wu*, Hui-Huang Hsu[†], Zixue Cheng*

University of Aizu, Aizuwakamatsu, Japan[*] Tamkang University, Tamsui, Taiwan[†]

ACRONYMS

ARM	Association rule mining
BS	Base station
CC	Cellular communication
CDR	Call detail record
CSR	Complete spatial randomness
EM	Expectation-maximization
MRF	Markov random field
PAM	Partitioning around medoids
QoS	Quality of service
SAR	Spatial autoregression

1 INTRODUCTION

Cellular communications (CCs) play a very important role in our daily lives by connecting people together through phone calls or data transmission. For example, a user can immediately transmit photos to their family during a trip. Meanwhile, with the development of modern communication behaviors, CC systems are encountering new challenges, such as unpredictable crowd behaviors, congested requests, and dynamic changes of the users' environments. The networking scale is growing, physical environments are changing, and social behaviors are varying. Therefore, traditional static supports are insufficient for the users in CC systems. Telecommunication operators have to plan a communication network cost-effectively to provide the necessary future capacity, to maintain real-time network requirements, and to make reliable responses to emergencies or disasters. CC systems are expected to carry out these communications goals with dynamic adjustments. However, none of those strategies can be simply done without a deep understanding of CC systems. Big data analytics provides a chance to solve the above problems. An example of the power of big data analytics is finding hidden information through deep learning or mining raw data [1]. Many applications have benefited from analyses of big data [2], and even predicting humans' futures becomes possible by data analyses [3].

CC systems are generating massive data every day and consequently initiating a new era of support from big data analytics. Generally, two kinds of data can be collected from CC systems: user-oriented and system-oriented data. Through analyses of user-oriented data in CC systems, including voice and text calls from mobile devices, short message service (SMS), and the data traffic of Internet applications, it is possible to understand and predict users' living habits. By analyzing system-oriented data from CC systems and the variations of CC systems, it is also possible to understand the development of high-density cities.

Furthermore, spatiotemporal information is gaining importance for providing more suitable support for CC systems to meet the various quality of service (QoS) requirements in complex situations. The reasons include the following: (1) most data generated in CC systems are integrated with time/location information; and (2) analyzing data from the time/location point of view provide understanding of the situation of CC systems, because people and base stations (BSs) are distributed randomly in space. Spatial big data analytics explores valuable information in spatial data by observing the spatial attributes, modeling the spatial autocorrelations (SACs), and inducing the spatial patterns of observed objects/phenomena.

Considering the importance of spatial big data analytics to CC systems, in this chapter, we comprehensively survey the foundations and methodologies of spatial big data analytics, and study possible typical applications to examine the feasibility of using spatial big data analytics for CC system support. Finally, we highlight the key challenging issues when adopting spatial big data analytics for CC systems.

2 CELLULAR COMMUNICATIONS AND GENERATED DATA

Variations of wireless networks arise from radio and spread spectrum technologies as well as communications satellites. CCs have experienced great growth along with the increasing popularity of mobile devices. We can easily and quickly find how CC is influences our daily lives. For example, we can make a phone call to a family member or transmit high-quality photos or videos to share our experiences with friends.

CC is distributed over land areas called cells, and each is served by at least one fixed-location transceiver, which is the BS. The BS provides the cell with network coverage that can be used for the transmission of voice, data, etc. CC is more advanced than a single large transmitter due to its higher capacity, larger coverage area, and lower power consumption by mobile devices.

Generally, a CC system generates two kinds of data: user-oriented data and system-oriented data.

- Call detail record (CDR) data are the main user-oriented data generated in CC systems. The data are recorded by telecommunication equipment such as a telephone exchanges or cell towers. These data are log files containing details of a single instance of communication activity, such as a voice call, SMS text, and data service initiated by the phone user. Each activity is processed by specific telecommunication equipment. Every single entry of CDR data includes parameters of the device and phone number, the exact time and date, and the call duration and location in terms of

Table 1 An Example of Call Detail Record

Call Detail	Sample Data	Unit
Calling number	123****1234	
Called number	111****1111	
Start time	May 14, 2016; 14:02:00	Second
Duration	3	Minute
Sector of each call	2048	

Table 2 An Example of Basic Information From the Cell Stations

Station	Location	No. of Calls	No. of Users
A	Commercial building	29,717	1655
B	Research institute	21,574	650
C	Commercial building	23,111	500
D	Commercial building	25,455	700

the latitude and longitude of the cell tower that provided the network signal for the communication activity of the mobile device, as well as other parameters, as shown in Table 1 as an example.

- The system-oriented information contains the information of cell stations, as shown in Table 2 as an example. The system-oriented data can provide understanding of city dynamics, changing environments of a city, and so on. For example, the data of varying locations of BSs and different communication generations can be useful for understanding the development of a city. By analyzing such data, it is possible to identify patterns and relations that reveal insightful information about the city and in turn provide authorities, service providers, and citizens with a better way of understanding, making decisions about, and exploring urban life.

3 SPATIAL BIG DATA ANALYTICS

In this section, we first review the statistical foundation for spatial big data analytics, and then we study spatial pattern mining for spatial big data analytics in detail.

3.1 STATISTICAL FOUNDATION FOR SPATIAL BIG DATA ANALYTICS

Spatial analytics, evolved from spatial data mining, looks for the fundamental spatiotemporal relations to discover the possible causes of various phenomena through the observed data. Generally, spatial data mining is divided into two classes: descriptive mining, which summarizes/characterizes the general properties of data in repositories, and perspective mining, which performs inference on current data to make predictions based on historical patterns/features. It is challenging to extract meaningful patterns from spatial data because of the complexities of spatial data types, spatial relations, and SACs, listed as follows [4]:

- The spatial data types, including the attributes of spatial location and extent of spatial objects, rely on different spatial frameworks such as set-based, topological, Euclidean, metric, and network spaces. Spatial data as input exceed the scope of classical data mining.
- Novel models or techniques are needed to incorporate spatial information into the data mining process in order to capture the implicit spatial relations, such as overlap and intersect.
- Spatial data are typically self-correlating, and so contradict the fundamental assumptions of traditional statistical analyses about the independence of samples.

To infer knowledge or evaluate hypotheses for a process, *statistical models* and *procedures* can be applied to observations. Spatial data can be considered to be the results of observations on a stochastic process $Z(s) : s \rightarrow D$, where s is a spatial location and D is a possible random set in a spatial framework. In spatial statistics, typical *statistical models* and *procedures* include *geo-statistics*, *point process*, and *lattice*, described as follows:

- *Geo-statistics* is a branch of statistics focusing on spatial or spatiotemporal datasets. It deals with the analysis of spatial continuity and weak stationarity, which are inherent characteristics of spatial data.
- *Point process* is a model for a spatial distribution of points in a point pattern, such as the positions of trees in a forest. Real point patterns are often compared with a random pattern (such as a Poisson point process) by using the average distance between a point and its nearest neighbor.
- *Lattice* is a model for a gridded space in a spatial framework. It refers to a countable collection of regular or irregular spatial sites related to each other via a neighborhood relation. Several statistical spatial analyses, for example, the spatial autoregression (SAR) model and Markov random field (MRF), can be applied to lattice data.

Several spatial models are quantified by measures such as Ripley's K-function, spatial scan statistics [5], Moran's I, local Moran index, Getis Ord, and Geary's C. The local measure of an SAC is defined as the spatial heterogeneity (or nonstationarity), namely, the variability of an observed process over space. SAC and spatial heterogeneity, which are two unique properties of spatial data, play important roles in spatial analysis. Examples of SAC are given in Section 4.

3.2 SPATIAL PATTERN MINING FROM SPATIAL BIG DATA ANALYTICS

Based on these statistical foundations, spatial analytics comprises a broad spectrum of techniques that deal with spatial objects and find important spatial patterns, such as *spatial predictive models*, *spatial outliers*, *spatial co-location rules*, and *spatial clusters* [4].

3.2.1 Spatial prediction models

Spatial prediction models are widely used as a guide to making practical decisions in crime analysis, cellular networking, and natural disasters such as fires, floods, droughts, plant diseases, and earthquakes. The spatial predictive models allow flexibility in representing the explicit spatial relations of objects in terms of distance, direction, and topology, and also in representing implicit spatial dependencies.

The SAC property represents the existence of statistical dependence in a collection of spatial variables, each of which is associated with a different geographical location. The measure of this statistical dependence is denoted as the spatial dependence. It is important in applications for postulating the existence of a corresponding set of random variables at locations that have not been observed. Based on the spatial dependence, spatial interpolation techniques are used to estimate the unobserved random outcomes of variables, for example, to estimate rainfall amounts at locations near the measured locations.

Kriging (Gaussian process regression) [6] is a typical interpolation method for spatial prediction. This method utilizes an observed spatial relation to determine the range of auto-correlation. The ordinary kriging method is most commonly used. In the kriging method, we assume that each point i in a space is associated with a value z_i. Let u represents a point whose value (i.e., z_u) is unknown. Then let $V(u) = \{1, ..., N_n\}$ be a set of neighboring points of point u, where the value z_i for each point $i \in V(u)$ is a priori. In ordinary kriging, the unknown value z_u at point u is estimated as a weighted linear combination (see Eq. 1) of the known values in $V(n)$. To produce the minimum estimation error, kriging calculates the optimal weights by using Eq. (2). In Eq. (2), $h_{i,j}$ is a distance function between points i and j, $\gamma(h_{i,j})$ is a semivariogram function for the spatial correlation measure that represents the spatial variance in the distance between all pairs of sampled locations in space, and λ is the Lagrange multiplier to minimize the kriging error. The ordinary kriging method assumes that the mean is constant in the neighborhood of a point. This means that the expected value of the estimation error at an unknown point u is zero (i.e., $E((\hat{z})_u - z_u) = 0$). The weights determined by Eq. (2) are optimal when they minimize the variance of the estimation error (i.e., $Var(\hat{z}_u - z_u)$).

$$\hat{z}_u = \sum_{i \in V(u)} w_i z_i, \quad \text{where} \sum_{i \in V(u)} w_i = 1 \tag{1}$$

$$\begin{pmatrix} w_1 \\ \vdots \\ w_{N_n} \\ \lambda \end{pmatrix} = \begin{pmatrix} \gamma(h_{1,1}) & \cdots & \gamma(h_{1,N_n}) & 1 \\ \vdots & \ddots & \vdots & 1 \\ \gamma(h_{N_n,1}) & \cdots & \gamma(h_{N_n,N_n}) & 1 \\ 1 & \cdots & 1 & 0 \end{pmatrix}^{-1} \begin{pmatrix} \gamma(h_{1,u}) \\ \vdots \\ \gamma(h_{N_n,u}) \\ 1 \end{pmatrix} \tag{2}$$

In addition to statistic approaches such as kriging, spatial classification, and regression models have been used as data mining methods for spatial prediction. Several studies (e.g., [7]) have shown that the modeling of spatial dependency (often called context) during the classification or regression process improves the overall accuracy. In most spatial datasets, variables are classified into two types, namely, independent or explanatory variables and dependent variables. Spatial classification deals with discrete dependent variables and the spatial regression deal with the continuous ones. For example, MRF is a popular classification model for incorporating spatial data into image segmentation and land-use classification problems. The SAR model incorporates the spatial dependence to extend the classical regression model for prediction problems.

3.2.2 Spatial outlier detection

Spatial outlier detection [8] (also referred to as identification of spatial outliers) is finding data with spatial features distinctive from their surrounding neighbors. Bipartite tests are typical multidimensional spatial outlier detection methods. Bipartite tests use the spatial attributes to characterize location, neighborhood, and distance, and the nonspatial attributes to compare a spatially referenced object to its neighbors.

Shekhar et al. [9] presented a unified definition for a spatial outlier. This definition does not simply abstract spatial objects as isolated points because of the neighborhood effects of the spatial properties of objects (such as boundary, size, volume, and locations) in many real applications (such as transportation, public, safety, and location-based services [10]). First, we consider a spatial framework $SF = \langle S, NB \rangle$, where $S = \{s_1, s_2, ..., s_n\}$ is a set of locations and $NB: S \times S \rightarrow \{True, False\}$ is an all-pair neighbor relation over S. Let $N(x)$ be a neighborhood relation of location x in S by referring to NB, specifically $N(x) = \{y | y \in S, NB(x, y) = True\}$.

The spatial outlier is then defined as an object O: $S\text{-outlier}(f, f_{aggr}^N, F_{diff}, ST)$.

This definition is valid if $ST\{F_{diff}[f(x), f_{aggr}^N(f(x), N(x))]\}$ is true, where R is a set of real numbers, $f: S \rightarrow R$ is an attribute function, $f_{aggr}^N: R^N \rightarrow R$ is an aggregation function for the values of f over the neighborhood, $F_{diff}: R \times R \rightarrow R$ is a difference function, and $ST: R \rightarrow \{True, False\}$ is a statistical test procedure for determining statistical significance.

As an example in the network traffic application domain, the neighborhood aggregate function $f_{aggr}^N(x) = E_{y \in N(x)}(f(y))$ is the average attribute value function over neighborhood $N(x)$. The difference function $F_{diff}(x)$ is newly expressed as $\mathcal{F}(x) = [f(x) - E_{y \in N(x)}(f(y))]$, which is the arithmetic difference between attribute function $f(x)$ and the new neighborhood aggregated function $E_{y \in N(x)}(f(y))$. If $\mu_{\mathcal{F}(x)}$ and $\sigma_{\mathcal{F}(x)}$ are the mean and standard deviation, respectively, of the new difference function $\mathcal{F}(x)$, then the significance test function ST can be defined as $Z_{\mathcal{F}(x)} = \left| \dfrac{\mathcal{F}(x) - \mu_{\mathcal{F}(x)}}{\sigma_{\mathcal{F}(x)}} \right| > 0$.

Given the mathematical definition, various statistical tools or methods are available for spatial outlier detection. The spatial statistics literature [11] provides two kinds of bipartite multidimensional tests, namely, graphical tests and quantitative tests. The graphical tests, which typically are variogram clouds [12], scatterplots [13], or Moran scatterplots [14], illustrate (visualize) the distribution of the neighborhood difference in a figure and identify points in particular portions of the figure as spatial outliers.

- Variogram clouds [12] display data points related by neighborhood. Locations that are near to one another but with large attribute differences might indicate a spatial outlier.
- Scatterplots [13] show attribute values on the X-axis and the average of the attribute values in the neighborhood on the Y-axis. A least squares regression line is used to identify spatial outliers.
- Moran scatterplots [14] plot the normalized attribute values against the neighborhood average values of the normalized attributes, and the outliers are the points surrounded by unusually high- or low-value neighbors.

However, graphical tests are limited by the lack of precise criteria to distinguish the spatial outliers. Although they share common technologies with the graphical tests, quantitative tests provide a more precise test to distinguish spatial outliers. The spatial outliers detected by scatterplots and Moran scatterplots are special cases. Shekhar et al. provided a general definition: the z-value. Further details are as follows.

- A Moran outlier is a special case of spatial outlier, and it is detected as a point located in the upper left or lower right quadrant of a Moran scatterplot.

- A scatterplot outlier is also a special case of a spatial outlier, and it is defined as a point with significant standardized residual error from the least squares regression line in the scatter plot.
- The z-value is used to detect spatial outliers for a normally distributed attributed value $f(x)$. For each location x with an attribute value $f(x)$, the outlier is detected if $Z_{\mathcal{F}(x)} = \left| \dfrac{\mathcal{F}(x) - \mu_{\mathcal{F}(x)}}{\sigma_{\mathcal{F}(x)}} \right| > \Theta$, where $\mathcal{F}(x)$ is the difference between the attribute value at location x and the average attribute value of x's neighbors, $\mu_{\mathcal{F}(x)}$ is the mean value of $\mathcal{F}(x)$, and $\sigma_{\mathcal{F}(x)}$ is the value of the standard deviation of $\mathcal{F}(x)$ over all stations. The choice of Θ depends on a specified confidence level, for example, $\Theta \approx 2$ given a confidence level of 95%.

Furthermore, due to the various formats and semantics in spatial data, spatial outlier detection algorithms are designed to accommodate the special properties of the given spatial data. For example, Shekhar et al. introduced a spatial outlier detection method for a graph dataset [15], and Zhao et al. proposed a wavelet-based method to detect region outliers in meteorological data [16].

3.2.3 Spatial co-location discovery

Spatial co-location discovery is a process to find the subsets of features that are frequently located together in the same geographic area [17]. Spatial co-location is different in the traditional association rule problem, because no natural notion of transactions in spatial datasets are embedded in continuous geographic space [18].

A spatial co-location pattern can be formalized as follows: *Assume the existence of several datasets (e.g., d_1, d_2, ..., d_k). These datasets have a spatial co-location relation if the areas with these datasets are frequently located near a neighborhood distance R_d.* For example, in the case of two datasets (d_i, d_j), we say (d_i, d_j) has a co-location pattern if for each area/point p_a with datum d_i, area/point p_b exists with datum d_j, and the distance between p_a and p_d is less than R_d.

In the literature, co-location pattern discovery is classified into two major categories: spatial statistics-based and data mining approaches. The *spatial statistics-based approaches* use the measures of spatial correlation to characterize the relation between different types of spatial events (or features). Measures of spatial correlation include the cross-K function with Monte Carlo simulation, the nearest-neighborhood and the spatial regression models [19].

In the *data mining approaches*, the clustering-based map overlay method treats every spatial attribute as a map layer and considers spatial clusters (regions) of point data in each layer as candidates for mining associations. Association rule mining (ARM) is another typical data mining method in spatial co-location discovery. ARM was first introduced in Agrawal et al. [20] as an efficient approach for finding frequent and meaningful relations, positive associations, and stochastic plus asymmetric patterns among sets of items in a large transactional database and a spatial database [21].

The spatial ARM for co-location detection is further divided into transaction-based ARM and distance-based ARM.

- The transaction-based ARM focuses on the creation of transactions over space. The transactions over space can be defined either by a reference-feature centric model [21] (if the spatial features are user-specified) or by a data-partition model [22] using a prevalence measure that is order-sensitive instead. However, it is difficult to generalize a reference-feature centric model when user-specified features simply are not available. The transactions are often implicit in the data partition model, for example, force fitting the notion of a transaction in a *continuous spatial framework* leads to the loss of the implicit spatial relations across the boundary of these transactions.

- The distance-based ARM uses the concept of a proximity neighborhood. Two representative models are the *k*-neighboring class sets proposed in Morimoto [22] and the event-centric model proposed in Shekhar and Huang [23]. The event-centric model is more advanced than the *k*-neighboring class model in addressing the limitations in the case of order-sensitive measures or no available reference features. The event-centric model can also find subsets of spatial features that occur in a neighborhood around instances of given subsets of event types.

3.2.4 Spatial clustering

The spatial clustering process labels similar objects based on similarity measures such as distance, connectivity, or their relative density in space.

Similar to *unsupervised learning* in machine learning and concept hierarchies, the cluster analysis in statistics aims at finding interesting structures or clusters from data based on natural notions of similarities without using much background knowledge. In contrast with complete spatial randomness (CSR) [11], the spatial clustered pattern is distributed dependently and attractively in space. The spatial clustering process labels similar objects based on similarity measure such as distance, connectivity, or their relative density in space. Generally, clustering methods can be categorized as *partitional clustering*, *hierarchical clustering*, or *density-based clustering*, described as follows.

1. *Partitional clustering* methods are typically *k*-means [24] methods that break *n* objects into *k* clusters to optimize a given criterion (such as the squared error function). The partitioning around medoids (PAM) algorithm [25] effectively finds the most centrally located objects as representatives of each cluster iteratively in $\mathcal{O}(k(n-k)^2)$ steps. Van der Laan et al. [26] optimized PAM for recognizing small clusters. To improve the efficiency, the sampling-based clustering large applications (CLARA) algorithm [25] was proposed to accelerate PAM to $\mathcal{O}(kS^2 + k(n-k))$ iterations on larger datasets. The CLARA based on randomized search (CLARANS) [27] algorithm outperforms CLARA and PAM both in efficiency and effectiveness by using a randomized search [28] constrained by the maximum number of neighbors, *maxneighbor*, and the number of local minima obtained, *numlocal*. However, the *k*-means algorithms only cluster single attributes at a time, and the resolution of the data model is also limited by the size of the memory buffer. Therefore, a scalable expectation-maximization (EM) [27] clustering algorithm was proposed to admit categorical and continuous attributes, and to outperform traditional in-memory implementations in large databases. Meanwhile, the outputs of partitional clustering algorithms are mostly hyperellipsoidal and of similar sizes. Therefore, it is not easy for these algorithms to find clusters with different sizes or shapes [29].

2. *Hierarchical clustering* produces a nested sequence of clusters with a single, all-inclusive cluster at the top and single-point clusters at the bottom. The agglomerative hierarchical clustering is a "bottom-up" approach with respect to a divisive one. The *centroid-* or *medoid*-based methods measure the *closeness* similarity represented by the *centroid/medoid* of clusters. For example, the balanced iterative reducing and clustering using hierarchies (BIRCH) method [30] outperforms the CLARANS algorithm for large datasets. However, the *centroid/medoid*-based methods fail in the situation that locations of data in a given cluster are closer to the center of another cluster

compared to the center of their own cluster. Such a situation occurs in the case of large variations in cluster size or concave cluster shapes [31]. Unlike the *centroid/medoid*-based methods, the *single-link* hierarchical methods such as clustering using representatives (CURE) [32] find clusters of arbitrary shapes and different sizes by measuring the similarity of the closest pair of data points belonging to different clusters. But hierarchical methods are susceptible to noise, outliers, and artifacts. The aggregate similarity-based methods such as robust clustering using links (ROCK) [33] consider new measures; for example, *interconnectivity* usually scales according to the size of clusters. However, methods such as ROCK are still limited in assuming a static user-specified *interconnectivity* model. Chameleon [29] overcomes the limitation by measuring both *interconnectivity* and *closeness* for identifying the most similar pair of clusters.

3. *Density-based clustering* finds clusters as dense regions of objects in data space. Density-based spatial clustering of applications with noise (DBSCAN) [34] defines a cluster to be a maximum set of *density-connected* points, which means that every core point in a cluster must have at least a minimum number of points *MinPts* within a given radius (EPS). As a result, DBSCAN can find clusters of arbitrary shapes if the cluster density can be determined beforehand and if the cluster density is uniform. The method of ordering points to identify the clustering structure (OPTICS) [34] extends the DBSCAN for an infinite number of distance parameters by ordering two values, *core-distance* and *reachability-distance*. The threshold estimation is still a problem in the above-mentioned model-based approaches. The density-based cluster method (DECODE) [35], which presumes the spatial data consist of different point processes and clusters with different densities, is capable of identifying the classification thresholds with little prior knowledge.

4 TYPICAL APPLICATIONS

In this section, we discuss typical applications by analyzing generated data from CC systems with the above methodologies/techniques.

4.1 BS BEHAVIOR UNDERSTANDING THROUGH SPATIAL BIG DATA ANALYTICS

First, we consider BS behavior understanding through spatial big data analytics with user- and system-oriented data. The work in Zhang et al. [36] presented an example to detect abnormal BSs from a spatial point of view. The example first measures SAC as introduced in Section 3.1, that is, Moran's indicator based on the volume of communication traffic, as defined below:

$$I = \frac{N}{\sum_i \sum_j w_{ij}} \frac{\sum_i \sum_j w_{ij}(x_i - \bar{x})(x_j - \bar{x})}{\sum_i (x_i - \bar{x})^2} \tag{3}$$

where x is the variable of interest (i.e., volume of communication traffic), x_i denotes the value of the volume of communication traffic in region i, and $\bar{x}$ represents the mean value in the whole area. N denotes the total number of observations, and w_{ij} represents the spatial weights [36].

The value of Moran's indicator ranges from -1 to 1. When Moran's indicator is 0, variable x is recognized as an independent distribution in space (e.g., a random distribution). A positive value of Moran's indicator indicates a positive spatial correlation, and conversely, a negative value indicates a negative spatial correlation of x.

Then the work in Zhang et al. [36] discovered the information behind the data, and found that BSs with positive correlation are of the same low-level traffic as their neighbors (please refer to Fig. 3 in Zhang et al. [36] for details). The results possibly support the ability to find abnormal BSs, because they found that the BSs that are different from their neighbors can be distinguished with spatial correlation detection.

The above study is rather important to help future cellular optimization and resource planning. However, the shortcoming is that automatic detection is not realized. The reason is that Moran's indicator is just a statistical foundation for spatial big data analytics, as introduced in Section 3.1. Without support from the spatial pattern mining methods introduced in Section 3.2, automatic detection is impossible. Because spatial big data analytics for CC systems are still at an emerging stage, not enough studies have investigated how spatial big data analytics support CC systems. As listed below, we explore further possible applications and study their possibilities with the assumed data and knowledge on spatial big data analytics introduced in Section 3.2.

- *Spatial prediction*: By adopting the spatial prediction models introduced in Section 3.2.1, the situations in unknown areas are possible to understand based on observations of the surrounding areas. Assume we collect information on the communication rate of each user and the geo-information when the user is served by the CC systems. Spatial dependency exists in the above data because the communication rate is mainly influenced by environments (e.g., heights of buildings). Users at the same regions possibly have a similar communication rate, if they are assumed to use mobile devices of similar performance. Then through the kriging method (Eq. 1), the value in the unknown areas can be modeled by using the observations in the surrounding areas. More complex spatial dependency can also be defined, for example, by adopting the MRF in spatial big data analytics and by considering neighboring subareas having similar communication situations [37].
- *Spatial outlier detection*: This can support automatic detection of BSs with abnormal behaviors. The coverage hole in a cellular network is a type of spatial outlier due to the distribution of BSs. According to the outlier model described in Section 3, BSs can be considered as spatial objects, which have spatial features such as size and boundary, and also nonspatial attributes such as communication traffic rate of multiple mobile operators. The communication traffic rate can be modeled as the attribute function $f(x)$, where x denotes the historical location of mobile operators, and the neighborhood effects can be modeled as the aggregated function F_{aggr}^{N}. Then a significance test for the difference between $f(x)$ and F_{aggr}^{N} helps to detect the existence of a spatial outlier after the test values are above the predefined threshold Θ. The coverage hole in a cellular network could be further indicated based on the BSs' spatial outlier detection.
- *Spatial co-location discovery*: The co-location of new generation BSs with existing older generation BSs such as 2G provides an effective way of achieving full coverage while fulfilling QoS requirements. Understanding the co-location patterns of existing BSs and their QoS performance can help to make plans or evaluate the distribution of new BSs.
- *Spatial clustering*: Spatial clustering of the BSs helps to break down a large-scale cellular network into smaller clusters. In each cluster, the BSs with similar features are close to each other. This can improve the maintenance efficiency of BSs by properly scheduling unified maintenance tasks to the clusters.

4.2 **USER BEHAVIOR UNDERSTANDING THROUGH SPATIAL BIG DATA ANALYTICS**

Another typical application for spatial big data analytics in CC systems is user behavior detection, which includes single-user and multiuser cases. For the single-user case, an anomaly detection method is proposed in Karatepe and Zeydan [38]. This method is based on CDR data from a mobile service provider in Turkey. The main idea is to detect suspicious CITY ID and CELL ID pairs by analyzing the details of the user's call activities through knowledge-based rules. For example, an abnormal trip can be detected due to a longer traveling time between two cities. The time stamps are collected through the call records of different cells.

Through understanding the behavior of multiusers in CC systems, it is possible to understand new communication or behavior trends, the spatial structure of a high-density city, and so on. For example, in Chen et al. [39], the urban spatial structure is identified through CDR data. The urban spatial structure often refers to the sets of human flows occurring from the regular interactions between different functional regions of an urban area, such as daily travel behaviors. The travel behaviors cause relatively frequently human flows, which can be considered as the hot lines between different functional regions. The study finally shows hot lines would be quantified as relatively popular channels that exist in two different functional regions.

Next, we further explore the possible application when adopting spatial pattern mining methods into an application as follows.

- *Spatial prediction*: As discussed in Section 3.2.1, spatial prediction models discover nonspatial values at unknown locations through observation of values at surrounding areas, based on spatial dependencies retrieved from domain knowledge. However, when we consider applications to detect users' behavior, the spatial dependency is unclear and too much of a contingency factor for modeling.
- *Spatial outlier detection*: This is expected to be adopted in this kind of application, to detect hot points where the people have abnormal behaviors. For example, suppose CC systems provide CDR data with very precise geo-location information; then the frequency of people going through each location/point can be calculated and used as spatial objects in the spatial outlier detection method. The nonspatial values (i.e., frequency of visiting) can be modeled by attribute function $f(x)$, and the neighboring effects are represented by the aggregated function F_{aggr}^{N}. Through further calculation, as shown in Section 3.2.2, spatial outliers can be detected. For example, a spatial outlier is a strange point with very few visits even when the surrounding locations are popular (i.e., high visiting frequency). The information behind the data could be a destroyed road, especially in a disaster scenario. The above detection can help users to find a better route.
- *Spatial co-location discovery*: This discovers features/data that are frequently located in the same areas. Assume we have the same data (i.e., frequency of visiting). Then, assume we have another dataset (e.g., store information around the street). The spatial co-location can help us to find the spatial relation between the frequency of visiting and the type of store. A possible result could be that young people often visit fashion shops at lunch time.
- *Spatial clustering*: This groups data with similar features together, and so this clustering has many applications considering multiuser behaviors. Spatial clustering supports a system to detect the areas where people often have similar specific behaviors and then discovers unobservable hidden information.

5 CONCLUSION AND FUTURE CHALLENGING ISSUES

In this chapter, we comprehensively review methodologies and techniques in spatial big data analytics. We classify typical applications in CC systems by adopting spatial data analytics. Furthermore, we analyze how big data analysis methodologies and techniques support CC systems. The spatial big data analysis techniques can possibly be adopted in CC systems, although this presents the following challenging issues [37].

(1) *Discovering and modeling spatial relations of data*: Spatial analytics, especially for spatial prediction, requires modeling of the spatial relations of the data first. The relations should be analyzed based on the domain knowledge or training dataset, but efficient and sufficient spatial relations have still not been studied adequately to support future applications of CC systems.

(2) *Incompleteness of data*: Spatial analytics faces barriers because the system may not collect enough crowd data from users in all subareas. It is expected that predicting undetectable data will be based on detected data, and so this becomes the second future challenge. Fortunately, associations/patterns of data from the spatial point of view can possibly be extracted from data collected in other areas, but the corresponding prediction models will need to be developed in the future.

(3) *Computation complexity*: The increasing size, variety, and update rate of spatial datasets exceed the capacity of commonly used spatial computing technologies to learn, manage, and process data within a reasonable response time. Efficient or parallel storing and analyzing of spatial big data is an important challenge. Currently, some cloud platforms have been built to store and query spatial big data efficiently, for example, SpatialHadoop, Hadoop-GIS, and GIS tools for Hadoop released by the Environmental Systems Research Institute (ESRI). However, the surveyed spatial data analysis methods are still conducted in the traditional way. A more efficient or parallel way to process spatial data analytics is another challenge.

ACKNOWLEDGMENTS

This research was supported by JST-NSF joint funding, Strategic International Collaborative Research Program, SICORP, entitled "Dynamic Evolution of Smartphone-Based Emergency Communications Network," from 2015 to 2018.

REFERENCES

[1] Chen X, Lin X. Big data deep learning: challenges and perspectives. IEEE Access 2014;2:514–25.
[2] Katal A, Wazid M, Goudar R. Big data: issues, challenges, tools and good practices. In: 2013 Sixth international conference on contemporary computing (IC3). IEEE; 2013. p. 404–9.
[3] Asur S, Huberman B, et al. Predicting the future with social media. In: 2010 IEEE/WIC/ACM international conference on web intelligence and intelligent agent technology. IEEE; 2010. p. 492–9.
[4] Shekhar S, Zhang P, Huang Y, Vatsavai RR. Trends in spatial data mining. In: Data mining: next generation challenges and future directions. CiteSeer; 2003. p. 357–80.

[5] Kulldorff M. A spatial scan statistic. Commun Stat Theory methods 1997;26(6):1481–96.

[6] Stein ML. Interpolation of spatial data: some theory for kriging. Springer Series in Statistics. Springer New York, NY: Springer Science+Business Media; 1999.

[7] Jhung Y, Swain PH. Bayesian contextual classification based on modified M-estimates and Markov random fields. IEEE Trans Geosci Remote Sens 1996;34(1):67–75.

[8] Shekhar S, Lu C, Zhang P. Detecting graph-based spatial outliers. Intell Data Anal 2002;6(5):451–68.

[9] Shekhar S, Lu C-T, Zhang P. A unified approach to detecting spatial outliers. GeoInformatica 2003;7 (2):139–66.

[10] Shekhar S, Chawla S. A tour of spatial databases. Upper Saddle River, NJ: Prentice Hall; 2002.

[11] Cressie N. Statistics for spatial data. New York, NY: Wiley; 1993.

[12] Haslett J, Bradley R, Craig P, Unwin A, Wills G. Dynamic graphics for exploring spatial data with application to locating global and local anomalies. Am Stat 1991;45(3):234–42.

[13] Anselin L. Interactive techniques and exploratory spatial data analysis. In: Longley P, Goodchild M, Maguire D, Rhind D, editors. Geographical information systems: principles, techniques, management and applications. Cambridge: Geoinformation Int; 1999.

[14] Anselin L. The Moran scatterplot as an ESDA tool to assess local instability in spatial association. Morgantown, WV: Regional Research Institute, West Virginia University; 1993.

[15] Shekhar S, Lu C-T, Zhang P. Detecting graph-based spatial outliers: algorithms and applications (a summary of results). In: Proceedings of the seventh ACM SIGKDD international conference on knowledge discovery and data mining. ACM; 2001. p. 371–6.

[16] Zhao J, Lu C-T, Kou Y. Detecting region outliers in meteorological data. In: 11th ACM international symposium on advances in geographic information systems. ACM; 2003. p. 49–55.

[17] Zala M, Rushirajsinh L, Mehta M, Brijesh B, Zala M, Mahipalsinh R. A survey on spatial co-location patterns discovery from spatial datasets. Int J Comput Trends Technol 2014;7(3):137–42.

[18] Huang Y, Shekhar S, Xiong H. Discovering colocation patterns from spatial data sets: a general approach. IEEE Trans Knowl Data Eng 2004;16(12):1472–85.

[19] Chou YH. Exploring spatial analysis in Gis. Onword Pr; 1996.

[20] Agrawal R, Imieliński T, Swami A. Mining association rules between sets of items in large databases. ACM Sigmod Record. vol. 22. No. 2. ACM; 1993.

[21] Koperski K, Han J. Discovery of spatial association rules in geographic information databases. International symposium on spatial databases. Springer Berlin Heidelberg; 1995.

[22] Morimoto Y. Mining frequent neighboring class sets in spatial databases. In: Proceedings of the seventh ACM SIGKDD international conference on knowledge discovery and data mining. ACM; 2001. p. 353–8.

[23] Shekhar S, Huang Y. Discovering spatial co-location patterns: a summary of results. International symposium on spatial and temporal databases. Springer Berlin Heidelberg; 2001.

[24] Singh SS, Chauhan N. K-means v/s K-medoids: a comparative study. In: National conference on recent trends in engineering & technology. vol. 13. 2011.

[25] Kaufman L, Rousseeuw PJ. Finding groups in data: an introduction to cluster analysis. vol. 344. John Wiley & Sons; 2009.

[26] Van der Laan M, Pollard K, Bryan J. A new partitioning around medoids algorithm. J Stat Comput Simul 2003;73(8):575–84.

[27] Bradley PS, Fayyad U, Reina C. Scaling EM (expectation-maximization) clustering to large databases. Microsoft Research Redmond; 1998. Technical Report MSR-TR-98-35.

[28] Ioannidis YE, Kang Y. Randomized algorithms for optimizing large join queries. ACM SIGMOD Rec 1990;19(2):312–21.

[29] Karypis G, Han E, Kumar V. Chameleon: hierarchical clustering using dynamic modeling. Computer 1999;32(8):68–75.

[30] Zhang T, Ramakrishnan R, Livny M. Birch: an efficient data clustering method for very large databases. ACM Sigmod Rec 1996;25(2):103–14.

[31] Han E-H, Karypis G, Kumar V, Mobasher B. Hypergraph based clustering in high-dimensional data sets: a summary of results. IEEE Data Eng Bull 1998;21(1):15–22.

[32] Guha S, Rastogi R, Shim K. CURE: an efficient clustering algorithm for large databases. 27; 1998. 73–84.

[33] Guha S, Rastogi R, Shim K. ROCK: a robust clustering algorithm for categorical attributes. In: IEEE 15th international conference on data engineering. 1999. p. 512–21.

[34] Ester M, Kriegel H-P, Sander J, Xu X. A density-based algorithm for discovering clusters in large spatial databases with noise. In: Knowledge discovery in databases. vol. 96. 1996. p. 226–31.

[35] Pei T, Jasra A, Hand DJ, Zhu A-X, Zhou C. DECODE: a new method for discovering clusters of different densities in spatial data. Data Min Knowl Disc 2009;18(3):337–69.

[36] Zhang S, Yin D, Zhang Y, Zhou W. Computing on base station behavior using Erlang measurement and call detail record. IEEE Trans Emerg Topics Comput 2015;3(3):444–53.

[37] Wang J, Wu Y, Yen N, Guo S, Cheng Z. Big data analytics for emergency communication networks: a survey. IEEE Commun Surv Tutorials 2016;18(3):1758–78.

[38] Karatepe IA, Zeydan E. Anomaly detection in cellular network data using big data analytics. In: 20th European wireless conference, European wireless 2014. Barcelona, Spain: VDE; 2014. p. 1–5.

[39] Chen S, Wu H, Tu L, Huang B. Identifying hot lines of urban spatial structure using cellphone call detail record data. In: 2014 IEEE 11th intl conf on ubiquitous intelligence and computing (UTC-ATC-ScalCom). IEEE; 2014. p. 299–304.

GLOSSARY

Spatial prediction This estimates values of target variable at a new location, using sampled values and auxiliary data (e.g., map) that can be used to explain variation of the target variable.

Spatial co-location This represents the subsets of spatial events whose instances are often located in close geographic proximity.

Spatial outlier A spatially referenced object whose nonspatial attribute values are significantly different from the values of its neighborhood.

Spatial clustering This permits a generalization of the spatial component like explicit location and extension of spatial objects which define implicit relations of spatial neighborhood, and groups similar spatial objects into classes.

COGNITIVE APPLICATIONS AND THEIR SUPPORTING ARCHITECTURE FOR SMART CITIES

Haytham Assem*, Lei Xu*, Teodora S. Buda*, Declan O'Sullivan†

IBM, Dublin, Ireland* Trinity College Dublin, Dublin, Ireland†

ACRONYMS

CPM	constrained Poisson model
CSE	cognitive smart engine
DA	deep autoencoder
DBNs	deep belief networks
FFNN	feed forward neural networks
IoT	Internet of Things
LBSN	location-based social network
LDA	latent Dirichlet allocation
OPEX	operating expense
PCA	principle component analysis
POIs	point of interests
RBM	restricted Boltzmann machine
RSM	replicated Softmax model
SLA	service level agreement

1 INTRODUCTION

A smart city is defined as a city where "investments in human and social capital and traditional (transport) and modern (ICT) communication infrastructure fuel sustainable economic development and a high quality of life, with a wise management of natural resources, through participatory governance" [1]. Sensors positioned on various objects such as vehicles, patients or smart devices falling under the broad definition of Internet of Things (IoT) can be an essential part of future smart cities since they provide monitoring systems state information that is the cornerstone of the management of smart cities. These sensors communicate with each other through high-speed networks. It is expected that there will be billions of devices connected to these networks, which will generate substantial amounts of data. The management system has to track these devices and their generated data to yield insights, detect meaningful events and conditions, and respond to them correctly.

The challenges of big data management can be tackled by machine learning techniques, which are supposed to deploy on a supporting architecture that enables both batch and real-time processing to meet demands of different smart city scenarios. This chapter will propose a cognitive smart engine (CSE) to support machine learning techniques. It consumes state records on the hardware and software resources gathered in real-time from multiple functional blocks. The collected records will be processed by the engine in (near) real-time or periodically. Real-time processing is one of the core contributions of this work that will be crucial to real-time smart city applications, since they aim to provide immediate response to changes.

The growth of devices and their supporting network and computer systems also bring more failures from both hardware and software perspectives, resulting in a discomfort in user experience and potentially in revenues losses for providers. Instead of over-provisioning resource that can produce very large cost, providers could track resource state and adjust provision dynamically to avoid this problem.

Manual inspection of the state of hardware and software systems is not feasible due to the sheer size of data. Autonomous anomaly detection—discovering unexpected pattern, which is empowered by big data ecosystems, such as our CSE—can be one solution. The chapter will introduce the concept of anomaly detection and its related work. It is supposed to detect abnormal events and respond to them correctly to mitigate negative impacts, which forms the basis for a dynamic and robust management system for smart cities.

The proliferation of wireless sensors and the popularity of social networks over the past few years has led to the significant rise of social network data, especially location-based social network (LBSN). These data can potentially bridge the gap between the physical and digital online world. The analysis of data generated from LBSN has been proved to facilitate the identification of urban patterns, understanding activity behaviors in urban areas, as well as producing novel suggestions on resource deployment and migration for smart city application providers.

Machine learning techniques are an ideal vehicle for yielding insights from LBSN. A typical domain area that can benefit from the analysis is urban planning, which utilizes both spatial (geo-tagged location) and temporal (time-stamped) information of LBSN to understand functionality of regions within cities. This chapter will review the state-of-the-art in the area and propose a new approach for discovering spatio-temporal functional regions in a city using LBSN data. This solution is a step towards urban planning to facilitate the design of urban environment and make the best use of available resources.

Meanwhile, recent advancements in machine learning techniques promise new deeper insights with the possibility of finding new spatio-temporal patterns in cities. This chapter will present one of the recent advancements in machine learning, deep belief networks (DBNs), which has the potential to discover a new type of pattern: the Socio-demographic Regional Pattern. Specifically, the presented work will explain how DBNs can be applied for urban pattern discovery. It is expected that this work can pave the way towards a deeper understanding about social commonalities and the geographical evolution of different regions and areas, within cities across the globe.

2 CSE FOR SMART CITY APPLICATIONS

The development of networks, hardware, and software technologies is enabling billions of smart devices, sensors, and controllers to be connected and share data and knowledge. This paves the way towards a new generation of smart city applications and services by harvesting huge amounts of available data. However, this new opportunity also raises challenges on fast and continuous processing of big data due to the dynamicity and unpredictability of city crowds.

To tackle the challenge on big data processing in the context of smart cities, this section presents a CSE, which takes account of the key features of big data on volume, velocity, variety, and veracity to yield insights from data efficiently and effectively. This engine is agonistic to any services/applications, and it is not dependent on any specific systems or implementation techniques. The CSE collects data from multiple resources, such as data streams generated by monitoring systems or sensors and frozen data sets. It is compatible with all services/applications of smart cities, and can be reused and redeployed between different cities. This enables data collection from both the resource provider-side and consumer-side. This double-sided data collection can potentially increase the openness and transparency of smart city applications/ services, and subsequently provide better user experiences.

The collected data are analyzed by CSE and then output some key values that will be consumed by certain components to adjust resource offering for various purposes, such as dynamic resource allocation, security threats and performance degradation detection, demand prediction, or to guide some components generating management policies.

2.1 ARCHITECTURE SPECIFICATION

The high-level architecture of the CSE is depicted graphically in Fig. 1, which consists of the following components:

- Data collector—this collects data from resources, and maps collected data into those that are suitable for further operations.
- Data cleaning and filtering—this cleans and refines received data, and then places them into the data storage or forwards them to the (near) real-time processing engine.
- Data storage—this stores data, and makes them available for multiple components constituting the CSE.

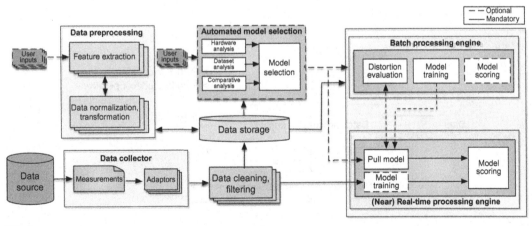

FIG. 1

High-level architecture of the Cognitive Smart Engine (CSE).

- Data pre-processing—this can work in either automatic or manual mode to pre-process collected data in the data storage and make them ready for further analysis. Feature extraction can be implemented with Deep Neural Networks, which are capable of generating highly informative features automatically. Such functionality is essential to support the overall flexibility of the architecture and to keep it adjustable to a constantly changing environment. It will help us control the complexity of models and reduce the processing time when dealing with big data applications.
- Algorithm selection—similar to data pre-processing, this component is able to identify the model(s) that will be deployed on processing engines automatically or based on customer requirements. In the automatic mode, it will take account into the features of given data sets, the performance of candidate algorithms, and available resources of the selected processing engine.
- Batch processing engine—this retrieves processed data from data storage, and applies these data to train a model based on pre-configuration or outputs from algorithm selection, or generate scores. In the former case, the batch processing engine will evaluate the distortion of the current model periodically. If the model has become "stale" or no model is available, it will generate a new model from scratch to facilitate the work of the (Near) Real-time Processing Engine. In the latter case, this engine works independently to analyze collected records in a more accurate but higher latency manner. Note that the scoring in both the batch processing engine and (near) real-time processing engine is not to simply apply one machine learning model but may involve a sequence of models associated with post-processing.
- (Near) real-time processing engine—this consumes processed data from the data collector directly instead of data storage, and scores the received data within a short period of time. This can be achieved by applying the model generated by the batch processing engine, or lightweight on-line learning approaches directly, such as some online clustering algorithms. Details on how the two processing engines can work cooperatively or independently are specified graphically in Fig. 2. Depending on the latency requirement of an application, this component can generate scores either in real-time if it is implemented and deployed in a distributed real-time computation system, such as Apache Storm, or near real-time if it is powered by a mini-batch system, such as Spark Streaming.

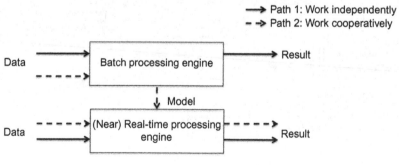

FIG. 2

Modes of Operations for the CSE.

2.2 **BIG DATA ANALYSIS AND MANAGEMENT**

This smart engine is designed to process substantial amounts of data that will be generated by a variety of devices and systems in smart cities. In practice, these data are collected based on different time intervals and diverse schemes, and the quality and accuracy of the data are less controllable. To solve the diversity of data sources, the CSE is able to transform different types of data into one that can be processed by the engine directly. This addresses the variety of big data.

The CSE is equipped with data pre-processing, which identifies suitable predictor variables and performs a number of operations, such as data transformation and normalization, to improve the quality of collected data and tackle the uncertainty of data—veracity. Meanwhile, due to the velocity of big data, the CSE may not have a priori knowledge on models suitable for given data sets, and algorithms need to be identified on-the-fly, which is addressed by the algorithm selection component. In addition, the CSE is supported by two processing engines to tackle the challenges raised by big data analysis. The batch processing engine aims to offer accurate insights on vast amounts of data but it comes with high latency, whereas the (near) real-time processing engine deal with a small amount of records with minimal latency. The two engines cooperate with each other to handle massive quantities of data by taking advantage of both batch and stream-processing methods.

The CSE addresses feature pre-processing including feature extraction and algorithms selection, and also supports both real-time and batch processing. It is able to support most machine learning techniques widely used today. Potentially, it is a key enabler for lots of sub-components of management systems for smart city applications, such as anomaly detection, from a big data analysis point of view.

3 **ANOMALY DETECTION IN SMART CITY MANAGEMENT**

Smart city services are typically supported by huge amounts of hardware and software resources, which are expected to be available at all times to ensure service level agreements (SLAs). This requires significant efforts in continuously monitoring large volumes of data in order to detect abnormal events, such as potential performance degradations and intrusions. Manual inspection of these data such as visual spikes detection has become infeasible due to the sheer size of the problem, whereas machine learning is a potential solution to discovering anomalies in an automated manner.

Anomaly detection refers to the problem of finding patterns in data that do not conform to expected behavior. These nonconforming patterns are often referred to as anomalies, outliers, discordant observations, exceptions, aberrations, surprises, peculiarities, or contaminants in different application domains [2]. There have been many anomaly detection techniques proposed in various smart city applications, such as: fraud detection for financial systems, health-related problems, performance optimization, etc. However, as the complexity of systems and size of collected data are constantly increasing, manual selecting and turning techniques become infeasible.

The most common existing techniques deployed in real systems employ threshold-based methods, which can be categorized into parametric and nonparametric ones. Parametric methods make assumptions of the underlying distribution of the data set and determine threshold values based on the distribution. However, this assumption is often violated in practice. Contrarily, nonparametric methods avoid making such assumptions but determine the threshold in an ad-hoc manner. However, both approaches cannot adapt to varying patterns in incoming data sets, and often require significant efforts in tuning the threshold value.

Machine learning-based methods for anomaly detections, which do not rely on assumption on thresholds, can be divided into three classes: supervised, semi-supervised, and un-supervised. Supervised learning detection requires a data set where each row is labeled and typically it involves training a classifier on a training set. Semi-supervised algorithms construct a model to represent the normal behavior from an input normal training data set; following the model is used to calculate the likelihood of the testing data set to be generated by the model. Unsupervised models do not require a labeled data set and operate under the assumption that the majority of the data points are normal (e.g., employing clustering techniques) and return the remaining ones as outliers. Recent efforts reveal systems that employ more than one existing anomaly detection techniques. They utilize an ensemble approach such as a voting mechanism for determining the result, for instance, Skyline [3] declares a metric as anomalous when a consensus of six techniques detecting it is reached.

3.1 RELATED WORK TO ANOMALY DETECTION

The anomaly detection survey [2] introduces several anomaly detection techniques based on certain categories: point anomalies, contextual anomalies, and collective anomalies:

- A point anomaly occurs when an individual point can be considered as an anomaly compared to the rest of the data. For example, points outside the boundary of a normal region (e.g., large clusters) could be anomalies.
- A contextual anomaly occurs when a data instance can be considered as an anomaly only in a specific context, and not otherwise. The context in this case can be, for instance, the latitude and longitude of a data point, as it determines its position in a location, or the time, as it determines its position in a sequence.
- A collective anomaly occurs when a collection of data instances can be considered anomalous compared to the entire data set. The individual data points might not be anomalies, but their appearing together as a collection is anomalous. For instance, a collective sequence of actions within a script on a computer could be considered anomalous while each individual command is not.

In particular, contextual anomalies have been most commonly explored in time-series data [4,5] and spatial data [6,7]. Considering a temperature time series showing the monthly temperature of an area, unusual temperatures can be discovered within a certain season. For instance, a temperature of 35°C might be normal during the summer at that place, but the same value is an anomaly during winter. The anomaly detection techniques typically focus on a particular application domain or research area (e.g., intrusion detection, fraud detection, medical and public health, image processing, text processing, sensor data, etc.). The survey [8] presents intrusion detection techniques in the cloud. Anomaly detection has been applied to several other domains such as speech recognition [9,10], novelty detection in robot behavior [11–14], traffic monitoring [7], click-through protection [15], detecting faults in web applications [16,17], detecting anomalies in biological data [18,19], detecting anomalies in census data [20], detecting associations among criminal activities [21], detecting anomalies in customer relationship management data [21], detecting anomalies in astronomical data [22,23], and detecting ecosystem disturbances [6,24].

The popularity of sensing techniques and high-speed connections has generated a diverse set of data on human activities and behaviors in cities, which may represent urban dynamics and rhythms. Detecting anomalies in different regions of a city enables us to better understand user behaviors and urban crowds, and to facilitate resource provision for better user experiences. Lots of research work has been done based on a single data source for various purposes, such as outlier trajectories detection [25,26], traffic anomaly identification [27], problematic design collection [28,29]. However, data sets collected in the context of smart cities can be very sparse in many cases due to the plurality of expected IoT devices and their diversity. Therefore, integrating multiple data sets can give us a wider and clearer picture on urban anomalies. Combining multiple data sets to detect anomalies can be performed successively [30,31] or simultaneously [32].

3.2 CHALLENGES AND BENEFITS OF ANOMALY DETECTION IN SMART CITIES

It is expected that a huge amount of data will be tracked by anomaly detections in smart cities. Therefore, the first challenge needs to be addressed by anomaly detection is how to handle, analyze, and manage this substantial amount of data efficiently. Moreover, the anomaly detection in a smart city focuses on applying anomaly detection algorithms on data collected for instance from networking services, in order to detect anomalies in these cases in a timely manner to allow sufficient time for corrective actions. These anomalies reflect potential performance degradations and thus early discovery and proactive correction can have a significant impact on the performance of the system under analysis. Therefore, another challenge encountered is the timely discovery of the anomalies, coupled with the appropriate corrective actions to take.

These challenges are supposed to be tackled by the analysis part of anomaly detection systems, such as the CSE introduced in Section 2. It should take into account the volume, velocity, variety, and veracity of the data and yield insights from data efficiently and effectively. It should also be able to scale horizontally or vertically to handle various smart cities scenarios.

Once the challenges have been addressed, anomaly detection can benefit IoT resource management in smart cities from the following aspects:

1. *SLA management*: Through the timely detection of anomalies within hardware or software resources and their associated corrective measures performed before the degradation occurs, the anomaly detection application can improve the SLA compliance of the environment.
2. *Operating expense (OPEX) management*: Anomaly detection can aid in discovering performance degradations that help lower the costs associated with downtime and revenue losses triggered by poor user experience. Through a detection and correction of performance degradations in a timely manner, this cost can be significantly reduced.
3. *Equipment cost and resources overprovisioning reduction*: Studies have shown that servers in many existing data centers are often severely underutilized due to overprovisioning for the peak demand in order to avoid performance degradations. Overprovisioning for the peak demand and redundancy are both measures taken for preparing the system for a demanding workload and to avoid performance degradations, such as downtime. However, these measures produce substantial costs. These measures need to be avoided in a smart city, and more efficient and less costly mechanisms need to be investigated. The Anomaly Detection application is expected to aid in reducing the need of overprovisioning and increasing the resources utilization, while minimizing the damaging effects of performance degradations.

4 FUNCTIONAL REGION AND SOCIO-DEMOGRAPHIC REGIONAL PATTERNS DETECTION IN CITIES

The research community is exploring the potential of harnessing the power of the data on human activities and behaviors to impact different domain areas including urban planning, marketing, urban energy, and economy. Urban planning focuses on planning the land use in cities. It relies on the knowledge on the functionality of regions within cities since this will facilitate the design of urban environments and make the best use of the available spaces to increase the well-being of citizens. Urban planning also interests in discovering regional patterns that is helpful to understand citizen behaviors and activity patterns. For many years, lots of approaches have been proposed to investigate both topics in a city using socio-demographic data.

4.1 DISCOVERING FUNCTIONAL REGIONS

To discover functional regions in cities, urban planners require huge amount of data on urban land use that is typically gathered from direct observations or questionnaires that captures how citizens interact with the urban environment. However, this approach has some obvious limitations in relation to the cost for running surveys and gathering such amount of data, in addition to privacy concerns from citizens for providing such information. An alternative approach for capturing functional regions and land use is geographic information systems, which provides satellite imagery, and has the possibility to capture land use through advanced vision techniques. Nevertheless, such techniques fail to capture real-time information as satellite images are not captured frequently.

An alternative type of data set to support urban planning is LBSN, which is collected by sensors widely deployed on mobile devices and smartphones. The LBSN empowers people to share their activity-related choices using their social networks (e.g., Facebook, Twitter, Foursquare). LBSN leads to the emergence of a type of uncontrolled experimental context resulting in data sets with novels characteristics by enabling anyone to participate in sharing data. Although previous mobility data featured geographical coordinates of users, LBSN comes with fundamentally different attributes [33]: first, LBSN not only reports the geographical coordinates of the user but also identifies the venues where users check-in, such as restaurants, outdoor activities, or a stadium. In other words, it has the power to correlate the location of the user along with their activity. In addition, these broadcasts contain semantically rich information such as tips, comments, or recommendations on the venues visited by the users. Finally, the scale of LBSN data is all based on the user level participation that itself gives some cultural, socio-demographic, and behavioral insights of different cities [34].

LBSN data represents a treasure that is still under-explored, especially the added location dimension on social networks that bridges the gap between the physical world and the digital online social network services. This addition has stimulated the research community into identifying new human-generated patterns in cities that can find a natural application for not only predicting events and providing novel recommender systems that facilitate users' choices and social interactions, but also discovering social commonalities among people [35]. In addition, by coupling real-time social systems like Twitter, Facebook, and Google Buzz with the location-sharing services like Foursquare, Gowalla, and Google Latitude, we can foresee an unprecedented access to activities, actions, and footprints of millions of people [34]. This has the potential for deeper insights and better geospatial understanding of cities' unique characteristics and the collective conscious of the people who reside, work, and play in different regions of cities.

4.1.1 Related work to functional region detections

Based on traditional human mobility and survey data, there have been several attempts to utilize human mobility in the form of spatial-temporal patterns to infer the functional regions by cell phone Erlang data [36,37], taxicab data [38,39], Wi-Fi data [39], and smart card data [40]. Besides the human mobility data, some other studies have relied on using activity-based survey data to explore the spatial-temporal pattern and then derive the functional regions of a city [39]. Unfortunately, human mobility and survey data have their own limitations. Human mobility data is subject to a lack of travel demand information that consequently impacts the detailed characteristics of regions that can be inferred. Hence, empirical analysis is needed to infer cluster of regions' type leading to an inability to distinguish between the non-home/work activities [39]. To overcome these challenges, Yuan et al. used human mobility among both regions and point of interests (POIs) located in a region [39]. They introduced a topic-based inference model that links the human mobility with POIs; however, this is not always the case in real scenarios. For instance, one user may go to a library that is beside a shopping center. If the library is not in the POI data, then that user's movement will be linked to shopping rather than an educational purpose.

Meanwhile, with the rise of LBSNs such as Foursquare, Twitter, and Flickr, it is feasible to record a user's surrounding along with their movement routes through so-called "check-in." Unlike data from cell phone and car trajectories data, check-in data contain not only the location but also the activity category of the user. False check-in is one of the obvious challenges in relying on this data, but Cheng et al. [39] proposed a series of rules to eliminate false check-ins, while We et al. [41] introduced five criteria to discover the fake/untrusted check-ins. Consequently, these data are a great source for discovering functional regions compared to the previous type of data. Justin et al. [42] relied on LBSN data to discover sub-urban areas from Foursquare data referred to as Livehoods. Thiago et al. [43] measured eight cities dynamics on a large scale using LBSN data. However, they did not consider the interdependence between the functional regions and human activities that has been studied in detail by Ye et al. in Ref. [44].

4.1.2 Discovering functional regions

The discovered spatio-temporal functions regions can not only help people better understand complex metropolitans but can also benefit a variety of applications, such as personalized recommendations, urban planning, and better deployment of resources in cities. This section proposes a clustering-based approach for discovering spatio-temporal functional regions in a city using LBSN data.

Problem definitions

Let $R_{|t|}$ denote all the physical regions that will act as the input to the clustering techniques based on interval $|t|$. The inputs to the clustering technique is defined as a normalized vector forming a matrix $R_{|t|}$:

$$R_{|t|} = \begin{bmatrix} r_{1,1} & r_{1,2} \cdots & r_{1,D} \\ \vdots & \ddots & \vdots \\ r_{N,1} & r_{N,2} \cdots & r_{N,D} \end{bmatrix}, \tag{1}$$

where N indicates the number of zip codes and D represents the number of keywords (functionality). Hence, the input vector for each functionality is represented as

$$\hat{r}_i = R_{:i} = [r_{1,i}, ..., r_{N,i}]. \tag{2}$$

According to the above notation, let C denote all regions of a given city; $R_{|t|}$ of a functionality i to a zip code j for all places p that belong to functionality i within j can be defined as

$$r_{i,j} = \sum_{a \in c} checkins(p), \quad \forall p \in C. \tag{3}$$

Other concepts used in this functional region detection are formalized as follows. Let ZC denote the zip code of a region; let kw denote a keyword (functionality) of a region; and let r_m and r_n denote two physical regions within the city this work is interested in, where $r_m \neq r_n$ if $ZC(r_m) \neq ZC(r_n)$. Each region is identified by its own set of keywords and a zip code, where $r_{i,:} = f(kw_1(t), kw_2(t), ..., kw_2(t); ZC(r_{i,:}))$, and values of these keywords may be changed with time. Let $fr_i(t)$ denote a time-based functional region that consists of one or multiple physical regions, where $fr_i(t) = g(r_{1,:}, r_{2,:}, ..., r_{n,:})$, n is the number of regions having functionality i. Any two functional regions within the same time slot are different in this work, i.e., $fr_i(t) \cap fr_j(t) = \varnothing$. Let $FR_{|t|,i}(t)$ denote all the functional regions generated by given clustering techniques on an interval $|t|$ for the time slot i, where $FR_{|t|,i}(t) = (fr_i(t); fr_j(t); ...; fr_w(t))$. Let $k_{|t|}$ denote the optimum number of clusters when splitting data based on interval $|t|$.

Proposed approach

Fig. 3 explains the proposed approach for generating spatio-temporal functional regions from raw LBSN data. Initially, the input data will be aggregated and mapped into a number of keywords to describe each physical region for given time slots. The optimum number of clusters will then be identified for each of the time intervals studied. These are depicted in lines 2–8. After concluding the optimum number of clusters, a clustering technique is applied on all time slots for a given interval. Based on the clustering results, the average value of key words will be calculated for each time slot of every cluster. Afterwards, the top key word, which is the most dominating functional feature of a region, will be identified. The calculation of the average values of keywords along with the top key words identification is specified in lines 13–17.

4.2 DEEP LEARNING AND REGIONAL PATTERN DETECTIONS

Recent advancements in machine learning hold new promises for detecting more complex and finer patterns in cities at various levels of spatial and temporal resolution. Deep learning is considered one of the most recent advancements in machine learning aiming at learning feature hierarchy formed by the composition of low-level features [45]. Deep learning provides an automatic feature selection at multiple levels of abstractions allowing a system to learn very complex functions mapping the input to output directly without depending completely on human-crafted features. The concept of automating the feature selection process will become more important with the rise of machine learning applications and the availability of complex data sets collected from smart cities in which building human-crafted features will become extremely expensive [45].

Algorithm 1 Functional region detection.

1: **procedure** REGIONDECTION($LBSNdata$, $|t|$)
2:   **for** $i = 0$ to $24/|t|$ **do**
3:     Generate $R_{|t|,i}$ from $LBSNdata$
4:     **for** $j = min$ to max **do**
5:       $cl_{|t|,i} = clustering(R_{|t|,i}, k_j)$
6:       Calculate $SC_{|t|,i}$ for $cl_{|t|,i}$
7:     **end for**
8:     Find $k_{|t|,i}$ equiv. to $max(SC_{|t|,i})$
9:   **end for**
10:   Find out optimum $k_{|t|} = \sum_{i=1}^{i=n} k_{|t|,i}/n$
11:   **for** $i = 0$ to $24/|t|$ **do**
12:     $FR_{|t|,i} = clustering(R|t|, i, k_{|t|})$
13:     **for** $\forall fr_k(t) \in FR_{|t|,i}$ **do**
14:       **for** $\forall kw_l(t) \in fr_k(t)$ **do**
15:         Calculate the average value $kw_l(t)$
16:       **end for**
17:       Find out the $topkeyword$ of $fr_k(t)$
18:     **end for**
19:   **end for**
20: **end procedure**

FIG. 3

Algorithm for Functional Regions Detection.

In 2006, Hinton et al. introduced DBNs, which was considered as a breakthrough [46]. DBNs uses an unsupervised learning algorithm that greedily trains one layer at a time where each layer forms a restricted Boltzmann machine (RBM) [47]. Shortly afterwards, auto-encoders [48] were proposed exploiting the same concept of training intermediate levels of representations using unsupervised learning performed for each layer. Since 2006, deep networks have seen huge success in several tasks and applications including but not limited to dimensionality reduction [49], natural language processing [50], collaborative filtering [51], classification tasks [52], and several more.

4.2.1 Related work to discovering regional patterns

In recent years, many approaches have been proposed for identifying patterns using mobility and LBSN data. In Ref. [53], Bicoocchi et al. proposed an approach based on clustering and segmenting GPS traces to infer the places of relevance to the user. In Ref. [54], Eagle et al. applied principle component analysis (PCA) to infer places and mobility patterns on the basis of nearby radio frequency beacons (e.g., WIF and GSM towers). The human activities termed as eigen behaviors are represented as the top eigenvectors of the PCA. Similarly, the work presented by Sigg et al. in Ref. [55] compared different data mining techniques for extracting patterns from mobility data where they found that independent component analysis (ICA) and PCA are most suitable for identifying humans' daily patterns.

Although the previous unsupervised learning methods showed a great success for detecting patterns in cities based on whole days, there is also a need for detecting such patterns for various time intervals [56]. Topic modeling is a useful tool in such a case that has been investigated by several works to extract individual recurrent patterns. It was introduced originally for finding underlying topics of words from a large collection of documents. latent Dirichlet allocation (LDA) is one of the implementations of topic modeling that has been widely used for extracting individual recurrent patterns in cities [57].

In Ref. [58], Laura et al. presented a method based on LDA to automatically discover users' routine behavior extracted from a Google Latitude mobility data set. They focused more on extracting the routine behaviors other than relevant places compared to what was proposed in Refs. [53] and [54]. In Ref. [56], authors presented an approach based on LDA for crowd detection using Twitter posts of data in New York that contains a large set of users but in a sparse way. In Ref. [59], Samiul et al. provided foundational tools that can be used to predict user-specific activity patterns. They addressed the main limitation for geo-location data for modeling individual behaviors and presented a topic model that can extract the activity patterns without the socio-demographic details of the individuals. Felix et al. in Ref. [60] combined textual and movement data, and they applied topic models to the combined data on an averaged week activity in which they were able to show how city modalities evolve over time and space.

In the past, neural networks have had the following drawbacks: they require labeled data that is difficult to obtain in most cases; the learning time does not scale well as it is very slow in networks with multiple hidden layers; and it has the tendency to get stuck in a poor local minima [61]. Smolensky introduced the RBM [62] and afterwards Hinton introduced a learning algorithm called Contrastive Divergence for the training RBM [46]. Hinton and Salakhutdinov introduced the pre-training process by stacking a number of RBMs [49] and being able to train each RBM separately using the Contrastive Divergence algorithm. This was found to provide a crude convergence for the parameters that can be used as an initialization for the fine-tuning process. The fine-tuning process is very similar to the learning algorithms that have been used in the feed forward neural networks (FFNNs). By using an optimization model, the parameters converge to reconstruct the input. Hinton and Salakhutdinov validated their method on the popular MNIST data set by demonstrating how it reduces the dimensionality of an input vector from 784 dimensions to 2 dimensions, but still represents the original data well [49].

Hinton and Salakhutdinov introduced the constrained Poisson model (CPM) as a core component of RBM to model word count data for performing a dimensional reduction on document data [63]. Afterwards, the authors replaced the CPM with the replicated Softmax model (RSM) due to the inability of the CPM when defining a proper distribution over word counts [64]. Later, the RSM was introduced to act as the first component in the DBN pertaining process [65]. Hinton and Salakhutdinov also introduced Semantic Hashing to produce binary values [63], which can be applied to measure the similarity between documents using hamming distance.

4.2.2 Modeling region pattern with deep learning

Deep learning can be used to discover socio-demographic regional patterns. This section introduces how the problem can be modeled and tackled by the selected approach. In particular, the following work leverages the power of deep learning for forming a complex automated feature hierarchy and adopts a DBN to identify the unique temporal region-footprints patterns. It is expected to identify new social-demographic commonalities between regions in various cases.

Problem definitions

Inferring unique patterns for different regions within the same city involves finding the complex multi-week patterns from an individual's activity everyday (individual-footprint) within each region. This new type of pattern is called a Socio-demographic Regional Pattern Model. Meanwhile, in this section, a region-footprint is a distribution of individuals-footprints within a particular region in the city where each individual-footprint can be represented by day of the week, category of activity, and time. Based on the above, the problem of inferring socio-demographic regional patterns can be defined as: given a set of individuals-footprints within a city for m weeks as $r_1^1, r_1^2, r_1^3, \ldots, r_1^{t_1}; r_1^2, r_1^3, \ldots, r_1^{t_2}; \ldots; r_m^1, r_m^2, r_m^3, \ldots, r_m^{t_m}$ where an individual on week 1, 2,..., m participates in activities $t_1, t_2, \ldots, t_m$, respectively, determine the K dimensional subspace through $\phi_k, k \in 1, 2, \ldots, K$ where each ϕ_k is a distribution of region-footprint so that weeks with similar region-footprint lie next to each other.

Deep belief nets

The main difference between the theory of the traditional FFNN and DBN is the training procedure, as training DBN is defined by two main steps: pre-training and fine-tuning. In the pre-training process, the neural network is separated pairwise to form two layered networks in which each forms an RBM. Each RBM is trained independently where the output of the lower RBM is provided as input to the next higher-level RBM, and so forth. The goal of this pre-training process is to perform rough approximations of the model parameters. These parameters are passed to the fine-tuning process. In the fine-tuning process, the network is transformed into a deep autoencoder (DA) by unrolling the whole DBN and by repeating the input and hidden layers and attaching it to the output of the DBN. Using this structure, the DA can perform back-propagation on the unlabeled data by computing the probability of the input data $p(\hat{x})$ rather than computing the probability of the label given the input data $p(\hat{y}|\hat{x})$.

In the context of this chapter, a document is modeled by its word count vector, which represents a week of region-footprint in a borough within a given city while the word represents individual-footprint captured for particular borough in that city. The number of times an individual-footprint appears in a week representing the document is relevant to this work. Thus, the bottom RBM is replaced by an RSM and stochastic binary units are used for all the hidden layers. In the RSM, each input of the visible units $v_1, \ldots, v_D$ is scalar values. The inputs of the visible units are defined as binary vectors forming a matrix U.

$$U = \begin{bmatrix} u_{1,1} & u_{1,2} \cdots & u_{1,D} \\ \vdots & \ddots & \vdots \\ u_{N,1} & u_{N,2} \cdots & u_{N,D} \end{bmatrix}, \tag{4}$$

where D indicates the size of the dictionary and N represents the length of the document. Note that the dictionary represents all different individual-footprints that exist in the whole data set. Hence, the input vectors can be represented as

$$\hat{u}_i = U_{:,i} = [u_{1,i}, \ldots, u_{N,i}]. \tag{5}$$

The energy of the RSM is defined as

$$e(U, \hat{h}; w) = -\sum_{n=1}^{N}\sum_{j=1}^{D}\sum_{D}^{i=1} w_{ijn} h_j U_{n,j} - \sum_{n=1}^{N}\sum_{i=1}^{D} U_{n,i} b_{n,j} - \sum_{j=1}^{M} h_j a_j, \tag{6}$$

where w_{ijn} is the weight between visible unit i at location n in the document $u_{i,j}$, and hidden unit j [66]. $b_{n,j}$ is the bias of $U_{n,i}$. a_j is the bias of hidden unit j. The conditional distribution of the hidden units h_j and visible units can be computed as

$$p(h_j = 1|U) = \sigma\left(a_j + \sum_{n=1}^{N}\sum_{i=1}^{D} U_{n,i} W_{ijn}\right), \tag{7}$$

$$p(U_{n,i} = 1|\hat{h}) = \frac{e^{b_{n,i} + \sum_{j=1}^{M} h_j W_{ijn}}}{\sum_{q=1}^{d} e^{b_{n,q} + \sum_{j=1}^{M} h_j W_{qjn}}}, \tag{8}$$

where σ represents the logistic sigmoid function and Eq. (8) denotes the softmax function. It is worth emphasizing that the softmax function can be applied to multinomial distribution only that is denoted by U.

The hidden units of RBM are stochastic binary units. The RBM's inference is conducted by finding representation of the hidden layer $\hat{h} = [h_1, ..., h_M]$ that minimizes the energy $e(\hat{v}, \hat{h}; w)$ with respect to the visible layer $\hat{v} = [v_1, ..., v_D]$ [67]. The energy is defined as in Ref. [68]:

$$e(\hat{v}, \hat{h}; w) = -\sum_{i=1}^{D} b_i v_i - \sum_{j=1}^{M} a_i h_j - \sum_{i=1,j=1}^{D,M} v_i h_j W_{ij}, \tag{9}$$

where v_i is the state of the visible unit, h_j is the state of the hidden unit, b_i is the bias of the visible layer, a_j is the bias of the hidden layer, and W_{ij} is the weight between v_i and h_j that represents a matrix comprising all the weights and biases. A joint distribution can describe the visible (v_i) and hidden layers (h_j) as follows:

$$p(\hat{v}, \hat{h}; w) = \frac{1}{Z(w)} e^{-e(\hat{v}, \hat{h}; w)}, \quad \text{where } Z(w) = \sum_{\hat{v}, \hat{h}} e^{-e(\hat{v}, \hat{h}; w)}, \tag{10}$$

where $p(\hat{v}, \hat{h}; w)$ is called the Boltzmann distribution and $Z(w)$ is the partition function used as a normalizing constant for the Boltzmann distribution. The probability the model reconstructs the visible vector $\hat{v}$ is calculated by [66]:

$$p(\hat{v}; w) = \frac{1}{Z(w)} \sum_{\hat{h}} e^{-e(\hat{v}, \hat{h}; w)}. \tag{11}$$

The conditional distribution over the hidden units and visible units are calculated using Eqs. (12), (13), respectively.

$$p(h_j = 1|\hat{v}) = \sigma\left(a_j + \sum_{i=1}^{D} v_i W_{i,j}\right), \tag{12}$$

$$p(v_j = 1|\hat{h}) = \sigma\left(b_i + \sum_{j=1}^{M} h_j W_{i,j}\right). \tag{13}$$

For training, the derivative of the log-likelihood is calculated with respect to the model parameters w as illustrated in Ref. [66]. This work relies on Contrastive Divergence for approximating the gradient of the objective function, as suggested by Hinton in Ref. [46]. Hence, the RBM update of the weights and biases is done by

$$\Delta W = \epsilon\left(\mathbb{E}_{p_{\text{data}}}\left[\hat{v}\hat{h}^T\right] - \mathbb{E}_{p_{\text{recon}}}\left[\hat{v}\hat{h}^T\right]\right), \tag{14}$$

$$\Delta \hat{b} = \epsilon \left(\mathbb{E}_{p_{\mathrm{data}}} \left[\hat{h} \right] - \mathbb{E}_{p_{\mathrm{recon}}} \left[\hat{h} \right] \right), \tag{15}$$

$$\Delta \hat{a} = \epsilon \left(\mathbb{E}_{p_{\mathrm{data}}} \left[\hat{v} \right] - \mathbb{E}_{p_{\mathrm{recon}}} \left[\hat{v} \right] \right), \tag{16}$$

where $\mathbb{E}_{p_{\mathrm{data}}} [\cdot]$ is the expectation of the joint distribution of the real data, $\mathbb{E}_{p_{\mathrm{recon}}} [\cdot]$ is the expectation with respect to the reconstructions, and $\mathcal{E}$ is the learning rate. The distribution of p_{recon} is calculated by using a Gibbs chain that has been proved to work well in Ref. [46].

After the pre-training, it is expected that the parameters estimated which will be passed to the fine-tuning process are already in proximity to a local minima on the error surface. The fine-tuning process will further apply an optimization algorithm to adjust these parameters to ensure convergence. The Conjugate Gradient is an ideal candidate for the optimization, which has been proved to be faster and more robust than the *Gradient Descent* [69].

5 SUMMARY

It is expected that substantial amount of sensors and devices will be connected and will share their data and knowledge in near future. This raises challenges on management systems of smart cities but also lead to a new type of social network data: LBSN. To tackle the challenge, this chapter proposed an architecture to deal with big data that is equipped with autonomous data pre-processing and model selection and is able to perform analysis periodically or in real-time. This architecture forms the basis for lots of applications that yield values from data collected in cities. One typical application, which can be facilitated by the proposed architecture and is crucial to management of smart cities, is anomaly detection. The concept and related work on anomaly detection have been introduced in this chapter, and the challenges specific to this topic have also been emphasized.

To facilitate the management of cities and also better understand human behaviors and activity patterns, this chapter presented solutions based on clustering and deep-learning techniques to harvest the LBSN data. They apply clustering techniques on both temporal and spatial information gathered from LBSN to discover functional regions that are varied with time. This offers a higher granularity compared with those based on spatial information only, and can benefit a variety of applications, such as personalized recommendations and telecom network planning. The proposed solutions also identify weekly urban patterns for various regions within a city by leveraging the power of deep learning. It is expected that this solution could yield a better understand and derive new insights on socio-demographic commonalities, which was not feasible heretofore.

REFERENCES

[1] Washburn D, Sindhu U, Balaouras S, Dines RA, Hayes NM, Nelson LE. Helping CIOs understand "smart city" initiatives: Defining the smart city, its drivers, and the role of the CIO. Cambridge, MA: Forrester Research, Inc.; 2010. http://public.dhe.ibm.com/partnerworld/pub/smb/smarterplanet/forr_help_cios_und_smart_city_initiatives.pdf.

[2] Chandola V, Banerjee A, Kumar V. Anomaly detection: A survey. ACM Comput Surv 2009;41(3):15.

[3] Stanway A. etsy/skyline, https://github.com/etsy/skyline; 2013.

[4] Weigend AS, Mangeas M, Srivastava AN. Nonlinear gated experts for time series: Discovering regimes and avoiding overfitting. Int J Neural Syst 1995;6(04):373–99.

[5] Salvador S, Chan P, Brodie J. Learning states and rules for time series anomaly detection. In: FLAIRS conference; 2004. p. 306–11.

[6] Kou Y, Lu C-T, Chen D. Spatial weighted outlier detection. In SDM. SIAM; 2006. p. 614–8.

[7] Sekar R, Bendre M, Dhurjati D, Bollineni P. A fast automaton based method for detecting anomalous program behaviors. In: Security and privacy, 2001. S&P 2001. Proceedings. 2001 IEEE symposium on. IEEE; 2001. p. 144–55.

[8] Modi C, Patel D, Borisaniya B, Patel H, Patel A, Rajarajan M. A survey of intrusion detection techniques in cloud. J Netw Comput Appl 2013;36(1):42–57.

[9] Albrecht S, Busch J, Kloppenburg M, Metze F, Tavan P. Generalized radial basis function networks for classification and novelty detection: Self-organization of optimal Bayesian decision. Neural Netw 2000;13 (10):1075–93.

[10] Emamian V, Kaveh M, Tewfik AH. Robust clustering of acoustic emission signals using the kohonen network. In: Acoustics, speech, and signal processing, 2000. ICASSP'00. Proceedings. 2000 IEEE international conference on. vol. 6. IEEE; 2000. p. 3891–4.

[11] Crook P, Hayes G. A robot implementation of a biologically inspired method for novelty detection. In: Proceedings of the towards intelligent mobile robots conference; 2001.

[12] Crook PA, Marsland S, Hayes G, Nehmzow U. A tale of two filters-on-line novelty detection. In: Robotics and automation, 2002. Proceedings. ICRA'02. IEEE international conference on. vol. 4. IEEE; 2002. p. 3894–9.

[13] Marsland S, Nehmzow U, Shapiro J. A model of habituation applied to mobile robots. In: Proceedings of Towards Intelligent Mobile Robots; 1999.

[14] Marsland S, Nehmzow U, Shapiro J. A real-time novelty detector for a mobile robot. arXiv preprint cs/0006006; 2000.

[15] Ihler A, Hutchins J, Smyth P. Adaptive event detection with time varying Poisson processes. In Proceedings of the 12th ACM SIGKDD international conference on knowledge discovery and data mining. ACM; 2006. p. 207–16.

[16] Id´e T, Kashima H. Eigenspace-based anomaly detection in computer systems. In Proceedings of the tenth ACM SIGKDD international conference on knowledge discovery and data mining. ACM; 2004. p. 440–9.

[17] Sun J, Qu H, Chakrabarti D, Faloutsos C. Neighborhood formation and anomaly detection in bipartite graphs. In Data mining, fifth IEEE international conference on. IEEE; 2005.

[18] Sun P, Chawla S, Arunasalam B. Mining for outliers in sequential databases. In SDM. SIAM; 2006. p. 94–105.

[19] Kadota K, Tominaga D, Akiyama Y, Takahashi K. Detecting outlying samples in microarray data: A critical assessment of the effect of outliers on sample classification. Chem-Bio Inf J 2003;3(1):30–45.

[20] Lu C-T, Chen D, Kou Y. Algorithms for spatial outlier detection. In: Data Mining, 2003. ICDM 2003. Third IEEE International Conference on. IEEE; 2003. p. 597–600.

[21] He Z, Xu X, Huang JZ, Deng S. Mining class outliers: Concepts, algorithms and applications in CRM. Expert Syst Appl 2004;27(4):681–97.

[22] Dutta H, Giannella C, Borne KD, Kargupta H. Distributed top-k outlier detection from astronomy catalogs using the demac system. In SDM. SIAM; 2007. p. 473–8.

[23] Escalante HJ. A comparison of outlier detection algorithms for machine learning. In Proceedings of the international conference on communications in computing; 2005. p. 228–37.

[24] Sun P, Chawla S. On local spatial outliers. In: Data mining, 2004. ICDM'04. Fourth IEEE international conference on. IEEE; 2004. p. 209–16.

[25] Lee J, Han J, Li X. Trajectory outlier detection: A partition-and-detect framework. In Proc. of ICDE'08; 2008. p. 140–9.

[26] Zhang D, Li N, Zhou Z, et al. iBAT: Detecting anomalous taxi trajectories from GPS traces. In Proc. UbiComp'11; 2011. p. 99–108.

[27] Chawla S, Zheng Y, Hu J. Inferring the root cause in road traffic anomalies. In Proc. ICDM'12; 2012. p. 141–50.

[28] Liu W, Zheng Y, Chawla S, Yuan J, Xie X. Discovering spatio-temporal causal interactions in traffic data streams. In Proc. KDD'11; 2011. p. 1010–8.

[29] Zheng Y, Liu Y, Yuan J, Xie X. Urban computing with taxicabs. In Proc. UbiComp'11; 2011. p. 89–98.

[30] Matsubara Y, Sakurai Y, Faloutsos C. FUNNEL: Automatic mining of spatially coevolving epidemics. In Proc. KDD'14; 2014.

[31] Pan B, et al. Crowd sensing of traffic anomalies based on human mobility and social media. In Proc. GIS'13; 2013. p. 334–43.

[32] Zheng Y, Zhang H, Yu Y. Detecting collective anomalies from multiple spatio-temporal datasets across different domains. In Proceedings of the 23rd SIGSPATIAL international conference on advances in geographic information systems (GIS'15). New York: ACM; 2015.

[33] Noulas A, Scellato S, Mascolo C, Pontil M. Exploiting semantic annotations for clustering geographic areas and users in location-based social networks. The Social Mobile Web 2011;11:02.

[34] Cheng Z, Caverlee J, Lee K, Sui DZ. Exploring millions of footprints in location sharing services. In: ICWSM. vol. 2011; 2011. p. 81–8.

[35] Bao J, Zheng Y, Wilkie D, Mokbel M. Recommendations in location-based social networks: A survey. GeoInformatica 2015;19(3):525–65.

[36] Reades J, Calabrese F, Ratti C. Eigenplaces: Analyzing cities using the space–time structure of the mobile phone network. Environ Plan B Plann Des 2009;36(5):824–36.

[37] Toole JL, Ulm M, Gonz´alez MC, Bauer D. Inferring land use from mobile phone activity. In Proceedings of the ACM SIGKDD international workshop on urban computing. ACM; 2012. p. 1–8.

[38] Qi G, Li X, Li S, Pan G, Wang Z, Zhang D. Measuring social functions of city regions from large-scale taxi behaviors. In Pervasive computing and communications workshops (PERCOM Workshops), 2011 IEEE international conference on. IEEE; 2011. p. 384–8.

[39] Liu Y, Wang F, Xiao Y, Gao S. Urban land uses and traffic 'source-sink areas': Evidence from gps-enabled taxi data in Shanghai. Landsc Urban Plan 2012;106(1):73–87.

[40] Pelletier M-P, Tr´epanier M, Morency C. Smart card data use in public transit: A literature review. Transport Res C Emerg Technol 2011;19(4):557–68.

[41] Wu L, Zhi Y, Sui Z, Liu Y. Intra-urban human mobility and activity transition: evidence from social media check-in data. PLoS ONE 2014;9(5):e97010.

[42] Cranshaw J, Schwartz R, Hong JI, Sadeh N. The livehoods project: Utilizing social media to understand the dynamics of a city. In International AAAI conference on weblogs and social media; 2012. p. 58.

[43] Silva TH, de Melo PO, Almeida JM, Salles J, Loureiro AA. Visualizing the invisible image of cities. In: Green computing and communications (GreenCom). 2012 IEEE international conference on. IEEE; 2012. p. 382–9.

[44] Zhi Y, Liu Y, Wang S, Deng M, Gao J, Li H. Urban spatial temporal activity structures: A new approach to inferring the intraurban functional regions via social media check-in data. arXiv preprint arXiv:1412.7253; 2014.

[45] Bengio Y. Learning deep architectures for AI. Found Trends Mach Learn 2009;2(1):1–127.

[46] Hinton GE. Training products of experts by minimizing contrastive divergence. Neural Comput 2002;14 (8):1771–800.

[47] Freund Y, Haussler D. Unsupervised learning of distributions of binary vectors using two layer networks, Technical Report. University of California at Santa Cruz, Santa Cruz, CA; 1994.

[48] Bengio Y, Lamblin P, Popovici D, Larochelle H, et al. Greedy layer-wise training of deep networks. In NIPS; 2007.

[49] Hinton GE, Salakhutdinov RR. Reducing the dimensionality of data with neural networks. Science 2006;313 (5786):504–7.

[50] Collobert R, Weston J. A unified architecture for natural language processing: Deep neural networks with multitask learning. In ICML; 2008.

[51] Salakhutdinov R, Mnih A, Hinton G. Restricted Boltzmann machines for collaborative filtering. In ICML; 2007.

[52] Larochelle H, Erhan D, Courville A, Bergstra J, Bengio Y. An empirical evaluation of deep architectures on problems with many factors of variation. In ICML; 2007.

[53] Bicocchi N, Castelli G, Mamei M, Rosi A, Zambonelli F. Supporting location-aware services for mobile users with the whereabouts diary. In MobilWare; 2008.

[54] Eagle N, Pentland AS. Eigenbehaviors: Identifying structure in routine. Behav Ecol Sociobiol 2009;63 (7):1057–66.

[55] Sigg S, Haseloff S, David K. An alignment approach for context prediction tasks in ubicomp environments. In: PERCOM; 2010.

[56] Ferrari L, Rosi A, Mamei M, Zambonelli F. Extracting urban patterns from location-based social networks. In SIGSPATIAL; 2011.

[57] Blei DM, Ng AY, Jordan MI. Latent Dirichlet allocation. J Mach Learn Res 2003;3:993–1022.

[58] Ferrari L, Mamei M. Discovering daily routines from Google latitude with topic models. In PERCOM; 2011.

[59] Halevy A, Norvig P, Pereira F. The unreasonable effectiveness of data. IEEE Intell Syst 2009;24(2):8–12.

[60] Kling F, Pozdnoukhov A. When a city tells a story: urban topic analysis. In SIGSPATIAL; 2012.

[61] Jain AK, Mao J, Mohiuddin K. Artificial neural networks: A tutorial. Computer 1996;3:31–44.

[62] Smolensky P. Information processing in dynamical systems: Foundations of harmony theory. In: David E. Rumelhart, James L. McClelland, PDP Research Group, CORPORATE, editors. Parallel distributed processing: Explorations in the microstructure of cognition, vol. 1. Cambridge, MA: MIT Press; 1986. p. 15–8.

[63] Salakhutdinov R, Hinton G. Semantic hashing. Int J Approx Reason 2009;50(7):969–78.

[64] Hinton GE, Salakhutdinov RR. Replicated Softmax: An undirected topic model. In NIPS; 2009.

[65] Hinton G, Salakhutdinov R. Discovering binary codes for documents by learning deep generative models. Top Cogn Sci 2011;3(1):74–91.

[66] Hinton G. A practical guide to training restricted Boltzmann machines. Momentum 2010;9(1):926.

[67] LeCun Y, Chopra S, Hadsell R, Ranzato M, Huang F. A tutorial on energy-based learning. Predicting structured data, 1:0; 2006.

[68] Hopfield JJ. Neural networks and physical systems with emergent collective computational abilities. Proc Natl Acad Sci 1982;79(8):2554–8.

[69] Anzai Y. Pattern recognition and machine learning. Academic Press, San Diego, CA; 1992.

GLOSSARY

Auto-encoders An artificial neural network used for learning efficient coding, which aims to learn a representation (encoding) for a set of data, typically for the purpose of dimensionality reduction.

Batch processing The execution of a series of jobs in a program on a computer without manual intervention.

Boltzmann distribution A probability distribution of particles in a system over various possible states.

Collaborative filtering A technique used by some recommender systems to filters information by using the recommendations of other people.

Dimensionality reduction A process of reducing the number of random variables under consideration through obtaining a set of "uncorrelated" principal variables.

Erlang A unit of telecommunications traffic measurement. Strictly speaking, an Erlang represents the continuous use of one voice path. In practice, it is used to describe the total traffic volume of 1 h.

Functional region A region made up of different places that are linked and function as a unit.

Independent component analysis A computational method to separate a multivariate signal into additive subcomponents.

Poisson model A form of regression analysis used to model count data and contingency tables. It assumes the response variable Y has a Poisson distribution, and assumes the logarithm of its expected value can be modeled by a linear combination of unknown parameters.

Principle component analysis A statistical procedure that uses an orthogonal transformation to convert a set of observations of possibly correlated variables into a set of values of linearly uncorrelated variables.

Real-time processing The execution of a series of jobs in a program on a computer within specified short time constraints.

Socio-demographic regional pattern A pattern described and explained by demographic data and methods, which can be used to predict social phenomena in given regions.

DEEP LEARNING FOR HUMAN ACTIVITY RECOGNITION

Phyo P. San[a], Pravin Kakar[a], Xiao-Li Li, Shonali Krishnaswamy, Jian-Bo Yang, Minh N. Nguyen

Institute for Infocomm Research, Agency for Science, Technology and Research (A*STAR), Singapore

ACRONYMS

AC	Accuracy
ADL	Activities of daily living
AF	Average F-measure
CNN	Convolutional neural network
CPU	Central processing unit
DBN	Deep belief network
DT	Decision tree
HA	Hand Gesture
HAR	Human activity recognition
KNN	K-nearest neighbors
LSTM	Long- and short-term memory
MV	Means and variance
NB	Naive Bayes
NF	Normalized F-measure
OAR	Opportunity activity recognition
RAM	Random access memory
ReLU	Rectified linear unit
REALDISP	Real displacement
RNN	Recurrent neural network
SVM	Support vector machine

1 INTRODUCTION

Automatically recognizing a human's physical activities which is commonly referred to as human activity recognition (HAR) has emerged as a key area of interest in several sectors such as the sports and entertainment sectors, office scenarios, and health care. For example, monitoring daily activities in supporting medical diagnosis, assisting patients with chronic impairments, etc., are the key enhancements to traditional medical diagnosis methods. In addition, a vast exploration of

---

[a]Both authors contributed equally to this work.

Big Data Analytics for Sensor-Network Collected Intelligence. http://dx.doi.org/10.1016/B978-0-12-809393-1.00009-X

related human activities made its debut as key components in several consumer products, such as the Nintendo Wii and the Microsoft Kinect which rely on the recognition of gestures or even full-body movements to fundamentally enhance an immersive gaming experience. All of these useful application examples highlight the significance of HAR in both academia and industry.

Various investigations were performed to study the recognition of human gestures and activities from images and videos in constrained environments or stationary settings [1, 2]. Advances in sensor technologies have given rise to more potential application areas for activity recognition beyond controlled indoor settings and they promise to provide smart assistance and interfaces virtually anywhere and at any time by observing activities from the perspective of users. The first feasibility studies on activity recognition using body-worn sensors [3] dealt with fairly arbitrarily chosen activities, which were not always relevant to real-world applications. To our best knowledge, there are no unified signal processing and classification frameworks for activity recognition that satisfy application and user requirements for scalability and ease of deployment. On the other hand, with the greater availability of data, the motivation to develop activity recognition systems for more challenging and application-oriented scenarios is greater than ever before. Therefore, in this work, we propose an effective and efficient system that is able to recognize a human's physical activities automatically through analysis of the signals acquired (in real time) from multiple body-worn (or body-embedded) inertial sensors.

In the past few years, body-worn sensor-based HAR has made promising progress in applications such as game consoles, personal fitness training, medication intake, and health monitoring. An excellent survey on this topic can be found at Bulling et al. [1]. The HAR signals used in the application acquired by on-body sensors are arguably favorable over the signals acquired by video cameras, due to several reasons: (i) On-body sensors alleviate the limitations of environment constraints and stationary settings that video cameras often suffer from Bulling et al. [1], Ji et al. [4], and Le et al. [5]; (ii) Multiple on-body sensors allow more accurate and effective deployment of signal acquisition sensors on the human body; and (iii) On-body sensors enjoy the advantages of information privacy, as their acquired signals are target-specific while the signals acquired by camera may also contain the information of other nontarget subjects in the scene.

On the other hand, sensor-based HAR systems can suffer several possible issues. One issue is intraclass variability, which is common in experiments done with multiple human subjects. As each subject may perform the same activity with somewhat different movements, it is often difficult for HAR systems to find the commonalities in such cases. Another issue that arises has to do with interclass similarity. Depending on the recognition requirements, some activities may be very similar to be distinguished effectively. As an example, jogging and running share considerable similarity in terms of the motion of human body parts, but may be required to be classified as distinct activities. Besides, class imbalance can also be a problem for training HAR systems, especially in data collected from loosely constrained settings [6, 7]. In such cases, it often happens that certain classes occur much more rarely, yielding fewer training data samples. For instance, in daily life, walking generally occurs far more frequently than running. Data collected from a human subject over the course of such a day will have more samples from the walking activity as compared to the running activity. In addition, annotation of the collected data can also be an issue. It is often difficult to pinpoint precisely when an activity has started and ended. Given the generally high sampling rate of sensors (tens of samples per second), this can result in considerable amounts of incorrectly annotated data. Sensors can also suffer from inherent variability depending on environmental conditions, and degrade over time which poses a problem for HAR systems.

The key factor attributed to the success of a HAR system is to find an effective representation of the time series collected from the on-body sensors. Though considerable research has been dedicated to investigating this issue, diminishing returns have been obtained. Conventionally, the HAR problem is often taken as one of specific applications of time series analysis. The widely used features in HAR include basis transform coding (e.g., signals with wavelet transform and Fourier transform) [8], statistics of raw signals (e.g, mean and variance of time sequences) [1, 9], and symbolic representation [10]. Although these features are widely used in many time series problems, they are heuristic and not task-dependent. It is worth noting that the HAR task has its own challenges as mentioned above, such as intraclass variability, interclass similarity, the NULL-class dominance (most sensor data arising from activities outside the scope of interest), and the complexity and diversity of physical activities [1]. All these challenges make it highly desirable to develop a systematic feature representation approach to effectively characterize the nature of signals relative to the activity recognition task.

Recently, deep learning has emerged as a family of learning models that aim to model high-level abstractions in data [11, 12]. In deep learning, a "deep" architecture with multiple layers is built up for learning highly discriminative feature representations. Specifically, each layer in a deep architecture performs a non-linear transformation on the outputs of the previous layer, so that the deeply learned model can represent the data by a hierarchy of features that can be interpreted as increasing in complexity from low-level to high-level. The well-known deep learning models include CNNs, deep belief networks (DBNs), and autoencoders. Depending on the usage of label information, the deep learning models can be learned in either a supervised or an unsupervised manner. Though deep learning models have achieved remarkable results in computer vision, natural language processing, and speech recognition, they have not been fully exploited in the field of HAR.

In this chapter, we tackle the HAR problem by adapting one particular deep learning model—the convolutional neural network (CNN) [13]. We build on the work of Yang et al. [13] by providing a more comprehensive experimental evaluation, a deeper analysis of the methods and issues involved with HAR and a more in-depth explanation of the choice of our CNN architecture. A CNN is constructed by stacking different processing units (e.g., convolution, pooling, sigmoid/hyperbolic tangent squashing, rectifier, normalization) in a repetitive manner. This stacking can yield an effective representation of local portions of the signals. Since the deep architecture allows multiple layers of these processing units to be stacked, it can characterize progressively wider portions of the signals by building on the representations learned in the lower layers. Therefore, the features extracted by the CNN are task dependent and nonhandcrafted. Moreover, these features also possess more discriminative power, since the CNN can be trained under the supervision of output labels. All these advantages of the CNN will be further elaborated in the following sections.

As detailed in the following sections, in the application on HAR, the convolution and pooling filters in the CNN are applied along the *temporal* dimension for each sensor, and all these feature maps for different sensors need to be unified as a common input for the neural network classifier. Therefore, a new architecture of the CNN is developed in this paper. In the experiments, we performed an extensive study on the comparison between the proposed method and the state-of-the-art methods on benchmark datasets. The results show that the proposed method is a very competitive algorithm for the HAR problems. We also investigate the efficiency of the CNN and conclude that the CNN is fast enough for online HAR.

2 MOTIVATIONS AND RELATED WORK

It is highly desirable to develop a systematic and task-dependent feature extraction approach for HAR. Though the signals collected from wearable sensors are time series, they are different from other time series like speech signals and financial signals. Specifically, in HAR, only a few parts of the continuous signal stream are relevant to the concept of interest (i.e., human activities), and the dominant irrelevant part mostly corresponds to the null activity. Moreover, depending on the sensor setup, not all the sensors are relevant to distinguishing each activity. Finally, considering how human activity is performed in reality, we observe that every activity is a combination of several basic continuous movements. Typically, a human activity could last a few seconds in practice, and only a few basic movements could be involved over any given duration in this window. From the perspective of sensor signals, the basic continuous movements are more likely to correspond to smoothly changing signals, and the transitions among different basic continuous movements may cause abrupt, significant changes in the signal values. These properties of signals in HAR require the feature extraction method to be effective enough to capture the nature of basic continuous movements as well as the salience of the combination of basic movements.

As such, we are motivated to build a deep architecture of a series of signal processing units for feature extraction. This deep architecture consists of multiple shallow architectures, and each shallow architecture is composed by a set of linear/nonlinear processing units on locally stationary signals. When these shallow architectures are stacked, the salience of signals in different scales is captured. This deep architecture is not only for decomposing a large and complex problem into a series of small problems, but more importantly for obtaining specific "representations" of signals at different scales. Here, the signal representations reflect the salient patterns of signals. As stated in Bengio [11], what matters for generalization of a learning algorithm is the number of such representations of signals we wish to obtain after learning.

In contrast to this, the traditional features extraction methods such as basis transform coding (e.g., signals with wavelet transform and Fourier transform) [8], statistics of raw signals (e.g., mean and covariance of time sequences) [1], and symbolic representation [10] are deemed to play a comparable role of transforming the data by one or a few of neurons in one layer of a deep learning model. Another type of deep learning model, called DBN [14–16], was also investigated for HAR by Plätz et al. [2]. However, this feature learning method does not employ the effective signal processing units (like convolution, pooling, and rectifier) and also neglects the available label information in feature extraction. The primary use of the CNN mainly lies in 2D image [17, 18], 3D videos [4], and speech recognition [19]. However, in this paper, we attempt to build a *new* architecture of the CNN to handle the unique challenges present in HAR. The most related work is Zeng et al. [20], in which a shallow CNN is used and the HAR problem is restricted to the accelerometer data.

3 CONVOLUTIONAL NEURAL NETWORKS IN HAR

CNNs have great potential to identify the various salient patterns in the sensor signals used for HAR. Specifically, the processing units in the lower layers obtain the local salience of the signals (to characterize the nature of each basic movement in a human activity). The processing units in the higher layers obtain the salient patterns of signals at high-level representations (to characterize the nature of a combination of several basic movements). Note that each layer may have a number of convolution or pooling operators (often with different input and output sizes) as described below, so multiple salient patterns learned from different sections of the signals are jointly considered in the CNN. When these operators with the same parameters are applied on local signals (or their representations) at different time segments, a form of translation invariance is obtained [11, 12, 21]. Consequently, what matters is only the salient patterns of signals instead of their positions or scales. However, in HAR we are confronted with multiple channels of time series signals, in which the traditional CNN cannot be used directly. The challenges in our problem include (i) processing units in CNN need to be applied along temporal dimension and (ii) sharing or unifying the units in CNN among multiple sensors. In what follows, we will define the convolution and pooling operators along the temporal dimension, and then presented the entire architecture of the CNN used in HAR.

We start with the notations used in the CNN. A sliding window strategy is adopted to segment the time series signal into a collection of short segments of signals. Specifically, an instance used by the CNN is a two-dimensional matrix containing r raw samples (each sample with D attributes). Here, r is chosen to be as the sampling rate, and the step size of sliding a window is chosen according to the experimental setup. In general, a CNN requires much more training data than conventional, shallower learning architectures due to the significantly larger number of free parameters involved in the learning process. A smaller step size increases the amount of training instances, but introduces greater redundancy between different instances which may not have an equitable impact in improving test-time performance for the CNN.

For training data, the true label of the matrix instance is determined by the most-frequently occurring label for r raw records. For the jth feature map in the ith layer of the CNN, it is also a matrix, and the value at the xth row for sensor d is denoted as $v_{ij}^{x,d}$ for convenience. This is explained as shown in Fig. 1. For convenience, we show the feature maps for the first convolutional layer. The $r \times D$ input matrix is convolved with J filters of length k along the temporal dimension. This gives rise to J feature maps of size $(r - k + 1) \times D$, each element of which can be referenced by the term $v_{ij}^{x,d}$.

3.1 TEMPORAL CONVOLUTION AND POOLING

In the convolution layers, the previous layer's feature maps are convolved with several convolutional kernels (to be learned in the training process). The output of the convolution operators along with a bias (to be learned) is passed through an activation function to form the feature map for the next layer. Formally, the value $v_{ij}^{x,d}$ is given by

$$v_{ij}^{x,d} = \tanh\left(b_{ij} + \sum_m \sum_{p=0}^{P_i-1} w_{ijm}^p v_{(i-1)m}^{x+p,d} \right), \quad \forall d = 1,...,D \tag{1}$$

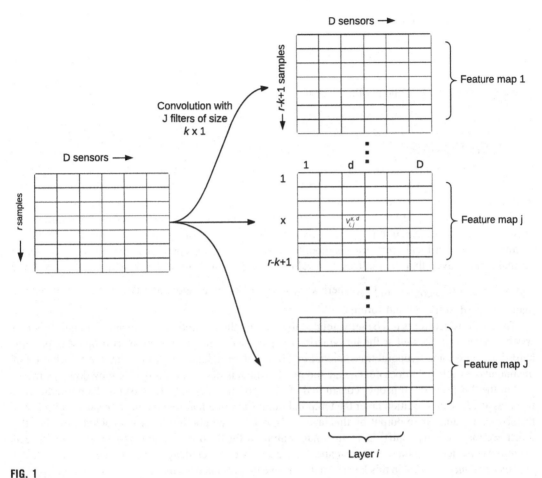

FIG. 1

Illustration of the computation of $v_{i,j}^{x,d}$ at an intermediate layer of the CNN.

where $\tanh(\cdot)$ is the hyperbolic tangent function, b_{ij} is the bias for this feature map, m indexes over the set of feature maps in the $(i-1)$th layer connected to the current feature map, w_{ijm}^{p} is the value at the position p of the convolutional kernel, and P_i is the length of the convolutional kernel.

In the pooling layers, the resolution of feature maps is reduced to increase the invariance of features to distortions on the inputs. Specifically, feature maps in the previous layer are pooled over local *temporal* neighborhood by either max pooling function

$$v_{ij}^{x,d} = \max_{1 \le q \le Q_i} \left(v_{(i-1)j}^{x+q,d} \right), \quad \forall d = 1,...,D \tag{2}$$

or a sum pooling function

$$v_{ij}^{x,d} = \frac{1}{Q_i} \sum_{1 \leq q \leq Q_i} \left(v_{(i-1)j}^{x+q,d} \right), \quad \forall d = 1,...,D \tag{3}$$

where Q_i is the length of the pooling region.

3.2 ARCHITECTURE

Based on the operators introduced in the above section, we construct a CNN shown in Fig. 2. For convenience, all layers of the CNN can be grouped into five sections. For the first two sections, each section consists of (i) a convolution layer that convolves the input or the previous layer's output with a set of kernels to be learned; (ii) a rectified linear unit (ReLU) layer that maps the output of the previous layer by the function $relu(v) = \max(v, 0)$; (iii) a max pooling layer that finds the maximum feature map over a local *temporal* neighborhood (a subsampling operator is often involved); (iv) a normalization layer that normalizes the values of different feature maps in the previous layer $v_{ij} = v_{(i-1)j} \left(\kappa + \alpha \sum_{t \in G(j)} v_{(i-1)t}^2 \right)^{-\beta}$, where κ, α, β are hyper-parameters and $G(j)$ is the set of feature maps involved in the normalization.

The use of ReLU units has benefits related to reducing the likelihood of vanishing gradients, which speeds up learning, as well as the introduction of sparsity that helps prevent overfitting. Max pooling helps introduce some temporal translational invariance. Normalization ensures that the distribution of the outputs of each layer does not change too much, which is important for not slowing down learning.

For the third section, it is only constituted of a convolution layer, ReLU layer and a normalization layer, as after the convolution layer the temporal dimension of a feature map becomes one (noting that the size of a feature map output by this layer is $D \times 1$) so the pooling layer is avoided here. For the fourth section, we aim to unify the feature maps output by the third section among all D sensors. Instead of simply concatenating these feature maps, we use a fully connected layer to unify them to achieve the *parametric concatenation* in this layer. An illustrative diagram is shown in Fig. 3. This scheme appears to lead to an explosion in the number of parameters at this layer (in total $d \times 20 \times 400$ parameters). Following the same strategy used in the previous convolution layers, we use different weights for d sensors but share these weights among hidden units in the third layer, as shown in Fig. 3. Mathematically, the value of the jth feature map in this layer is computed by:

$$v_{ij} = \tanh \left(b_{ij} + \sum_{m} \sum_{d=1}^{D} w_{ijm}^d v_{(i-1)m}^d \right) \tag{4}$$

and this unification is also followed by the ReLU layer and normalization layer.

The fifth section is a fully connected network layer. This layer is same as a standard multilayer perceptron neural network that maps the latent features into the output classes. The output of this layer is governed by the softmax function. This softmax function provides the posterior probability of the classification results. Then, an entropy cost function can be constituted based on the true labels of training instances and probabilistic outputs of softmax function.

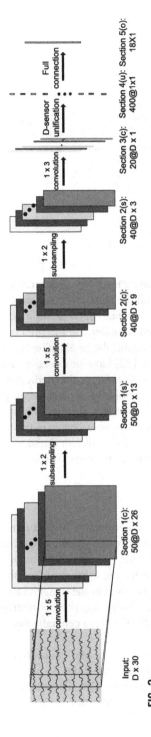

Input:
D x 30

1 x 5
convolution

Section 1(c):
50@D x 26

1 x 2
subsampling

Section 1(s):
50@D x 13

1 x 5
convolution

Section 2(c):
40@D x 9

1 x 2
subsampling

Section 2(s):
40@D x 3

1 x 3
convolution

Section 3(c):
20@D x 1

D-sensor
unification

Full
connection

Section 4(u):
400@1x1

Section 5(o):
18X1

FIG. 2

Illustration of the CNN architecture used for a multisensor based human activity recognition problem. We use the Opportunity Activity Recognition dataset presented in Section 4 as an illustrative example. The *symbols* "c," "s," "u," and "o" in the parentheses of the layer tags refer to convolution, subsampling, unification, and output operations, respectively. The *numbers before and after* "@" refer to the number of feature maps and the dimension of a feature map in this layer. Note that pooling, ReLU and normalization layers are not shown due to the limitation of space.

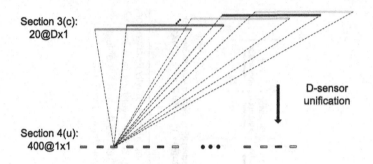

Section 3(c):
20@Dx1

Section 4(u):
400@1x1

D-sensor
unification

FIG. 3

Illustration of unification layer (i.e., the fourth section in Fig. 2).

$$v_{ij} = \frac{\exp\left(v_{(i-1)j}\right)}{\sum_{j=1}^{C} \exp\left(v_{(i-1)j}\right)} \tag{5}$$

where C is the number of output classes.

To convert the matrix-level prediction given by the CNN to originally desired sample-level predictions, the following two steps are used. First, all the samples in a matrix-level instance are labeled by the same predicted label for this matrix-level instance. Second, for a sample lying in the overlapped matrix-level instances, a voting method is used to determine the final predicted label of this sample.

Due to the temporal dependence of sensor signals, the labels of instances often have a smooth trend, as mentioned in Section 2. Recently, Cao et al. [22] have proposed a simple but effective smoothing method to postprocess the predicted labels so as to enhance the prediction performance. The idea is to employ a low-pass filter to remove the impulse noise (potential wrong prediction) and maintain the edges (i.e., the position of activity transition). Specially, for the ith instance, a smoothing filter with a predefined length u_i is applied on the sequence whose center is the ith instance. This filter finds the most frequent label in this sequence and assign it to the ith instance. We shall investigate the prediction results with/without this smoothing method in the experiments.

3.3 ANALYSIS

Note that the ReLU and normalization layers are optional in the first four layers of the CNN in Fig. 2. In our experiments, we found that incorporating these two layers can lead to better results. Furthermore, to avoid overfitting, dropout operations [23] and other regularization methods might be employed in the CNN, though they are not used in our experiments due to the resultant minor performance difference.

Remark 1. The conventional CNN [4, 17, 24] used in the image/video case does not have the unification layer shown in Fig. 3, because the image/video signal is considered to come from a single sensor channel. Thus, the proposed architecture of the CNN is a generalization of the conventional CNN by considering multiple channels of data.

In the CNN, the parameters in all processing units and connection weights are jointly learned through a global objective function (i.e., entropy cost function). In other words, this is an optimization to be performed over a large number of unknown variables. This global objective function can be efficiently optimized by a so-called back-propagation algorithm [25]. The idea of this algorithm is using the chain rule to derive the gradients of the cost function with respect to the variables in the CNN and then updating these variables by a simple gradient descent method. To speed up the algorithm, a stochastic gradient descent method is often adopted in updating the variables. Investigation on the efficiency of parallel computing of the back-propagation algorithm has attracted considerable research efforts and excellent work along this direction can be found at Jia et al. [26] and Donahue et al. [27].

Remark 2. The global objective function is related to the training error that is computed based on the ground truth labels as well as the outputs of the softmax function in the last layer of the CNN. This function's variables control the various feature maps of the signals. Consequently, through the optimization model, the two tasks of feature learning and classification are mutually enhanced, and the learned features by the CNN have more discriminative power with respect to the ultimate classification task.

4 EXPERIMENTS, RESULTS, AND DISCUSSION

In the experiments, we consider three datasets for HAR with different focuses. The first dataset—the Opportunity Activity Recognition (OAR) dataset—is related to the entire body's movement, the second dataset—the Hand Gesture dataset—particularly focuses on the hand's movement, while the third dataset—the REALDISP dataset—focuses on the impact of wearer-introduced sensor displacement on classification frameworks trained under ideal scenarios. The architecture of the CNN used in the OAR dataset is shown in Fig. 2. The detailed descriptions of the three data sets will be introduced later in this section. The same architecture of the CNN is used for the other two datasets with the only differences in the number of feature maps and the sizes of convolution kernels, since the dimensions of the input and output of the datasets are different. In the normalization operator of the CNN, the parameters are chosen as $\kappa = 1$, $\alpha = 2 \times 10^{-4}$, $\beta = 0.75$ and the size of $G(\cdot)$ is 5 in all experiments. We follow the rules of thumb shown in LeCun et al. [25] to choose other parameters, as how to find the optimal parameters in CNN is still an open question.

4.1 EXPERIMENT ON OAR DATASET

The OAR dataset[1] [22, 28, 29] is about the human activities related to a breakfast scenario. This dataset contains the data collected from the sensors configured on three subjects who perform activities of daily living (ADL). There are 18 classes in this activity recognition task.[2] The Null class refers to the either nonrelevant activities or nonactivities. The used sensors include a wide variety of body-worn, object-based, and ambient sensors—in total, 72 sensors from 10 modalities—with 15 wireless and wired sensor network in home environment. The sampling rate of the sensor signals is 30 Hz. Each record is comprised of 113 real-valued sensory readings excluding the time information. With these sensors, each subject performed one drill session (Drill) which has 20 repetitions of some predefined actions

---

[1]http://www.opportunity-project.eu/challenge.
[2]The 18 classes are Null, open door 1, open door 2, close door 1, close door 2, open fridge, close fridge, open dishwasher, close dishwasher, open drawer 1, close drawer 1, open drawer 2, close drawer 2, open drawer 3, close drawer 3, clean table, drink cup, and toggle switch.

in one sequence of sensory data, and five ADLs. Following Cao et al. [22], we use Drill and first two sets of ADLs as the training data, and use the third set of ADL as the testing data.

We further remove the time series from six faulty sensors for Subject 1 and also remove the time series from three faulty sensors for Subjects 2 and 3 as suggested in Cao et al. [22]. All these faulty sensors have more than 30% of missing data. For other missing sensor data, we fill the missing values using cubic spline fitting in the temporal dimension. We use a step size of 3 for the training data, and 1 for the testing data in order to have better resolution in the latter case. The network is trained for eight epochs with a learning rate profile of 0.1 for the first two epochs, 0.01 for the next three, and 0.001 for the last three. While a constant learning rate (say, 0.01) can also be used, it is generally found that the number of epochs required in this case is much larger. This would necessitate a much longer training time for a large dataset such as this one. We do demonstrate the use of a constant learning rate for the REALDISP dataset below. The number of epochs and the learning rate profile is determined by using a validation set held out from the training data, and the network is retrained with the entire training data, once the appropriate parameters are determined.

We compare the proposed method with the following four baselines, namely support vector machine (SVM) [22], K-nearest neighbors (KNN) classifier [22, 30], means and variance (MV) [1], and DBN [2]. Among them, the first two methods and the third method show the state-of-the-arts results on the OAR dataset and Hand Gesture datasets, respectively. The fourth method is a recently developed deep learning method for HAR.

- *SVM* with radial basis function (RBF) kernel is used as the classifier. In this baseline, the raw time series samples are directly used as the input of SVM. Additionally, the cross-validation procedure is used to tune the parameters of SVM.
- *KNN* performed a comprehensive empirical evaluation on time series classification problems. Interestingly, the simple technique KNN (specifically, 1NN, i.e., classification based on the top one nearest neighbor) with Euclidean distance was shown to be the best technique. Therefore, we incorporate the KNN with $K = 1$ as the classifier. Same as the SVM baseline, the raw time series samples are directly used as the input of KNN.
- *MV*, which is the same as the proposed CNN method, the sliding window strategy is used to generate a set of $r \times D$ matrix-level instances first. Then the mean and the variance of the signals over the r samples in every $r \times D$ matrix are extracted to constitute the features of the input data for the classifier. The classifier used is the KNN with $K = 1$.
- *DBN*, similar to the CNN and MV methods, a set of $r \times D$ matrix-level instances are generated first. Then, the mean of the signals over the r samples in every $r \times D$ matrix is used as the input of the DBN.[3] The classifier used in this method is chosen between KNN with $K = 1$ and a multilayer perceptron neural network, and the one with better performance is reported.

For MV and DBN methods, matrix-level predictions are converted to the sample-level predictions based on the same strategy used in the CNN method as introduced in Section 3.2. We evaluate all methods' performance under the both settings of with/without the smoothing method mentioned in Section 3.2. As suggested in Cao et al. [22], the parameter u_i in the smoothing method is recommended to be chosen in the range of [60, 100].

---

[3]The experiment of using the raw inputs as the features in DBN is also performed, but the results are substantially worse than the reported one.

Table 1 AF, NF, and AC Results of the Proposed CNN Method and Four Baselines for the OAR Dataset

	Subject 1			Subject 2			Subject 3		
	AF	NF	AC	AF	NF	AC	AF	NF	AC
Without smoothing									
SVM (quoted from Cao et al. [22])	45.6	83.4	83.8	44.4	75.6	79.4	32.1	76.8	78.1
1NN (quoted from Cao et al. [22])	42.7	80.3	79.3	41.1	73.5	73.9	28.5	67.5	63.8
MV	54.2	83.9	83.7	50.8	74.6	74.3	48.6	80.9	80.7
DBN	14.3	75.0	80.0	7.0	66.7	74.1	20.0	73.4	79.3
CNN	**55.5**	**86.4**	**87.0**	**57.1**	**79.5**	**82.5**	**55.8**	**84.0**	**85.8**
With smoothing									
SVM	48.6	84.7	85.9	43.8	75.9	80.4	27.6	76.7	79.2
1NN	53.9	84.1	84.6	53.2	78.2	79.8	34.0	71.8	69.7
MV	47.9	83.3	84.3	54.3	75.7	75.7	49.6	81.9	82.1
DBN	12.9	74.5	79.5	7.3	66.9	74.9	21.1	73.0	79.7
CNN	**51.6**	**86.5**	**87.7**	**60.0**	**79.7**	**83.0**	**52.6**	**84.7**	**86.7**

Notes: *The best result for each metric is highlighted in bold.*
AC, accuracy; AF, average F-measure; NF, normalized F-measure.

The results of the proposed CNN method and the four baseline methods on OAR dataset are shown in Table 1. Following Cao et al. [22], average F-measure (AF), normalized F-measure (NF), and Accuracy (AC) are used to evaluate the performance of different methods in all experiments. The best performance for each evaluation metric is highlighted in bold.

From the results, we can see that the proposed CNN method consistently performs better than all four baselines in both settings of with/without the smoothing strategy on both datasets in terms of all three evaluation metrics. Remarkably, for Subject 3 in the first dataset and Subject 2 in the second dataset, the proposed method outperforms the best baseline by 5% or so in terms of accuracy both in the absence as well as presence of smoothing. When the smoothing strategy is used, the performance of all methods generally is improved, but the performance ranking of all methods remains almost invariant. The class imbalance issue is a main challenge for all methods. This can be seen from the confusion matrix generated by the proposed CNN method shown in Fig. 4. Due to the dominant Null class, all signals samples, except for the ones in class close drawer 2, tend to be classified into the Null class. Similar phenomena caused by the class imbalance issue exist in all methods but they are more severe for the other baseline methods.

The better performance of the CNN over DBN demonstrates that the supervised deep learning outperforms the unsupervised one for HAR. This observation has also been seen in other applications like image classification and speech recognition. Note that SVM and KNN use the raw instances in this paper while in Plätz et al. [2] they use the matrix-level instances whose amount is smaller than that of the raw instances. This may explain why DBN is a bit worse than SVM and KNN in our experiments while it is slightly better than SVM and KNN in the experiments shown in Plätz et al. [2]. The evidence

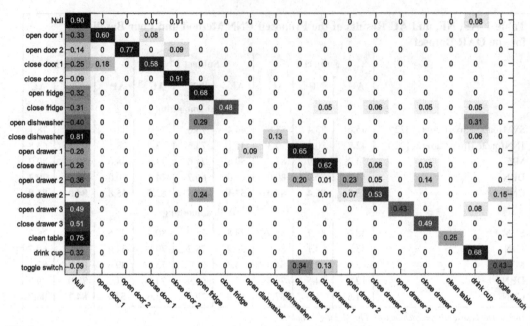

FIG. 4

Confusion matrix yielded by the proposed CNN method (without temporal smoothing) on the Opportunity Activity Recognition dataset for Subject 1 (the larger the value, the *darker the background*).

that the CNN has the better performance than SVM, KNN, and MV suggests that the CNN is closer to finding the nature of signals in terms of feature representation than the methods with shallowing learning architectures and heuristic feature designs for the HAR problem.

4.2 EXPERIMENT ON HAND GESTURE DATASET

The Hand Gesture dataset [1][4] is about different types of the human's hand movements. In this dataset, two subjects perform hand movements with eight gestures in daily living and with three gestures in playing tennis. In total, there are 12 classes in this hand gesture recognition problem.[5] Similar to the first dataset, the Null class refers to the periods with none of the predefined activities. The used body-worn sensors include a three-axis accelerometer and a two-axis gyroscope, and the sampling rate is 32 samples per second. Then, each record has 15 real-valued sensor readings in total. Every subject repeated all activities about 26 times. We randomly select one repetition as the testing data and the rest repetitions as the training data. The parameters for the CNN used for this dataset are obtained in a similar manner as the OAR dataset, and have similar values.

---

[4]https://github.com/andyknownasabu/ActRecTut.
[5]The 12 classes are Null, open a window, close a window, water a plant, turn book page, drink from a bottle, cut with a knife, chop with a knife, stir in a bowl, forehand, backhand, and smash.

Table 2 The AF, NF, and AC Results of the Proposed CNN Method and Four Baselines for the Hand Gesture Dataset

	Subject 1			Subject 2		
	AF	NF	AC	AF	NF	AC
	Without smoothing					
SVM	76.0	85.0	85.6	71.1	83.5	82.6
1NN	64.8	73.2	71.8	66.2	79.3	77.9
MV	87.5	91.3	91.2	84.1	90.1	89.3
DBN	71.8	82.1	82.8	69.0	81.4	80.1
CNN	**89.2**	**92.0**	**92.2**	**90.7**	**95.0**	**95.0**
	With smoothing					
SVM	85.1	89.2	89.6	86.0	89.3	88.5
1NN	**92.2**	93.3	93.2	86.1	89.8	89.2
MV	91.5	93.3	93.3	84.4	90.5	89.6
DBN	78.5	84.9	85.8	73.2	83.4	82.0
CNN	**92.2**	**93.9**	**94.1**	**87.0**	**95.5**	**96.0**

Similar to the results for the OAR dataset, we present the results on the Hand Gesture dataset in Table 2. Again, the CNN is able to consistently outperform the various baselines with Subject 2 showing a performance margin of about 5% in terms of accuracy both with and without smoothing.

We also conducted the experiments that the magnitudes of Fourier Transform of the raw data are taken as the inputs for all methods. However, no performance improvement can be made. Similar results have been observed in Cao et al. [22].

4.3 EXPERIMENT ON REALDISP DATASET

The REALDISP dataset [31, 32][6] is a HAR dataset that focuses on identifying a wide range of 33 different activities[7] across 17 different subjects. The data capture setup using 39 tri-axial accelerometers worn on the subject's body, under three different scenarios.

In the first scenario called the ideal displacement scenario, the dataset creators placed the various sensors precisely on the subjects' bodies. In the second scenario called the self-displacement scenario, the subjects were allowed to place the sensors themselves, after having been given general guidelines

[6]https://archive.ics.uci.edu/ml/datasets/REALDISP+Activity+Recognition+Dataset.
[7]The categories include Walking, Jogging, Running, Jump Up, Jump Front & Back, Jump Sideways, Jump Legs/Arms open/closed, Jump Rope, Trunk Twist (Arms Outstretched), Trunk Twist (Elbows Bent), Waist Bends Forward, Waist Rotation, Waist Bends (Foot Reach with other Hand), Reach Heels Backward, Lateral Bend, Lateral Bend with Arm Up, Repetitive Forward Stretching, Upper Trunk and Lower body opposite twist, Lateral elevation of arms, Frontal elevation of arms, Frontal hand claps, Frontal crossing of arms, Shoulders high-amplitude rotation, Shoulders low-amplitude rotation, Arms inner rotation, Knees to the breast, Heels to the backside, Knees bending, Knees bending forward, Knee Rotation, Rowing, Elliptical bike, and Cycling.

about which body part each sensor was supposed to be placed on. In the third scenario called the induced displacement scenario, the dataset creators placed multiple sensors with predefined displacements from their ideal settings in order to analyze performance in a controlled setting.

In this work, we use data only from the first two scenarios as they most closely correspond to a real-world usage example. Specifically, the algorithm is trained by using data from the ideal displacement scenario but tested on the self-displacement scenario. In other words, we demonstrate the impact on performance that moving away from an ideal laboratory setting has on various HAR algorithms.

The REALDISP dataset differs from the previous two datasets in that the NULL activity is not a label that is used for evaluating HAR performance. It is assumed by the dataset creators in their evaluation setup that the sensor data will be predivided into NULL and non-NULL sections. We follow the same methodology in our experiment and report the results for HAR using non-NULL activities. We compare our proposed experiment with the results from Baños et al. [32] using various methodologies:

- *Single sensor*: HAR performance is evaluated by using a single sensor at a time as the input to the system, and the reported performance is the average across the performance of all the sensors, taken one at a time.
- *Feature fusion*: HAR performance is evaluated by using a framework that unifies all the sensor inputs before passing the fused inputs to a classifier.
- *Decision fusion*: HAR performance is evaluated based on fusing together the decisions obtained from the Single Sensor scenario above, but using a hierarchical weighted classifier to assign weights to the decision of each sensor based on its performance on a validation set.

All three methodologies are evaluated using three widely used classifiers—C4.5 Decision Trees (DT) [33], KNN [34] with $k = 3$, and Naive Bayes (NB) [35]. The sensor signals are processed prior to being fed into the HAR framework. In general, the best performance is obtained when a relatively rich set of hand-crafted features consisting of the mean, standard deviation, maximum, minimum, and mean crossing rate (effective frequency) are used.

The work of Baños et al. [32] uses a 6-second sample window with no overlap in their evaluation. The length of the time window is chosen "to sufficiently capture cycles in activities" [36]. We too choose to use windows with no overlap; however, this presents a problem for using a CNN in the form of very limited data for training. On average, the REALDISP dataset contains about 13 minutes of non-NULL activity in the ideal displacement setting (training data) and about 14 minutes of such activity in the self-displacement setting (testing data) for each subject. Combined with missing data (due to sporadically faulty sensors), this translates to less than 2000 six-second windows for 33 activities for training, which results in overfitting for the CNN.

In order to circumvent this problem, we choose to use 1-second windows with no overlap to augment the data. Using a shorter-time window should result in several cycles not being captured in the data, which should make the HAR problem even more challenging for our proposed method. Indeed, several of the activities present in the dataset (such as Elliptical Bike and Cycling) can share many of the same basic movements. Despite this potential limitation, we show below that our method outperforms all the compared techniques.

A constant learning rate profile of 0.01 for 25 epochs is used for training the CNN used for this dataset, again determined by using a held-out validation set. While not directly comparable with the CNN trained on the OAR dataset (due to different dataset complexities), it can be seen that in general, a constant learning rate requires considerably more epochs than a variable learning rate profile.

Table 3 Accuracy of the Proposed CNN Method and Nine Baselines on the REALDISP Dataset for Self-Displaced Sensors

Method	DT	KNN	NB
Single sensor [32]	36.6	46.0	45.3
Feature fusion [32]	50.7	79.3	60.0
Decision fusion [32]	76.9	88.0	63.3
CNN		**90.1**	

Table 4 Accuracy of the Proposed CNN Method With Various Smoothing Methods

Smoothing Method	Accuracy
None	90.1
Blockwise	92.8
Median	91.4

The performance of our proposed method is shown in Table 3. It can be seen that the CNN-based HAR system outperforms the compared baseline methods, despite the limitation of working with shorter-time windows. This is presumably because the CNN is able to discover better feature representations than the hand-crafted features used by the compared baselines.

It is also interesting to note the effect of smoothing on the output of the proposed CNN. As NULL activities are not considered in this dataset, the smoothing strategy is slightly different from that explained earlier. Specifically, one may assume that every contiguous block of non-NULL activity corresponds to the same activity. This may be a reasonable assumption whenever there is a pause between activities. In such a case, the most frequently occurring activity in the block is assigned to all the data samples present in the block. Alternatively, one can consider each contiguous non-NULL block as composed of multiple non-NULL activities. In this case, median filtering can be applied within each block to remove singly misclassified observations. Note that an "observation" in this case corresponds to a 1-second interval. Since the smallest contiguous non-NULL block in the data is of 7 seconds, we use 7 as the size of the median filter. We refer to the above two cases as "Blockwise" and "Median" smoothing, respectively, in Table 4.

It can be seen that using median smoothing gives an improvement of about 1.3% in accuracy. On the other hand, using blockwise smoothing more than doubles the improvement to 2.7%. This indicates that instances of multiple labels for a single contiguous block do not occur very frequently in the data. Thus, having prior knowledge of how the data is obtained can help with choosing the correct smoothing strategy. In either case though, smoothing does help boost performance as with the previous two datasets.

4.4 COMPUTATIONAL REQUIREMENTS

All experiments are conducted on a PC, which has an Intel i5-2500 3.30 GHz CPU and 8 GB RAM. We report the timing results of the CNN on the OAR dataset for Subject 1 as this dataset is the largest one in all experiments. The training and testing raw samples for this dataset are 136,869 and 32,466, respectively, and the input dimension is 107. The training time of the CNN is around 1 hour, while the testing time is 8 minutes. On average, within a second the CNN can predict 56 raw instances' labels. Thus, the efficiency of the CNN is good enough for online HAR.

4.5 FUTURE DIRECTIONS

The training and testing times for CNNs can be significantly reduced when the parallel computation of the CNN [26, 27] is implemented. This research topic will be fully investigated in our future work.

Additionally, it will be interesting to see if deep learning architectures for sequential data such as recurrent neural networks (RNNs) [37], long short-term memory networks (LSTMs) [38], etc., will be useful when applied to the HAR problem. These have been extensively used in other sequential tasks such as speech recognition, where it is important to label a group of sound samples with the right word or sound (phoneme). However, the HAR problem cannot be directly mapped to a sequential problem, since each sample (rather than only a well-defined group of samples) possesses a ground-truth activity label. Nevertheless, the use of such sequential networks holds some promise in bypassing the need for the sliding window approach, which is a heuristic parameter used in CNNs.

5 CONCLUSION

In this chapter, we have proposed a new method to automate feature extraction for the HAR task. The proposed method builds a novel deep architecture for the CNN to investigate the multichannel time series data. This deep architecture mainly employs the convolution and pooling operations to capture the salient patterns of the sensor signals at different time scales. All identified salient patterns are systematically unified among multiple channels and finally mapped into the different classes of human activities. The key advantages of the proposed method are: (i) feature extraction is performed in a task-appropriate and nonhand-crafted manner; (ii) extracted features have more discriminative power w.r.t. the classes of human activities; and (iii) feature extraction and classification are unified in one model so their performances are mutually enhanced. In the experiments, we demonstrate that the proposed CNN method outperforms other state-of-the-art methods, and we therefore believe that the proposed method can serve as a competitive tool of feature learning and classification for the HAR problems.

REFERENCES

[1] Bulling A, Blanke U, Schiele B. A tutorial on human activity recognition using body-worn inertial sensors. ACM Comput Surv 2014;46(3):33:1–3.
[2] Plätz T, Hammerla NY, Olivier P. Feature learning for activity recognition in ubiquitous computing. In: IJCAI; 2012.
[3] Reddy S, Mun M, Burke J, Estrin D, Hansen M, Srivastava M. Using mobile phones to determine transportation modes. ACM Trans Sens Netw 2010;6(2):13:1–13:27.
[4] Ji S, Xu W, Yang M, Yu K. 3D convolutional neural networks for human action recognition. In: ICML; 2010.
[5] Le QV, Zou WY, Yeung SY, Ng AY. Learning hierarchical invariant spatio-temporal features for action recognition with independent subspace analysis; 2011. p. 3361–8.

[6] Cao H, Li XL, Woon YK, Ng SK. Structure preserving oversampling for imbalanced time series classification. In: Proceedings of IEEE 11th international conference on data mining; 2011.

[7] Cao H, Li XL, Woon YK, Ng SK. Integrated oversampling for imbalanced time series classification. IEEE Trans Knowl Data Eng 2013;12(25):2809–22.

[8] Huynh T, Schiele B. Analyzing features for activity recognition. In: Proceedings of the 2005 joint conference on smart objects and ambient intelligence: innovative context-aware services: usages and technologies; 2005. p. 159–63.

[9] Nguyen MN, Li XL, Ng SK. Positive unlabeled learning for time series classification. In: Proceedings of the 22nd international joint conference on artificial intelligence; 2011.

[10] Lin J, Keogh E, Lonardi S, Chiu B. A symbolic representation of time series, with implications for streaming algorithms. In: SIGMOD workshop on research issues in data mining and knowledge discovery; 2003.

[11] Bengio Y. Learning deep architectures for AI. Found Trends Mach Learn 2009;2(1):1–127.

[12] Deng L. A tutorial survey of architectures, algorithms, and applications for deep learning. APSIPA Trans Signal Inf Process 2014;3:1–29.

[13] Yang JB, Nguyen MN, San PP, Li XL, Krishnaswamy SP. Deep convolutional neural networks on multichannel time series for human activity recognition. In: Proceedings of the 24th international joint conference on artificial intelligence; 2015.

[14] Hinton GE, Osindero S. A fast learning algorithm for deep belief nets. Neural Comput 2006;18(7):1527–54.

[15] Le Roux N, Bengio Y. Representational power of restricted Boltzmann machines and deep belief networks. Neural Comput 2008;20(6):1631–49.

[16] Tieleman T. Training restricted Boltzmann machines using approximations to the likelihood gradient. In: ICML; 2008. p. 1064–71.

[17] Krizhevsky A, Sutskever I, Hinton GE. ImageNet classification with deep convolutional neural networks. In: NIPS; 2012. p. 1097–105.

[18] Zeiler M, Fergus R. Visualizing and understanding convolutional networks; 2014.

[19] Deng L, Li J, Huang JT, Yao K, Yu D, Seide F, et al. Recent advances in deep learning for speech research at Microsoft. In: ICASSP; 2013.

[20] Zeng M, Nguyen LT, Yu B, Mengshoel OJ, Zhu J, Wu P, et al. Convolutional neural networks for human activity recognition using mobile sensors. In: MobiCASE; 2014.

[21] Fukushima K. Neocognitron: a self-organizing neural network model for a mechanism of pattern recognition unaffected by shift in position. Biol Cybern 1980;36(4):193–202.

[22] Cao H, Nguyen MN, Phua C, Krishnaswamy S, Li XL. An integrated framework for human activity classific. In: ACM international conference on ubiquitous computing; 2012.

[23] Srivastava N, Hinton G, Krizhevsky A, Sutskever I, Salakhutdinov R. Dropout: a simple way to prevent neural networks from overfitting. J Mach Learn Res 2014;15(1):1929–58.

[24] Wan J, Wang D, Hoi SCH, Wu P, Zhu J, Zhang Y, et al. Deep learning for content-based image retrieval: a comprehensive study. In: ACM MM; 2014. p. 157–66.

[25] LeCun Y, Bottou L, Orr G, Muller K. Efficient BackProp. In: Orr G, Muller K, editors. Neural networks: tricks of the trade; Springer; 1998. p. 9–50.

[26] Jia Y, Shelhamer E, Donahue J, Karayev S, Long J, Girshick R, et al. Caffe: convolutional architecture for fast feature embedding. In: ACM MM; 2014. p. 675–8.

[27] Donahue J, Jia Y, Vinyals O, Hoffman J, Zhang N, Tzeng E, et al. DeCAF: a deep convolutional activation feature for generic visual recognition. In: ICML; 2014.

[28] Sagha H, Digumarti ST, del R. Millán J. Chavarriaga R, Calatroni A, Roggen D, et al. Benchmarking classification techniques using the opportunity human activity dataset. In: IEEE international conference on systems, man, and cybernetics; 2011.

[29] Roggen D, Calatroni A, Rossi M, Holleczek T, Förster K, Tröster G, et al. Collecting complex activity data sets in highly rich networked sensor environments. In: Proceedings of the seventh international conference on networked sensing systems (INSS), Kassel, Germany; 2010.

[30] Keogh E, Kasetty S. On the need for time series data mining benchmarks: a survey and empirical demonstration. In: SIGKDD; 2002. p. 102–11.

[31] Baños O, Damas M, Pomares H, Rojas I, Tóth MA, Amft O. A benchmark dataset to evaluate sensor displacement in activity recognition. In: Proceedings of the 2012 ACM conference on ubiquitous computing. ACM; 2012. p. 1026–35.

[32] Baños O, Toth MA, Damas M, Pomares H, Rojas I. Dealing with the effects of sensor displacement in wearable activity recognition. Sensors 2014;14(6):9995–10023.

[33] Duda RO, Hart PE, Stork DG. Pattern classification. Hoboken, NJ: John Wiley & Sons; 2012.

[34] Cover TM, Hart PE. Nearest neighbor pattern classification. IEEE Trans Inf Theory 1967;13(1):21–7.

[35] Theodoridis S, Koutroumbas K. Pattern recognition and neural networks. Machine learning and its applications. Springer; 2001. p. 169–95.

[36] Bao L, Intille SS. Activity recognition from user-annotated acceleration data. Pervasive computing. Berlin, Heidelberg: Springer; 2004. p. 1–17.

[37] Graves A. Supervised sequence labelling. Berlin, Heidelberg: Springer; 2012.

[38] Hochreiter S, Schmidhuber J. Long short-term memory. Neural Comput 1997;9(8):1735–80.

GLOSSARY

Cost function Objective function to be minimized in the model learning process.

Feature map A representation of data that can be used to find salient information.

Feature representation learning A method to automatically learn useful representations of raw data without the need for hand-crafted features.

Free parameters Parameters of the model to be learned.

Hyper-parameters Parameters used to control the learning process of the model.

Ideal displacement Scenario for the REALDISP dataset where sensors are placed in their ideal positions.

Induced displacement Scenario for the REALDISP dataset where sensors are offset from ideal positions by a fixed amount.

Learning rate Hyper-parameter that controls the step size in the objective minimization process.

NULL class A class of human activities that is outside the scope of interest of a given task.

Overfitting A process occurs when a model is excessively complex, having too many parameters relative to the number of observations.

Self-displacement Scenario for the REALDISP dataset where sensors are offset from ideal positions by subject-determined random amounts.

Sigmoid function A function is a bounded differentiable real function that is defined for all real input values and has a positive derivative at each point.

Sliding window strategy A method to subset data into contiguous segments, possibly with some overlap.

Smoothing A postprocessing method to improve performance by filtering out short, spurious misclassifications.

Tri-axial accelerometer A sensor to record accelerations along three (typically, two horizontal and one vertical) axes.

NEONATAL CRY ANALYSIS AND CATEGORIZATION SYSTEM VIA DIRECTED ACYCLIC GRAPH SUPPORT VECTOR MACHINE

10

Szu-Ta Chen*, Kathiravan Srinivasan[†], Chen Lin[‡], Chuan-Yu Chang[‡]

National Taiwan University Hospital Yun-Lin Branch, Douliu City, Yunlin County, Taiwan[*] National Ilan University, Yilan City, Yilan County, Taiwan[†] National Yunlin University of Science and Technology, Douliu City, Yunlin County, Taiwan[‡]

1 INTRODUCTION

The cry is an inherent characteristic of a neonatal and it is the means through which they connect with the outside world. Generally, the neonatal cries for 2 h a day, as per the data collected by a group of child physicians. The cry typically signals out the problem of the neonate. Nevertheless, care takers seldom identify the reason for the neonate's cry. The major causes are comprised of the factors like hunger, distress due to gas or intestinal contractions, indigestion, uneasiness because of a damp diaper, anguish owing to hot or cold weather, and disturbances from the external environment [1]. The requirements of neonates can be recognized from the kind of cry; for instance, a cry out of hunger is diminutive and small-pitched, whereas the distressed cry is uneven. If the care takers can segregate the crying behavior into different classes, it becomes easy for them to respond to the neonate needs. Therefore, a neonatal cry analysis and categorization system is proposed for detecting the behavioral characteristics of the cry, which helps in the enhancement of neonatal care.

Commonly, the language is the widely utilized tool for conveying some information or the feelings of an individual. A smart audio emotion recognition scheme, which employed jointly the prosodic and spectral features to identify the six widespread emotions comprising happiness, fear, disgust, anger, surprise, and sadness, was established by Ooi et al. [2]. Nevertheless, neonates can merely use crying as a natural contrivance for conveying their emotions and requirements. The cry's acoustic features are the prime source for constructing the neonatal cry estimation model. The features like timber, intensity [3], Mel-frequency cepstrum coefficients (MFCCs) [4], formant, zero crossing rate (ZCR), linear prediction cepstrum coefficients (LPCCs) [5], octave and pitch [3,6], etc. Nevertheless, employing an extensive range of features to identify and classify the neonate's cry is still arduous, while ambiguity prevails over the prominence of each of these features in the categorization of the crying behavior. Therefore, to decide on the more specific authentic features, the sequential forward floating selection (SFFS) [7] approach is employed.

Typically, an artificial neural network (ANN) is mostly adopted as a classifier for categorization and grouping of data. The ANN is an algorithm established on the principles that deal with the functions and structure of biological neural networks. Support vector machines (SVMs) are a collection of supervised learning approaches employed for categorization and regression, which is uncomplicated and superior when compared with alternative classifiers. Consequently, in this work, the SVM is employed to classify and group the neonatal cry into three different categories [8]. The 10 MFCCs were extracted by Petroni et al. for investigating crying behavior [9]. Moreover, they categorized neonate emotions like pain, anger, and fear by means of the neural networks. Baeck et al. investigated the cry caused by hunger for neonates aged below 6 months [1]. In addition, they assessed the association between the growth and crying frequency of the neonate. The fundamental frequency of a neonate's hunger cry is well-known to lie in the range between 350 and 550 Hz. Runefors et al. investigated the neonatal cry due to pain. In addition, they evaluated the pitch and time period of the neonates cry triggered owing to needle piercing [10]. The investigation indicates the fact that after injecting the needle, the neonate's first cry has an extremely greater pitch and elongated time duration than the fifth cry. The proposed approach is elaborated in Section 2. The experimental results are portrayed in Section 3 and Section 4 gives the conclusion.

2 NEONATAL CRY ANALYSIS AND CATEGORIZATION SYSTEM

This work establishes a neonatal cry analysis and categorization system, which classifies the neonates cry into three different categories comprising of sleepiness, hunger, and pain. The flow chart of the proposed neonatal cry analysis and categorization system is depicted in Fig. 1. The four major stages in the proposed approach are signal preprocessing, feature extraction, feature selection, and neonatal cry analysis and categorization. The subsequent subdivisions elaborate the particulars of all stages.

2.1 CRY SIGNAL PREPROCESSING

The signal preprocessing is the first stage that is employed for removing the disturbances and interferences from the cry signal [11]. This stage further has seven substages: normalization of audio; framing process; endpoint diagnosis; automatic detection of cry units; preemphasis; windowing–hamming window; and fast Fourier transformation. The flow diagram of the cry signal preprocessing stage is illustrated in Fig. 2.

2.1.1 Normalization of audio

The sampling rate, format, and bit resolution rate of the audio signal are normalized to a similar style, so as to decrease the dissimilarity between the neonatal cries. The recorded cry signals are transformed to Waveform Audio format (WAV), and correspondingly, the sampling rate and bit resolution of these signals are set at 8 and 16 kHz in this work.

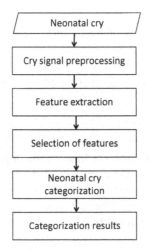

FIG. 1

Flow chart of the neonatal cry analysis and categorization system.

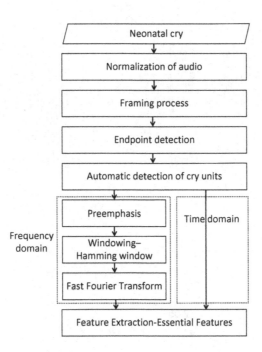

FIG. 2

Cry signal preprocessing—flow diagram.

2.1.2 Framing process

Generally, investigating a bigger quantity of signal information might be an arduous task. Comparatively, petite audio signals are stable and easier to process. Hence, the neonatal cry signal is chopped into numerous short time frames. In this work, each frame encompasses 256 sampling points (32 ms) and consecutive frames have an overlap of 50 percentage (16 ms). Fig. 3 demonstrates the schematic diagram of the framing process.

2.1.3 Endpoint diagnosis

Normally, silence or environmental disturbances form the major part of the noncrying fragments of the neonatal cry. Therefore, for identifying the endpoints of the cry, the end point detection method is employed. Moreover, this approach removes the unnecessary signals in the cry and it retains the crying fragments required for further investigation. The data quantity and computational time can be narrowed by adopting this technique. The frame intensity is calculated as follows:

$$Intensity = \sum_{i=0}^{N-1} |S_i| \tag{1}$$

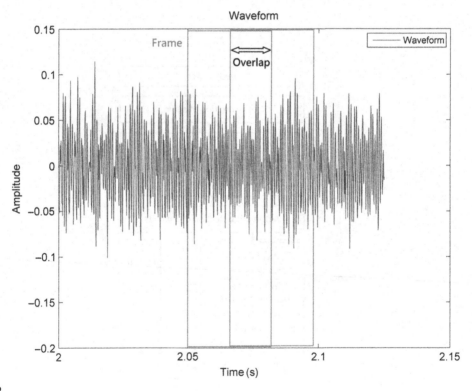

FIG. 3

Framing process—schematic diagram.

where N represents the amount of sampling point of a frame, and S_i denotes the intensity of the ith sampling point in the frame. The crying fragment is obtained from the frame that has a greater intensity, when compared with the set threshold value.

2.1.4 Automatic detection of cry units
The neonate's breathing and whining signals are normally the part of the crying fragments. The main objective of the automatic detection of cry units is to diagnose and segregate the cry signals from unwanted disturbances [12]. Furthermore, frames with time duration below 250 ms are eliminated for accomplishing this objective [1,13]. The threshold is computed by using the subsequent expression:

$$Threshold = \frac{t \times (fs) - Overlap}{FrameStep} \tag{2}$$

where t represents the predefined threshold of time length, fs denotes the signal sampling rate, *Overlap* indicates the coinciding sampling points between successive frames, and *FrameStep* exemplifies the difference between the frame size and overlap. Fig. 4 demonstrates a case for the automatic detection of cry units.

2.1.5 Preemphasis
The high frequency portion of the signal gets curbed during the sound generation process of the neonatal cry. However, the high frequency portion of the cry signal is boosted by employing a high-pass filter, which completes the process of preemphasis. The subsequent equation illustrates the preemphasis process:

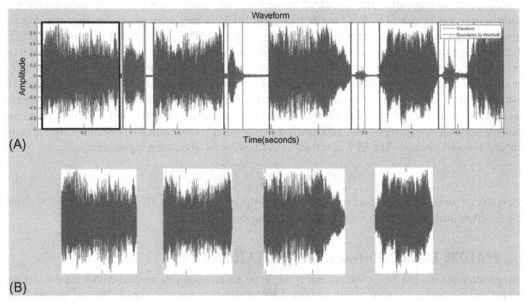

FIG. 4

Automatic detection of cry units. (A) Neonatal cry signal. (B) Elimination of frames with time duration below 250 ms.

$$S'(n) = S(n) - \alpha \cdot S(n-1) \tag{3}$$

where $S(n)$ represents the magnitude of the nth sampling point inside a frame. Usually, the α value is fixed in the range 0.9–1.0.

2.1.6 Windowing—Hamming window

During the preceding substage, the neonatal cry fragments are chopped into several frames. Consequently, this act ascends the problem of incoherence between the anterior end and rear end of every frame. Therefore, it becomes significant to allow the energy of the frame to concentrate on the spectrum, thereby subsiding the signal edge disparity. The spectral noise can be eliminated or diminished by multiplying each and every frame with a windowing function. In this work, the windowing process is expressed by the following equation:

$$Y(n) = S'(n) \times W(n) \tag{4}$$

where $W(n)$ represents the windowing function. Hamming window is employed in this proposed approach. The hamming window is portrayed by the following equation:

$$W(n) = \begin{cases} 0.54 - 0.46 \times \cos\left(\dfrac{2\pi n}{N-1}\right) & 0 \leq n \leq N-1 \\ 0 & \text{otherwise} \end{cases} \tag{5}$$

2.1.7 Fast Fourier transformation

In general, processing the neonatal cry signal in the time domain is a lengthy and laborious task. Comparatively, the assessment of the cry signal in the frequency domain for extracting various essential features is an easier task. The fast Fourier transform (FFT) is employed to convert the time domain signal to frequency domain information, in this research [14]. The discrete Fourier transform (DFT) of the cry signal is determined using the FFT algorithm. This algorithm quickens the computational speed and lessens the complexity of the whole process. Due to the fact that the FFT algorithm splits the transform into two components with a size $N/2$ at every step. Consequently, the number of frames is restricted to the power of two. The sampling frequency is set as 8 kHz and the length of the frame is fixed as 16 ms, in this research. Therefore, it leads to 256 samplings points. Moreover, the frames are split into odd and even components, and finally a pair of complex information is obtained after accomplishing the FFT process. The FFT spectrum is defined by the following expression:

$$S'(n) = \sqrt{s'(n)^2 + is'(n)^2} \tag{6}$$

where $s'(n)$ represents the real part, and $is'(n)$ denotes the imaginary part. The spectrum of the cry signal that is determined the fast Fourier transform is illustrated in Fig. 5.

2.2 FEATURE EXTRACTION—ESSENTIAL FEATURES

The quantity of data can be enormous and it might be an arduous task to deal with such data, if the categorization of the neonatal cry is restricted to merely the acoustic signal. Hence, the neonatal cry information is transformed into a comparatively petite feature vector. Consequently, the characteristic parameters, which denote the neonatal cry signal, are extracted. In the time domain, merely lesser amount of features can be extracted, even though the neonatal acoustic signal remains undamaged and it never loses information. On the other hand, in the frequency domain, the cry signal may get slightly

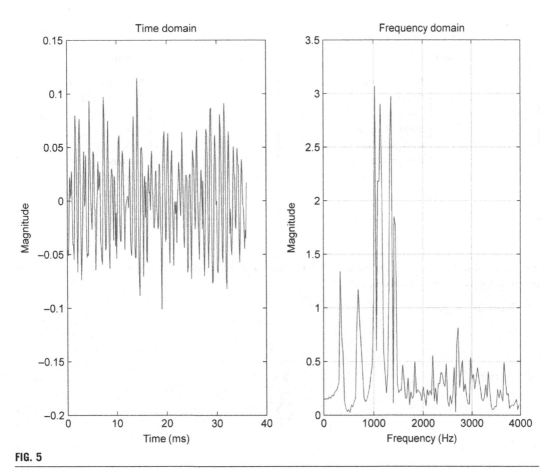

FIG. 5

FFT spectrum of the cry signal.

damaged or lost, due to that fact that the neonatal cry signal is transformed from the time domain to the frequency domain. However, several features can be extracted from the signal in the frequency domain. For that reason, in this research, features from both the time and frequency domain are extracted, thereby enhancing the process of infant cry recognition.

Primarily, from every frame, 15 features are extracted. Moreover, six features from the time domain and nine features from the frequency domain are extracted, respectively. Henceforth, to elaborate the features adopted in this work, the subsequent five terminologies are established:

$S_j(n)$: the signal of the jth frame in the time domain;
$S'_j(n)$: the signal of the jth frame in the frequency domain after framing, Hamming windowing, and fast Fourier transformation;
T: the features extracted in time domain;
F: the features extracted in the frequency domain; and
N: the number of samples in a frame.

Table 1 The 15 Extracted Features

Time Domain		Frequency Domain	
1	Intensity magnitude	1	Spectral centroid
2	Average	2	Roll-off frequency
3	Variance	3	Bandwidth
4	Standard deviation	4	Peak
5	Root mean square	5	Valley
6	Zero crossing rate	6	Contrast
		7	Formant
		8	LPCC
		9	MFCC

Table 1 exhibits the details of the extracted 15 features. The particulars of every feature are summarized as given by the subsequent expressions:

1. Intensity magnitude

$$TM_j = \sum_{i=0}^{N-1} |S_j(i)| \tag{7}$$

2. Average

$$TA_j = \frac{1}{N} \sum_{i=0}^{N-1} (S_j(i)) \tag{8}$$

3. Variance

$$TV_j = \frac{1}{N} \sum_{i=0}^{N-1} (S_j(i) - TA_j)^2 \tag{9}$$

4. Bandwidth

$$FB_j = \sqrt{\frac{\sum_{i=0}^{N-1} \left(\left|S_j'(i)\right|^2 \times (i - FC_j)^2 \right)}{\sum_{i=0}^{N-1} \left(\left|S_j'(i)\right|^2 \right)}} \tag{10}$$

5. Spectral centroid

$$FC_j = \frac{\sum_{i=0}^{N-1} \left(\left|S_j'(i)\right|^2 \times i \right)}{\sum_{i=0}^{N-1} \left(\left|S_j'(i)\right|^2 \right)} \tag{11}$$

6. Roll-off frequency

$$\sum_{i=0}^{FR_j} \left| S'_j(i) \right|^2 = 0.85 \times \sum_{i=0}^{N-1} S'_j(i) \tag{12}$$

7. Root mean square

$$TRMS_j = \sqrt{\frac{\sum_{i=0}^{N-1} (S_j(i))^2}{N}} \tag{13}$$

8. Zero crossing rate

$$ZCR = \sum_{i=1}^{N-1} \left| \text{sgn}(S_j(i)) - \text{sgn}(S_j(i-1)) \right| \tag{14}$$

9. Peak

$$FPeak_{j,k} = \log \left\{ \frac{1}{\alpha N} \sum_{i=0}^{\alpha N-1} S'_{j,k,i} \right\} \tag{15}$$

10. Valley

$$FValley_{j,k} = \log \left\{ \frac{1}{\alpha N} \sum_{i=0}^{\alpha N-1} S'_{j,k,N-i+1} \right\} \tag{16}$$

11. Contrast

$$FContrast_{kj,k} = FPeak_{j,k} - FValley_{j,k} \tag{17}$$

where k denotes the number of subbands and α value is a constant. Furthermore, in this work, the factors k and α are fixed with values of 7 and 0.2, respectively.

12. Pitch

Pitch is the notion of seeing the low or high acoustic signal as a frequency, which is similar to the fundamental frequency (f_0). The best rudimentary method to assess f_0 is to investigate the waveform in the time domain. Autocorrelation calculation is used to extract the pitch of the neonates cry signal, in this research [15].

13. Formant

Formant is defined as the assortment of frequencies of a complex sound, in which there is an absolute or a relative maximum in the acoustic spectrum. Formant can mean either a resonance or the spectral maximum that the resonance generates. The formants are usually measured as amplitude peaks in the frequency spectrum of the sound, using a spectrogram or a spectrum analyzer. The first six formants are extracted from the signal frame as per the characteristic parameter, and they are represented as F1~F6.

14. Linear Prediction Cepstrum Coefficients (LPCC)

In several audio recognition applications, the LPCC [5] is widely employed. The idea embracing the LPCC is to model the human vocal tract using a digital all-pole filter. There will be p number of the LPCC. The LPCC will be clustered together to establish one feature vector for a specific neonatal cry signal frame. In this work, factor p is fixed to a value 12, and the extracted 12 features are represented as $LPCC_1 \sim LPCC_{12}$.

15. Mel-frequency Cepstrum Coefficients (MFCC)

In the audio recognition systems, the MFCC [4] is one of the best frequently adapted feature extraction. Moreover, from the frequency spectrum of the windowed neonatal cry signal frames, the feature vectors are extracted. Assume that p is the order of the Mel scale cepstrum. These feature vectors are attained with bearing in mind the first p Discrete Cosine Transform (DCT) coefficients. In this research, factor p is fixed to a value 12, and the extracted 12 features are represented as $MFCC_1 \sim MFCC_{12}$.

2.3 SELECTION OF FEATURES

In this research, from every frame, 15 features are extracted. Nevertheless, training the classifier by employing these 15 features is a very lengthy process and it takes a very long time for completion. Therefore, the discriminative features are chosen to decrease the computational time and to enhance the categorization accuracy.

In general, the optimum feature set is determined by employing the SFFS approach. In the year 1994, Pudil et al. established this SFFS algorithm by merging the sequential forward selection (SFS) algorithm with the sequential backward selection (SBS) [16] algorithm. During the search process, the dynamic capability of finding the number of forward or backward steps makes SFFS approach better and outstanding, when compared with SFS and SBS algorithms. The algorithm will terminate the searching process, once it determines the feature set with maximum classification rate. Fig. 6 illustrates the flow diagram of the feature selection process.

With the proposed system, the 15 features are primarily supplied as input to the SVM classifier. Furthermore, the categorization accuracy is determined by employing the k-fold cross-validation and the discriminative features are chosen by using the SFFS approach. Lastly, the four discriminative features, comprising the pitch, spectral centroid, peak, and contrast, are chosen. The neonatal cry signals will be trained and classified based on these four features, in all the subsequent experiments.

2.4 CATEGORIZATION AND VALIDATION

The support vector machine is a supervised learning approach and the selected optimal feature set is employed to train the SVM classifier. Fig. 7 demonstrates the concept of mapping the feature vectors of distinct categories in a higher dimensional feature space, to determine an optimal hyperplane for segregating the two classes and that is alienated by a widespread perfect gap. The SVM is a more universally and efficaciously employed in classification and identification applications like signal/image assessment, pattern classification, or character recognition.

The SVM classifier forecasts the test data as associated with any one of two categories, because the SVM is a classic two-type classifier. Nevertheless, the neonatal cries are classified into three different categories, in this research. Therefore, the directed acyclic graph SVM (DAG-SVM) approach is employed as the classifier for validation, in the testing phase [17]. In comparison with the alternative multiclass SVM techniques, the DAG-SVM approach outperforms all its counterparts in terms of computational time. While considering a problem with N classes, only $N-1$ decision nodes shall be assessed for determining a solution. Fig. 8 illustrates the DAG decision tree for determining the best

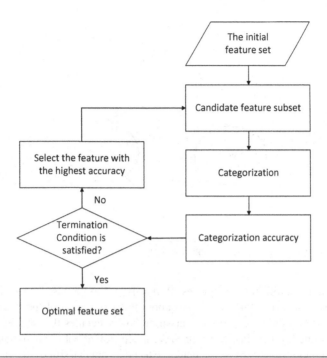

FIG. 6

Feature selection—flow diagram.

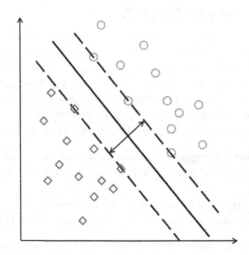

FIG. 7

Hyperplane—schematic diagram.

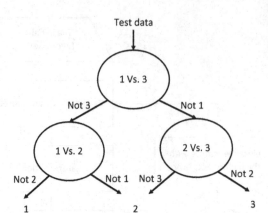

FIG. 8

DAG decision tree for determining the best category amongst the three categories.

category amongst the three different categories. Primarily, when the test data is directed to the classifier, the layer-1 classifier will make a decision about the association of the test data with category 1 or category 3. Subsequently, if the layer-1 classifier finally decides that the test data is associated with category 1, then the layer 2 classifier will make a decision about the association of the test data with category 1 or category 2. Moreover, all available test data are classified into any one of these three categories using the two classifier approach.

3 EXPERIMENTAL RESULTS AND DISCUSSION

3.1 ENVIRONMENT OF THE EXPERIMENTS

Thirty-seven neonates comprising of 15 females and 22 males were involved in this research. The neonates with ages ranging from 1 to 10 days old were considered for these experiments, and they were born in the department of Obstetrics and Gynecology at National Taiwan University Hospital Yun-Lin Branch, Taiwan. Furthermore, these neonates encountered no impediments during birth, and their gestational ages, birth weights, and ages were absent of any pathological background. In addition, from these normal neonates, three different kinds of cry encompassing the sleep-induced, hunger-induced, and pain-induced cries were acquired. The three different kinds of cry are:

- sleep-induced cry (sleepiness): triggered by drowsiness, and the neonatal sleeps after the crying;
- hunger-induced cry (hungry): triggered by hunger, and the neonatal stops crying after consuming milk; and
- pain-induced cry (pain): triggered by a sharp pierce that is adequate to draw blood, also consequential from a precautionary vaccination or tape confiscation [11,18].

In addition to the above, the data set employed in these investigations encompasses 138 sleep-induced cries, 176 hunger-induced cries, and 176 pain-induced cries. Each neonatal cry was acquired in a supine position with a sampling rate of 44.1 kHz and a bit resolution of 16 bits on a SONY HDR-PJ10 HD

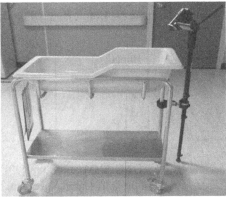

FIG. 9

Experimental arrangement for collecting neonatal cries.

digital video recorder (with a built-in microphone). The microphone was placed around 40 cm from the neonate's mouth. All recorded files were 10–60 s long. Fig. 9 demonstrates the experimental arrangement for recording the neonatal cries. The Ethical Review Committee of National Taiwan University Hospital granted official permission for this research. Each and every parent of the neonates offered their written concurrence for taking part in this investigation. All the experiments were implemented on a computer with an Intel(R) Core(TM) i7-2600 processor (3.4GHz) and 4 GB of main memory, running Microsoft Windows 7 Professional.

Predominantly, four experiments were done to illustrate the performance of the proposed approach. Experiment 1 employs the 15 extracted features for portraying the accuracy of the neonatal cry analysis and categorization system. In experiment 2, the four selected features were employed to exemplify the accuracy of the neonatal cry analysis and categorization system. Experiment 3 describes the robustness of the neonatal cry analysis and categorization system for male and female babies. Finally, in experiment 4, the results of the proposed approach were compared with that of Y. Abdulaziz's method [19].

3.2 EXPERIMENT 1: NEONATAL CRY ANALYSIS AND CATEGORIZATION—EMPLOYING 15 EXTRACTED FEATURES

The extracted 15 features were deployed in this experiment. Considering all the cry signals, half the quantity of the cry signals were employed for training and the remaining were utilized for testing. Table 2 encapsulates the amount of cries deployed for training and testing purposes. The LIBSVM

Table 2 Training and Testing Data			
	Training Data	**Testing Data**	**Total**
Hunger	88 cries	88 cries	176 cries
Sleepiness	69 cries	69 cries	138 cries
Pain	88 cries	88 cries	176 cries

Table 3 Categorization Accuracy—Employing All the Extracted 15 Features

Actual Categorization	System Categorization			
	Hunger	Sleepiness	Pain	Accuracy (%)
Hunger	76	0	12	86.3636
Sleepiness	6	53	10	76.8116
Pain	4	0	84	95.4545
Average				86.9388

was adapted to accomplish the DAG-SVM algorithm [20]. The optimal cost factor c and the kernel function γ were chosen based on the grid search algorithm. In this experiment the factors c and γ were fixed to values of 0.8 and 0.5, respectively. Table 3 demonstrates the confusion matrix for the categorization. The experimental results portray the fact that the categorization accuracy rate of being hungry, sleepy, and in pain is 86%, 77%, and 95%, respectively. The proposed system deprived of feature selection has an average categorization accuracy around 86.94%.

The accuracy can be computed from the following expression:

$$Accuracy = N_T/N \tag{18}$$

where N_T indicates the number of correct categorization, and N signifies the total number of testing cries.

3.3 EXPERIMENT 2: NEONATAL CRY ANALYSIS AND CATEGORIZATION—DEPLOYING THE SELECTED FOUR FEATURES

In this experiment, the data set exemplified in Table 2 was employed. Moreover, identical factor values for LIBSVM was deployed in this investigation. The features employed constitute the major distinction between experiments 1 and 2. The four discriminative features such as contrast, peak, spectral centroid, and pitch were deployed for training and testing purposes, in this trial. Table 4 describes the confusion matrix for the categorization. The proposed system achieves an average categorization accuracy of around 92.17% for all the experimental results that are superior, when compared with that of experiment 1.

Table 4 Categorization Accuracy—Deploying the Selected Four Features

Actual Categorization	System Categorization			
	Hunger	Sleepiness	Pain	Accuracy (%)
Hunger	81	0	7	92.0454
Sleepiness	3	63	3	91.3043
Pain	6	0	82	93.1818
Average				92.1771

Table 5 Categorization Accuracy for Different Genders				
	Correct	**Incorrect**	**Total**	**Accuracy (%)**
Male	103	10	113	91.1504
Female	123	9	132	93.1818

3.4 EXPERIMENT 3: COMPARISON OF NEONATAL CRY ANALYSIS AND CATEGORIZATION BETWEEN MALE AND FEMALE BABIES

In experiment 3, the categorization scenario of experiment 2 is deployed for understanding the variation in cries between male and female neonates. An aggregate of 245 cries comprising of 113 male and 132 female neonatal cries was tested, in this investigation. The categorization accuracy for distinct gender is displayed in Table 5. The cry categorization accuracy of male and female neonates is 91.15% and 93.18%, respectively. Since both the categorization accuracies are greater than 91%, this indicates the point that the discrepancy between male and female neonates is inconsequential.

3.5 EXPERIMENT 4: COMPARISON OF PROPOSED SYSTEM WITH Y. ABDULAZIZ'S APPROACH

The competence of the proposed system can be depicted by comparing it with Y. Abdulaziz's approach [19]. In addition, from the neonatal cries, the MFCC and LPCC were extracted for further processing. The in-pain/non-pain classifier was trained by deploying the scaled conjugate gradient and an aggregate of 88 in-pain and 88 non-pain cries were employed for testing purposes. The performance of the proposed system was assessed by employing five measurements: negative predictive value (NPV), specificity, accuracy, positive predictive value (PPV), and sensitivity. These five measurements can be computed using the subsequent expressions:

$$Accuracy = \frac{N_{TP} + N_{TN}}{N_P + N_N} \tag{19}$$

$$Sensitivity = \frac{N_{TP}}{N_P} \tag{20}$$

$$Specificity = \frac{N_{TN}}{N_N} \tag{21}$$

$$PPV = \frac{N_{TP}}{N_{TP} + N_{FP}} \tag{22}$$

$$NPV = \frac{N_{TN}}{N_{TN} + N_{FN}} \tag{23}$$

where N_P and N_N signifies the number of neonatal cries induced by pain and other reasons, respectively. N_{TP} indicates the number of cries that the system categorizes as true pain. N_{FP} exemplifies the number of cries that the system categorizes as false pain. N_{TN} depicts the number of cries that the system categorizes as true not-in-pain. N_{FN} represents the number of cries that the system categorizes as false not-in-pain. The compared confusion matrix of Y. Abdulaziz's approach and the proposed system are

Table 6 The Compared Confusion Matrix of Y. Abdulaziz's Approach and the Proposed System

Actual Categorization	System Categorization			
	In Pain		Not in Pain	
	Y. Abdulaziz's Method	Proposed System	Y. Abdulaziz's Method	Proposed System
In-pain	75	82	3	5
Not in pain	13	6	85	83

Table 7 Compared Five Measurements of Y. Abdulaziz's Approach and the Proposed System

Method	Accuracy (%)	Sensitivity (%)	Specificity (%)	PPV (%)	NPV (%)
Y. Abdulaziz's approach	91.43	85.23	96.59	96.15	86.73
Proposed system	93.75	93.18	94.32	94.25	93.26

illustrated in Table 6. The compared five measurements of Y. Abdulaziz's approach and the proposed system are summarized in Table 7.

Based on the investigational outcomes, the average accuracy rate of Y. Abdulaziz's approach, categorized by LPCC and MFCC, is around 91.43%. The average accuracy rate of our proposed system, categorized by pitch, spectral centroid, contrast, and peak is around 93.75%. Investigational outcomes demonstrate the fact that the proposed system attains greater accuracy. Table 7 exemplifies the point that all the evaluations (PPV, accuracy, NPV, specificity, and sensitivity) employing the proposed system are above 93% and greater than Y. Abdulaziz's approach. The evaluation of sensitivity and NPV are below 87%, in the Abdulaziz's approach. The proposed system displays a greater accuracy for categorizing the neonatal cry due to pain that is superior, when compared with Y. Abdulaziz's approach.

4 CONCLUSION

The neonates exhibit their feelings and needs solitarily through the cry. The cry is normally classified into three different kinds: hunger, sleepiness, and a response to environmental stimulus (e.g., piercing from an injection or tape confiscation pain). The distinct cry behavior of neonates conveys their varied needs. In this work, a neonatal cry analysis and categorization system is proposed. The SFFS algorithm was deployed to pick out the four discriminative features (pitch, spectral centroid contrast, and peak). In addition, for each neonate, the SVM classifier was trained using the selected features and validation was accomplished using the DAG-SVM algorithm. The investigational outcomes clearly demonstrate that the proposed system exhibits greater categorization accuracy than that of Abdulaziz's approach.

ACKNOWLEDGMENT

This work was supported by the Ministry of Science and Technology, Taiwan, under the grants NSC 100-2218-E-224-007-MY3.

REFERENCES

[1] Baeck HE, Souza MN. Longitudinal study of the fundamental frequency of hunger cries along the first 6 months of healthy babies. J Voice 2007;21(5):551–9.

[2] Ooi CS, Seng KP, Ang LM, Chew LW. A new approach of audio emotion recognition. Expert Syst Appl 2014;41:5858–69.

[3] Silva M, Mijovic B, et al. Decoupling between fundamental frequency and energy envelope of neonate cries. Early Hum Dev 2010;86:35–40.

[4] Jothilakshmi S, Ramalingam V, Palanivel S. Unsupervised speaker segmentation with residual phase and MFCC features. Expert Syst Appl 2009;36:9799–804.

[5] Sheng XC, Maddage NC, Xi S. Automatic music classification and summarization. IEEE Trans Speech Audio Process 2005;13(3):441–50.

[6] Prukkanon N, Chamnongthai K, Miyanaga Y, Higuchi K. VT-AMDF, a pitch detection algorithm. In: International symposium on intelligent signal processing and communication systems; 2009. p. 453–6.

[7] Pudil P, Ferri FJ, Novovicova J, Kittler J. Floating search methods for feature selection with nonmonotonic criterion functions. Pattern Recogn 1994;2:279–83.

[8] Dhanalakshmi P, Palanivel S, Ramalingam V. Classification of audio signals using SVM and RBFNN. Expert Syst Appl 2009;36:6069–75.

[9] Petroni M, Malowanyl AS, Johnston CC, Stevens BJ. A comparison of neural network architectures for the classification of three types of infant cry vocalizations. In: Engineering in Medicine and Biology Society, IEEE 17th annual conference, vol. 1; 1995. p. 821–2.

[10] Runefors P, Arnbjörnsson E, Elander G, Michelsson K. Newborn infants' cry after heel-prick: analysis with sound spectrogram. Acta Paediatr 2000;89:68–72.

[11] Orlandi S, Dejonckere PH, Schoentgen J, Lebacq J, Rruqja N, Manfredi C. Effective pre-processing of long term noisy audio recordings: an aid to clinical monitoring. Biomed Signal Process Control 2013;8:799–810.

[12] Díaz MAR, García CAR, Robles LCA, Altamirano JEX, Mendoza AV. Automatic infant cry analysis for the identification of qualitative features to help opportune diagnosis. Biomed Signal Process Control 2012;7:43–9.

[13] Gilbert HR, Robb MP. Vocal fundamental frequency characteristics of infant hunger cries: birth to 12 months. Int J Pediatr Otorhinolaryngol 1996;34:231–43.

[14] Cooley JW, Tukey JW. An algorithm for the machine calculation of complex Fourier series. Math Comput 1965;19:297–301.

[15] Baeck HE, Souza MN. Study of acoustic features of newborn cries that correlate with the context, In: IEEE international conference Engineering in Medicine and Biology Society, vol. 3; 2001. p. 2174–7.

[16] Guyon I, Gunn S, Nikravesh M, Zadeh LA. Feature extraction: foundations and applications. Secaucus, New Jersey: Springer-Verlag New York; 2006.

[17] Platt JC, Cristianini N, Taylor JS. Large margin DAGs for multiclass classification. In: Advances in neural information processing systems. Cambridge: MIT Press; 2000. p. 547–53.

[18] Etz T, Reetz H, Wegener C, Bahlmann F. Infant cry reliability: acoustic homogeneity of spontaneous cries and pain-induced cries. Speech Comm 2014;58:91–100.

[19] Abdulaziz Y, Ahmad SMS. Infant cry recognition system: a comparison of system performance based on Mel frequency and linear prediction cepstral coefficients. In: Proceedings of the 2010 international conference on Information Retrieval & Knowledge Management; 2010. p. 260–3.

[20] Chang CC, Lin CJ. LIBSVM: a library for support vector machines. Available at http://www.csie.ntu.edu.tw/~cjlin/libsvm.

BIG DATA INTELLIGENCE AND IoT SYSTEMS

IV

SMART BUILDING APPLICATIONS AND INFORMATION SYSTEM HARDWARE CO-DESIGN

11

Qian Huang, Chao Lu, Kang Chen

Southern Illinois University, Carbondale, IL, United States

ACRONYMS

AHU	air handler unit
AP	access point
DRAM	dynamic random access memory
HVAC	heating, ventilation, air conditioning
LED	light emitting diode
Li-Fi	light fidelity
NAT	network address translator
OOK	on off keying
PAM	pulse amplitude modulation
RFID	radio frequency identification
RSSI	received signal strength indicator
SDN	software defined network
TCP	transmission control protocol
TEG	thermal electrical generation
TSV	through silicon via
UDP	user datagram protocol
WSN	wireless sensor network

1 SMART BUILDING APPLICATIONS

1.1 THE EVER-INCREASING NEED FOR SMART BUILDINGS

Building is an art of architecture design, interior design, fashion design, safety management, civil engineering, mechanical engineering, electrical engineering and information system. Nowadays, buildings are required to integrate cutting-edge concepts and novel technologies to satisfy diverse needs of residents or users through providing excellent quality of service. According to the U.S. Green Building Council, more than 39% of carbon dioxide and 70% of electricity of the United States are consumed by buildings. Of various energy usage sources in buildings, HVAC (heating, ventilation, and air conditioning) equipment typically accounts for as much as 50% [1]. In many old houses, inefficient operation

Big Data Analytics for Sensor-Network Collected Intelligence. http://dx.doi.org/10.1016/B978-0-12-809393-1.00011-8

of existing HVAC systems leads to significant energy loss. Researchers have revealed that much of these green gas emissions and electricity energy usage could be avoided through increased energy efficiency when providing intelligent control of heating, ventilation, cooling, and lighting.

Nowadays, sustainable building design and energy conservation have become global concerns. Most people agree that next-generation advanced buildings should be energy efficient ones. In future, building architects and design professionals should consider the impact and consequence of building operation on the environment and society. A series of environmentally friendly standards has been erected to tackle these great challenges in areas of energy efficiency, gas emission, indoor air quality, and waste water recycle. Most people believe that joint optimization of energy/water/material efficiency, indoor air quality, building construction and life-cycle maintenance should be taken into account during the initial design stage of buildings.

In recent years, with rapid growth of semiconductor industry and information system, many innovative technologies have been proposed for building applications, which further leads to the emerging idea of "smart buildings." A smart building has to achieve high energy efficiency and maintain environmental sustainability. Yet smart buildings go far beyond the goals of saving energy and contributing to sustainability. Smart buildings should also include the function of improving the comfort and experience of residents. Smart buildings are expected to deeply understand daily activities of residents, and adjust its operation accordingly to satisfy the residents. For instance, a distributed network of miniature wireless sensors can be deployed inside buildings to collect real-time values of a rich set of environmental parameters including air temperature, air humidity, carbon oxide level and volatile organic compounds level. It is commonly believed that these parameters are critical to human health and disease. A building is usually divided into multiple thermal zones by mechanical engineers or HAVC professionals. If temperature values of each room are obtained and monitored in a real-time manner through wireless sensor network, HVAC equipment has great potential to alter its operation setup parameters to optimize energy usage for each individual room or thermal zone. One good example is a wireless sensor network installed in Danville, CA, which enables automatic closing off air vents for real-time HVAC control through wireless sensor-actuator networks [2]. As a result, the energy efficiency of HVAC systems was boosted.

At the time of writing, a wireless sensor node is in the size of several cm^2 or cm^3, which is very easy to be placed in or attached to the points of interest in buildings. As a consequence, distributing hundreds or thousands of tiny wireless nodes does not bring much inconvenience to building users or residents. Such a small form-factor of wireless node is mainly attributed to aggressive technology scaling of semiconductor fabrication process, through which the channel length of a transistor has shrunk into 10–20 nm from a few micron meters. The other benefit of a wireless sensor network is achieving wireless data communication through radio-frequency electromagnetic waves. Comparing with conventional wire or cable-connected sensor network, where electrical cables or optical fibers are used to interconnect sensor nodes, the novel wireless sensor network is more cost-effective and environmentally friendly. Based on these advantages of wireless sensor network, researchers treat it as an indispensable technology for smart building applications to realize intelligent building environmental sensing and monitoring.

While the basic idea of smart buildings has been widely proposed and demonstrated in some case studies, the design of optimized smart building applications require a fully understanding of smart building and information system. Due to the high complexity of this problem, the overall design and architecture of smart buildings requires a systematic and comprehensive approach.

Despite the increasing interests, current research focus has mainly been at a particular design area (e.g., smart building applications), while assuming other design areas (e.g., information system) as black boxes. As the performance of a smart building application heavily depends on the choice and option of information hardware systems, it is very attractive to consider both design fields at early design stages to maximize their benefits. Therefore, the aim of this chapter is to provide an overview of smart building applications and introduce several examples of new information hardware systems. The "co-design" issue between smart building applications and information system hardware is addressed and emphasized. Through a case study and in-depth discussion, it is clear that in order to obtain efficient design of smart buildings, it is absolutely necessary to consider design options and constraints of information hardware at the early design phase.

In this chapter, we first overview typical smart building applications and extract their fundamental features. Next, we carry out an overview of popular information hardware systems, and focus on their inherent characteristics and design challenges. Then, the concept and practice of "co-design" are illustrated through one dedicated case study, followed by the conclusions.

1.2 SMART BUILDING APPLICATIONS

1.2.1 Demand-driven HVAC operation management

As we have introduced earlier, maximizing HVAC operation efficiency is one of the basic requirements in smart buildings. Therefore, one typical smart building application is intelligent control of HVAC operation with the assistance of wireless sensor network, which measures or detects variable environmental parameters (e.g., air temperature or relative humidity) and offers user-centric demand-driven quality of service.

Researchers have shown that the lack of visibility into real-time building operating conditions is a root cause for low energy efficiency of buildings [3]. Here, visibility indicates getting accurate values of environmental parameters for each location of interest, such as air temperature, air humidity and so on. Due to the various benefits of wireless sensor network, such as ease of use, low deployment cost, fine grain of non-intrusive monitoring, modern building management systems start to integrate wireless sensor network into the existing building operation.

Room occupancy estimation is a useful way to realize demand-driven HVAC systems [4]. The basic mechanisms of room occupancy estimation is to install various sensors including CO_2 concentration sensor, RFID sensor, motion sensor, image capture sensor, infrared sensor, or acoustic sensor. Once the central control computer obtains the information of room occupancy from a wireless sensor network, it starts to search or calculate the best settings of HVAC facilities, such as air handler fan or air duct damper, to meet the demands of building residents.

In practice, theoretical analysis or empirical look-up tables are used to ensure that HVAC systems do not provide excessive level of service to users, because more-than-needed quality of service results in unnecessary energy waste. In extreme cases, where nobody is detected in a room or a thermal zone, a minimum level of heating, cooling, and ventilation service is supplied, instead of running HVAC equipment at typical service level. As depicted in Fig. 1, a wireless sensor network has been proposed to detect room occupancy condition, which is sent to a central control computer. Thus, performance demand of HVAC systems could be regulated to meet the room occupancy estimation. Examples of HVAC equipment are heat pumps, air vents, air valves, fans, controllers, condensers, chillers, sensors, etc.

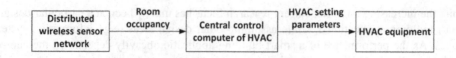

FIG. 1

Demand-driven HVAC operation management.

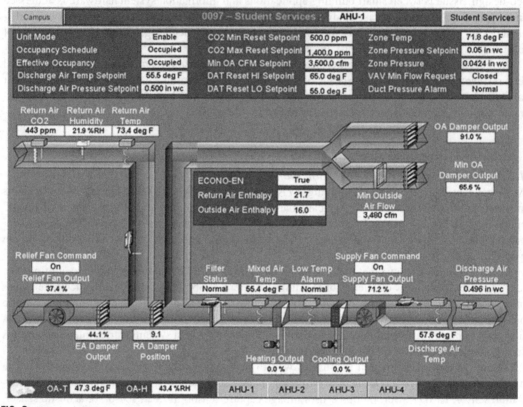

FIG. 2

HVAC components and sensors depicted in a building automation system.

Fig. 2 shows the structure and components of an air handler unit (AHU) at student service building of Southern Illinois University Carbondale. We can see that there are air filters, heating pipes, cooling pipes, fans, and many sensors. Because these HVAC devices are placed at different locations of a building, it is cumbersome to connect them with wires or cables. A wireless sensor network is the most attractive approach to connect these HVAC components.

1.2.2 Indoor localization-based smart building service

A smart building adapts itself to accommodate users' or residents' daily lives. It is very desirable for smart buildings to know the locations of each occupant and then provide location-based services, such as intelligent car parking, health monitoring, indoor navigation, logistics tracking, access control, and

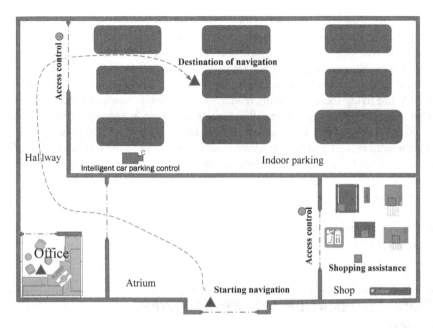

FIG. 3

Overview of indoor location services in smart buildings.

shopping assistance [5]. Due to the wide use of wearable hardware devices, such as the Apple watch and Fitbit wristband, the demand of location-based smart building services is increasing rapidly.

Fig. 3 is an illustration of potential indoor location services in smart buildings. The dashed line indicates that once a person enters a building, indoor location service can guide to his/her car in the parking lot. When a person walks close to a door, the smart building detects his/her position and offers security access control. When a person stays in a shop, their movements are tracked and the smart building provides recommended shopping advice based on the past shopping history. With the presence of accurate indoor positioning technique, smart buildings help business retailers to maximize in-store marketing through location-based advertisement. Therefore, localization-based shopping assistance in smart buildings is viewed as an effective approach to understand the shopping preference and decision-making process. Users also benefit a lot from these indoor-localization smart applications, especially in large or complex shopping centers, museums, airports, and convention centers.

Considering the overwhelming popularity of smartphones, various business retailers have implemented smartphone based indoor localization technology, whose computation algorithm is based on received signal strength indicator (RSSI) of Wi-Fi signals on shoppers' smartphones. As we have discussed earlier, the benefits of location-based shopping assistance include knowing a shopper's location and trajectory, conducting shopping history data analysis, learning shopping interest and preference, and then offering appropriate product recommendations and advertisements. Under such circumstances, the effectiveness of shopping assistance heavily depends on the estimation accuracy of indoor localization technology. An inefficient indoor positioning system can negatively impact the business. Therefore, companies are developing their sophisticated Wi-Fi based indoor positioning applications for smartphones [6].

In addition to smart shopping assistance, location-based service plays a crucial role in reduction of buildings' energy cost. In past decades, mechanical engineers have been striving to boost energy efficiency of HVAC facilities, so users can save substantial energy bill. Given an occupant's accurate indoor position, a building management system is capable to offer highly efficient heating, cooling, ventilation, and lighting service to the occupant. For example, when an occupant sits down in a chair and watches TV in a living room, a building management system is aware of their accurate location; it may then turn down the operation of ventilation fans or air valves in bedrooms of this house to reduce energy consumption. When the occupant moves to another room (i.e., different thermal zone), the building management system will keep tracking their location and adaptively adjust HVAC operation status. From this example, it is apparent that accurate indoor localization is of great importance for location-based HVAC facility operation.

Overall, new smart building applications are deployed based on integrating various innovative information systems into conventional buildings. Thus, a smart building seems to own a "brain" to merge physical and computational resources and realize intelligent control to enhance the life quality of building users or residents.

2 EMERGING INFORMATION SYSTEM HARDWARE
2.1 OVERVIEW
The hardware systems or technologies that we envision in future smart building applications include wireless sensor networks, 3D stacking integrated circuits, and Li-Fi communication infrastructure.

2.2 EXAMPLES
2.2.1 Miniature energy-harvesting wireless sensor node
Wireless sensor network is an emerging technology to enable distributed sensing function inside buildings. Today, the concepts of smart meter and smart appliance rely on a wireless sensor network. Hereafter, we review and discuss the hardware of a wireless sensor network.

As shown in Fig. 4, a wireless sensor node is usually composed of several parts: an antenna, a radio transceiver (e.g., CC2500 chip), and microcontroller circuit (e.g., MSP430F2274), and an energy supply source (e.g., battery pack). The wireless sensor network was initially reported to monitor living habits of outdoor animals. Later, researchers presented to install wireless sensor networks inside buildings for building operation management. Through a comprehensive interview with building operation staff and managers, ten key design challenges have been identified and shown in Table 1 [7]. Power consumption (battery lifetime) and data communication of a wireless sensor node are two of the primary concerns. As wireless sensor nodes have been increasingly utilized in smart building applications, the inherent challenge on energy availability leads to prohibitive labor expense and maintenance inconvenience [8].

Note that in Fig. 4, the battery pack occupies most of the size and volume of a wireless sensor node. Due to the low energy density of battery material, a battery pack has limited energy capacity. Therefore, the battery energy is depleted in several months and frequent battery replacement is needed. To overcome this severe challenge, energy harvesting wireless sensor node is gaining more and more attention.

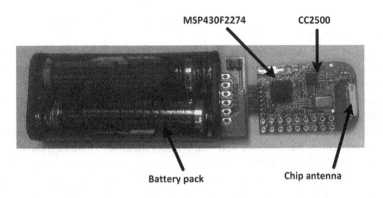

FIG. 4

Wireless sensor node from TI eZ430-RF2500-SHE.

Table 1 Challenge Factors of a Wireless Sensor Network in Building Management [7]	
Rank	**Concern**
1	Lack of installation ease/ease of use
2	Lack of/concerns about reliability or robustness
3	Concerns about interference
4	Lack of standards/interoperability
5	Power consumption still too high/battery life too short
6	Overall costs too high
7	Lacking encryption and other means of security
8	Bit rate too low/high
9	Applications not understood/clearly defined
10	Size of node/endpoints too big

Environmental energy sources are ubiquitous in household or industrial surroundings. Such as solar irradiance, thermal gradients, mechanical vibrations, radio frequency waves, etc. Energy harvesting is an energy process of converting ambient energy sources into electrical energy [9,10]. Scavenging environmental energy to extend the operational lifetime of a wireless sensor node is highly appealing. Even though the power density is from hundreds of nanowatts to a few milliwatts, researchers have found that the harvested power is sufficient to sustain a typical wireless sensor [8].

2.2.2 3D stacking integrated circuits

The key driver of modern semiconductor industry is technology scaling. The physical dimension of transistors has been shrinking for several decades and now enters nanometer era. Technology scaling enables integration of more and more transistors in a single chip, and hence increases the function over cost per chip. Nowadays, people have the capability of integrating and implementing a full system onto a single chip. A shrunk transistor runs faster and consumes less power due to less parasitic capacitance and inductance. However, technology scaling beyond 10 nm is hard to achieve, due to process variation, leakage and lithography limitations. Considering all these non-trivial factors, technology scaling has been a big challenge in production yield.

A new solution to continue the trend of integration and lower power consumption is required in industry. 3D chip stacking is a potential approach where multiple dies or chips are stacked vertically and interconnected through wire-bonds, or flip-chip bumps or through silicon vias. Among three kinds of interconnection approaches, through silicon via (TSV) is most promising, since it has very fine pitches and little parasitic capacitance. Although the fabrication cost of TSV is very expensive, this technology offers the best performance, footprint, power, and density. As a consequence, 3D stacking integrated circuit technology has been viewed as a feasible method to maintain the trend of integrated circuit performance after Moore's law.

In fact, TSV-based 3D stacking has been studied for many years. Many big semiconductor companies have been investigating the development of mature TSV process and materials to achieve high density and reliable TSV fabrication. For instance, IBM, Samsung, Micron Technology, Intel, and Tezzaron Semiconductor have presented their prototypes of 3D IC products. Worldwide universities and research institutions also pay much attention to 3D stacking IC. For example, Fermi National Accelerator Laboratory of United States collaborated with Tezzaron Semiconductor and fabricated 3D sensor chips for high energy particle detection [11]. 3D IC results in a smaller footprint and faster processing speed, as well as lower power.

3D IC has a few design challenges:

(1) Extreme design complexity. The circuit designers must consider different processes, heat flow, reliability, package, yield, etc.
(2) Bottom-up design methodology is inefficient for complex 3D IC.
(3) New computer-aided design tools for 3D IC are not mature.
(4) Designers suffer from tight time-to-market pressure.

System-level modeling and optimization has great potential to help and mitigate these design difficulties, so recently system-level optimization has gained more and more attention. While challenges remain, it is expected that 3D stacking integrated circuits will be widely used in future smart building systems, such as wireless sensor nodes, biosensors, and ubiquitous embedded computing systems. Thanks to the tiny connection of through silicon via (TSV), these sensors or computing devices are becoming smaller and cheaper. As a result, it is possible to integrate a larger number of 3D stacking integrated circuits to smart building systems.

For instance, 3D DRAM is a critical component in next-generation smart building applications, especially for big data storage and access. Several choices for the storage of huge data in electronics systems exist. DRAM (dynamic random access memory) has a simple structure to build. Modern DRAM is based on a structure of one transistor and one capacitor. There is one capacitor for charge storage, and one transistor for a switch to charge or discharge the capacitor. Once this capacitor is charged to high voltage level, it indicates data "1." Otherwise, this capacitor is discharged to low voltage level, and indicates data "0." Compared with other memory cells (such as SRAM), DRAM cell has the highest integration density and hence is very cost-effective.

2.2.3 High throughput Li-Fi communication infrastructure

Most people are aware of Wi-Fi, which utilizes magnetic field of radio waves as wireless communication medium. Instead of using radio frequency waves, Li-Fi (Light Fidelity) utilizes visible light as the wireless carrier of data. The most common frond-end devices in Li-Fi are commercial LEDs, which

Table 2 Wi-Fi Standards and Their Maximum Data Throughput

Wi-Fi standard	Maximum data throughput (Mbps)
802.11b	11
802.11a	54
802.11g	54
802.11n	600
802.11ac	1300

ensures the easy-deployment of Li-Fi technology. As those devices can hardly modulate the phase and amplitude of visible light wave, Li-Fi mainly adopts intensity modulation and direct detection to transmit data. This indicates that data needs to be positive in order to be modulated as a light intensity. Therefore, existing real-valued modulation schemes in radio frequency communication technologies such as on-off keying (OOK) and pulse-amplitude modulation (PAM) can be imported into Li-Fi directly. Various 802.11 Wi-Fi standards and their corresponding maximum speeds are shown in Table 2. The data throughput of Wi-Fi network is limited below 1 Gbps. In contrast, the reported Li-Fi data throughput is much higher than 1 Gbps.

In a smart building environment, either low or high bandwidth data transmission in indoor network infrastructure should be supported by information hardware. For example, high definition TV video signal needs high bandwidth, and indoor temperature value is classified into low bandwidth signal. To this end, Li-Fi technology, which utilizes visible light for high-speed wireless data communication, has gained much attention in recent years due to many potential advantages such as high speed, simplicity, security, etc. Many Li-Fi application scenarios have also been developed by both academia and industry to exploit its advantages for high speed, low cost, and reliable wireless communication.

In the smart building domain, we also foresee several unique network needs that can be potentially satisfied by Li-Fi. Therefore, we propose a high throughput Li-Fi communication infrastructure for smart buildings. The system can well support smart building applications, while naturally avoiding certain drawbacks of visible light communication. In the following, we first introduce more details about Li-Fi which include its basic principles and potential application scenarios. We then present details of the proposed Li-Fi communication infrastructure in smart buildings.

Due to the properties of visible light, Li-Fi presents several natural advantages compared to current wireless communication technologies (e.g., Wi-Fi).

- High speed: Li-Fi can easily realize gigabit level wireless data communication. It currently has reached about 100 times higher speed of Wi-Fi.
- Low cost: Li-Fi can readily utilize commonly available LED lights as the transmit front ends, which indicates a low deployment cost.
- Secure communication: visible light communication can hardly be overheard by eavesdroppers outside the room due to its low penetration ability. In addition, visible light does not interfere with radio-frequency waves, which means that it can hardly be interrupted remotely.
- Rich bandwidth resources: the frequency bandwidth in the visible light can reach several hundred terahertz, which is more than 10,000 times of the frequency bandwidth of the radio spectrum.

On the other hand, Li-Fi suffers from certain limitations due to the usage of visible light. We briefly introduce those drawbacks in the following:

• Low penetration ability: visible light can hardly penetrate walls and even small objects due to the short wave length. Those factors limit the coverage of Li-Fi.
• Interference with ambient light: there are a lot of visible light sources in public places, which may greatly degrade the signal-to-noise ratio of the Li-Fi system.

Although it has certain limitations, Li-Fi technology can potentially be deployed in many scenarios (particularly in indoor environments) to offer fast and secure wireless data communication. We introduce some application scenarios in the following:

• Underwater communication system: Li-Fi technology can effectively support high throughput data communication between nearby submarine devices.
• Inside airplane communication system: Li-Fi technology can offer fast data transfer to passengers without creating interference to the airplane's wireless communication system.
• Surgery room communication system: Li-Fi technology can offer high-throughput transfer of video/audio data for remote surgery consultancy.
• Office data communication system: Li-Fi technology can offer wireless network in the office environment through LED front ends mounted on the ceiling.

In a building, there are usually many lighting bulbs, which offers a good base for deploying Li-Fi technology. Li-Fi-enabled bulbs can offer wireless network connectivity to sensors, control blocks, and digital devices (e.g., computers) inside the building. Therefore, we propose a Li-Fi communication infrastructure for smart buildings, as illustrated in Fig. 5. The general idea of this system is to

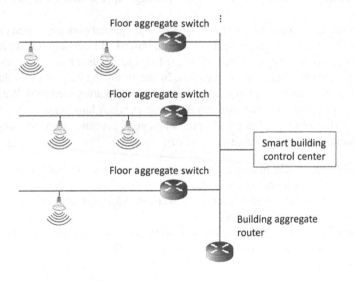

FIG. 5

Li-Fi communication infrastructure in a building.

replace the last hop wireless connection with Li-Fi technology. It consists of three major components: (1) building aggregate router; (2) floor aggregate switch; and (3) Li-Fi-enabled LED bulbs. The first two components are the same as current Ethernet based LAN with Li-Fi supported features.

The building aggregate router is the gateway connecting the building to the internet. It also connects to all floor aggregate switches as well as the smart building control center internally. Note that in reality, different floor aggregate switches connect to different ports of the building aggregate router, which is not reflected in the figure for simplicity. The number of aggregate router can be expanded by adding inter-connected routers at the building level. This can add redundancy for fault tolerance, and support a large number of floor aggregate switches.

There is at least one floor aggregate switch on each floor responsible for connecting all Li-Fi-enabled LED front ends. Again, in reality, different Li-Fi LED bulbs actually connect to different ports on the aggregate switch. When there are more Li-Fi LED bulbs than the number of ports on an aggregate switch, multiple interconnected aggregate switches can be deployed on the same floor to enhance the capacity.

Finally, Li-Fi-enabled LED bulbs function as the access point for client devices. Due to the limitation of Li-Fi, we mainly consider fixed devices under this infrastructure such as desktop and sensors. For mobile devices, when it moves under the coverage of a Li-Fi-enabled bulb, it can exploit Li-Fi technology to get access to the network. A hybrid Wi-Fi and Li-Fi system will be discussed in the next subsection to offer better mobility support.

In addition to interconnecting floor aggregate switches and building aggregate routers with Ethernet links, we can also utilize Li-Fi for this purpose. As shown in Fig. 6, two floor aggregate switches can be interconnected through a Li-Fi link. Due to the limited coverage and the low penetration capability of Li-Fi technology, the interference caused by such a point-to-point wireless link can be effectively controlled. Therefore, it can be used to rearrange network topology at a low cost, i.e., without the necessity of costly rewiring.

In summary, Li-Fi technology can be used to realize the last hop wireless link in the building scenario. Such a system can offer several beneficial features compared to current Wi-Fi network. For example, the confidentiality of data transmission can be limited inside rooms. The cost of deploying such a system is also low, as existing LED bulbs can be used directly. In addition, Li-Fi technology can help us build point-to-point connections easily.

3 BIG DATA APPLICATION AND INFORMATION HARDWARE CO-DESIGN
3.1 MOTIVATION AND CHALLENGE

As smart buildings are equipped with a great number of sensors, controllers and actuators, smart building applications have to involve in the processes of big data collection, storage, and analysis. Future big data applications require dedicated hardware and software platforms to accelerate processing speed of data points.

FIG. 6

Exploiting Li-Fi to bridge switches/routers.

A wireless sensor network was used to collect temperature data at points of interest in a building [8]. Even though the number of sensor nodes are limited to two, for a certain operation time, the number of collected data sets is huge (e.g., 87,106 points in 18 days). Assuming the number of wireless sensor nodes are a few hundred or even several thousand, the accumulated data points are tremendous. Therefore, machine learning algorithms are indispensable to analyze and interpret these big data. For example, researchers proposed a two-phase machine learning algorithm, including a training phase and a testing phase. During the data training phase, statistical characteristics and features of data points are studied and extracted. Later, in the data testing phase, the learned features and characteristics are applied to verify new observations. Using machine learning algorithms, the intrinsic features of data (e.g., mean value, statistical distribution, or correlation) are discovered easily. These features help the detection of any potential abnormal behaviors of building operation, such as indoor fire hazard detection [8].

In addition to the co-design between software and application layers, we envision the necessity of using 3D stacking integrated circuits in next-generation embedded computing systems for big data applications. Existing hardware approaches are difficult to meet all the end-user requirements, such as small size, low power, higher performance, and low latency. The emerging 3D stacking DRAM is highly attractive to work as high throughput data storage block. 3D DRAM is easy to integrate with micro-processor chips to build a processor-in-memory architecture. With these great advantages of 3D stacked IC, it is potential to design and realize advanced embedded computing within the constraints and requirements of power, performance, latency and footprint. For example, in collaboration with Micron Technology, Intel's Xeon processor has on-package memory integrated with computation logic blocks using 3D IC fabrication process. In this processor-in-memory architecture, all collected data from smart buildings are stored in an ultra-high capacity 3D DRAM chip, and the processor/logic is able to fetch data directly from this 3D DRAM though on-chip interconnects. This processor-in-memory architecture enables high memory density, large energy savings, high memory bandwidth, and a small system footprint.

Indoor miniature energy harvesting a wireless sensor network will also closely collaborate with big data applications. Since the future smart buildings run in data-driven mode, optimization of smart building operation will depend heavily on the quantity and quality of collected data points. A wireless sensor network is the most convenient and flexible approach to sense various building operation information. However, due to the size constraints of wireless sensor nodes, the maximum available energy capacity is small; the battery pack will therefore run out in a few months. To mitigate this challenge, we foresee that the adoption of various energy harvesting technologies in wireless sensor nodes to extend the operation lifetime of a wireless sensor network.

We also expect that high throughput Li-Fi hardware systems will be widespread in smart building systems. One good example is to integrate Li-Fi wireless communication and energy harvesting wireless sensors for next generation building management [12]. The basic idea is to replenish ambient harvested power to wireless sensor nodes, while Li-Fi LED communication is active. In this way, Li-Fi hardware provides both wireless data communication and energy replenishment at the same time. The long-term energy availability issue of a wireless sensor network is resolved. With the rapid growth of Li-Fi technology, big data applications can exploit Li-Fi hardware systems. For example, when a building maintenance staff member investigates a failure of HVAC operation, they usually need to access many documents, drawings, and historical data. The size of these building information documents can be very huge, in the range of gigabytes. Wi-Fi can be an approach to connect the building information database remotely. Since the bandwidth of Wi-Fi is limited in the range of megabytes, it will take tens of minutes to complete the download process of these building information documents, leading to inconvenience for staff. Since the data throughput of Li-Fi technology has been reported to reach a gigabyte per second, which is 100 times faster than Wi-Fi, we expect these building maintenance staff will love Li-Fi technology.

The designers of big data applications should learn and understand these emerging hardware system technologies, particularly at benefits and drawbacks. Besides, the information hardware designers need to consider how to modify and improve the hardware platforms to meet the requirements of big data applications in smart building systems, particularly at cost and reliability. For example, if designers want to choose energy harvesting wireless sensor network, the design choices include thermal, solar, vibration, acoustic energy scavenging. Designers need to investigate building structures and environments to find the best approach of energy harvesting. Vibration or thermal energy harvesting rather than solar energy is a better choice in HVAC ducts. Solar energy harvesting is easier to implement in offices or classrooms. Since 3D DRAM is expensive compared with conventional 2D DRAM, from a cost perspective, big data application designers may need to balance performance and cost. Performance-critical blocks such as micro-processors are preferred to integrate with 3D stacking DRAMs, while other non-critical blocks may use low-cost 2D DRAMs.

3.2 CASE STUDY AND DISCUSSION

To better illustrate and understand the interaction between big data application and information hardware, we introduce and discuss a case study in this section.

3.2.1 Big data rapid download application with hybrid Li-Fi/Wi-Fi communication network

Li-Fi can offer high-throughput wireless data communication at Gbps level, which makes it a favorable technology for emerging big data applications. However, it suffers from a limited coverage and thereby cannot support mobility well. This limits the flexibility of big data applications on mobile devices. On the contrary, Wi-Fi offers a reasonable coverage to allow network connectivity under moderate mobility, though its speed currently is much lower than that of Li-Fi.

Therefore, we propose a hybrid Li-Fi and Wi-Fi communication network to exploit the advantages of both technologies at the same time. The general idea is to utilize Wi-Fi to let mobile devices gain constant connectivity to the network, and exploit Li-Fi only when high-throughput data transmission is needed. The connectivity offered by Wi-Fi can also help guide mobile devices to the coverage area of a nearby Li-Fi access point for fast data transmission. Furthermore, we envision a future in which mobile devices are equipped with both Wi-Fi and Li-Fi interfaces, which is reasonable as mobile devices current already have multiple wireless interfaces such as Wi-Fi and Cellular network. The proposed system consists of three major components parts: (1) Wi-Fi/Li-Fi access points (APs); (2) traffic anchor point; and (3) software defined network (SDN) based handoff center. Fig. 7 shows the overall structure of the proposed hybrid Wi-Fi/Li-Fi network. There are multiple Wi-Fi/Li-Fi access points (APs) in such a network. Generally, the placement of Wi-Fi APs needs to ensure full coverage in the deployment site, while the placement of Li-Fi APs depends on actual needs. For example, Li-Fi APs can be deployed only in places where potentially big data applications need to have high-throughput wireless data communication. All Wi-Fi/Li-Fi APs connect to the SDN switch in this network.

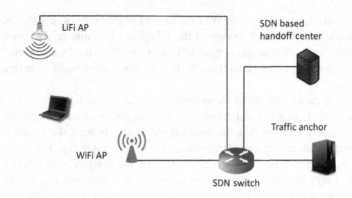

FIG. 7

Hybrid Wi-Fi/Li-Fi wireless network.

The traffic anchor functions as the anchor point for all traffic to or from the mobile device, which can go through either Wi-Fi APs or Li-Fi APs. It includes a network address translator (NAT) that translates the source IPs of all outgoing packets from the mobile devices as if those packets originate from the traffic anchor. Such a function is needed for the mobile device to switch between Li-Fi APs or Wi-Fi APs seamlessly without interrupting ongoing TCP/UDP connections. For example, suppose the mobile device currently is uploading high-definition video through a TCP connection over the Wi-Fi AP and wants to switch to the Li-Fi AP for higher throughput. With the proposed system, the mobile device can conduct the handoff directly without disconnecting the connection. This is because the upload traffic, no matter which network it goes through, appear to originate from the traffic anchor. As a result, the server receiving the video cannot sense the change of the network happened on the mobile device.

The SDN switch and the SDN based handoff center are designed to take care of the downlink handoff. This is because it is impractical to rely on the corresponding host, i.e., the server that sends the data to the mobile device, to determine which way (Wi-Fi or Li-Fi) to forward the data back to the mobile device. This component exploits the dynamic route control of the SDN switch. When the mobile device notifies the handoff center that it is in the coverage of a Li-Fi AP and wants to a correct TCP downloading to Li-Fi, the center would insert a new flow entry in the SDN switch. The new flow entry will forward all incoming packets of the TCP connection to the port connecting to the corresponding Li-Fi AP. The mobile device can then enjoy the high speed download from the Li-Fi. In this process, in order for the mobile device to successfully receive the traffic that has switched to the Li-Fi, we need to offer a virtualized interface above the two actual interfaces (i.e., Wi-Fi and Li-Fi) to applications running on the mobile device.

In summary, the proposed hybrid Wi-Fi/Li-Fi network can allow mobile devices to utilize both Wi-Fi and Li-Fi based on its network needs. The wide coverage of Wi-Fi enable the mobile device to obtain network connection anywhere in the deployment site. When it needs high throughput data transfer, it can use the Wi-Fi network to identify the position of the nearest Li-Fi AP. After it moves to the Li-Fi AP, the data transfer can be switched to the Li-Fi network seamlessly without being interrupted. The data transfer can also switch back to Wi-Fi just as seamlessly when the mobile device moves out of the coverage of Li-Fi.

4 CONCLUSIONS

Smart buildings are a key contributor to a future low-carbon economy, where information system and smart building applications will combine and merge perfectly. More and more researchers agree that smart building applications need to be hardware system conscious. In the long run, smart building applications will require multi-layer software/hardware adaptability to achieve both high quality of service and energy/cost reduction. Significant improvement requires new hardware solutions, understanding the whole system problem, and joint consideration.

Through this chapter, readers may get the introduction of emerging hardware systems for smart buildings, such as energy harvesting powered wireless sensor network, high throughput Li-Fi data communication, and three-dimensional stacking integrated circuits. Moreover, we envision and discuss the necessity of co-design of smart building applications and hardware systems. We believe that, to ensure cost-effective and high-performance smart building applications, the entire system must consider the features of information hardware at the early design stages.

Last but not least, software also plays a key role in the energy consumption and quality of service of smart buildings. Software is the interface between information hardware layer and smart application layer. Among many different software options, big data analytics is very important and more research attention is needed for this area. In the near future, building operation data will be collected by the distributed wireless sensor networks and meanwhile is analyzed through big data analytics and prediction with the support of 3D stacking integrated circuits and high throughput Li-Fi infrastructure.

REFERENCES

[1] Lombard L, Ortiz J, Pout C. A review on buildings energy consumption information. Energ Buildings 2008;40(2):394–8.
[2] Watts W, Koplow M, Redfern A, Wright P. Application of multizone HVAC control using wireless sensor networks and actuating vent registers. Technical Report, Energy System Laboratory, Texas A & M University; 2007.
[3] Li J, He J, Arora A. ThermoNet: wireless solution for fine-grain building comfort-efficiency assessment. OSU-CISRC-10/11-TR33, Electronic Report; 2011.
[4] Huang Q, Ge Z, Lu C. Occupancy estimation in smart buildings using audio-processing techniques. In: International Conference on Computing in Civil and Building Engineering, Osaka, Japan; 2016. p. 1413–20.
[5] Greene N, Hand L. Location-based services: an important building block to enhance the customer experience. white paper, CISCO; 2014.
[6] Huang Q, Zhang Y, Ge Z, Lu C. Refining Wi-Fi based indoor localization with Li-Fi assisted model calibration in smart buildings. In: International Conference on Computing in Civil and Building Engineering, Osaka, Japan; 2016. p. 1358–65.
[7] Healy W, Jang W. Practical challenges in wireless sensor network use in building applications. NIST Technical Note; 2008.
[8] Huang Q. Feasibility study of energy harvesting based wireless sensor network for building environment monitoring and management. PhD thesis, Purdue University; 2013.
[9] Lu C, Raghunathan V, Roy K. Efficient design of micro-scale energy harvesting systems. IEEE J Emerg Selected Top Circ Syst 2011;1(3):254–66.

[10] Lu C, Raghunathan V, Roy K. Micro-scale energy harvesting: a system design perspective. In: 15th Asia and South Pacific Design Automation Conference, Taipei, Taiwan; 2010. p. 89–94.

[11] Yarema R, Deptuch G, Lipton R. Recent results of 3D pixel integrated circuits using copper-copper and oxide-oxide bonding. In: 22nd International Workshop on Vertex Detector, Lake Starnberg, Germany; 2013. p. 1–10.

[12] Huang Q, Li X, Shaurette M. Intelligent Li-Fi wireless communication and energy harvesting wireless sensor for next generation building management. High Performance Building Conference, Purdue University; 2014.

GLOSSARY

3D IC An integrated circuit manufactured by stacking silicon wafers vertically to achieve smaller size and higher performance.

Air handler unit A mechanical device that regulates and circulates air for heating, ventilation, and air conditioning purpose.

DRAM A type of random access memory that has high density of memory cells.

Energy harvesting A process to scavenge electrical energy from ambient energy sources.

Indoor localization A technique for determining the location of a person inside a building.

Li-Fi A technique of wireless data communication through visible light.

Microcontroller A small microchip containing a processor core, memory or input/output peripherals.

Moore's law An observation that the number of transistors in an integrated circuit doubles approximately every two years.

RFID A wireless communication technique for automatic identification and tracking.

SDN A technique that offers several benefits compared with traditional, router-based network.

Smart building An intelligent building achieving significant energy savings and advanced services to building residents or users.

Thermal zone A space within a building that has its own thermostat control.

Through silicon via A vertical electrical connection passing through a silicon wafer or die.

Wireless sensor network Distributed autonomous sensors to monitor physical or environmental conditions.

SMART SENSOR NETWORKS FOR BUILDING SAFETY

12

Xuefeng Liu, Jiannong Cao

The Hong Kong Polytechnic University, Kowloon, Hong Kong

ACRONYMS

CCF	Cross-correlation function
CSD	Cross-spectral density
DAC	Data acquisition system
DOF	Degrees of freedom
ERA	Eigensystem realization algorithm
FEM	Finite element model
FFT	Fast Fourier Transform
LSWT	Lifting scheme wavelet transform
PSD	Power spectral density
RDT	Random decrement technique
RFP	Rational fraction polynomial
SHM	Structural health monitoring
SVD	Singular value decomposition
WPT	Wavelet packet transform
WSN	Wireless sensor network
WT	Wavelet transform

1 INTRODUCTION

Civil structures, such as dams, long-span bridges, skyscrapers, etc., are critical components of the economic and industrial infrastructure. Therefore, it is important to monitor their integrity and detect/pinpoint any possible damage before it reaches to a critical state. This is the objective of structural health monitorings (SHMs) [1].

Traditional SHM systems are wire-based and centralized. In a typical SHM system, different types of sensors, such as accelerometers or strain gauges, are deployed on the structure under monitoring. These sensor nodes collect the vibration and strain of the structure under different locations, and transmit the data through cables to a central station. Based on the data, SHM algorithms are implemented to extract damage associated information to make corresponding decisions about structural condition [1].

According to the duration of deployment, SHM systems can be largely divided into two categories: short- and long-term monitoring. Short-term SHM systems are generally used in routine annual inspections or urgent safety evaluations after unexpected events, such as earthquakes, overloads, or collisions. These short-term systems are usually deployed on structures for a few hours to collect enough amounts of data for offline diagnosis afterwards. Examples of short-term SHM systems can be found in the Humber Bridge of the UK [2] and the National Aquatic Centre in Beijing, China [3]. The second category of SHM systems is those used for long-term monitoring. Sensor nodes in these systems are deployed on structures for months, years, or even tens of years to monitor the structures' healthy condition. Different from short-term monitoring systems where data are processed offline by human operators, most long-term SHM systems require the healthy condition of the structure to be reported in a real-time or near real-time manner. Examples of long-term monitoring SHM systems can be found in the Tsing Ma Bridge and Stonecutters Bridge in Hong Kong [4].

The main drawback of traditional wire-based SHM systems is the high cost. The high cost mainly comes from the centralized data acquisition system (DAC), long cables, sensors, and in-field servers. Particularly for DAC, its price increases dramatically with the number of channels it can accept. As a result, the cost of a typical wire-based SHM system is generally high. For example, the cost of the systems deployed on the Bill Emerson Memorial Bridge and Tsing Ma Bridge reach $1.3 and $8 million, respectively [4].

In addition, deploying a wire-based SHM system generally takes a long period of time. This drawback is particularly apparent in SHM systems used for short-term purposes. Considering the length of cables used in an SHM system deployed on a large civil infrastructure can reach thousands or even tens of thousands of meters, deployment can take hours or even days to obtain measurement data just for a few minutes. Moreover, constrained by the number sensor nodes and the capability of DAC, it is quite common that an SHM system is repeatedly deployed in different areas of a structure to implement measurements. This dramatically increases the deployment cost. We have collaborated with civil researches to deploy a wire-based SHM system on the Hedong Bridge in Guangzhou, China (see Fig. 1). The DAC system we used can only support inputs from seven accelerometers simultaneously. To measure the vibration at different locations across the whole bridge, the system was hence moved to 15 different areas of the bridge to implement measurements in each location. For each deployment, it took about 2 hours for sensor installation, cable deployment, and initial debugging.

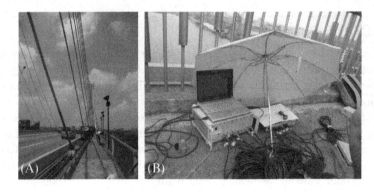

FIG. 1

A wired-based SHM system deployed on the Hedong bridge, China (A) Hedong bridge, (B) deploying a wired system.

Table 1 Difference Between SHM and Environmental Monitoring

	SHM	Env. Monitoring
Sensor type	Accelerometers, strain gauges	Temperature, light, humidity
Sampling pattern	Synchronous sampling round by round	Not necessarily synchronized
Sampling frequency	$\times 00$ to $\times 000$ per second	$\times$ per second, minute
Processing algorithms	On a bunch of data ($> \times 0000$) centralized, computationally intensive	Simple, easily to distribute

Recent years have witnessed a booming advancement of wireless sensor networks (WSNs) and an increasing interest of using WSNs for SHM. Compared with the traditional wire-based SHM systems, wireless communication eradicates the need for wires and therefore represents a significant cost reduction and convenience in deployment. A WSN-based SHM system can achieve finer grain of monitoring, which potentially increases the accuracy and reliability of the system.

However, SHM is different in many aspects from most existing applications of WSNs. Table 1 summarizes the main differences between an SHM and a typical application of WSNs, environmental monitoring, in terms of sensing and processing algorithms. Briefly speaking, sensor nodes in an SHM system implement synchronized sensing with relatively high sampling frequency. Moreover, SHM algorithms to detect damage are based on a bunch of data (at a level of thousands and tens of thousands), and are usually centralized and complicated.

Moreover, the difficulty of designing a WSN-based SHM system is different for short- and long-term applications. Designing a WSN for short-term SHM is relatively easy. Generally speaking, short-term SHM systems only need to address synchronized data sampling and reliable data collection. The former task can be realized using various time synchronization protocols [5] and resampling techniques [6]. In addition, considering the high cost of wireless transmissions in WSNs, wireless sensor nodes in a short-term SHM system can be equipped with a local storage device, such as a μ SD card or USB, to save the measured data in a real-time manner. The locally stored data in wireless sensor nodes can be retrieved afterwards by human operators.

In contrast, designing a WSN for long-term SHM purpose is much more challenging. A long-term SHM system not only needs to have a longer system lifetime and higher system reliability, embedding SHM algorithms within the network becomes a necessity. This task is difficult mainly due to the two factors below.

First, although there exist some SHM algorithms which are intrinsically distributed, most traditional SHM algorithms are centralized. The implementation of these algorithms requires the availability of the raw data from all the deployed sensor nodes. However, considering the high cost of transmitting raw data in a wireless environment, it is desirable that deployed wireless sensor nodes use their local information only or at most, exchange the information only with their nearby neighbors. Distributing these centralized SHM algorithms is a challenging task.

Moreover, unlike in many applications of WSNs where simple aggregation functions, such as average, max, min, etc., are widely used, most classic SHM algorithms involve complex matrix computation techniques such as singular value decomposition (SVD), eigenvalue decomposition, as well as other time-domain or frequency-domain signal processing methods. Some of these algorithms can be computationally very intensive and require a large auxiliary memory space for computation. For example, it was reported in Nagayama and Spencer [6] that implementing the SVD on a small 48-by-50 data matrix which includes data only from a few sensor nodes would take 150 seconds in Imote2 running at 100 MHz. Further considering the time complexity of SVD on a data matrix $\mathbf{H} \in \mathbb{R}^{n \times n}$ is $\Theta(n^3)$ [7], the SVD on a $\mathbf{H}$ including data from a large number of sensor nodes is essentially infeasible for most of the available off-the-shelf wireless sensor nodes. How to modify these resource-consuming SHM algorithms and make them lightweight is also a challenging task.

In this chapter, we target the WSN-based SHM systems used for long-term monitoring purposes and mainly focus on how to design and implement SHM algorithms in resource-limited wireless sensor nodes. We first give a summary review of the recent efforts of embedding SHM algorithms within the WSNs. We then select an SHM algorithm which is widely used in the civil engineering field, modal analysis, and describe how to implement it within WSNs.

2 RELATED WORKS

What distinguishes WSNs from traditional tethered structural monitoring systems is that the wireless sensor nodes are "smart" and able to process the response measurements they have collected or received from others. Autonomous execution of damage detection algorithms by the wireless sensor represents an important step toward automated SHMs.

Numerous SHM algorithms exist developed by civil engineers, and they have shown advantages in different structures and environmental conditions. However, in terms of difficulties of implementing them in a typical WSN, they can be largely divided as: (1) inherently distributed and lightweight; (2) inherently distributed but computationally intensive; and (3) centralized.

Some SHM algorithms can be implemented in a WSN directly without any modification. These algorithms share two properties: (1) they are inherently distributed, which means that each sensor node, based on its own measured data, can make a decision on the condition of the structure; and (2) the complexity of the algorithms is low. For example, to detect damage, some SHM algorithms rely on examining the change of a vibration characteristic called natural frequency. This natural frequency is a global parameter of structures and under some assumptions on the input excitation and environmental noise, it can be estimated based on time history data from each sensor node [8]. One rough but simple approach to extract natural frequencies is peak-picking [9]. In the peak-picking method, the power spectral density (PSD) of the measured time history from a sensor node is calculated using the Fast Fourier transform (FFT), and then the some "peaks" on the PSD are selected whose locations are selected as the identified natural frequencies. In a WSN-based SHM system implementing this strategy, any wireless sensor node is able to identify a set of natural frequencies using peak-picking without sharing data with each other. The peak-picking method itself is light-weight. However, a drawback of using this peak-picking method is that it can only give an approximate estimation of natural frequencies. An example of such a WSN system can be found in Monroig and Fujino [10].

Some SHM algorithms, although inherently distributed, cannot be directly implemented in a WSN due to the high computational complexity and large memory space required. Examples of these algorithms include the AR-ARX method [11], the DLAC method [12, 13], and the wavelet method [14, 15]. The AR-ARX method is based on the premise that if there were damage in a structure, the prediction model previously identified using the undamaged time history would not be able to reproduce the newly obtained time series. In the AR-ARX method, a sensor node (1) first identifies an AR model based on its collect data, and (2) then searches through a database which stores the AR models of the structure under a variety of environmental and operational conditions to find a best match and then, based on this, (3) identifies an ARX model to obtain the decision on the healthy status. The last two tasks are computationally intensive and require large memory space. To address this problem, Lynch [16] modified the AR-ARX method and made it applicable for WSNs. The basic idea is very simple: after a sensor node identifies its AR model, it will send the corresponding parameters to a central server and let the server finish the two remaining cumbersome tasks.

The DLAC method is also a distributed SHM algorithm. In the DLAC, each sensor node collects its own data, calculates its PSD, identifies natural frequencies, and obtains damage information by comparing identified natural frequencies with the reference ones. In the DLAC, the natural frequencies are identified using the rational fraction polynomial (RFP) method [17] instead of the peak-picking method mentioned above, since the RFP can provide a more accurate estimation. However, implementing the DLAC is much more time consuming than the peak-picking and hence not applicable for most of the off-the-shelf wireless sensor nodes. To address this problem, the DLAC is tailored for WSNs and within this, the most time-consuming task of the DLAC, the RFP, is offloaded to a central server. After the server has finished the RFP, the natural frequencies are transmitted back to the sensor nodes for the remaining tasks.

The wavelet transform (WT) or the wavelet packet transform (WPT) of the time histories collected from individual sensor nodes have been also used for damage detection [14, 15]. Wavelet-based approaches are based on the assumption that the signal energy at some certain frequency spectrum bands extracted from the WT/WPT will change after damage. However, traditional WT and WPT are computationally intensive, requiring large auxiliary memory space and thus they are not suitable for WSNs. To address this problem, the lifting scheme wavelet transforms (LSWTs) is proposed in Zhang and Li [18]; this has the advantages of fast implementation, fully in-place calculation without auxiliary memory, and integer-to-integer mapping. This modification on WT and WPT has proven very effective to improve the efficiency of WSNs using WT/WPT to detect damage.

Different from the distributed SHM algorithms mentioned above, by which decisions can be made based on data from individual sensor nodes, a large percentage of SHM algorithms are centralized. They require the raw data from all the deployed sensor nodes. Embedding centralized SHM algorithms within a WSN is not an easy task. In this chapter, we give an example of how centralized SHM algorithms can be distributed in a WSN. Since there exist a large variety of algorithms for SHM have been proposed by civil engineers, we select one technique called modal analysis. This is one of the most fundamental techniques in SHM. Using modal analysis, structural vibration characteristics, called the modal parameters, are identified; these will in turn give damage-associated information.

3 BACKGROUND: MODAL ANALYSIS

In this section, we first give some basic background associated with modal analysis and then describe, in a step-by-step manner, how this can be embedded within wireless sensor nodes.

3.1 MODAL PARAMETERS

Every structure has a tendency to oscillate with a much larger amplitude at some frequencies than others. These frequencies are called **natural frequencies**. (This concept was mentioned in the related works.) When a structure is vibrating under one of its natural frequencies, the corresponding vibration pattern it exhibits is called a **mode shapes** for this natural frequency.

For example, for a structure with n-degrees of freedom (DOFs), its natural frequency set and mode shapes are denoted, respectively, as:

$$\mathbf{f} = [f^1, f^2, \ldots, f^n]' \tag{1}$$

$$\mathbf{\Phi} = [\mathbf{\Psi}^1, \mathbf{\Psi}^2, \ldots, \mathbf{\Psi}^n] = \begin{bmatrix} \phi_1^1 & \phi_1^2 & \cdots & \phi_1^n \\ \phi_2^1 & \phi_2^2 & \cdots & \phi_2^n \\ \vdots & \vdots & \ddots & \vdots \\ \phi_n^1 & \phi_n^2 & \cdots & \phi_n^n \end{bmatrix} \tag{2}$$

where f^k ($k = 1, \ldots, n$) is the kth natural frequency, and $\mathbf{\Psi}^k$ ($k = 1, \ldots, n$) is the mode shape corresponding to f^k. ϕ_i^k ($i = 1, 2, \ldots, n$) is the value of $\mathbf{\Psi}^k$ at the ith DOF. For convenience, f^k and $\mathbf{\Psi}^k$ are also called **modal parameters** corresponding to the kth **mode** of a structure. As an example, Fig. 2 illustrates the first three mode shapes of a typical cantilevered beam, extracted from the measurements of the deployed 12 sensor nodes. Each mode shape corresponds to a certain natural frequency of this cantilever beam.

Modal parameters are only determined by the physical property of structure (i.e., mass, stiffness, damping, etc.). When damage occurs on a structure, its internal property will be changed, and consequently, modal parameters will be deviated from those corresponding to this structure in its healthy condition. Therefore, by examining the changes in these modal parameters, damage on the structure can be roughly detected and located. Modal parameters can also be used as the inputs for finite element model (FEM) updating [19], which is able to precisely locate and quantify structural damage.

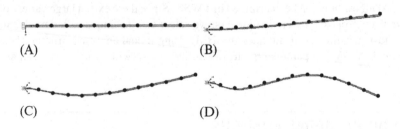

(A)   (B)

(C)   (D)

FIG. 2

Mode shapes of a typical cantilevered beam (A) original beam, (B) mode shape 1, (C) mode shape 2, and (D) mode shape 3.

It should also be noted that different from natural frequency vector $\mathbf{f}$, mode shape vector $\mathbf{\Psi}^k$ has an element corresponding to each sensor node. Moreover, elements in $\mathbf{\Psi}^k$ only represent the relative vibration amplitudes of structure at corresponding sensor nodes. In other words, two mode shape vectors $\mathbf{\Psi}^k$ and $\mathbf{\Psi}^j$ are the same if there exists a nonzero scalar ζ, which satisfies $\mathbf{\Psi}^k = \zeta \mathbf{\Psi}^j$. This property leads to one of the important constraints when designing distributed modal analysis. Details about this constraint will be given in the next section.

To identify modal parameters, civil engineers have developed a larger number of classic modal analysis algorithms including stochastic subspace identification [20], the Eigensystem realization algorithm (ERA) [21], the frequency domain decomposition [22], and the enhanced frequency domain decomposition [23]. In this chapter, we choose the ERA for modal parameter identification and briefly introduce how the modal parameters are identified using the ERA.

3.2 THE ERA

In this section, we briefly introduce the ERA. This is able to give accurate modal parameter estimates using output data only and has been widely used by civil engineers for many years.

Assume a total of m sensor nodes are deployed on a structure and the collected data are denoted as $\mathbf{y}(k) = [y^1(k), y^2(k), \dots, y^m(k)]'$ $(k = 1, \dots, N_{\mathrm{ori}})$ where $y^i(k)$ is the data sampled by the ith sensor at the kth time step and N_{ori} is the total number of data points collected in each node. To obtain modal parameters, the ERA first identifies, from measured responses $\mathbf{y}(k)$, a series of parameters $\mathbf{Y}(k)$ called **Markov parameters**. The Markov parameters $\mathbf{Y}(k)$ are calculated as the cross-correlation functions (CCFs) of the measurement $\mathbf{y}$ and a reference signal y^{ref}:

$$\mathbf{Y}(k) = CCF_{\mathbf{y}y^{\mathrm{ref}}}(k) = \begin{bmatrix} CCF_{y1\,y^{\mathrm{ref}}}(k) \\ CCF_{y2\,y^{\mathrm{ref}}}(k) \\ \vdots \\ CCF_{ym\,y^{\mathrm{ref}}}(k) \end{bmatrix} \tag{3}$$

where $CCF_{yi\,y^{\mathrm{ref}}}$ is the CCF between the ith measurement y^i and the reference y^{ref}. Generally speaking, measured signal from any deployed sensor node can be selected as y^{ref}. To estimate $CCF_{yi\,y^{\mathrm{ref}}}$ accurately, we first use Welch's averaged periodogram method [24] to calculate the cross-spectral density (CSD) between y^i and y^{ref}, then Inverse Fast Fourier Transform (IFFT) is implemented on the CSD to obtain the CCF.

In Welch's method, to calculate the CSD of two signals x and y, x and y are first divided into n_d number of overlapping segments. The CSD of x and y, denoted as G_{xy} is then calculated as

$$G_{xy}(\omega) = \frac{1}{n_d \cdot N} \sum_{i=1}^{n_d} X_i^*(\omega) \cdot Y_i(\omega) \tag{4}$$

where $X_i(\omega)$ and $Y_i(\omega)$ are the Fourier Transforms of the ith segment of x and y, and "*" denotes the complex conjugate. N is data points in each segment of x (or y) as well as the obtained $G_{xy}(\omega)$. N is generally taken as a power of two value 1024 or 2048 to give reasonable results. To decrease the noise, n_d practically ranges from 10 to 20.

After we obtain the CSD of y^{ref} with each response in $\mathbf{y}$, the Markov parameters $\mathbf{Y}(k)$ is then calculated as the IFFT of the obtained CSD:

$$\mathbf{Y}(k) = \begin{bmatrix} IFFT(G_{y1_{y\text{ref}}}) \\ IFFT(G_{y2_{y\text{ref}}}) \\ \vdots \\ IFFT(G_{y^m_{y\text{ref}}}) \end{bmatrix}(k) \tag{5}$$

Having obtained the Markov parameters $\mathbf{Y}(1)$, $\mathbf{Y}(2)$, ..., the ERA begins by forming the Hankel matrix composed of these Markov parameters and implements the SVD to obtain modal parameters. The detailed procedure of the ERA is summarized in Fig. 3. The ERA can be largely divided into two stages. In the first stage, the Markov parameters are identified. These Markov parameters are then used to identify the modal parameters in the second stage.

In the following three sections, we shall introduce, in a step-by-step manner, how these centralized modal analysis algorithms are tailored for WSNs.

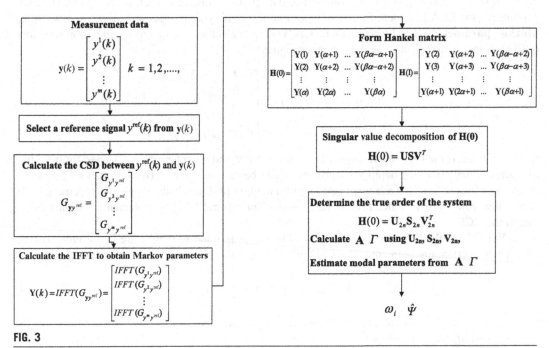

FIG. 3

The procedures of the ERA algorithm.

4 DISTRIBUTED MODAL ANALYSIS

4.1 STAGE 1: TRY TO DISTRIBUTE THE INITIAL STAGE OF MODAL ANALYSIS ALGORITHMS

To design a distributed version of centralized modal analysis algorithms, the detailed procedures in the ERA should be analyzed. It can be seen from Fig. 3 that the CSD estimation between the time history of a reference sensor and that of each sensor is first calculated. Therefore, if the CSDs can be calculated in a way suitable for WSNs, the efficiency of these algorithms in a WSN can be significantly improved. Nagayama and Spencer [6] proposed a decentralized approach illustrated in Fig. 4A to calculate the CSDs without necessitating the collection of all the measured data. In this strategy, the reference node broadcasts its measured time history record to all the remaining nodes. After receiving the reference signal, each node calculates a CSD estimation and then transmits it back to a sink node where the remaining portions of the algorithms are implemented. Considering that the amount of data in the CSDs is much smaller than the original time history record, the amount of transmitted data in this approach is much smaller than the traditional one where all the raw data are transmitted to the sink. Moreover, part of the computation load that was concentrated at the sink node (i.e., the one responsible for calculating the CSD) is partially offloaded to the other nodes, which is favorable for a homogeneous WSN in which no "super nodes" exist in the network.

This decentralized approach is further improved in Sim et al. [25] where the decentralized random decrement technique (RDT) is adopted to calculate the CSDs. With the help of the RDT, the reference node does not even need to send all the measured time history record; only some trigger points in the time history found by the RDT need to be broadcast. Once the trigger points are received, each node calculates the CSD that are subsequently collected at the sink node to continue remaining damage identification procedures. Considering the trigger information is in general much shorter than the time history record broadcast by the reference node; therefore, this RDT-based decentralized approach can considerably reduce wireless data transmissions. This approach is illustrated in Fig. 4B.

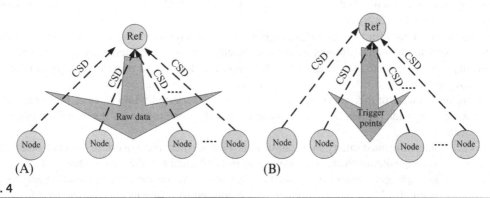

FIG. 4

Two approaches of calculating the CSDs in a distributed way: (A) the approach proposed in Nagayama and Spencer [6]; (B) the approach proposed in Sim et al. [25].

4.2 STAGE 2: DIVIDE AND CONQUER

If only the CSD estimation in the modal analysis algorithms are made to be distributed, there remain some problems, since the CSDs of all the nodes still need to be wirelessly transmitted to a sink where the remaining steps of the ERA are finished. First, transmitting the CSDs of all the sensor nodes to the sink is a challenging task, considering that the CSD of each node contains thousands of points which are usually in a double-precision floating-point format. In addition, in a large civil structure, the CSDs usually needs to be transmitted in a multihop manner, which considerably downgrades the performance of the system. The second problem is associated with computation. When the sink node receives the CSDs for the deployed sensor nodes, the computational resources required to identify modal parameters usually exceed the capacity of the most existing off-the-shelf wireless sensor nodes, especially when the number of sensor nodes is large. Therefore, a PC is generally used as the sink node, which can increase the system cost and difficulties in deployment.

To address the problems mentioned above, instead of using data from all the sensor nodes in a batch manner, we can divide the deployed sensor nodes into clusters and implement the ERA in each cluster. We then obtain a set of natural frequencies and "local" mode shapes, and these cluster-based modal parameters will be "merged" together afterwards. This is very similar to the divide and conquer strategy widely adopted by computer scientists to solve various mathematical problems. A minor difference might be that in the original divide and conquer algorithms, the original problem is solved by dividing the original problem in a *recursive* way, while in this cluster-based ERA, the division of a WSN only needs to be carried out once.

This cluster-based ERA is illustrated in Fig. 5. In this approach, the whole network is partitioned into a number of clusters. A cluster head (CH) is designated in each cluster to perform intracluster modal analysis using traditional centralized modal analysis algorithms. The identified modal parameters in all clusters are then assembled together to obtain the modal parameters for the whole structure. Compared with the centralized approach, the cluster-based approach has at least two advantages. The first advantage of this cluster-based approach is associated with the wireless communication. By dividing sensor nodes into single-hop clusters in which sensor nodes in each cluster are within single-hop communication with their CH, we can avoid multihop relay and thus reduce the corresponding wireless communications.

Second, compared with the centralized approach, the computational resources required in each cluster to compute the modal parameters are significantly decreased. By reducing the computational complexity, it is possible to use common wireless sensor nodes instead of a PC to implement modal analysis algorithms.

The third advantage of this approach is that by dividing sensor nodes into clusters, the computation of the ERA can be made parallel. All the CHs can work at the same time, thus the overall computation time is decreased.

However, clustering must satisfy some constraints. First, clusters must overlap with each other. This constraint is a prerequisite for the local mode shapes to be stitched together. As we have introduced in Section 3, mode shape vectors identified using the ERA only represent the relative vibration amplitudes at sensor nodes involved. Therefore, mode shapes identified in different clusters cannot be directly assembled together. This can be demonstrated in Fig. 6A, where the deployed 12 sensor nodes in Fig. 2 are partitioned into three clusters to identify the third mode shape. Although the mode shape of each cluster is correctly identified, we still cannot obtain the mode shapes for the whole structure.

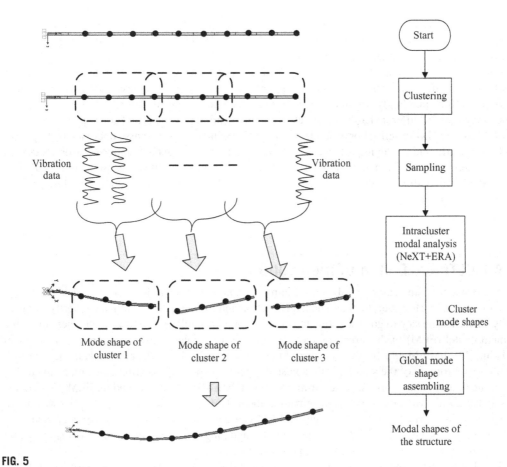

FIG. 5

Overview of cluster-based modal analysis process.

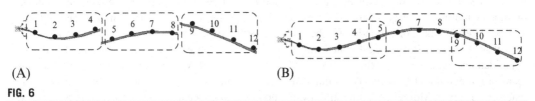

(A)   (B)

FIG. 6

Mode shape assembling when (A) clusters do not overlap and (B) clusters overlap.

The key to solve this problem is overlapping. We must ensure that each cluster has at least one node which also belongs to another cluster and all the clusters are connected through the overlapping nodes. For example, in Fig. 6B, mode shapes identified in each of the three clusters can be assembled together with the help of the overlapping nodes 5 and 9. This requirement of overlapping must be satisfied when divided sensor nodes into clusters.

Another constraint is the number of sensor nodes in a cluster. To avoid the under-determined problem, the ERA also requires that the number of sensor nodes in each cluster should be larger than the number of modal parameters to be identified.

Given a WSN, different clustering strategy will generated clusters with different sizes and network topologies, and therefore can result in different energy consumption, wireless bandwidth consumed, delay, etc. Correspondingly, clustering can be optimized according to different objective functions which may vary for different hardware, wireless communication protocols, and other specific scenarios of WSN-based SHM systems. For example, for a WSN in which wireless sensor nodes are battery powered, energy efficiency is an important issue. Therefore, how to divide the deployed sensor nodes such that the energy consumption is minimized is important. This optimal clustering problem is studied in Liu et al. [26]. In addition to energy consumption, other possible objective functions for clustering can be wireless transmissions, load-balance, delay, etc.

5 A MULTISCALE SHM USING CLOUD

In the SHM algorithms described above, we introduced how to use wireless sensor nodes to estimate modal parameters. However, to obtain damage location and further quantify damage severity, we generally still have one step to go. The estimated modal parameters will be sent to a server where the finite element model (FEM) of the structure under monitoring is updated. This procedure is called model updating [19]. In FEM updating, parameters of the structure's FEM, which are directly associated with the physical property of the structure, are adjusted to reduce a penalty function based on residuals between the modal parameters estimated from measured data and the corresponding FEM predictions. The updated FEM directly provides information about damage location and severity. However, for a large civil infrastructure where an accurate FEM can contain tens of thousands or even hundreds of thousands of small "structural elements," model updating is extremely resource-demanding and can take hours or perhaps days even for a powerful PC.

To alleviate the computational burden of the server as well as to decrease the associated delay, civil engineers have proposed a scheme called a multiscale SHM [27, 28]. In this strategy, two different FEMs, one coarse and one refined, are established for a given structure. The former FEM consists of smaller number of large-sized structural elements and the latter contains a small-sized but large number of elements. Correspondingly, the updating of the coarse FEM takes much less computation time than the latter. Initially, estimated modal parameters are used to update the coarse FEM. Only when damage is detected on this coarse FEM is the refined FEM updated for the detailed damage localization and quantification. This multiscale strategy can significantly decrease the computational load for the server. Moreover, in this strategy, the updating of the coarse FEM only require the "coarse" modal parameters, whose identification does not need all the deployed sensor nodes. Therefore, it is possible that only part of the deployed sensor nodes need to work. This can increase the lifetime of the WSN.

However, the server of the SHM systems using this multiscale strategy still needs to be powerful enough to handle the task of updating the refined FEM when the damage is suspected to occur. Considering most of the time, the server is running coarse-FEM updating where the computational load is low; it is thus a waste to purchase a powerful server which is under-loaded most of the time.

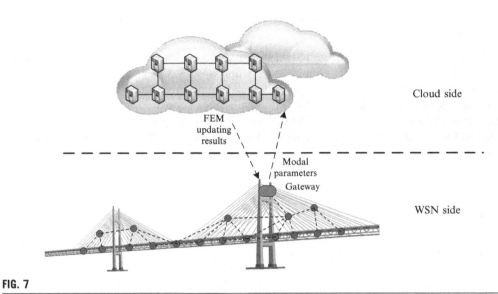

Cloud side

FEM
updating
results

Modal
parameters

Gateway

WSN side

FIG. 7

Architecture of WSN-Cloud SHM.

Cloud computing, being able to provide dynamically scalable resources, can be a perfect substitute for the server used in SHM system mentioned above. Instead of purchasing a powerful server, we can buy the computation resources from cloud provider and only pay for the resources we have used. This "pay as you go" business pattern can dramatically reduce the total cost of SHM systems. The property of dynamic scaling of multiscaled SHM makes cloud computing a perfect platform in this application.

A future SHM system is envisioned as shown in Fig. 7. A large number of wireless sensor nodes are deployed on the different locations of the structure under monitoring and a gateway node, serving as in-field commander, is able to communicate with both the WSN and the Internet. Initially, under the command of the gateway node, part of the wireless sensor nodes are activated to sample and compute the modal parameters. The modal parameters are sent to the gateway and then are forwarded to the cloud servers where the model updating is implemented. The updating will be transmitted back to the gateway. If damage is not detected, the procedures above repeated every predetermined period of time. Once damage is found on the coarse FEM, more wireless sensor nodes will be activated by the gateway nodes and a refined modal parameters will then send from the gateway to the cloud side to implement FEM updating on the refined FEM. We call this hybrid architecture as the "WSN-Cloud SHM."

There remains much space for us to explore to realize a practical WSN-Cloud SHM system. For example, most of the existing applications of cloud computing, particularly web-based applications, can use the "MapReduce" programming model [29]. However, different from web-associated applications such as text tokenization, indexing, and search, implementing FEM updating in the form of MapReduce is not straightforward and needs in-depth investigation. Moreover, from a cloud user's point of view, how to provide different levels of cloud-based SHM services for infrastructure owners is an interesting question. The answers to these questions will lead to great economic benefits in the future.

6 CONCLUSION

In this chapter, we introduced WSNs-based SHM systems, with the focus on how to design distributed versions of SHM algorithms that can be implemented within a WSN. Using the example of distributed modal analysis, a classic algorithm widely adopted in civil engineering, this chapter described how a distributed modal analysis is designed to achieve the similar accuracy of the centralized counterpart but uses much less wireless transmission cost. The examples shown in this chapter can serve as a guideline for more SHM algorithms. Finally, we proposed a WSN-Cloud system architecture which we believe is a promising paradigm for the future SHM.

ACKNOWLEDGMENTS

This research is partially supported in part under Hong Kong RGC under GRF (Grant No. Polyu152244/15E), the NSF of China with Grant 61332004 and 61572218.

REFERENCES

[1] Farrar CR, Worden K. An introduction to SHM. Philos Trans R Soc 2007;365(1851):303.

[2] Brownjohn JMW, Bocciolone M, Curami A, Falco M, Zasso A. Humber bridge full-scale measurement campaigns 1990–1991. J Wind Eng Ind Aerodyn 1994;52:185–218.

[3] Ou J, Li H. Structural health monitoring in mainland China: review and future trends. Struct Health Monit 2010;9(3):219.

[4] Wong KY. Instrumentation and health monitoring of cable-supported bridges. Struct Control Health Monit 2004;11(2):91–124.

[5] Maróti M, Kusy B, Simon G, Lédeczi Á. The flooding time synchronization protocol. In: Proceedings of the 2nd international conference on embedded networked sensor systems. ACM; 2004. p. 39–49.

[6] Nagayama T, Spencer Jr BF. Structural health monitoring using smart sensors. Newmark Structural Engineering Laboratory, University of Illinois at Urbana-Champaign; 2008. Tech. Rep. N.S.E.L. Series 001.

[7] Golub GH, Van Loan CF. Matrix computations (Johns Hopkins Studies in Mathematical Sciences). The Johns Hopkins University Press; 1996.

[8] Farrar CR, Doebling SW. An overview of modal-based damage identification methods. In: Proceedings of DAMAS conference; Sheffield, UK; 1997.

[9] Bendat JS, Piersol AG. Engineering applications of correlation and spectral analysis. New York, Wiley-Interscience; 1980.

[10] Monroig E, Fujino Y. Multivariate autoregressive models for local damage detection using small clusters of wireless sensors. In: Proceedings of the third European workshop on structural health monitoring, Granada, Spain; 2006.

[11] Sohn H, Farrar CR. Damage diagnosis using time series analysis of vibration signals. Smart Mater Struct 2001;10:446.

[12] Messina A, Jones IA, Williams EJ. Damage detection and localization using natural frequency changes. In: Proceedings of conference on identification in engineering systems; 1996. p. 67–76.

[13] Messina A, Williams EJ, Contursi T. Structural damage detection by a sensitivity and statistical-based method. J Sound Vib 1998;216(5):791–808.

[14] Hou Z, Noori MN, St Amand R. Wavelet-based approach for structural damage detection. J Eng Mech 2000;126(7):677–83.

[15] Sun Z, Chang C. Structural damage assessment based on wavelet packet transform. J Struct Eng 2002; 128(10):1354–61.

[16] Lynch JP, Sundararajan A, Law KH, Kiremidjian AS, Carryer E. Embedding damage detection algorithms in a wireless sensing unit for operational power efficiency. Smart Mater Struct 2004;13:800.

[17] Richardson MH, Formenti DL. Parameter estimation from frequency response measurements using rational fraction polynomials. In: Proceedings of the 1st international modal analysis conference. vol. 1; 1982. p. 167–86.

[18] Zhang Y, Li J. Wavelet-based vibration sensor data compression technique for civil infrastructure condition monitoring. J Comput Civ Eng 2006;20:390.

[19] Friswell MI, Mottershead JE. Finite element model updating in structural dynamics. Netherlands: Kluwer Academic Publishers; 1995.

[20] Peeters B, De Roeck G. Reference-based stochastic subspace identification for output-only modal analysis. Mech Syst Signal Process 1999;13(6):855–78.

[21] Juang JN, Pappa RS. An eigensystem realization algorithm for modal parameter identification and model reduction. J Guid 1985;8(5):620–7.

[22] Brincker R, Zhang L, Andersen P. Modal identification from ambient responses using frequency domain decomposition. In: Proceedings of the 18th international modal analysis conference; 2000. p. 625–30.

[23] Jacobsen NJ, Andersen P, Brincker R. Using enhanced frequency domain decomposition as a robust technique to harmonic excitation in operational modal analysis. In: Proceedings of ISMA2006: international conference on noise & vibration engineering; 2006. p. 18–20.

[24] Welch P. The use of fast Fourier transform for the estimation of power spectra: a method based on time averaging over short, modified periodograms. IEEE Trans Audio Electroacoust 1967;15(2):70–3.

[25] Sim SH, Carbonell-Márquez JF, Spencer Jr BF, Jo H. Decentralized random decrement technique for efficient data aggregation and system identification in wireless smart sensor networks. Probab Eng Mech 2011;26(1):81–91.

[26] Liu X, Cao J, Lai S, Yang C, Wu H, Xu Y. Energy efficient clustering for WSN-based structural health monitoring. In: IEEE INFOCOM. vol. 2; 2011. p. 1028–37.

[27] Li ZX, Chan THT, Yu Y, Sun ZH. Concurrent multi-scale modeling of civil infrastructures for analyses on structural deterioration part I: modeling methodology and strategy. Finite Elem Anal Des 2009; 45(11):782–94.

[28] Chan THT, Li ZX, Yu Y, Sun ZH. Concurrent multi-scale modeling of civil infrastructures for analyses on structural deteriorating part II: model updating and verification. Finite Elem Anal Des 2009;45 (11):795–805.

[29] Dean J, Ghemawat S. MapReduce: simplified data processing on large clusters. Commun ACM 2008; 51(1):107–13.

GLOSSARY

Divide and conquer A divide and conquer algorithm works by recursively breaking down a problem into two or more subproblems of the same (or related) type.

Modal analysis The study of the dynamic properties of structures under vibrational excitation.

Mode shape A specific pattern of vibration executed by a mechanical system at a specific frequency.

Natural frequency The frequency at which a system tends to oscillate in the absence of any driving or damping force.

Structural health monitoring The process of implementing a damage detection and characterization strategy for engineering structures.

Wireless sensor networks Spatially distributed autonomous sensors to monitor physical or environmental conditions and to cooperatively pass their data through the network to a main station.

THE INTERNET OF THINGS AND ITS APPLICATIONS

13

Chung-Nan Lee, Tian-Hsiang Huang, Chen-Ming Wu, Ming-Chun Tsai

National Sun Yat-sen University, Kaohsiung, Taiwan

ACRONYMS

ANN	artificial neuron network
CoREs	constrained resource environments
CRFs	conditional random fields
D2D	device-to-device
DTW	dynamic time warping
GA	genetic algorithm
GPS	global positioning system
ICGA	island-based cloud genetic algorithm
IP	Internet protocol
KNN	k nearest neighbor
MAP	maximum a posteriori probability
QoC	quality-of-content
QoS	quality of service
S2N	signal-to-noise
SVM	support vector machine

1 INTRODUCTION

As identified by Kevin Ashton in 1999 the Internet of Things (IoT) has become a popular term in IT technology these days. The IoT involves in connecting a variety of ubiquitous sensors, protocols, devices, and machines together. Recent terms similar to IoT include the Internet of Everything and the Internet of Human. It requires everything, including objects, devices, machines, animals, and human beings, to have unique identifiers (UIDs), so they can communicate with each other through a wired or wireless network. The interaction can be human-to-human, human-to-machine, machine-to-machine (M2M), and even device-to-device (D2D) to complete certain tasks. Gartner predicts that the IoT market will reach 20.8 billion by 2020 [1].

"Things," in the IoT sense, can produce, transfer, and exchange data. But why does a thing need to be connected to the network? The main reason is that people want to know the information that these

Big Data Analytics for Sensor-Network Collected Intelligence. http://dx.doi.org/10.1016/B978-0-12-809393-1.00013-1

things can provide, such as temperature, pressure, or battery power. People are interested in such information, and want to keep tracking and gathering. Therefore, how can we get the data that these things provide? Putting these "things" on the Internet makes it easy to gather and store data. When we are gathering these data, they may pass through a variety of devices or protocols. In this chapter, we shall discuss two typical D2D protocols: MQ telemetry transport (MQTT) and constrained application protocol (CoAP).

As more and more devices are connected, a massive amount of data is generated by a wide range of sources such as M2M, radio frequency identification (RFID), and sensors. However, this mass of data may not have much meaningful value unless we can find an effective way to analyze and understand it. Big data analytics are expected to offer promising solutions. In this chapter, we shall discuss some major techniques, such as statistics, Naïve Bayesian classification, artificial neuron networks (ANNs), conditional random fields (CRFs), decision trees, and support vector machines (SVMs), to classify and extract meaning from a huge volume of data generated from the IoT.

There are many IoT applications. In this chapter, we shall use intelligent transportation systems and intelligent manufacturing systems as examples. Modern vehicles are equipped with many advance devices, such as Internet protocol (IP) surveillance systems, global positioning system (GPS), CAN bus, onboard devices, and sensors, to deliver real-time driving information to the control center. One can analyze this information to find the behavior of the driver to enhance safety. In the intelligent manufacturing systems, a key method to improve product quality is to analyze the existing logs and find out the probable causative parameters affecting the yield of products. Due to the huge amount of data and large amounts of parameters that are collected from the IoT, it is difficult for traditional statistical analysis and relational analysis to process such big data to find out the critical parameters affecting the yields. In order to conquer the analysis bottleneck of big data, we take advantage of the high performance computing of MapReduce and design a novel cloud technique with MapReduce, called the island-based cloud genetic algorithm (ICGA), to mine the critical information.

An IoT-centric cloud system, as shown in Fig. 1, can consist of three levels. The first level consists of the IoT; the second level is the communication for interconnection; and the third level is the cloud computing with analytics. The first level of the IoT is composed of data-gathering devices: I/O modules and edge-computing devices whose main purpose is to collect all the different data and environmental conditions from sensors, wearable devices, surveillance video, etc. Then, all data are transmitted through a wired or wireless communication infrastructure. The cloud computing level is used to analyze all the collected data and transform them into useful information for users, and store the information in the data center.

2 COLLECTION OF BIG DATA FROM IoT

In general, the IoT is a system of combining everything around people, including furniture, vehicles, machines, and even all wearable devices. These things can be connected to the network, and are able to transfer data without manual manipulation.

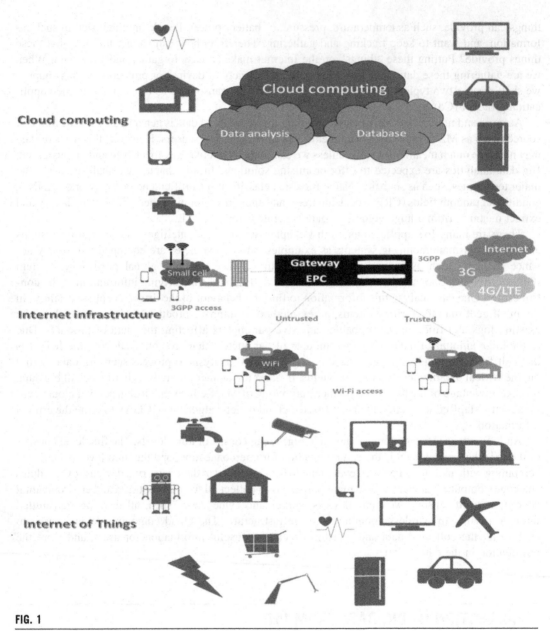

FIG. 1

IoT-centric cloud system.

With the evolution of the IoT and the Internet, more and more IoT devices enter our lives. These devices all have their own service models. It can be imagined that if the number of IoT devices has an explosive growth in the future, then we shall face problems such as:

1. a shortage of IP addresses;
2. a shortage of network bandwidth; and
3. the loading of a server being too heavy.

IPv6 has solved the first problem temporarily, but it is still very possible that we shall encounter this IP address shortage problem again in the future. It is therefore important to develop new IP address allocation methods.

Ongoing IoT devices installation and data transformation have led to an exponential rise in network traffic. Fortunately, many researchers are dedicated to working on next-generation network protocols. To date, the network bandwidth has always increased and been able to support the usage of the IoT.

As indicated above, massive data can be gathered from IoT devices. But how do we deal with these massive data? All these data are useless if we cannot analyze them. For example, a data store records the location of all cars in a whole city. If we do not analyze these data, we will only see that the data about the location of cars increase infinitely and messily. That is, these data mean nothing, and we cannot track a single car's path.

Fortunately, we can use big data analytics to filter or analyze the IoT data. We can identify useful trends, and then follow these to make a final decision. Meanwhile, we use the technologies of cloud computing to offer computing ability, storage space, software and hardware platforms, and so on.

Going one step further, we shall discuss about how to collect the data. Based on the structure of the IoT network, most IoT devices use a battery as their power source. This means that the lifetime of a device is limited. It is important to find out the most efficient usage of a battery. In addition, a lot of IoT devices may access the base station in the same time because of the characteristics of IoTs, meaning that the bandwidth each device can use is limited. Therefore, we should find out a network protocol which is energy saving and requires less bandwidth.

Hypertext transfer protocol (HTTP) [2] is the most common protocol on the Internet. To guarantee quality of service (QoS) of data transformation, HTTP sets its header to 41 bytes. However, a single IoT device usually produces a few data bytes so that the packet ends up having a long header with very short data. This phenomenon may cause the usage of network resource to be inefficient and the device will take more time and power to encapsulate the packet.

Since the energy is important for the IoT, a lightweight protocol is needed in order to reduce the transmitted packet. Here we describe two protocols, MQTT and CoAP, that could be used for communication in the IoT in the following.

2.1 MQ TELEMETRY TRANSPORT

MQTT [3] is a data transmission protocol based on lightweight "Publish-and-Subscribe." It means that MQTT have the characteristic of transferring the data in low size packets, and this is helpful to develop the remote technology with restricted device. The noted feature of MQTT is its mechanism of "publish/subscribe (P/S)," and it is comprised of three main elements:

1. subscriber;
2. publisher; and
3. broker.

Subscriber. The principle of "Publish-and-Subscribe" is that some elements are interested in the specific information and want to subscribe it. This process is known as "Subscription" and the element who wants to subscribe information is known as the "Subscriber."

Publisher. In this mechanism, the element is responsible for generating data to the others is known as the "Publisher." It will do the action known as "Publication" to combine a predefined "Topic" with the data it produces and transfers to "Broker."

Broker. The use of "Broker" is responsible for ensuring that the data the publisher produces can be passed to the subscriber, and for coordinating the process of subscription. After the subscription, the subscriber will set a network connection with the broker to get the information it wants. In addition, the broker will ensure each online element, and carry out the cyclical behavior according to the status of these elements.

Topic. As mentioned above, an element subscribes the information it interested in, and this information is presented in a special string which is known as a "Topic." As long as the subscriber indicates which kind of topic of the data it wants, the broker will transfer the data with the topic to the subscribers who subscribe the topic according to its record.

There are three types of Publish-and-Subscribe mechanisms:

1. topic-based: the topic is known in the step of programing;
2. type-based: the subscriber will indicate what topic of the information it is interested in; and
3. content-based: this type is relatively universal. The subscriber will describe the content of the information it wants. This kind of subscription can include any content such as the temperature or pressure of a place.

The process of data delivery. Fig. 2 depicts the process of data delivery. At first, the subscriber sends a *Sub*(*Topic*) message to the broker to inform them what topic it is interested in. Afterward, if a publisher wants to make a publication, it will send a *Pub*(*Topic*, *Data*) message to the broker. Finally, the broker will send this data to the subscribers, who subscribe the topic according to its record.

After the introduction of the "P/S" mechanism, we shall now discuss the MQTT itself. MQTT is a Topic-based "Publish-and-Subscribe" protocol, offering one-to-many messages allocation by the

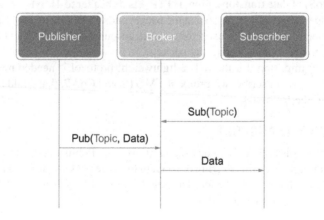

FIG. 2

The process of the Publish-and-Subscribe mechanism.

support of the string of the topic. In the process of transferring data, it offers a basic network connection by TCP/IP. MQTT also provides three basic QoS levels:

1. Level 0 provides the most efficient delivery service, but message loss may occur or the repeated sending of packets.
2. Level 1 guarantees the message will arrive, but it may repeatedly send packets.
3. Level 2 not only guarantees the message will arrive, but also delivers only once. (Usually, because of the system is very strict at calculation, such as a billing system.)

The header of a MQTT packet is only 2 bytes so that it can reduce the loading to the bandwidth for transferring data. In the situation that the device is staying online, it can prolong the life of the battery because of the small-sized packet.

In addition, MQTT enables a "Last Will and Testament" mechanism to inform the subscribers when an abnormal disconnection has happened. The device can request that the broker store its "Will" message and "Will" topic when the device connects to the broker. If an abnormal disconnection happens, the broker will transfer the "Will" publication to the subscribers. This mechanism can be used to debug and formulate the action after the disconnection.

2.2 CONSTRAINED APPLICATION PROTOCOL

CoAP [4] is developed in an IoT-motivated demand. It specializes in the architecture of the constrained resource environments (CoREs). The device in the CoRE usually has low network bandwidth and limited battery power can be used; there is a shortage of storage, and less CPU power. In response to the above requirements, the CoAP packet has a small footprint in the RAM and ROM, so that it is very suitable for the M2M network too.

The architecture showed in Fig. 3 is a common client-server model. Compared with MQTT, which uses TCP, the CoAP uses UDP to transfer its packet. The CoAP is developed based on HTTP, and it reduces the oversize header to make itself suitable for the IoT. The client-server model allows a device to set a proxy server to reduce the overloading of the network gateway and server. In terms of UDP transmission, it is suitable for devices that produce a large amount of repetitive data. It will also not retransmit data when there is packet loss in the CoRE, and then leads the network congestion.

We can observe that the client communicates with the others by the CoAP in the CoRE, and by HTTP in the Internet whose condition is better than CoRE to ensure the reliability of transferring data. It can also reduce the overloading of the server by setting a proxy server. In addition, the CoAP transfers data by UDP, so it is not reliable. However, research nowadays has improved the reliability and security by using the Datagram Transport Layer Security (CoRE) in UDP. Meanwhile, the stream control transmission protocol (SCTP), which combines the advantages of TCP and UDP, is under discussion to be adopted in the CoAP. Similar to HTTP, the CoAP also has its "Message types," such as GET, POST, PUT, and DELETE, to provide standardized services.

In the phase of packet format, as in Fig. 4:

1. the size of the CoAP packet's header is only 4 bytes;
2. CoAP provides option fields; and
3. CoAP provides payload fields, including unsigned integer (uint), string, and opaque.

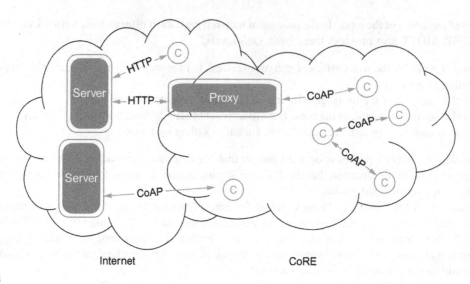

FIG. 3

The architecture of the CoAP.

```
bit: 0 1 2 3 4 5 6 7|0 1 2 3 4 5 6 7|0 1 2 3 4 5 6 7|0 1 2 3 4 5 6 7
    |Ver| T | OC  |    Code      |        Transaction ID        |
    |Options (optional) ...                                     |
    |Payload (if any) ...                                       |

Ver - CoAP version (2-bit)
T - Transaction type (2-bit)
OC - Option count (4-bit)
Code - Request method (1-10) or response code (40-255) (8-bit). E.g:
       - GET: 1
       - POST: 2
       - PUT: 3
       - DELETE: 4
Transaction ID - Unique identifier for matching response (16-bit)
```

FIG. 4

Packet format of the CoAP [5].

2.3 MQTT VS. CoAP

MQTT and CoAP are suitable for the IoT because they both reduce the size of the network packet. In addition, they both reduce the overloading of the network bandwidth, save battery power and storage space, reduce the amount of data the CPU operates, and significantly improve the life cycle of the IoT. Table 1 shows the comparisons Between MQTT and CoAP.

Both protocols have their own advantages, and are suitable for different scenarios. Before gathering the data, we should evaluate the quality of the network, the object to serve, and the service to provide, in order to identify which protocol is more suitable.

Table 1 Comparisons Between MQTT and CoAP

MQTT	CoAP
Use TCP to be the method of network connection Advantage: It guarantees the reliability of packet transmission Disadvantage: When the network environment is poor, it will retransmit the packet; this causes more network congestion	Use UDP to be the method of network connection Advantage: The mechanism is easier and tolerate at packet loss Disadvantage: Data transmission is not reliable
P/S	Client-server
One-to-one service	One-to-one service
One-to-many service	
No hierarchical structure	
Need to maintain the connection with broker for a long time	Transfer the data when needed
Need user (or programmer) to define "Topic." The service is more elastic	Provide fixed message type
No particular definition of proxy server services	Can set a proxy server to reduce the overloading of servers

3 IoT ANALYTICS

3.1 RELATED WORKS

To analyze the data collected from the IoT, many techniques can be used, such as classification, statistics, such as Naïve Bayesian models, ANNs, CRFs, decision trees, and SVM [6]. These machine learning-based methods are often applied to data classification. SVM is used to find out a hyperplane in high dimension data for the purpose of separating the two different sets. Fig. 5 is an example of SVM in two dimensions. We hope to find a line to separate a circle and triangle, and this separating line is as far as possible from data points from each set. We can then clearly distinguish to which set the object belongs. To implement SVM, software such as LIBSVM is a popular tool used to support research about classification [7].

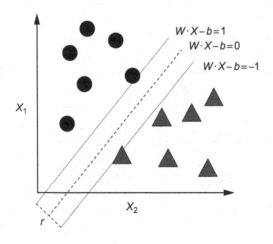

FIG. 5

A SVM hyperplane with margin.

Naïve Bayesian classification [8], based on probability inference, uses an uncertain variety of conditions in the presence. Moreover, it only knows the probability of the event to complete the decision-making tasks. Depending on the classification decision rules, Naïve Bayesian classification has various forms. Naïve Bayesian used in emotion classification mostly adopts maximum a posteriori probability (MAP), and the formula is defined as follows:

$$e_{MAP} = \arg\max_{e \in E} P(e|d) = \arg\max_{e \in E} \frac{P(d|e)p(e)}{P(d)}, \tag{1}$$

where e_{MAP} is the maximum a posteriori probability category, E denotes the set of all types of emotions (positive, negative), e is the type of category, and d is the unknown classification input document. Using Eq. (1), we can infer the most probability category e_{MAP} by computing $P(e|d)$. The variant of Naïve Bayesian classification is designed to model the word-emotion associations.

Outlier detection and anomalous detection are a statistical approach to find the data that deviate from normal distribution. For the outlier detection, we can find whether there are some parameter values acting differently from others. As shown in Fig. 6, in the same preference setting, parameter values in every machine should act alike. However, the figure shows clearly that tool B has some different parameter values from other tools. Tool B is hence regarded as an outlier tool. These parameters showing the extraordinary values in the outlier machines are thought to be sensitive on defective products. As a result, we should perform the outlier detection to find out which sensitive parameter is affected by the outlier machines.

To find out some further critical parameters we use a novel ICGA [9] to mine the critical parameters that affect the product. Eventually, the critical parameters discovered by ICGA and the sensitive parameters detected by outlier detection are cross-verified to obtain the most discriminative parameters. The system architecture of the mining methods is shown in Fig. 7.

The analysis procedure is split into two parts. One is the outlier detection without knowing classification information of data in advance, and the other is the anomalous detection with the ground truth of data. The outlier detection uses the MapReduce technique [10,11] to detect the sensitive

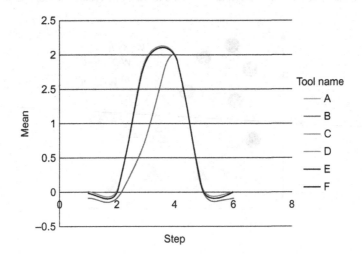

FIG. 6

A diagrammatic curve of outlier machines.

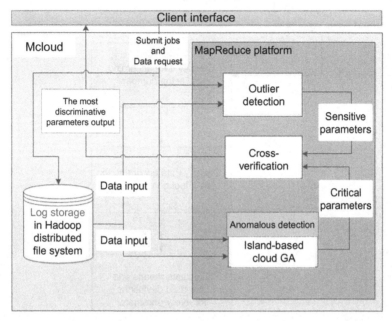

FIG. 7

System architecture.

parameters that are affected by the outlier tools. On the other hand, for anomalous detection, the algorithm performs the ICGA to obtain the critical parameters according to the ground truth. In the proposed cloud genetic algorithm (GA), we can apply the island GA to search for optimal solutions from different solution spaces.

After the results are returned from the outlier detection and the anomalous detection, cross-verification is applied to pick out the parameters that appear in both outlier detection and anomalous detection. As a result, these parameters are regarded as the most discriminative parameters that affect the wafer yield. In the following, the details of the outlier detection and the anomalous detection are described.

3.2 OUTLIER DETECTION FOR BIG DATA

Outlier detection is a primary step in many data mining tasks. The purpose of the outlier detection procedure here is to identify the parameters that are affected by outlier tools from thousands of parameters. There are several approaches for outlier detection. In order to determine the outliers from high-dimensional data without prior knowledge, we obtain outliers based on distance measures that are capable of handling large data sets.

The flowchart of outlier detection is shown in Fig. 8. Different parameters and machines will affect the yield of products. Consequently, as the selected data are input into the outlier detection module, it first separates the log files to several files according to the recipe number and then tool number. After

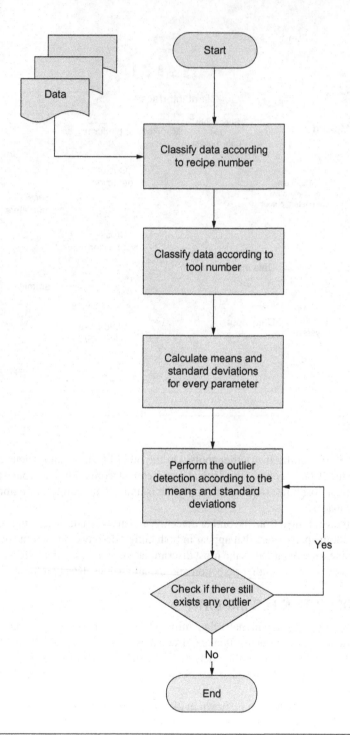

FIG. 8

Flowchart of outlier detection.

obtaining the separated files, the outlier detection module then processes the separated files to calculate means and standard deviations using the MapReduce technique. After obtaining means and standard deviations of every single parameter, the outlier detection module then performs outlier detection.

The results are categorized into two groups, where zero represents an outlier and one represents a normal one. The outlier criterion is defined as follows:

$$\text{outlier}(x) = \begin{cases} 1, & |x_i - \bar{x}| < 2\sigma, \\ 0, & |x_i - \bar{x}| \geq 2\sigma. \end{cases} \tag{2}$$

where x_i is the parameter value of ith tool, $\bar{x}$ is the mean of parameter values within all tools in an arbitrary parameter, and σ is its standard deviation.

Here, there are two different MapReduce computations in this module, as shown in Fig. 9. The first MapReduce job is to calculate means and standard deviations, and the second MapReduce job is to check the values according to Eq. (2) for finding outliers.

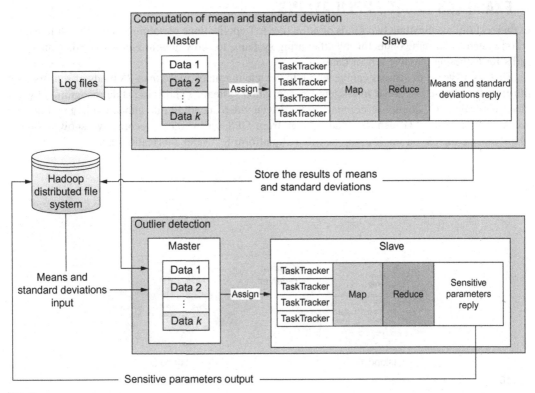

FIG. 9

Outlier detection with MapReduce.

3.3 ISLAND-BASED CLOUD GA

Since the GA is able to search several areas in solution spaces and island GA [12] is a popular way for searching different solutions from diverse populations, it is thus suitable for parallel implementation and provides more power when performing in a distributed environment, such as the cloud system. We extend the concept to design a novel distributed algorithm and implement it in the cloud platform. The MapReduce technique enhances the design to maximize its ability of parallelism. Such a parallel model offers many benefits over the traditional GAs, such as speed, ability to search on larger search spaces, and being less likely to run into a local optimum.

We design a hierarchical scheme where a multideme GA is at a higher level and a master-slave global parallelization on each deme (island) is at a lower level. The proposed algorithm is the ICGA using the MapReduce technique for improving computational efficiency. The scheme of ICGA is shown in Fig. 10. There are two islands where cloud GA performs its own genetic operations in parallel. They realize migration through the central receiver. This approach is popular when working with complex applications that need a considerable amount of computation time.

4 EXAMPLES OF IoT APPLICATIONS

In this section, we illustrate two kinds of attractive IoT applications pertaining to intelligent transportation systems and semiconductor manufacturing systems, to show how to employ big data analytics skills for gathering massive sensor data.

First, as a swarm of sensors can be set up in vehicle internals (more than 28 kinds of sensors), we illustrate three scenarios about intelligent transportation systems: (1) driving style recognition by vehicle sensor data; (2) quality-of-content (QoC)-driven video encoding rate allocation in a mobile surveillance cloud; and (3) identify "bad" driver from GPS sensor data. Second, we show a simple MapReduce example on the Hadoop distributed platform for wafer fabrication data.

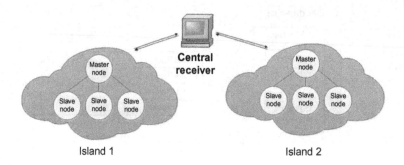

FIG. 10

Scheme of ICGA.

4.1 APPLICATIONS ON INTELLIGENT TRANSPORTATION SYSTEMS

4.1.1 Driving style recognition by vehicle sensor data

During the last decade, auto insurance companies have started placing cameras in vehicles to lower insurance rates, and they have also observed that people drive better when being monitored. In addition, this also can assess performance of drivers during training sessions. In brief, understanding and recognizing driving events that fall into two categories, nonaggressive and aggressive, can aid in vehicle safety systems. In particular, drivers are usually unaware that they commit potentially aggressive actions daily.

Several companies offer products for fleet management and individual use in order to monitor driving behavior using expensive cameras and equipment. Fortunately, in recent years, IoT technologies have promoted research for driver safety and assistance systems, such as sensors available in smartphones. Johnson and Trivedi [13] proposed a system named a mobile-sensor-platform for intelligent recognition of aggressive driving (MIROAD) that is inexpensive, effective, and intelligently uses the sensors available on a cell phone. They fused related interaxial data from multiple sensors into a single classifier based on the dynamic time warping (DTW) algorithm [14], which was designed to find an optimal alignment of two signal vectors. In the MIROAD system, DTW aligned the currently detected event signal with the prerecorded template signals.

The latest cell phones are equipped with many useful inputs for research, including but not limited to:

- camera (often multiple);
- microphone (often multiple);
- 3-axis accelerometer;
- 3-axis gyroscope;
- proximity;
- ambient light;
- touch;
- magnetometer; and
- GPS.

The MIROAD system focuses on the rear-facing camera, accelerometer, gyroscope (sampled at 25 Hz), and GPS (sampled at 1 Hz), but GPS is not always available. The types of events detected by MIROAD are:

- right turns (90 degree);
- left turns (90 degree);
- U-turns (180 degree);
- aggressive right turns (90 degree);
- aggressive left turns (90 degree);
- aggressive U-turns (180 degree);
- aggressive acceleration;
- aggressive braking;
- swerve right (aggressive lane change);
- swerve left (aggressive lane change);
- device removal; and
- excessive speed.

When trying to determine whether or not a driving event is typical (nonaggressive) or aggressive, the DTW algorithm finds the closest match between the different styles of templates. The aggressive templates consisted of high-jerk movements and turns that caused loss of traction.

With regard to device implementation, when the MIROAD application is started, it can be in one of two modes: active or passive. In the active mode, MIROAD monitors driving events and does not keep record of any sensor or video data unless a potentially aggressive event is detected. In the passive mode, the system records and stores all data for further analysis. The data consists of video and an archive of the raw device motion (acceleration, rotation, attitude, time stamps) with GPS data (longitude, latitude, speed, altitude, timestamps). The data is broken up into 5 min segment, just as in the active mode.

4.1.2 QoC-driven video encoding rate allocation in a mobile surveillance cloud

Video-based IoT, which integrates image processing, computer vision and network frameworks, is a new challenging scientific research area at the intersection of video and network technologies. Such research areas include surveillance systems, automatic behavior analysis, event detection, etc. [15].

Due to the large computational cost of video analysis applications and the intercooperating properties among multiple cameras, a cloud server collects videos from multiple moving cameras through wired and/or wireless networks. However, it is predicted that by 2019, more than 70% of all consumer mobile Internet traffic will be video [16]. In the foreseeable future, high packet loss/error rate, large delay, and jitter experienced in wireless networks will cause tremendous quality degradation of received videos. The bandwidth-limited and error-prone nature of wireless communication environments creates challenges for wireless video streaming applications. Unfortunately, transmitting video optimized for QoS based on existing designs are no longer optimal. Therefore, it is necessary to develop more efficient video transmission schemes specifically for video analysis and computer vision applications.

Chen et al. [17] proposed a joint source and channel coding rate allocation scheme for the mobile surveillance network. Their scenarios, set in a mobile surveillance network, have multiple mobile nodes that are randomly distributed, moving around in the area with different pedestrian densities. Each mobile node can capture, encode, and upload videos via wireless wide area networks to a cloud server for video analyses such as suspicious persons detection. The captured camera view of each node is encoded with high-efficiency video coding [18], using encoders with different encoding data rates. The parameter estimation module determines the necessary parameters required by the cloud server. The cloud server receives the transmitted APP-FEC block [19,20] with some packet loss due to either wireless transmission errors or network congestion.

The APP-FEC decoder decodes the APP-FEC block and feeds the video packets to the video decoder. The undecodable video frames will be dropped. The video decoder can conceal the lost video frames by copying the last successfully decoded video frame. After decoding the video, an object detection module performs the human detections and sends the detection results (content information) to the rate allocation module. Since the pedestrian density is different in the view of each mobile node, the human detection result is therefore different. Based on the content information and the necessary parameters delivered by the mobile nodes, the rate allocation module jointly optimizes the source coding rate and the APP-FEC coding rate for each mobile node under a predetermined total data rate constraint, which is assumed to be affordable by the wireless network. The rate allocation result is then fed back to the mobile nodes for the video encoding. Note that Chen et al. adopted a human detector based on the histogram of oriented gradient feature, which can effectively represent the shape of a human proposed by Dalal and Triggs [21].

The main contribution of Chen et al. is their proposed QoC-driven joint source and channel coding scheme, which was evaluated using plenty of simulations. The proposed scheme maximizes the overall true-positive human detection probability under a total data rate constraint and minimum data rate requirements for each moving node. This objective can be shown as a convex optimization problem, but we skip the complicated mathematics formulas in this section.

The proposed scheme only considers human detection as the video analytics purpose, which is the first step for more sophisticated systems such as human tracking and behavior understanding. Therefore, plenty of future studies can be conducted in computer vision, video compression, and video transmission areas.

4.1.3 Identify "bad" driver from GPS sensor data

It is conceivable that each driver has their own driving style, which could affect safety, road congestion, etc. In recent years, many active researchers have worked hard to develop systems that make driving safer. For example, suppose that most of the drivers have safe driving style with similar statistical characteristics. Kuhler and Karstens [22] introduced 10 aggregate driving behavior parameters for research in terms of driving cycles characteristics. These 10 parameters are "average speed," "average speed excluding stop," "average acceleration," "average deceleration," "mean length of a driving period," "average number of acceleration deceleration changes within one driving period," "proportion of standstill time," "proportion of acceleration time," "proportion of deceleration time," and "proportion of time at constant speed."

An interesting study on a large real-world GPS sensor data set was considered by Zhang et al. [23] to investigate how optimal the trajectory of the trip is, connecting two different points. Moreover, the wide use of GPS sensors in smartphones encourages people to record their personal trajectories and share them with others on the Internet. A recommendation service is required to help people process the large quantity of trajectories and select potentially interesting ones [24].

In this example, we consider just basic driving trajectories to estimate the probability that the current driver is bad (or has significant deviations from usual statistical characteristics), and download a data set of 547,200 anonymized driver trips (200 trips per any particular driver) from the Internet [25]. The total size of data is about 5.5 GB, and there are no traditional split train/tests, and there are no any labels available. The time difference (a few seconds) between two sequential 2D-point is fixed. In order to protect the privacy of the drivers' locations, the trips were centered to start at the origin $(0, 0)$, randomly rotated, and short lengths of trip data were removed from the start/end of the trip.

The most established method for assessing driving distractions is to analyze the frequency of critical driving events. They can be aggregated by summation and normalized over the driven distance, and are thus suitable metrics of driving behavior [26]. We propose to evaluate distractions with three different indicators: acceleration, braking, and turning.

In order to embark the driving trajectories, we can describe data in mathematical terms:

$$\{x_{d,t,i}, y_{d,t,i}\}, \tag{3}$$

where x and y represent horizontal and vertical coordinates, $1 \leq d \leq n_d$ is the index of the driver, and $n_d = 2736$; $1 \leq t \leq n_t$ is the index of the trip, $n_t = 200$; $1 \leq i \leq n_{d,t}$ is the sequential index of the point within particular trip, where $200 \leq n_{d,t} \leq 2000$ is the variable length.

It is essential here to note that the time difference for any two sequential points in Eq. (3) is fixed. Using this fact as a main ground, we can approximate the speed of the driver:

$$v_i = \sqrt{(x_{i+sv} - x_i)^2 + (y_{i+sv} - y_i)^2}, \tag{4}$$

where $1 \le i \le n_{d,t} - sv, sv \ge 1$ is the shift parameter for speed.

Additionally, we can take into account acceleration:

$$a_i = v_{i+sa} - v_i, \tag{5}$$

where $1 \le i \le n_{d,t} - sv - sa, sa \ge 1$ is the shift parameter for acceleration. Generally, shift parameters for speed sv and for accelerations sa are not necessarily the same and may be different. Let us consider 2D-vectors of speed:

$$\vec{v}_i = \{x_{i+sv} - x_i, y_{i+sv} - y_i\}. \tag{6}$$

It is essential that the vector of speed in Eq. (6) is used as a measurement of the direction of the movement. In the case if driver is changing direction, it will be very important to measure and to take into account how fast this change is. To do this, we shall consider the following difference of speed vectors:

$$\vec{dv_i} = \vec{v}_{i+sa} - \vec{v}_i. \tag{7}$$

Consequently, we can consider three new features:

$$L\left(\vec{dv_i}\right) = length\left(\vec{dv_i}\right), \tag{8}$$

$$Lv_i = L\left(\vec{dv_i}\right) \cdot v_i, \tag{9}$$

$$La_i = L\left(\vec{dv_i}\right) \cdot a_i, \tag{10}$$

where $L\left(\vec{dv}\right)$ is length of the vector $\vec{dv}$, which is measured according to Euclidean distance.

In order to apply the most efficient classification models such as *xgboost* [27], we have to transform data to the rectangular format. We find minimum and maximum values for any vector (speed, acceleration, turning speed) into equal-sized subintervals, and compute numbers of entries in any subinterval divided by total number of entries or length of the vector. In other words, we compute fractional empirical probabilities.

After data preprocess, we go through the list of all drivers, assuming that the current driver is "bad." We add to the database five randomly selected drivers, assuming that they are "good." Consequently, we shall form a training data table with 1200 rows, where 200 are labeled as one (bad) and remaining 1000 are labeled as zero (good). Further, we apply *xgboost* model (can also run on major distributed environment such as Hadoop and MPI). Consequently, we produce vector of 200 scores, corresponding to the current driver. After completion of the global cycle around all 2736 drivers, we shall calculate required vector of all 547,200 scores. The result of the area under receiver operating curve is 0.93606 [28].

4.2 APPLICATIONS ON INTELLIGENT MANUFACTURING SYSTEMS

Many researchers from academia as well as industries are getting involved in identifying the most probable causative factors in manufacturing field. However, thousands of parameters of each product may need to be stored properly and accessed in time. This cannot be easily accomplished by the traditional computing architecture. For example, the wafer fabrication process for producing integrated circuit consists of a lengthy sequence of complex physical and chemical processes. Therefore, semiconductor fabrication facilities have already collected the parameters of the fabrication processes, materials, and equipment involved in the product manufacturing [29].

In real-world applications, there are two main problems to solve. The first problem is how to access and storage huge data quickly, even how to recover it, when the storage disk is broken. The second one is how to figure out the impacting factor for the yield rate of automation product in a short time.

In order to conquer the analysis bottleneck of big data, we take advantage of the high-performance computing of MapReduce and use the ICGA to mine the critical information. ICGA is integrated of the cloud GA and k nearest neighbor (KNN) classifier. In addition, we adopt the concept of statistics to perform the outlier detection to find out the sensitive parameters.

Extended from Fig. 10, the flowchart of ICGA shown in Fig. 11 describes how we perform the proposed algorithm with MapReduce on each island. First of all, in order to obtain the most significant parameters that will be used as the individuals to ICGA, preliminary parameter analysis helps us to select the most significant parameters and reduce the burden of computation. The selected parameters are then sent to each island for the analysis of ICGA.

In the proposed ICGA, each population size is 100, and the number of generations of each separated GA are 1000. For the island model, each independent island carries out migration by exchanging the best individuals through the central receiver. In the migration process, we design a master-slave model for collecting diverse optimal solutions and leaving the best one to every separated island and to precede the next generation.

In the preliminary parameter analysis, we adopt a signal-to-noise (S2N) ratio [30] to select the most significant parameters, and this is implemented with MapReduce.

Each parameter is represented by an expression vector $v(p) = (w_1, w_2, w_3, ..., w_n)$, where w_i denotes a parameter value of parameter p in ith wafer in the data sets. A class distinction is described by a pattern $c = (c_1, c_2, c_3, ..., c_n)$, where $c_i \in \{0,1\}$ according to the ith wafer that belongs to a good class or a bad one. According to the ground truth generated before, we classify the bad wafers into class 0, and we group good and fair wafers into class 1.

In order to pick out the most discriminative parameters, we applied a measure of correlation, Pearson correlation coefficient, $P(p, c)$, which indicates a correlation between the parameter expression and the class distinction. Eq. (11) reflects the difference between the classes relative to the standard deviation within the classes. The larger $|P(p, c)|$ is, the stronger the class distinction is.

$$P(p,c) = \frac{\mu_0(p) - \mu_1(p)}{\sigma_0(p) + \sigma_1(p)}, \tag{11}$$

where $\mu_0(p) = \frac{\sum_{i=1}^{n}(1-c_i)w_i}{\sum_{i=1}^{n}(1-c_i)}$ and $\sigma_0(p) = \sqrt{\frac{1}{\sum_{i=1}^{n}(1-c_i)}\sum_{i=1}^{n}[(1-c_i)w_i - \mu_0(p)]^2}$ when $c_i = 0$;

$\mu_1(p) = \frac{\sum_{i=1}^{n}c_i w_i}{\sum_{i=1}^{n}c_i}$ and $\sigma_1(p) = \sqrt{\frac{1}{\sum_{i=1}^{n}c_i}\sum_{i=1}^{n}[c_i w_i - \mu_1(p)]^2}$ when $c_i = 1$.

The following describes how we use the MapReduce technique to implement S2N.

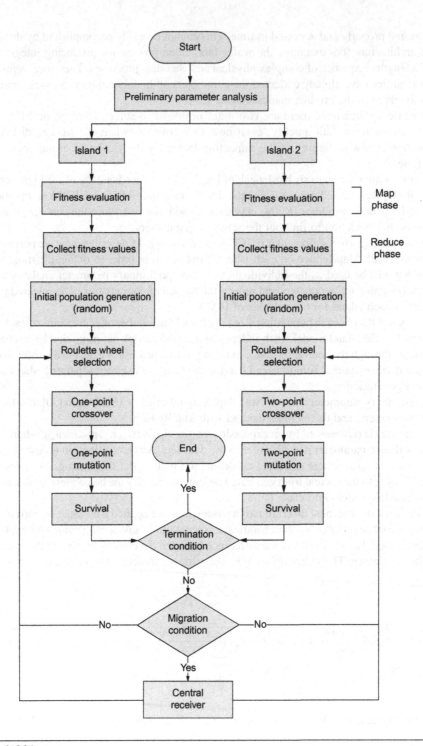

FIG. 11

Flowchart of ICGA.

4.2.1 Map phase for S2N

As the map function obtains the ground truth, it divides the data into two classes: one good, the other bad. The map function copes with the data line by line, and a parameter value displayed by several wafers is shown in one line. Therefore, as the map function processes one line, we calculate the Pearson value of one parameter according to the classification information of classes. The output ⟨*key, value*⟩ pairs are hence set so that the parameter number is the key and the Pearson value is the value.

4.2.2 Reduce phase for S2N

The reduce phase collects all the keys and sorts the results in a descending order according to the values. The corresponding Pearson value of a parameter is then outputted for the subsequent analysis.

Here, we keep the top 25% parameters according to their Pearson values. These selected parameters are so-called preliminary significant parameters. In order to obtain the most critical parameters that affect the wafer yield, we further perform ICGA to identify the most critical parameters from these preliminary significant parameters.

As shown in Fig. 12, there are several islands where their own populations independently evolve from one generation to another. Each island acts like a cloud, performing an independent GA. While islands need to communicate with each other, the master of each island transmits its information to the central receiver. In that way, the receiver can organize the communications and resend the required information to each master.

The following describes how we performed ICGA based on MapReduce. It is worth noting that our data are randomly located in different data nodes, so data transmission and communication rely on network transfer. In the global parallelization on each deme (island) at a lower level, we have to move data among different data nodes in order to evaluate the fitness of individuals. However, this method leads to a severe efficiency bottleneck due to its frequent I/O. Consequently, we should design a MapReduce model that can decrease such an overhead.

First, for the first generation, 100 individuals are generated randomly on the islands. The presentation of individuals here is a binary string. One represents the critical parameter, and zero means the regular one. The length of one individual is the number of those selected parameters through S2N. Next, the evaluation procedure is performed via the fitness function. This procedure is the most time-consuming and needs massive computing resources, so we parallelize the fitness evaluation to slave nodes for better performance. Here, the parallelization is executed with MapReduce. Although the MapReduce technique can increase the computational efficiency, nevertheless, the less MapReduce procedure is called for, the better the performance shows. Therefore, we design a MapReduce model to calculate the fitness evaluation just once.

Before performing the fitness evaluation with MapReduce, we use n-fold cross-validation to partition data into n equal size subsamples. In each fold, a single subsample is retained as the testing data for testing the model, and the remaining $(n-1)$ subsamples are used as the training data. Here, we use 10-fold cross-validation.

We apply the training data as the input of ICGA. In the training set, in order to verify the proposed ICGA is good enough, we use n-fold cross-validation once again, a model validation for using in settings where the goal is prediction, and we want to estimate how accurately a predictive

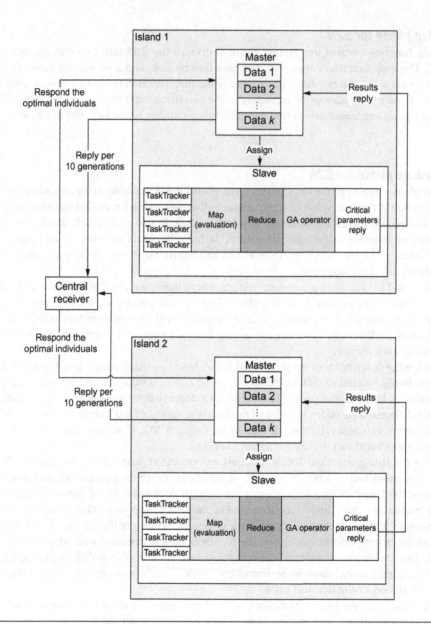

FIG. 12

The architecture of ICGA with MapReduce.

model will perform in practice. Here, we also use 10-fold cross-validation. In each fold, we perform ICGA to obtain a set of critical parameters and accuracy. The fitness function of ICGA is given in Eq. (12):

$$\text{Maximize}\ \ f(I) = Accuracy(I) \times \left(1 + \frac{1}{p(I)}\right),$$

$$\text{Subject to}\ \ p(I) \geq 50. \tag{12}$$

where I is the individual, $Accuracy(I)$ means the accuracy of the individual, and $p(I)$ represents the number of selected bits (critical parameters) in one individual. We apply the KNN classifier to calculate the accuracy.

5 CONCLUSIONS

In this chapter, we discussed two typical lightweight D2D protocols: MQTT and CoAP. These protocols are important for big IoT data collection. After that we presented some of major techniques to classify and reason the meaning from a huge volume of data generated from IoT. Finally, we used intelligent transportation systems and intelligent manufacturing systems as examples to show how to employ big data analytics skills for analyzing huge quantities of sensor data. As the usage of the IoT will very likely experience a tremendous increase in the future, the efficient collection and analysis of data is key for a company to stay competitive.

REFERENCES

[1] Smith T. Gartner: IoT market to hit 20.8 billion connected devices by 2020 [Online]. Available: http://www.peer1hosting.co.uk/industry-news/gartner-iot-market-hit-208-billion-connected-devices-2020; 2016.
[2] Wikipedia. Hypertext transfer protocol [Online]. Available: https://en.wikipedia.org/wiki/Hypertext_Transfer_Protocol; 2016.
[3] MQTT.ORG. Message queuing telemetry transport [Online]. Available: http://mqtt.org/; 2016.
[4] CoAP. RFC 7252 constrained application protocol [Online]. Available: http://coap.technology/; 2016.
[5] Sparkfun. Exploring the protocols of IoT [Online]. Available: https://www.sparkfun.com/news/1705; 2016.
[6] Cortes C, Vapnik V. Support-vector networks. Mach Learn 1995;20:273–97.
[7] Chang C-C, Lin C-J. LIBSVM: a library for support vector machines. ACM Trans Intell Syst Technol 2011;2.
[8] Russell SJ, Norvig P. Artificial intelligence: a modern approach. 3rd ed. New Jersey: Prentice Hall; 2010.
[9] Wu J-S, Tsai M-C, Chu S-W, Lee C-N. Big parameter data analysis for semi-conductor manufacture [Online]. Available: http://worldcomp-proceedings.com/proc/p2014/GCA2578.pdf; 2014.
[10] Dean J, Ghemawat S. MapReduce: simplified data processing on large clusters. Commun ACM 2008;51:107–13.

[11] Yahoo. Yahoo applied Hadoop to process 4PB data [Online]. Available: http://www.ithome.com.tw/itadm/article.php?c=49410&s=4; 2016.

[12] Deshpande P, Gupta A, Kondekar R, Maru R, Rokde A, Saluja G. A MapReduce based hybrid genetic algorithm using island approach for solving time dependent vehicle routing problem. In: International conference on computer & information science (ICCIS), Kuala Lumpur; 2012. p. 263–9.

[13] Johnson D, Trivedi M. Driving style recognition using a smartphone as a sensor platform. In: 14th international IEEE conference on intelligent transportation systems, Washington, DC, October 5–7; 2011. p. 1609–15.

[14] Sakoe H, Chiba S. Dynamic programming algorithm optimization for spoken word recognition. IEEE Trans Acoust Speech Signal Process 1978;26:43–9.

[15] Gubbi J, Buyya R, Marusic S, Palaniswami M. Internet of Things (IoT): a vision, architectural elements, and future directions. Futur Gener Comput Syst 2013;29:1645–60.

[16] Cisco. Cisco visual networking index: forecast and methodology, 2014–2019 [Online]. Available: http://www.cisco.com/c/en/us/solutions/collateral/service-provider/ip-ngn-ip-next-generation-network/white_paper_c11-481360.html; 2015.

[17] Chen X, Hwang J-N, Meng D, Lee K-H, Queiroz RLD, Yeh F-M. A quality-of-content (QoC)-based joint source and channel coding for human detections in a mobile surveillance cloud. IEEE Trans Circuits Syst Video Technol 2016. http://dx.doi.org/10.1109/TCSVT.2016.2539758.

[18] Sullivan GJ, Ohm J-R, Han W-J, Wiegand T. Overview of the high efficiency video coding (HEVC) standard. IEEE Trans Circuits Syst Video Technol 2012;22:1649–68.

[19] Baccaglini E, Tillo T, Olmo G. Slice sorting for unequal loss protection of video streams. IEEE Signal Process Lett 2008;15:581–4.

[20] Wu J, Shang Y, Huang J, Zhang X, Cheng B, Chen J. Joint source-channel coding and optimization for mobile video streaming in heterogeneous wireless networks. EURASIP J Wirel Commun Netw 2013;2013:283.

[21] Dalal N, Triggs B. Histograms of oriented gradients for human detection. In: IEEE computer society conference on computer vision and pattern recognition. San Diego, CA: IEEE; 2005. p. 886–93.

[22] Kuhler M, Karstens D. Improved driving cycle for testing automotive exhaust emissions. SAE technical paper 780650; 1978.

[23] Zhang D, Li N, Zhou Z, Chen C, Sun L, Li S. iBAT: detecting anomalous taxi trajectories from GPS traces. In: Proceedings of the 13th international conference on ubiquitous computing, New York, NY; 2011. p. 99–108.

[24] Yin P, Ye M, Lee W, Mining ZL. Mining GPS data for trajectory recommendation. Lect Notes Comput Sci 2014;8444:50–61.

[25] AXA. Data for driver telematics analysis [Online]. Available: https://www.kaggle.com/c/axa-driver-telematics-analysis/data; 2014.

[26] Bergasa L, Almeria D, Almazan J, Yebes J, Arroyo R. DriveSafe: an app for alerting inattentive drivers and scoring driving behaviors. In: IEEE intelligent vehicles symposium proceedings, Dearborn, MI; 2014. p. 240–5.

[27] XGBoost. XGBoost: an extreme gradient boosting library [Online]. Available: https://xgboost.readthedocs.org/en/latest/#xgboost-documentation; 2016.

[28] Huang TH, Nikulin V, Chen LB. Detection of abnormalities in driving style based on moving object trajectories without labels. In: International congress on advanced applied informatics, Kumamoto, Japan; 2016.

[29] Ooi MP-L, Sim EKJ, Kuang YC, Demidenko S, Kleeman L, Chan CWK. Getting more from the semiconductor test: data mining with defect-cluster extraction. IEEE Trans Instrum Meas 2011;60:3300–17.

[30] Bloomfield CD, Caligiuri MA, Coller H, Gaasenbeek M, Golub TR, Huard C, et al. Molecular classification of cancer: class discovery and class prediction by gene expression monitoring. Science 1999;286:531–7.

GLOSSARY

Big data analytics The analytical process of examining large amounts of data containing a variety of data types to uncover hidden patterns, correlations and other insights.

MapReduce A parallel programing model for processing and generating large data sets. Programmers express the computation as two functions: map and reduce. The former takes an input pair and produces a set of intermediate key/value pairs, and then applying the latter to all the values that shared the same key in order to combine the derived data appropriately.

Outlier detection An outlier is an observation that appears to deviate markedly from other observations in the sample. Outlier detection is the process of detecting outliers from a given set of data.

Signal-to-noise ratio A measure that compares the level of a desired signal to the level of background noise.

XGBoost An acronym short for "Extreme Gradient Boosting," which is used for supervised learning problems.

SMART RAILWAY BASED ON THE INTERNET OF THINGS

14

Qingyong Y. Li, Zhangdui D. Zhong, Ming Liu, Weiwei W. Fang

Beijing Key Lab of Transportation Data Analysis and Mining, Beijing Jiaotong University, Beijing, China

ACRONYMS

CBTC	communications-based train control
GSM-R	global system for mobile communication for railways
IoT	Internet of Things
IRIS	intelligent rail inspection system
LTE-R	long-term evolution for railways
NDE	nondestructive evaluation
VIS	visual inspection system

1 INTRODUCTION

The requirements of "higher speed, higher capacity of transport, higher degree of safety, higher quality of services, and higher efficiency of operation (five-higher)" have never stopped being pursued in the railway industry [1]. The industry has gone from the mode based on mechanics and electronics to the mode based on informatics in recent years [2]. In many countries, ITs and infrastructures have become core issues for railway transportation systems. For example, China has developed and implemented various kinds of advanced train operation and control systems and other large-scale railway information systems, such as the transportation management information system, the dispatching management information system, the Chinese train control system, and the global system for mobile communication for railways (GSM-R). These information systems have promoted the development of the railway industry, such as increasing speed and improving capacity; furthermore, the railway industry seems destined to move towards the so-called smart railway, facing the five-higher requirement. A smart railway will leverage advanced computing and sensing capabilities to meet the increasing transportation demands. State-of-the-art ITs (e.g., Internet of Things (IoT), big data, and cloud computing) can make the development of the smart railway feasible [3,4].

The IoT is the network of physical objects (such as devices, vehicles, buildings, and other items) embedded with electronics, software, sensors, and network connectivity that enables these objects to collect and exchange data [5]. Things can be regarded as inextricable devices with hardware, software, data, and services, such as heart monitoring implants, biochip transponders on farm animals, electric clams in coastal waters, and automobiles with built-in sensors. These devices collect useful data with the help of various existing technologies and then autonomously flow the data between other devices or

Big Data Analytics for Sensor-Network Collected Intelligence. http://dx.doi.org/10.1016/B978-0-12-809393-1.00014-3

humans. Each thing is uniquely identifiable through its embedded computing system but is able to interoperate within the existing Internet infrastructure. The IoT allows objects to be sensed and controlled remotely across the existing network infrastructure, and creates opportunities of integrating the physical world into computer-based systems (also called cyberspace).

Big data usually includes data sets with sizes beyond the ability of commonly used software tools to manage and process data within a tolerable span of time [6,7]. Big data requires a set of techniques and technologies with new forms of integration to reveal insights from datasets that are diverse, complex, and of a massive scale. With the accumulation of sensor data, operation data, and user data, big data is eventually becoming the main drive and fundamental property for the railway industry.

The modern railway system is a classic complex cyber physical system, which is composed of physical entities controlled by computer-based algorithms [8]. For example, a train management system turns trains into interconnected communication hubs that not only collect information from their own on-board devices and equipment, but also exchange information among trains and railway control centers, in order to report real-time operating status to and receive instructions from the control centers. A smart railway adopting the IoT and big data should be the right choice of the next generation of modern railway systems, aiming to improve the safety and performance of railway systems.

The reminder of this chapter is organized as follows. Section 2 presents the architecture of smart railway, and Section 3 introduces the intelligent rail inspection system (IRIS) based on the framework of smart railway. Lastly, the conclusions are made.

2 ARCHITECTURE OF THE SMART RAILWAY

This section proposes the architecture of smart railway, which is divided into four layers: perception and action layer, transfer layer, data engine layer, and application layer. The advanced and mostly concerned technologies for each layer are discussed in the corresponding subsections.

2.1 OVERVIEW

A modern railway transportation system requires better safety, operational efficiency, and passenger experience. To this end, more and more smart devices such as environmental sensors, key status detectors, and the associated actuators are integrated into railway transportation networks. It can be foreseen that the future railway transportation system will be covered by a comprehensive network of smart "things," which can help to improve all parts of the transportation system through efficiently and effectively applying emerging ITs to interconnected trains, infrastructures, and people. All these interconnected smart devices form an enormous IoT for the railway transportation system.

In general, the smart devices enrolled in a smart railway network can be classified into four main categories depending on their applications, namely on-board equipment monitoring devices, infrastructure inspection and maintenance devices, surrounding environment sensing devices, and transportation participant serving devices, as illustrated in Fig. 1. Massive devices of different categories are connected to the smart railway networks via various network-access means, such as wired or wireless data connections. For instance, the key parameters of a train, such as bearing temperatures, air brake pressure, and supply voltage, are transmitted through the wireless data link to the control center of the train in order to report the real-time operating status of the train. Online data analysis is then performed to

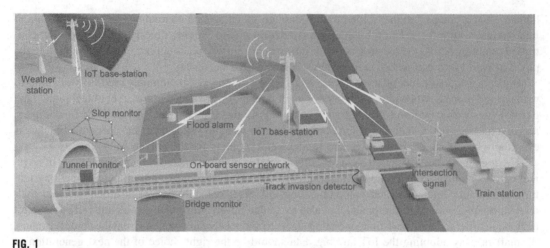

FIG. 1

Future smart railways scenarios.

discover potential equipment failure. The train operation is adjusted accordingly to improve operational efficiency and punctuality rate. In the meantime, various sensors deployed along or beside the railway collect the status of infrastructures such as the track, bridges, tunnels, and revetments, so that the safety of the train operation is guaranteed. Moreover, monitoring systems are deployed in the key nodes of the railway such as train stations, road intersections, and urban areas to ensure the safety of both the train and passengers. In addition, some sensing networks are also implemented in some critical parts of the railway to monitor the surrounding environments, so that an alarm will be triggered when geological disasters (such as earthquakes, floods, mudslides, or fierce wind) may hinder the safety of the railway operation.

The network of the smart devices should be elastic and versatile enough to embrace all these comprehensive functionalities. Fig. 2 presents a generic architecture of the future smart railway networks. The architecture is divided into four layers: perception/action layer, transfer layer, data engine layer, and application layer. These will be discussed in more detail in the following subsections.

2.2 PERCEPTION AND ACTION LAYER

The network gathers information that is perceived by its distributed sensors from different sources, including but not limited to the on-board sensor networks, sensors deployed in infrastructure, environmental sensors, and the detectors that are used to capture information from passengers and other transportation participants.

In a modern train, diverse sensors are mounted to acquire a series of key parameters, such as the bearing temperature, air brake pressure, power-supply voltage, and bogie condition. These parameters are used to determine the condition of the train. Some other information like geographical location, train speed, and acceleration is also collected to reflect the operation of the train. Meanwhile, many sensors such as fire alarms and door-lock alarms are deployed to ensure the security of the passengers

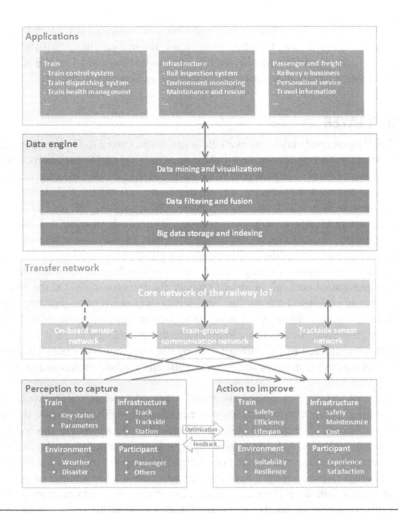

FIG. 2

The architecture of the smart railway based on the IoT.

as well as the train. In addition, a couple of sensors are employed to report the malfunctioning of the on-board equipment like toilets and air conditioners, in order to guarantee the quality of passenger services.

Apart from the on-board devices, a large amount of sensors are deployed beside rail tracks to monitor the infrastructure and the surrounding environment. For example, several types of sensors including piezometers, inclinometers, displacement sensors, and vibration sensors are used in tunnels, bridges, and mountainous areas to ensure that the infrastructure is in a fit state for the train to pass. Obstacle detectors are used to ensure sure the track is still clear. Meanwhile, weather stations and earthquake detectors are deployed to detect extreme weather and geological disasters in the critical areas.

Sensors serving passengers are also very useful to provide passengers with better experience and service. For example, we can deploy some beaconing devices based on Bluetooth to provide services like indoor localization and information recommendation to passengers with smartphones in a railway station. From the management side, the officers can know the motion characteristics and the services that are of interest to passengers. Meanwhile, the low-cost Radio Frequency Identification (RFID) technique offers a possible alternative or complement to existing paper-based tickets.

2.3 TRANSFER LAYER

Once captured by the perception layer, the raw data is first preprocessed to fit the requirements of upper layers. The collected data is then transmitted to the core network via different means. For instance, the key operational status of a train is transferred to the on-board data server. The critical parameters, like bearing temperature and air brake pressure, are sent to the core network through the train-ground wireless communication networks, which can be the classic GSM-R network, the state-of-the-art long-term evolution for railways (LTE-R) network, the upcoming 5G network, or other dedicated wireless networks. In the meantime, the status of infrastructure is capture by wired or wireless track-side sensor networks, and is then transferred to the core network as well. On the one hand, some critical information, such as an earthquake alarm or strong wind alarm, is sent to the affected trains through the direct train-ground communication network in order to reduce the response time. On the other hand, some sensing information is exchanged among the local sensors via machine-to-machine communication links. As the data may contain some correlation due to the proximity of the sensors' geographical locations, necessary processing is carried out to eliminate the redundancy in the data. The compressed information is then transmitted to the core network by the representative node. This can effectively avoid the number of concurrent network access and significantly reduce the amount of data exchanging between network and sensors.

The coexistence of various data sensing and transfer networks means that the overall network possesses a heterogeneous architecture. The data transfer needs to be highly efficient so that the key status can be reported to the control center and the reaction can be made within the shortest time possible. Moreover, the data transmission link needs to be highly robust, even in face of the extremely complicated wireless communication scenarios like fast-fading, high Doppler frequency shift and shadowing. Furthermore, the smart railway network needs to accommodate a large number of sensors and monitors. As a result, the network should be elastic enough to simultaneously maintain massive connections with various quality of service demands. In general, the idea information transmission needs to be stable, seamless, robust, and efficient, with very strong adaptability to various scenarios.

2.4 DATA ENGINE LAYER

The heterogeneous and huge data coming from different sources needs to be processed properly before it can be exploited further by applications. The data in smart railways have three characteristics.

(1) The data has large variety, including number, text, images, audio, and video. Some data are structured while other data are semistructured or unstructured.
(2) The data has big volume, ranging from a few dozen terabytes to many petabytes. For example, the high speed trains operating on the Beijing-Shanghai high-speed railway produce over 10 million of key status records every day.
(3) The data may locate in different places, including headquarters, divisions and local offices.

The data engine layer carries out the functions of intelligent data processing, including distributed storage, information indexing, noise filtering, data fusion, data mining, visualization, etc.

The collected data should be effectively stored in the network so that it can be accessed easily. Data sources with distributed and decentralized controls are a main characteristic of a smart railway. Each data source is able to generate and collect information automatically without involving (or relying on) any centralized control. Data collection should be accessed by parallel and concurrent ways. The MapReduce proposed by Google provides a parallel processing model, and an associated implementation was released to process huge amounts of data. Recent studies show that a multiple-layer architecture is one option to address the issues that big data presents [9]. A distributed parallel architecture saves data across multiple servers; these parallel execution environments can dramatically improve data processing speeds, using the MapReduce and Hadoop frameworks. Such multiple-layer storage architecture seems a good choice for a smart railway.

Data indexing is a necessary procedure to retrieve intended information effectively [10]. In the application of a smart railway, data should be basically indexed according to time, spatial information, and events. Of course, established data structure or customized algorithms should be applied for specific tasks. It should be noted that it is a big challenge to make an index for images or videos.

Data collected by sensors are inevitably noised or incomplete, because the sensors always work in an open dynamic environment and the objects associated with sensors are often both complex and uncertain. Thereafter, the collected data should be filtered first, in order to get rid of noises or to discard incomplete and contaminated data. Unsupervised learning methods and signal processing algorithms can be used for this stage.

The data fusion module aims to merge multisource information or to align heterogeneous data [11]. On the one hand, data captured for an object from different positions should be aligned for spatial dimension; meanwhile, data captured from different times should be aligned from temporal dimension. On the other hand, data fusion can be carried out not only for raw data, but also for feature representation. Feature fusion is a higher-level information processing procedure.

Data mining is the core module of the data engine. It is the process of finding useful information and deriving patterns by using certain machine learning algorithms. It uses the knowledge discovery process, which involves data integration, feature selection, and data transformation. Mining big data to perform predictive and prescriptive analytics will be a key drive of smart railways in the future, enabling better decisions and increased efficiency and safety of transportation systems. The well-established machine learning methods have great potential for smart railways, including clustering, classification methods, regression models, and graph mining algorithms [12].

Data visualization is a valuable tool to display important data or results of data mining for smart railways, because big data are often voluminous and tend to change and morph rapidly [13]. Data visualization is the presentation of data in a pictorial or graphical format. It enables decision-makers to see analytics presented visually, so they can grasp difficult concepts or identify new patterns. With interactive visualization, analysts can take the concept a step further by using technology to drill down into charts and graphs for more detail, interactively changing what data they see and how it is processed. Visualization-based data discovery solutions typically enable users to explore data without much training, making them accessible to a wider range of employees than traditional business analysis tools do.

2.5 APPLICATION LAYER

Smart railways brings together advanced technologies such as sensor, communications, computing, and intelligent control to address various aspects of railway systems, such as train control and dispatching, infrastructure inspection, and customer service. Applications of smart railway can be divided into three categories: train-related, infrastructure-related, and passenger- and freight-related.

2.5.1 Train-related applications

Aiming to increase the speed, safety, and density of train traffic, smart railways should pay more attention to train control and dispatching systems, train health management systems, etc.

The train control module is the brain and nerve system of a railway transportation system. Communications-based train control (CBTC) is a modern railway signaling system that makes use of the telecommunications between the train and track equipment for the traffic management and infrastructure control. By means of the CBTC systems, the exact position of a train is known more accurately than with the traditional signaling systems. This results in a more efficient and safe way to manage the railway traffic. Advanced communication technologies are the key components of CBTC, and LTE-R is regarded as the core communication way for smart railways.

The train dispatching management system transparently manages operational trains by applying signaling, communications, computing, and multimedia technologies. This system can raise traffic-control efficiency and customer-service quality, but it can be improved further by using advanced machine learning models and artificial intelligence technologies [14].

The train health management system is used to monitor the status of a running train itself with the help of various sensors and ITs. The real-time status data about bearing temperatures, air brake pressure, supply voltage, etc. are captured by certain sensors and transferred to on-board server for analysis. Online data analysis is then carried out to discover potential equipment failure and to control the operation of the train.

2.5.2 Infrastructure-related applications

These applications mainly concern the inspection and maintenance of infrastructure, monitoring of environment, emergency rescue, etc. To prevent accidents and to reduce losses if accidents take place, these applications track the current status of railway infrastructure and support decisions for maintenance and rescue. In the following section, we present the IRIS for smart railways.

In addition, smart railways can provide solutions to minimize the negative impacts and to maximize the benefits of the railway to the environment. The environmental impact of high-speed railway, either in the construction or operation process, has attracted more and more attention in recent years. Investigations should be conducted on the topics, such as noise, vibration, pollution, protection of biodiversity, and land-use change. Smart railway systems should pursue initiatives to achieve long term reductions in carbon emissions based on advanced information technology and lower carbon power sources.

2.5.3 Passenger- and freight-related applications

These applications help passengers make optimal travel plans, and help owners of freight arrange optimal shipment schedules. In the framework of smart railways, passengers and owners can easily obtain information about train timetables, ticket prices, and train operation statuses by web services or cell phone applications. Furthermore, they can make easier and better decisions with the help of recommendation systems of smart railways.

Except for information release and recommendation, smart railways would pay more attention to understanding and responding to the requirements and expectations of customers. Basically, passengers are concerned with the safety and reliability of railway services. In addition, they also consider other aspects, such as punctuality, journey quality, prices, and connectivity with other transportation modes. A smart railway makes it feasible to provide a highly sophisticated passenger service by way of the Internet, cell phones, and so on.

According to freight transportation, freight owners are often concerned about cost, connectivity, time duration, and restriction of volume, size, and weight. Smart railways should help to design affordable and accessible transportation systems to meet these requirements. A railway e-business system has been developed in recent years, and realizes door-to-door cargo transportation by electronic order, payment, and check.

3 IRIS FOR SMART RAILWAYS

Rail inspection is one of the most important tasks for railway operation, and an IRIS is a significant aspect of the smart railway. This section introduces the state-of-the-art and trends of IRIS. Note that rail inspection covers a large number of tasks, such as rail defect detection [15], corrugation recognition [16], and fastener anomaly detection [4]. This chapter will focus on rail defect detection.

3.1 RAIL DEFECTS

Rail defects can develop in any rail type and any position of a rail, because of the rail manufacturing process, cyclical loading, impact from rolling stock, rail wear, plastic flow etc. [17]. Rail defects can occur in any portions of a rail, which is composed of head, web, and base. According the occurring position of defects, they can be roughly grouped into two types: internal and surface.

3.1.1 Internal defects

An internal defect mostly has internal origins, and it can only identified by a certain nondestructive inspection process, unless the defect has progressed to the rail running surface and has cracked out. According to the plane that sustains defects, internal defects include transverse defects and longitudinal defects. A transverse defect is the type of fatigue that has developed in a plane transverse to the cross-sectional area of the rail head. A longitudinal defect is any progressive fracture that has a longitudinal separation. Some typical internal defects are depicted in Fig. 3.

Transverse fissure refers to a progressive crosswise fracture originating from a nucleus located inside the head. It can spread outward as a smooth, bright or dark, round or oval surface at the rail head. Its origin is an imperfection in the steel, such as a shatter crack or a minute inclusion. Wheel impact or bending stresses often incurs the growth of a transverse separation around the originating imperfection.

Engine burn fracture is a progressive fracture originating in spots where driving wheels have slipped on top of the rail head. The defect initiates when a slipping engine driver wheel heats a portion of the rail surface, and then rapid cooling forms thermal cracks.

Horizontal split head means a horizontal progressive defect originating inside of a rail head, usually one-quarter of an inch or more below the running surface. The defect appears as a crack lengthwise of a rail when it reaches the side of the rail head. A horizontal split head originates from an internal longitudinal seam or inclusion inherent from the manufacturing process.

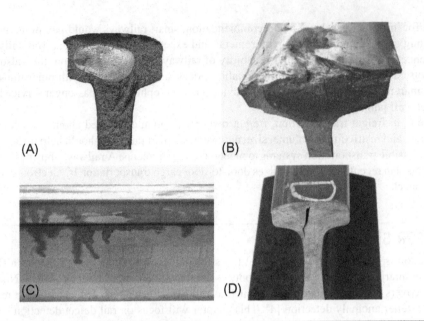

FIG. 3

Typical internal defects. (A) Transverse fissure, (B) engine burn fracture, (C) horizontal split head, and (D) vertical split head.

From Li Q, et al. Rail inspection meets big data: methods and trends, In: Network-based information systems (NBiS), 2015 18th international conference on. IEEE; 2015.

Vertical split head denotes a vertical split through or near the middle of the head, extending into or through it. A crack may show under the head, or close to the web. The origin is an internal longitudinal seam, or inclusion inherent from the manufacturing process, just like a horizontal split head.

3.1.2 Surface defects

A surface defect is any imperfection, damage, or deformation at or near the exterior surface of a rail. rolling contact fatigue (RCF), developed in rails at the wheel/rail interface, is the main surface defects in most railroad systems. Most surface defects can be detected by visual inspection. Some critical types of surface conditions are displayed in Fig. 4.

Shelling is identified as progressive horizontal separations, generally on the gauge side of the rail head. Shelling may turn down to form a transverse separation. The exact origin of shelling has not been definitely determined. It is prevalent at curves and is accelerated if streaks or small seams are present.

Flaking is a progressive horizontal separation of the running surface of a rail near the gauge corner, with scaling or chipping of small slivers. Flaking originates at the surface of a rail and is commonly found near the rail stock area of a switch.

Burned rail is a rail head condition that is the result of intense friction from slipping locomotive wheels, which overheats and displaces tread metal on the running surface. The damaged area can gradually chip out and roughen under repeated traffic.

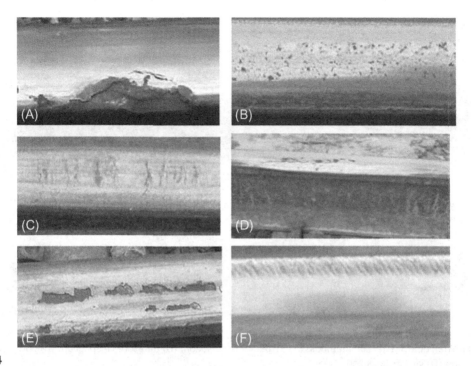

FIG. 4

Typical surface defects. (A) Shelling, (B) flaking, (C) burned rail, (D) flattened rail, (E) spalling, and (F) corrugation.

From Li Q, et al. Rail inspection meets big data: methods and trends, In: Network-based information systems (NBiS), 2015 18th international conference on. IEEE; 2015.

Flattened rail is a short length of rail that has flattened out across the width of the rail head to a depth of three-eighths of an inch or more below the rest of the rail. A flattened rail has no apparent localized cause such as a weld or engine burn.

Spalling is generally referred to as the displacement of parent metal from the rail head because of high contact stresses associated with cyclical loading. Further deterioration of the rail head can increase the amount of metal displacement, resulting in a significant spalling condition.

Corrugation is cyclic (wave-like) irregularities on the running surface of the rails. Corrugation is generally attributed to a repetitive wheel sliding action, such as braking and lateral motion across the rail surface.

3.2 THE STATE-OF-THE-ART FOR RAIL INSPECTION

Nowadays, rails are systematically inspected for internal and surface defects using various nondestructive evaluation (NDE) techniques [18]. During the manufacturing process, rails are examined visually for any surface damage, and assessed for internal defects through ultrasonic inspection. During the service time, rails are also examined visually by experienced rail inspectors. Furthermore, they are assessed periodically with various NDE devices as well. Fig. 5 demonstrates typical rail defect detection methods.

FIG. 5

The typical rail defect detection methods. (A) Inspector observation, (B) ultrasonic inspection, (C) eddy current testing, and (D) visual inspection.

Traditionally, rails are mainly inspected by inspectors, who walk along the rail track and detect potential defects with their intuitive observation and experience. Note that such inspection is also extensively applied in most railway networks nowadays. Ultrasonic inspection is a well-established technology to detect internal defects, but it always fails to identify surface defects [19]. Alternatively, eddy current probes are capable of detecting surface cracks accurately. Nonetheless, their performance is largely affected by lift-off variations, which means that certain surface defects can still be missed during inspection [20]. Recently, extensive research has got under way for the development of novel high-speed NDE equipment, involving high-speed cameras [15], alternating current field measurement probes [21], and electromagnetic acoustic transducers [19]. Although several rail inspection technologies have been developed according to different types of rail defects, their accuracy is not sufficient to meet the actual need of rail inspection. For that reason, the rail industry has invested considerably in the research and development of better NDE methodologies. We shall briefly introduce the state-of-the-art of NDE techniques for rail inspection.

3.2.1 Visual inspection methods

A visual inspection system (VIS) includes an image acquisition subsystem and defect identification subsystem (DIS). The image acquisition subsystem is mainly composed of hardware, and its main function is to capture rail images in real-time. The DIS analyzes the obtained rail images and judges whether an image is defective or not.

Image acquisition subsystem

The image acquisition subsystem is the hardware part of VIS, including a high-speed line-scan camera, digital frame grabber, and LED light sources. Fig. 6 shows the hardware device used in [15] and an example of captured track image. The core component of acquisition subsystem is a Dalsa Spyder high-speed line-scan camera, which has the maximum horizontal frequency of 65 k lines/s and 1024 pixels in each row. A PC-Camlink frame grabber connects the camera and an on-board computer, and it is responsible for coding and transmission of images captured by the camera at a high speed. In order to reduce the influence of external light sources as much as possible, several groups of LED light sources are installed. In addition, the camera is triggered by a wheel encoder to ensure that each pixel of a captured image has the same physical size. The acquisition system is installed under a train carriage. It automatically generates one image per meter as the testing trains are moving on the rail. Note that external factors, such as sunlight and camera shaking, will unavoidably affect the quality of the captured rail images.

FIG. 6

The illustration of image acquisition subsystem. (A) The schematic diagram of image acquisition, (B) the real scene picture of image acquisition subsystem, and (C) an example of track images captured by this system.

Defect identification subsystem

The DIS analyzes the images generated by the image acquisition subsystem, and determines whether there is a defect on the rail surface. It mainly includes three modules: rail localization, feature extraction, and defect recognition. The pipeline of DIS is displayed in Fig. 7.

(1) *Rail localization.* A track image obtained by the image acquisition subsystem includes not only the rail area but also other components (such as fasteners, sleepers, and ballast) on both sides of the rail, as shown in Fig. 7. DIS should first extract the exact rail area that is the only region to be dealt by the subsequent procedures, in order to reduce interference of irrelevant information and to improve detection performance. Generally, the gray values of rail area are greater than those of background, so the rail can be localized based on its projection profile [15]. This method can accurately localize the position of rail under normal conditions, but deviation would appear when a rail is rusted or in the condition of uneven illumination.

(2) *Feature extraction.* Surface defects should be first described by certain feature vectors. Discrete defects (e.g., shelling, spalling, and flaking) are often represented by gray histograms or shape descriptors [22]. Meanwhile continuous defects (e.g., corrugation and burned rail) are ready to be described by texture features [16]. For example, corrugation is a kind of wavelike surface defect, and a corrugation image is characterized by the periodic pattern with an alternation of light and dark. Gabor feature is an effective representation for corrugation, though it is time-consuming.

(3) *Defect recognition.* Defects are identified automatically applying pattern recognition methods, including a supervised learning scheme [23] and an unsupervised analysis approach [22]. Pattern recognition has achieved exciting progress in recent years, but rail defect detection remains still a great challenge because of the complex open situation, such as uneven illumination, camera shaking, and large variety of defects.

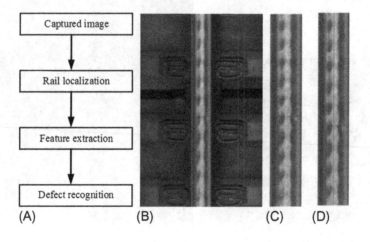

(A) (B) (C) (D)

FIG. 7

The process diagram of defect identification subsystem. (A) The pipeline of defect identification, (B) a track image captured by image acquisition subsystem, (C) the rail subimage segmented by a localization algorithm, and (D) the detected defect (e.g., corrugation) marked with the two solid vertical lines.

VIS has the merit of high detection speed, which can vary from 1 to 240 km/h depending on the type of inspection carried out and the quality of image resolution required. In addition, the cost of VIS is low, and its detection procedure can be reproduced. However, VIS does not provide any information with regards to the presence of internal defects.

3.2.2 Ultrasonic inspection

In this method, a beam of ultrasonic energy generated by a piezoelectric element is transmitted into a rail, and then the reflected or scattered energy of the transmitted beam is detected by a collection of transducers. Finally, the amplitude of collected signal together with its temporal information is used to recognize defects [19]. The energy is transmitted at several different incident angles to improve the detection performance, because defects can locate in various planes of a rail. Commonly used angles are 0, 37, 45, and 70 degrees.

Ultrasonic inspection can be manually performed with dedicated portable ultrasonic equipment or by special high-speed testing trains carrying ultrasonic probes. The transducers are contained within a liquid-filled tire, which is known as a roller search unit in established products. An ultrasonic probe is joined with a rail using water sprayed on the rail surface by a special sprinkler, as the testing train moves along the track. The inspection speeds achieved by testing trains varies from 10 up to 100 km/h.

Ultrasonic inspection methods are good at detecting internal defects, particularly in the rail head and web, but they always fail to detect surface defects that are smaller than 4 mm deep. Moreover, such surface defects can shadow critical internal defects and thus incur false alarm. Ultrasonic inspection also misses some defects in the rail base.

3.2.3 Other NDE techniques

Eddy current testing is an important technology for surface inspection, and it has been applied to rail inspection in recent years. A typical eddy current sensor comprises one exciting and one sensing coil. An alternating current is fed into the exciting coil to generate a magnetic field near the running surface. Changes of the magnetic field induce eddy currents below the rail surface, and changes in the secondary magnetic field generated by the eddy currents are detected by the sensing coil. If an inspected area is free of defects, then the impedance of the eddy current sensor remains constant. If an inspected area presents a near-surface or surface defect, the eddy currents would be disturbed and result in fluctuation in the secondary magnetic field, which would subsequently give rise to changes in the impedance. Consequently, such changing signals in the impedance are recorded and analyzed to figure out defects.

Magnetic flux leakage (MFL) inspection is the other important and sensitive method for electromagnetic nondestructive testing of surfaces and near-surface area in ferromagnetic materials [24]. In the scheme of MFL rail inspection, search coils, which are positioned at a constant distance from the rail, are used to detect any changes in the magnetic field that is generated by a DC electromagnet near a rail head. If a certain area on rail surface or near-surface presents a transverse defect, its ferromagnetic domain would show MFL. Therefore, the coils detect and record the change in the magnetic field, and defects are recognized based on these signals. An online MFL inspection system consists of a high-speed MFL signal acquisition subsystem and a fast signal processing module. The former can be achieved by some well-established equipment, e.g., the bobbin-type magnetic camera [25]. The latter module needs advanced signal processing algorithms.

These two methods do well in detecting near-surface defects or RCF cracking. However, they are sensitive to the position of sensors and the environment.

3.3 RAIL INSPECTION BASED ON THE IoT AND BIG DATA

With the development of advanced sensor and information technology in railway infrastructure inspection, big data has recently emerged as a potential methodology to improve the productivity and reliability of current rail inspection systems [3]. Currently, inspection equipment collects enormous quantities of data through ultrasonic probes, eddy current probes, video cameras, and acoustic emission transducers. Furthermore, the data are growing in both quantity and quality, but traditional inspection software always uses only the temporal and single-source data. Data of extremely large size are difficult to be analyzed using traditional approaches because they may exceed the limits of a typical computational platform for most NDE systems. However, big data technologies offer a new direction for rail inspection.

We can observe that within rail inspection, two trends have appeared: multisensors monitoring and data-center analysis. Firstly, many types of sensors are applied in rail inspection. These sensors can divide into on-board sensors and ground sensors. On-board sensors are installed on a testing train, including but not limited to ultrasonic probes, cameras, MFL, and eddy current detectors. Ground sensors are fixed on certain position to monitor some special objects, for example, rail bridges and tunnels. In addition, some meteorological sensors are used to observe weather disasters. However, these sensors are often used separately, and identify defects based on single-source data. Like the blind feeling a giant elephant, these systems alone are not adequate to diagnose the service status of rails thoughtfully. Secondly, the collected data are archived to form a large database, while traditional inspection is based on single-source data or instant data. Of course, such a database is very useful for defect detection and statistical modeling, since it integrates multiple-source data that are captured by different sensors, and historical data as well.

According to these trends, we proposed the research framework of intelligent rail inspection based on big data in [2]. Fig. 8 demonstrates the pipeline of the rail inspection system. This system includes three layers as follows:

(1) The first layer carries out the sensing function. On-board sensors capture the status of rail infrastructure from different aspects, for example, cameras obtain the images of rail surface, whereas ultrasonic probes detect the state of internal structure of rails. Ground sensors monitor specific objects (such as rail bridges and tunnels) and capture their real-time status. In addition, some meteorological sensors are used to observe and predict weather disasters.

(2) The second layer collects and processes the sensing data. The data captured by on-board sensors are firstly transmitted to an on-board server by wired data link, and are then synchronized to a data center in an offline way. The data obtained by ground sensors are usually transferred to an on-site server by wired or wireless networks. Note that these data are heterogeneous and they should be spatially and temporally correlated. Furthermore, some preprocessing is necessary to remove noise and to check the integrity of sensing data.

(3) The third layer analyses and exploits the database in order to construct maintenance planning models. Basically, pattern recognition methods are performed to verify if the concerned rail has defects. Furthermore, historical monitoring, trend analysis, and forecasting of degradation or

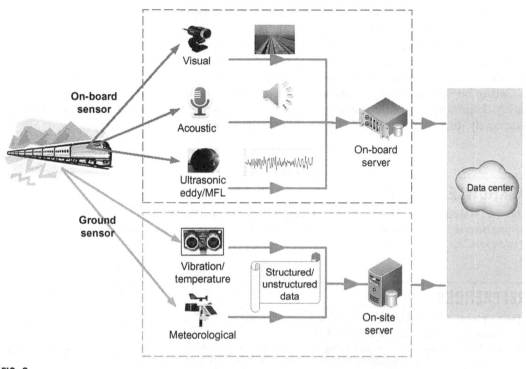

FIG. 8

The pipeline of rail inspection based on the IoT and big data.

failure can be conducted after multisource data is collected and archived to form large databases. Advanced statistical analyses (e.g., multivariate regression analysis) and data mining methods are feasible to develop higher-order models for forecasting and trend analysis. Lastly, rail life prediction models can be derived from big data and such basic models. These models, integrated with the databases, make up the basis for building maintenance planning models, which determine maintenance requirements and schedule maintenance activities.

4 CONCLUSION

The busier railway networks have yielded higher requirements in terms of safety, speed, and efficiency. In modern railway systems, ITs and infrastructure have become core components. Intelligent sensors are extensively applied in all parts of railway networks, and big data has become the inevitable trend for the railway industry. This chapter proposes the architecture of smart railway, which is built on the IoT and big data, and introduces the IRIS as an application of smart railway. The architecture of smart railway is divided into four layers: perception and action layer, transfer layer, data engine layer, and application layer. In the framework of a smart railway, intelligent sensors of different categories are connected to railway networks via various network-access means, such as wired or wireless data connections. The captured sensor data combined with other information (e.g., operation data and user data) constructs big data collection, and therefore knowledge can be discovered from the data collection by data mining and artificial intelligence technologies. Based on the collected data and discovered knowledge, applications can be developed to meet the requirements of railway systems.

Although the smart railway concept is in its infancy for the railway industry, smart devices and associated big data processing techniques are rapidly developing in other sectors of the global IoT industry. Therefore, it is the right time for the railway operators to develop smart railway technologies extensively for a more secure and efficient future railway network.

ACKNOWLEDGMENT

This work is supported by Fundamental Research Funds for the Central Universities (2014JBZ003, 2016JBZ006), Beijing Natural Science Foundation (No. 4142043, J160004), and National Natural Science Foundation of China (No. 61501022).

REFERENCES

[1] Li Y, et al. Rail component detection, optimization, and assessment for automatic rail track inspection. IEEE Trans Intell Transp Syst 2014;15(2):760–70.
[2] Li Q, et al. Rail inspection meets big data: methods and trends. In: Network-based information systems (NBiS), 2015 18th international conference on. New York, USA: IEEE; 2015.
[3] Zarembski AM. Some examples of big data in railroad engineering. In: Big data (big data), 2014 IEEE international conference on. New York, USA: IEEE; 2014.
[4] Aytekin C, et al. Railway fastener inspection by real-time machine vision. IEEE Trans Syst Man Cybern Syst Hum 2015;45(7):1101–7.
[5] Atzori L, Iera A, Morabito G. The internet of things: a survey. Comput Netw 2010;54(15):2787–805.
[6] Seife C. Big data: the revolution is digitized. Nature 2015;518(7540):480.
[7] Wu X, et al. Data mining with big data. IEEE Trans Knowl Data Eng 2014;26(1):97–107.
[8] Khaitan S, Mccalley J. Design techniques and applications of cyberphysical systems: a survey. IEEE Syst J 2015;9(2):350–65.
[9] Boja C, Pocovnicu A, Batagan L. Distributed parallel architecture for "Big Data". Inform Econ 2012;16(2):116.
[10] Gani A, et al. A survey on indexing techniques for big data: taxonomy and performance evaluation. Knowl Inf Syst 2016;46:241–84.
[11] Varshney P. Multisensor data fusion. Electron Commun Eng J 1997;9(6):245–53.
[12] Bishop C, Nasrabadi N. Pattern recognition and machine learning. J Electron Imaging 2007;19(4):461–2.
[13] Byrne L, Angus D, Wiles J. Acquired codes of meaning in data visualization and infographics: beyond perceptual primitives. IEEE Trans Vis Comput Graph 2016;22(1):509.
[14] Ning B, et al. Intelligent railway systems in China. IEEE Intell Syst 2006;21(5):80–3.
[15] Li Q, Ren S. A real-time visual inspection system for discrete surface defects of rail heads. IEEE Trans Instrum Meas 2012;61(8):2189–99.
[16] Mandriota C, et al. Filter-based feature selection for rail defect detection. Mach Vis Appl 2004;15(4):179–85.
[17] Federal Railroad Administration. Track inspector rail defect reference manual. Washington, DC: U.S. Dept. of Transportation; 2011.

[18] Clark R. Rail flaw detection: overview and needs for future developments. NDT&E Int 2004;37(2):111–8.

[19] Edwards RS, et al. Ultrasonic detection of surface-breaking railhead defects. Insight-Non-Destr Test Cond Monit 2008;50(7):369–73.

[20] Thomas H, Heckel T, Hanspach G. Advantage of a combined ultrasonic and eddy current examination for railway inspection trains. Insight-Non-Destr Test Cond Monit 2007;49(6):341–4.

[21] Topp D, Smith M. Application of the ACFM inspection method to rail and rail vehicles. Insight-Non-Destr Test Cond Monit 2005;47(6):354–7.

[22] Li Q, Ren S. A visual detection system for rail surface defects. IEEE Trans Syst Man Cybern Part C Appl Rev 2012;42(6):1531–42.

[23] Feng H, et al. Automatic fastener classification and defect detection in vision-based railway inspection systems. IEEE Trans Instrum Meas 2014;63(4):877–88.

[24] Priewald RH, et al. Fast magnetic flux leakage signal inversion for the reconstruction of arbitrary defect profiles in steel using finite elements. IEEE Trans Magn 2013;49(1):506–16.

[25] Le M, et al. Quantitative evaluation of corrosion in a thin small-bore piping system using bobbin-type magnetic camera. J Nondestruct Eval 2014;33(1):74–81.

GLOSSARY

Rail inspection The process to verify whether the rails are in healthy condition or not by means of manual detection or automatic detection with equipment.

Railway infrastructure The collection of devices and facilities used for railway transportation, such as rail track, fasteners, bridges, and tunnels.

Smart railway The modern railway system leveraging advanced information technologies (e.g., Internet of Things, big data, and artificial intelligence) to achieve better safety, efficiency, and capacity.

Index

Printed in the United States
By Bookmasters